ETHICS AND TECHNOLOGY

ETHICS AND TECHNOLOGY

Ethical Issues in an Age of Information and Communication Technology

HERMAN T. TAVANI

Rivier College

WILEY

John Wiley and Sons, Inc.

For my parents, Flora and Herman Tavani, Sr.

Acquisitions Editor   *Paul Crockett*
Marketing Manager   *Katherine Hepburn*
Senior Production Editor   *Valerie A. Vargas*
Senior Designer   *Karin Kincheloe*

This book was set in 10/12 Times Roman by Argosy and printed and bound by Malloy Lithograph. The cover was printed by Phoenix Color.

This book is printed on acid-free paper.

Library of Congress Cataloging-in-Publication Data
Tavani, Herman T.
    Ethics and technology : ethical issues in an age of information & communication technology / Herman T. Tavani
        p. cm.
    ISBN 0-471-24966-1 (pbk.)
    1. Computer networks—Moral and ethical aspects. I. Title.
    TK5105.5.T385 2003
    174'.90904—dc21

                                        2003045098

ISBN 0-471-24966-1
ISBN 0-471-45250-5 (WIE)

Printed in the United States of America
10 9 8 7 6 5 4 3 2 1

CONTENTS AT A GLANCE

TABLE OF CONTENTS

PREFACE

The purpose of *Ethics and Technology* is to introduce students to issues and controversies that comprise the relatively new field of *cyberethics*. The term "cyberethics" is used in this textbook to refer to the field of study that examines moral, legal, and social issues involving cybertechnology. *Cybertechnology*, in turn, refers to a broad spectrum of computing and information technologies that range from stand-alone computers to the cluster of networked computing, information, and communications technologies. Many of these technologies include devices that are connected to privately owned computer networks as well as to the Internet itself.

This textbook examines a wide range of cyberethics issues—from specific issues of moral responsibility that directly affect computer professionals to broader social and ethical concerns that affect each of us in our day-to-day lives. Questions about the roles and responsibilities of computer professionals in developing safe and reliable computer systems are examined under the category of professional ethics. Broader social and ethical concerns associated with cybertechnology are examined under topics such as privacy, security, crime, intellectual property, Internet regulation, and so forth.

Because cyberethics is an interdisciplinary field, this textbook aims at reaching several audiences and thus easily runs the risk of failing to meet the needs of any one audience. I have nonetheless attempted to compose a textbook that addresses the needs of computer science, philosophy, social/behavioral science, and library/information science students. Computer science students need a clear understanding of the ethical challenges they will face as computer professionals when they enter the workforce. Philosophy students, on the other hand, should understand how moral issues involving cybertechnology can be situated in the field of applied ethics in general. Social science and behavioral science students will want to assess the sociological impact of cybertechnology on our social and political institutions (government, commerce, and education) and sociodemographic groups (affecting gender, race, ethnicity, and social class). And library science and information science students should be aware of the complexities and nuances of current intellectual property laws that threaten unfettered access to electronic information, and should be informed about recent regulatory schemes that threaten to censor certain forms of electronic speech.

Students from other academic disciplines should also find many issues covered in this textbook pertinent to their personal and professional lives; some undergraduates may elect to take a course in cyberethics to satisfy one of their general education requirements. Although *Ethics and Technology* is intended mainly for undergraduate students, it could be used, in conjunction with other texts, in graduate courses as well.

We examine ethical controversies using actual case examples and hypothetical scenarios, wherever appropriate. In some instances I have deliberately constructed controversial scenarios and selected controversial cases to convey the severity of the ethical issues we consider. Some readers may be uncomfortable with, and possibly even offended by, these scenarios and cases, for example, unethical practices that negatively affect children and minorities. Although it might have been politically expedient to skip over issues and cases that could unintentionally offend certain individuals, I believe that no textbook in applied ethics would do justice to its topic if it failed to expose and examine issues that adversely affect vulnerable groups in society.

Exercise questions are included at the end of each chapter. First, basic "review questions" quiz the reader's comprehension of key concepts, themes, issues, and cases covered in that chapter. These are followed by higher-level "discussion questions" designed to encourage students to reflect more deeply on some of the controversial issues examined in the chapter. In certain cases students are asked to compare and contrast arguments and themes that span multiple chapters; for example, they may be asked to relate arguments used to defend intellectual property rights, considered in one chapter of the book, to arguments for protecting privacy rights, examined in an earlier chapter. Other discussion questions ask students to apply foundational concepts and frameworks, such as ethical theory and critical thinking techniques introduced in Chapters 2 and 3, to the analysis of specific cyberethics issues examined in subsequent chapters. In some cases, these discussion questions may generate lively debate in the classroom. Perhaps some of these questions will also serve as a point of departure for various class assignments and group projects.

▶ ORGANIZATION AND STRUCTURE OF THE BOOK

Ethics and Technology is organized into eleven chapters. Chapter 1, "Introduction to Cyberethics: Concepts, Perspectives, and Methodological Frameworks," defines key concepts and terms that will appear throughout the book. For example, definitions of terms such as *cyberethics* and *cybertechnology* are introduced in this chapter. Also included is a brief historical sketch of the field of cyberethics in terms of four developmental "phases," from its informal beginning as a loosely defined area of applied ethics (in the 1950s and 1960s) to the present. We then examine whether any ethical issues involving computers and the Internet are unique ethical issues. We also consider how we can approach cyberethics issues from three different perspectives: professional ethics, philosophical ethics, and descriptive ethics, each of which represents the approach generally taken by a computer scientist, a philosopher, and a social/behavioral scientist. Chapter 1 concludes with a proposal for a comprehensive and interdisciplinary methodological scheme for approaching cyberethics issues from these perspectives. This methodological scheme includes a strategy that will be used to identify, analyze, and evaluate the specific moral issues we encounter in Chapters 4 through 11.

In Chapter 2, "Ethical Concepts and Ethical Theories: Establishing and Justifying a Moral System," we examine some of the basic concepts that make up a moral system. We draw a distinction between "ethics" and "morality" by defining "ethics" as the study of morality. "Morality," or a moral system, is defined as an informal, public system comprising rules of conduct and principles for evaluating those rules. Before beginning our examination of ethical theory, we critically analyze challenges posed by four "discussion stoppers," which cause debates about ethical issues to break down prematurely. We then examine consequence-based, duty-based, character-based, and contract-based ethical theories. Chapter 2 concludes with a proposal that integrates elements of competing ethical theories into one comprehensive and unified theory, which we will use, wherever possible, in our examination of specific cyberethics issues in the later chapters.

Chapter 3, "Critical Thinking Skills and Logical Arguments: Tools for Evaluating Cyberethics Issues," includes a brief overview of basic concepts and strategies that are essential for debating moral issues in a structured and rational manner. We begin by examining some informal logical fallacies that occur in everyday reasoning and by providing a list of "fallacy-types" as well as a technique for spotting these informal fallacies. Next, we examine a technique for distinguishing between arguments that are valid and invalid, sound and unsound, and inductive and fallacious. We illustrate examples of each type with topics and issues involving cybertechnology and cyberethics. Chapter 3 concludes with a seven-step procedure for analyzing and evaluating arguments.

Chapter 4, "Professional Ethics, Codes of Conduct, and Moral Responsibility," examines issues related to professional responsibility for computer professionals. We consider whether there are any special moral responsibilities that computer professionals have *as* professionals. To address issues of responsibilities for computer professionals in general, and software engineers in particular, many computer organizations have adopted professional codes of conduct, and we consider whether these professional codes can adequately guide computer professionals in critical decisions that may affect them. We also ask: To what extent are software engineers responsible for the reliability of the computer systems they design and develop, especially applications that include "life-critical" and "safety-critical" software? Are computer professionals ever permitted, or perhaps even required, to "blow the whistle" when they have reasonable evidence to suggest that a computer system is unreliable? What are the acceptable levels of risk that we should tolerate in the development of safety-critical software?

We discuss privacy issues involving cybertechnology in Chapter 5. First, we examine the concept of privacy as well as some arguments for why privacy is considered an important human value. We then look at how personal privacy is threatened by surveillance techniques and data-collection schemes that involve cybertechnology. Specific data-gathering and data-exchanging techniques, such as computerized merging and matching, are then examined in detail. We contrast traditional record-matching operations used by the federal government to identify welfare cheats and deadbeat parents with recent biometric-based matching techniques used to identify criminals and terrorists. We next consider some challenges that a computerized technique commonly referred to as "data mining" poses for protecting personal privacy in public space. In Chapter 5 we also consider whether technology itself, in the form of privacy-enhancing technologies (or PETs), can provide an adequate solution to privacy issues in cyberspace. Finally, we examine some recent and pending privacy legislation in the United States as well as some international privacy laws and data-protection principles.

Chapter 6, "Security in Cyberspace," discusses security threats involving cybertechnology. Initially, we draw a distinction between two different senses of "security" as applied to computers: systems security and data security. We also examine security questions as they relate to anonymity in cyberspace; for example, how can we allow individuals engaged in on-line activities to be anonymous and at the same time protect against certain kinds of criminal and terrorist activities that can also take place on-line. Other security-related topics surround cryptography and current methods of data encryption used as security countermesures. And we ask in Chapter 6 whether any meaningful distinctions can be drawn between "cyberterrorism" and "information warfare."

We begin our analysis of cybercrime in Chapter 7 by considering whether we can construct a profile of a "typical" computer criminal. We examine criminal activities such as "denial-of-service" attacks on commercial Web sites and the launching of computer viruses. We propose a definition of cybercrime that enables us to distinguish between "cyberspecific" and "cyberrelated" crimes to see whether a such distinction would aid in the formulation of more coherent cybercrime laws. We also consider legal jurisdiction in cyberspace, especially with respect to the extradition of cybercriminals and the prosecution of cybercrimes that involve interstate and international venues. In addition, we examine technological efforts to combat cybercrime, such as controversial uses of encryption and biometric technologies.

Chapters 8 and 9 examine legal issues involving intellectual property and free speech, respectively, as they relate to cyberspace. One objective of Chapter 8, "Intellectual Property Disputes in Cyberspace," is to show why an understanding of the concept of intellectual property is important in an information age. We consider three theories of property rights and make important distinctions among legal concepts such as copyright law, patent protection, and trademarks. Additionally, we consider specific cases involving intellectual property disputes, including the Napster controversy, and we examine the implications of the Digital Millennium Copyright Act (DMCA) for continued access to information in cyberspace.

Chapter 9, "Regulating Commerce and Speech in Cyberspace," looks at additional legal issues, especially as they involve regulatory concerns in cyberspace. We draw distinctions between two different senses of "regulation" as it applies to cyberspace, and in our analysis of cyberspace regulation we also examine whether the Internet should be understood as medium or as a "place." We argue that the model used to view cyberspace will ultimately influence which types of regulations will and will not apply there. We also consider in Chapter 9 a cluster of regulatory issues that pertain to the assignment of Internet domain names, the use of (HTML) metatags, and the practice of hyperlinking on the Web. We also examine social and moral questions surrounding electronic spam, which some believe can be viewed as a form of "speech" in cyberspace. We then ask whether all forms of on-line speech should be granted legal protection; for example, should child pornography, hate speech, and speech that can cause physical harm to others be tolerated in on-line forums? We also consider whether software filters provide an adequate solution to the problems underlying the debate over free speech vs. censorship in cyberspace. Finally, we examine the issue of on-line defamation, and we consider whether Internet Service Providers (ISPs) should be held legally liable and possibly morally responsible as well for the content of information conveyed in their various on-line forums.

Chapters 10 and 11 examine a wide range of social issues, many of which we analyze from the perspective of descriptive ethics. Issues in Chapter 10 span several categories, from equity and access to employment and work. The chapter begins with an analysis of domestic and international aspects of the "digital divide," and then analyzes the debate involving the need for a universal Internet service policy, as well asequity-and access-issues affecting race, gender, and disabled persons. We also examine access-and-equity issues affecting employment in the contemporary workplace, and we ask whether cybertechnology has transformed our conventional understanding of employment and work. We consider the implications of robotics and expert systems for the workplace, as well as the impact that remote work and "virtual organizations" are beginning to have for both the meaning of work and the quality of work in an information age. Chapter 10 closes with a brief discussion and analysis of employee privacy and autonomy issues that arise because of surveillance and monitoring techniques used in the computerized workplace.

We conclude with Chapter 11, where we examine issues pertaining to two broad themes: *community* and *identity* in cyberspace; we analyze the impact of cybertechnology for our conventional understanding of "community" and community life. In particular, we ask whether on-line communities raise any special ethical or social issues. Next, we explore the relationship between the Internet and democracy and consider whether Internet technology facilitates democracy and whether the Internet should be used as a tool to spread democracy. We then examine social and ethical issues involving virtual environments and virtual reality (VR) applications. The final two sections of Chapter 11 consider the implications of cybertechnology for personal identity and for our sense of self (i.e., what it means to be a human being). We close on a speculative note by attempting to anticipate social and ethical issues in view of future directions and predictions, especially concerning research and development in artificial intelligence (AI) and nanocomputing.

Five appendices and a glossary complete the book. Appendices A, B, and C include the full text of three professional codes of ethics: the IEEE Code of Ethics, the ACM Code of Ethics and Professional Conduct, and the IEEE-CS/ACM Software Engineering Code of Ethics and Professional Practice. The Glossary defines terms commonly used in the context of computer ethics and cyberethics, but it is by no means an exhaustive list of such terms. Appendices D and E are only available on-line at www.wiley.com/college/tavani. Appendix D contains the section of the IEEE-CS/ACM Computing Curricula 2001 Final Report that describes the social, professional, and ethical units of instruction mandated in their computer science curriculum. Appendix E provides some additional critical thinking techniques that expand on the strategies introduced in Chapter 3.

▶ A NOTE TO STUDENTS

If you are taking an ethics course for the first time, you might feel uncomfortable with the prospect of embarking on a study of moral issues and controversies—topics that might initially cause you discomfort because ethics is sometimes perceived to be "preachy," and its subject matter is sometimes viewed as essentially personal and private in nature. Because these are common concerns, we address them early in the textbook. We make a distinction between an ethicist, who studies morality, and a moralist who may assume to have the correct answers to all of the questions; note that a primary objective of this book is to examine and analyze ethical issues, not to presume that any of us already has *the* correct answer to any of the questions we consider. To accomplish this objective, I introduce three types of conceptual frameworks early in the textbook: In Chapter 1, I provide a methodological scheme that enables you to identify controversial problems and issues involving cybertechnology *as* ethical issues. The conceptual scheme included in Chapter 2, based on ethical theory, provides some general principles that guide your analysis of specific cases as well as your deliberations about which kinds of solutions to problems should be proposed. A third, and final, conceptual framework is introduced in Chapter 3 in the form of critical thinking techniques, which provides rules and standards that you can use for evaluating the strengths of competing arguments and for defending a particular position that you reach on a certain issue.

This textbook was designed and written for you, the student! Whether or not it succeeds in helping you to meet the objectives of a course in cyberethics is very important to me, so I welcome your feedback on this textbook; and I would sincerely appreciate hearing your ideas for how this textbook could be improved. Please feel free to write to me with your suggestions, comments, etc. My e-mail address is htavani@rivier.edu. I look forward to hearing from you!

▶ NOTE TO INSTRUCTORS: A ROADMAP FOR USING THIS BOOK

The chapters that make up *Ethics and Technology* are sequenced so that readers are exposed to foundational issues and conceptual frameworks before they examine specific problems in cyberethics. In some cases, it may not be possible for instructors to cover all of the material in Chapters 1–3. It is strongly recommended, however, that before students are assigned material in Chapters 4–11, they at least read Sections 1.1, 1.4–1.5, 2.4–2.8, and 3.2. Instructors using this textbook can determine which chapters best accommodate their specific course objectives. Computer science instructors, for example, will likely want to assign Chapter 4, on professional ethics and responsibility, early in the term. Social science instructors, on the other hand, will likely examine issues discussed in Chapters 10 and 11 early in their course. Philosophy instructors may wish to structure their courses beginning with a thorough examination of the material on ethical concepts and ethical theory in Chapter 2 and techniques for evaluating logical arguments in Chapter 3.

Many textbooks in applied ethics include a requisite chapter on ethical concepts/theory at the beginning of the book. Unfortunately, they often treat them in a cursory manner; furthermore, these ethical concepts and theories are seldom developed and reinforced in the remaining chapters. Thus, readers often experience a "disconnect" between the material included in the book's opening chapter and the content of the specific cases and issues discussed in subsequent chapters. By incorporating elements of ethical theory into my discussion and analysis of the specific cyberethics issues I examine, I have tried to avoid the disconnect between theory and practice that is commonplace in many applied ethics textbooks.

Ethics and Technology was designed to be a stand alone textbook. For those who wish to supplement this text with primary readings, however, a number of anthologies in computer ethics are available. These include Baird, Ramsower, and Rosenbaum's *Cyberethics: Social and Moral Issues in the Computer Age* (Amherst, NY: Prometheus, 2000); Hester and Ford's *Computers and Ethics in the Cyberage* (Upper Saddle River, NJ: Prentice Hall, 2001); Johnson and Nissenbaum's *Computing, Ethics & Social Values* (Englewood Cliffs, NJ: Prentice Hall, 1995); and Spinello and Tavani's *Readings in CyberEthics* (Sudbury, MA: Jones and Bartlett, 2001).

▶ A NOTE TO COMPUTER SCIENCE INSTRUCTORS

Ethics and Technology can be used as the main text in a course dedicated to ethical and social issues in computing, or it can be used as a supplementary textbook for computer science courses in which one or more ethics modules are included. As I suggested in the preceding section, instructors may find it difficult to cover all of the material included in this book in the course of a single semester. And as I also previously suggested, computer science instructors will likely want to ensure that they allocate sufficient course time to the professional ethical issues discussed in Chapter 4. Also of special interest to computer science instructors and their students will be the sections on computer security and risk in

Chapter 6, open source code and intellectual property issues in Chapter 8, and Internet-regulation issues affecting software code in Chapter 9. Because computer science instructors may need to limit the amount of class time they devote to covering foundational concepts included in the earlier chapters, I recommend covering at least the critical sections of Chapters 1–3 described previously. This should provide computer science students with some of the tools they will need as professionals to deliberate on ethical issues and to justify the positions they reach.

In designing this textbook, I took into account the recent guidelines on ethical instruction included in the *Computing Curricula 2001 Final Report*, issued in December 2001 by the IEEE-CS/ACM Joint Task Force on Computing Curricula, which recommends the inclusion of sixteen core hours of instruction on social, ethical, and professional topics in the curriculum for undergraduate computer science students. (See the on-line Appendix D at www.wiley.com/college/Tavani for detailed information about the SP units in the Computing Curricula 2001.) Each topic prefaced with an SP (Social/Professional) designation defines one "knowledge area" or a "CS body of knowledge." They are distributed among the following ten units:

SP1: History of computing (e.g., history of computer hardware, software, and networking)

SP2: Social context of computing (e.g., social implications of networked computing, gender-related issues, and international issues)

SP3: Methods and tools of analysis (e.g., identifying assumptions and values, making and evaluating ethical arguments)

SP4: Professional and ethical responsibilities (e.g., the nature of professionalism, codes of ethics, ethical dissent, and whistle-blowing

SP5: Risks and liabilities of computer-based systems (e.g., historical examples of software risks)

SP6: Intellectual property (e.g., foundations of intellectual property, copyrights, patents, and software piracy)

SP7: Privacy and civil liberties (e.g., ethical and legal basis for privacy protection, technological strategies for privacy protection)

SP8: Computer crime (e.g., history and examples of computer crime, hacking, viruses, and crime prevention strategies)

SP9: Economic issues in computing (e.g., monopolies and their economic implications; effect of skilled labor supply)

SP10: Philosophical frameworks (e.g., ethical theory, utilitarianism, relativism)

All ten SP units are covered in this textbook. Material described in SP1 is included in Chapters 1 and 10; and topics included in SP2 are also discussed in those two chapters. The methods and analytical tools mentioned in SP3 are described at length in Chapters 2 and 3. The professional issues involving codes of conduct and professional responsibility described in SP4 are included in Chapter 4 and in the final section of Chapter 11. Also discussed in Chapter 4, as well as in Chapter 6, are issues involving risks and liabilities (SP5). Intellectual property issues (SP6) are discussed in detail in Chapter 8 and in certain sections of Chapter 9. Privacy and civil liberty concerns (SP7), on the other hand, are discussed mainly in Chapter 5. Chapter 7, on computer crime, is devoted to material described in SP8. Economic issues (SP9) are considered in Chapters 9 and 10. And philosophical frameworks of ethics, including ethical theory (SP10), are included in Chapter 2.

Table 1 illustrates the corresponding connection between SP units and the chapters of this book.

TABLE 1   SP ("Knowledge") Units and Corresponding Book Chapters

SP (Social/ Professional) Unit	1	2	3	4	5	6	7	8	9	10
Chapter(s)	1, 10	1, 10	2, 3	4, 11	4, 6	8, 9	5	7	9, 10	2

ACKNOWLEDGMENTS

In composing this textbook, I have drawn from several of my previously published papers. Chapter 1 incorporates material from three articles: "The State of Computer Ethics as a Philosophical Field of Inquiry," *Ethics and Information Technology* (Vol. 3, No. 2, 2001); "Applying an Interdisciplinary Approach to Teaching Computer Ethics," *IEEE Technology and Society* (Vol. 21, No. 3, 2002), and "Some Ethical Reflections on Cyberstalking" (coauthored with Frances Grodzinsky), *Computers and Society* (Vol. 32, No. 1, 2002). In Chapter 2, I drew from material in "Social and Ethical Aspects of Information Technology" in the *Wiley Encyclopedia of Electrical and Electronics Engineering* (New York: John Wiley and Sons, 1999) and "The Uniqueness Debate in Computer Ethics," *Ethics and Information Technology* (Vol. 4, No. 1, 2002). Chapter 3 draws from material in my article "Facts, Opinions, and Value Judgments," *InSight* (Vol. 1, No. 2, 1994). In Chapter 4, I incorporated material from "Professional Ethics and Codes of Conduct" (coauthored with Richard Spinello) in *Readings in CyberEthics* (Sudbury, MA: Jones and Bartlett Publishers, 2001), Chapter 5 draws from material in four papers: "Internet Search Engines and Personal Privacy" in Jeroen van den Hoven's *Computer Ethics: Philosophical Enquiry* (Rotterdam, The Netherlands: Erasmus University Press, 1998); "Informational Privacy, Data Mining, and the Internet," *Ethics and Information Technology* (Vol. 1, No. 2, 1999); "Privacy-Enhancing Technologies as a Panacea for On-line Privacy Concerns: Some Ethical Considerations," *Journal of Information Ethics* (Vol. 9, No. 2, 2000); and "Privacy Protection, Control of Information, and Privacy-Enhancing Technologies" (coauthored with James Moor), *Computers and Society* (Vol. 31, No. 1, 2001). In Chapter 6, on security, I drew from my chapter on "Privacy and Security" in Duncan Langford's book *Internet Ethics* (London: Macmillan, 2000). Chapter 7, on cybercrime, incorporates material from "Defining Computer Crime: Piracy, Break-ins, and Sabotage in Cyberspace," *Computers and Society* (Vol. 30, No. 3, 2000). In my discussion of intellectual property issues in Chapter 8, I drew from my article "Information Wants to Be Shared: An Alternative Framework for Approaching Intellectual Property Disputes in an Information Age," *Catholic Library World* (Vol. 72, No. 2, 2002). Chapter 9 incorporates material from "Computer Matching and Personal Privacy: Can They Be Compatible?" in Proceedings of the Symposium on Computers and the Quality of Life (New York: ACM Press, 1996) and "Cyberstalking, Moral Responsibility, and Legal Liability for Internet Service Providers" (coauthored with Frances Grodzinsky) in the *Proceedings of the International Symposium on Technology and Society* (Los Alamitos, CA: IEEE Computer Society Press, 2002). In Chapter 10, I incorporated material from "Ethical Reflections on the Digital Divide," *Journal of Information, Communication and Ethics in Society* (Vol. 1, No. 2, 2003). And in Chapter 11, I drew from material in my chapter on "The Impact of the Internet on Our Moral Condition: Do We Need a New Framework of Ethics?" included in Robert Cavalier's forthcoming book, *The Impact of the Internet on Our Moral Lives* (Albany, NY: State University of New York Press, in press).

I wish to thank Rivier College for granting me a sabbatical leave during the fall 2002 term to complete this textbook. I also wish to thank my colleagues in the philosophy department at Rivier who, in providing a supportive and intellectually stimulating environment in which to teach and conduct research, have contributed significantly to this book. Many students in my computer ethics classes at Rivier College have also contributed directly or indirectly to this textbook. In particular, I would like to thank Casey Cheshire, Nathan Duclos. Erica Moncada, and Michael Scaife for their helpful suggestions. I am also grateful for the comments I received from students in Toby Teory's class at the University of Michigan, who used an interim version of this textbook during the fall 2002 term.

This book has benefited from many helpful comments and suggestions by colleagues who reviewed the entire text or specific sections of it. I wish to thank the following reviewers: Alison Adam, John Artz, Philip Brey, Elizabeth Buchanan, Terrell Bynum, Lloyd Carr, Steve Cooper, Richard Epstein, Eduardo Fernandez, Rob Freidman, Frances Grodzinsky, Chuck Huff, Tom Jewett, Tamara Maddox, Mark Manion, Keith Miller, James Moor, Brian O'Connell, Toby Teory, and John Weckert. I also wish to thank many anonymous reviewers for their valuable comments and suggestions as well. Special thanks to Fran Grodzinsky and Jim Moor for an extraordinary amount of support on this project.

I also wish to thank the editorial staff at John Wiley & Sons, including Simon Durkin and Katherine Hepburn, for their support and attention to important details throughout the various stages of this book's production. I am especially grateful to Paul Crockett, senior editor at Wiley, who believed in this book and who managed to keep me focused on it during a crucial period when I began to have some doubts about this project. I am grateful to Jennifer Albert and Kathleen Byrne, in the copyedit/production group at Argosy Publishing, for allowing me to make several last-minute changes while this manuscript was being converted into a book.

Finally, I would like to thank the two most important people in my life: my wife Joanne, and our daughter, Regina. Without their unwavering support and extraordinary patience, this book could not have been completed.

Herman T. Tavani

Nashua, NH

FOREWORD

The computer/information revolution is shaping our world in ways it has been difficult to predict and to appreciate. When mainframe computers were developed in the 1940s and 1950s, some thought only a few computers would ever be needed in society. When personal computers were introduced in the 1980s, they were considered fascinating toys for hobbyists but not something serious businesses would ever use. When Web tools were initially created in the 1990s to enhance the Internet, they were a curiosity. Using the Web to observe the level of a coffee pot across an ocean was intriguing, at least for a few moments, but not of much practical use. Today, armed with the wisdom of hindsight, the impact of such computing advancements seems obvious, if not inevitable, to all of us. What government claims that it does not need computers? What major business does not have a Web address? How many people, even in the poorest of countries, are not aware of the use of cellular phones?

The computer/information revolution has changed our lives and has brought with it significant ethical, social, and professional issues; consider the area of privacy as but one example. Today, surveillance cameras are abundant, and facial recognition systems are effective even under less-than-ideal observing conditions. Information about buying habits, medical conditions, and human movements can be mined and correlated relentlessly using powerful computers. Individuals' DNA information can easily be collected, stored, and transmitted throughout the world in seconds. This computer/information revolution has brought about unexpected capabilities and possibilities. The revolution is not only technological but also ethical, social, and professional. Our computerized world is perhaps not the world we expected, and, even to the extent that we expected it, it is not a world for which we have well-analyzed policies about how to behave. Now more than ever we need to take cyberethics seriously.

Herman Tavani has written an excellent introduction to the field of cyberethics. His text differs from others in at least three important respects: First, the book is extraordinarily comprehensive and up-to-date in its subject matter. The text covers all of the standard topics such as codes of conduct, privacy, security, crime, intellectual property, and free speech, and also discusses sometimes-overlooked subjects such as democracy, employment, access, and the digital divide. Tavani more than anyone else has tracked and published the bibliographical development of cyberethics over many years, and his expertise with this vast literature shines through in this volume. Second, the book approaches the subject matter of cyberethics from diverse points of view. Tavani examines issues from a social science perspective, from a philosophical perspective, and from a computing professional perspective, and then he suggests ways to integrate these diverse approaches. If the task of cyberethics is multidisciplinary, as many of us believe, then such a diverse but integrated methodology is crucial to accomplishing the task. His book is one of the few that constructs such a methodology. Third, the book is unusually helpful to students and teachers because it contains an entire chapter discussing critical thinking skills and is filled with review and discussion questions.

The cyberage is going to evolve. The future details and applications are, as always, difficult to predict. But it is likely that computing power and bandwidth will continue to grow while computing devices themselves will shrink in size to the nanometer scale. More and more information devices will be inserted into our environment, our cars, our houses, our clothing, and us. Computers will become smarter. They will be made out of new materials—possibly biological. They will operate in new ways—possibly using quantum properties. The distinction between the virtual world and the real world will blur more and more. We need a good book in cyberethics to deal with the present and prepare us for this uncertain future. Tavani's *Ethics and Technology* is such a book.

James H. Moor

Dartmouth College

1

INTRODUCTION TO CYBERETHICS: CONCEPTS, PERSPECTIVES, AND METHODOLOGICAL FRAMEWORKS

Our primary objective in Chapter 1 is to introduce some foundational concepts and methodological frameworks that will be used in our analysis of specific cyberethics issues in subsequent chapters of this textbook. To accomplish this objective, we

- define key terms such as *cyberethics* and *cybertechnology*;
- describe the development of cyberethics as a separate field of applied ethics;
- consider whether there is anything unique or special about cyberethics issues;
- examine three distinct perspectives for identifying and approaching cyberethics issues;
- propose a comprehensive methodological scheme for analyzing cyberethics issues.

We begin with a reflection on a recent cyberstalking incident, which illustrates several of the ethical issues that will be examined in this book.

▶ **CASE ILLUSTRATION:** Internet Stalking

In October 1999, twenty-year-old Amy Boyer was murdered by a young man who had stalked her via the Internet. The stalker, Liam Youens, was able to carry out most of the stalking activities that eventually led to Boyer's death by using a variety of tools available on the Internet. Using standard on-line search facilities available to any Internet user, Youens was able to gather personal information about Boyer. For example, Youens was able to find out where Boyer lived, where she worked, and what kind of vehicle she drove. Youens was also able to use another kind of on-line tool that was available to Internet users to construct two Web sites, both dedicated to his intended victim. On one site he posted personal information about Amy Boyer as well as a photograph of her. And on the other Web site Youens described, in explicit detail, his plans to murder Boyer.

The cyberstalking incident involving Amy Boyer raises a wide range of ethical and social issues, including concerns about privacy and security, free speech and censorship, and moral responsibility and legal liability. Consider a few of the questions that arise: Was Boyer's right to privacy violated because of the way in which personal information about her could be so easily gathered by Liam Youens? Was Youens' "right" to set up a Web site about Amy Boyer without Boyer's knowledge, and without first getting her explicit consent, also a violation of Boyer's rights? And was Youens' alleged right to place on that Web site any kind of information about Boyer he wished to include, regardless of whether that information might be false or defamatory, a right that is protected by free speech? Should the two Internet Service Providers (ISPs) that allowed Youens to post such information to Web sites that reside in their Internet space be held legally liable? And should one of those ISPs be held liable, at least in some contributory sense, for the murder of Amy Boyer, because of the death threat posted on one of the Web sites in its Internet space? Do ordinary users who happen to come across a Web site that contains a posting of a death threat directed toward one or more individuals have a moral responsibility to inform those individuals whose lives are threatened?

The Amy Boyer case provides us with a context to begin thinking about the wide range of ethical issues involving computer and Internet technology. A number of alternative contemporary examples could also have been used to illustrate moral and legal concerns involving the use of computer and Internet technologies. For instance, we could have briefly considered the case of the ILOVEYOU computer virus, which wreaked havoc worldwide in May 2000. Or we could have considered the cyberattacks (i.e., the "denial of service" attacks) that crippled major commercial Web sites in February 2000. We also could have used scenarios involving Internet pedophilia or Internet pornography to illustrate certain points of controversy and contention. Or perhaps we could have selected the recent Napster case. In fact, examples abound. One has only to read a daily newspaper or view regular television news programs to be informed about controversial issues involving the Internet, including questions that pertain to property, privacy, security, anonymity, crime, and jurisdiction. We will examine each of these issues in detail in later chapters of this textbook.

▶ 1.1 DEFINING KEY TERMS: CYBERETHICS AND CYBERTECHNOLOGY

For our purposes, *cyberethics* can be defined as the study of moral, legal, and social issues involving cybertechnology. Cyberethics examines the impact of cybertechnology on our social, legal, and moral systems, and it evaluates the social policies and laws that have been framed in response to issues generated by its development and use. To grasp the significance of these reciprocal relationships, it is important to understand what is meant by the term *cybertechnology*.

1.1.1 What Exactly Is Cybertechnology?

Cybertechnology, as used throughout this textbook, refers to a wide range of computing and communications devices, from stand-alone computers to "connected," or networked, computing and communications technologies. These technologies include, but need not be limited to, hand-held devices (such as Palm Pilots), personal computers (desktops and laptops), and mainframe computers. Networked devices can be connected directly to the Internet, or they can be connected to other devices through one or more privately owned computer networks. Privately owned networks, in turn, include Local Area Networks (LANs) and Wide Area Networks (WANs). A LAN is a privately owned network of computers that span a limited geographical area, such as an office building or a small college campus. WANs, on the other hand, are privately owned networks of computers that are interconnected throughout a much broader geographic region.

How exactly are LANs and WANs different from the Internet? In one sense, the Internet can be understood as *the network of interconnected computer networks*. A synthesis of contemporary information and communications technologies, the Internet evolved from an earlier United States Defense Department initiative (in the 1960s) known as the ARPANET. Unlike WANs and LANs, which are privately owned computer networks, the Internet is generally considered to be a public network, in the sense that much of the information available on the Internet resides in "public space" and is thus available to anyone. The Internet, which should be differentiated from the World Wide Web, includes several applications. The Web, based on Hyper Text Transfer Protocol (HTTP), is one application; other applications include File Transfer Protocol (FTP), Telnet, and e-mail. Because many users access the Internet by way of the Web, and because the majority of users conduct their on-line activities almost exclusively on the Web portion of the Internet, it has become very easy to confuse the Web with the Internet.

The Internet and privately owned computer networks, such as WANs and LANs, are perhaps the most common and well-known examples of *cybertechnology*. However, "cybertechnology" is used in this book to represent the entire range of computing systems, from stand-alone computers to privately owned networks to the Internet itself. And, "cyberethics" refers to the study of moral, legal, and social issues involving those technologies.

1.1.2 Why the Term "Cyberethics"?

Many authors have used the term "computer ethics" to describe the field that examines moral issues pertaining to computing and information technology (see, for example, Moor 1985; Gotterbarn 1991; and Johnson 2001). Because of recent concerns about ethical issues involving the Internet in particular, some have also begun to use the term "Internet ethics" (Langford 2000). Ethical issues examined in this textbook, however, are not limited to the Internet or to computing machines, they also include privately owned computer networks and interconnected communications technologies. Hence we use the relatively new term "cyberethics" (Baird et al. 2000; Halbert and Inguilli 2002; Spinello 2003; Spinello and Tavani 2001; and Willard 1997) to capture the wide range of moral issues involving cybertechnology.

For our purposes, "cyberethics" is more accurate than either "computer ethics" or "Internet ethics" for two reasons: First, the term "computer ethics" can connote ethical issues associated with computing *machines*, and thus could be construed as pertaining to stand-alone or "unconnected" computers. Because computing technologies and communications technologies have converged in recent years, resulting in networked systems, a computer system may now be thought of more accurately as a new kind of *medium* than as a machine. Second, the term "computer ethics" might also suggest a field of study that is concerned exclusively with ethical issues involving computer professionals. Although these issues are very important, and are examined in detail in Chapter 4, we should note that the field of cyberethics is not limited to an analysis of moral issues that affect only professionals.

Given the wide range of moral issues examined in this book, the term "cyberethics" is also more comprehensive than "Internet ethics." Although many of the issues considered under the heading "cyberethics" often pertain to the Internet , some issues examined in this textbook do not involve the Internet per se; for example, issues associated with computerized monitoring in the workplace, with professional responsibility for designing reliable computer hardware and software systems, and with the implications of cybertechnologies for gender and race. We examine ethical issues that will cut across the spectrum of devices and networked communication systems comprising cybertechnology, from stand-alone computers to networked systems.

▶ 1.2 THE CYBERETHICS EVOLUTION: FOUR DEVELOPMENTAL PHASES

Cyberethics had its informal and humble beginnings in the late 1940s, when some analysts confidently predicted that no more than six computers would ever need to be built. Although still a relatively young field, cyberethics has now matured to a point where articles about its historical development have recently appeared in books and scholarly journals (see Bynum 1999). The evolution of cyberethics can be summarized in four distinct *technological phases* (Tavani 2001). Note that what I am calling a technological phase is not to be confused with something as precise as the expression "computer generation," which is often used to describe specific stages in the evolution of computer hardware systems.

Phase 1 (1950s and 1960s), computing technology consisted mainly of huge mainframe computers that were unconnected and thus existed as stand-alone machines. One set of ethical and social questions raised during this phase had to do with the impact of computing machines as "giant brains." Today, we might associate these kinds of questions with the field of artificial intelligence (or AI). In Phase 1, these kinds of questions arose: Can machines think? If so, should we invent thinking machines? If machines can be intelligent entities, what does this mean for our sense of self, for what it means to be human?

Another set of ethical and social concerns that arose during Phase 1 could be catalogued under the heading "privacy threats and the fear of Big Brother." For example, some people in the United States feared that the federal government would set up a national database in which extensive amounts of personal information about its citizens would be stored as electronic records. A strong centralized government could then use that information to monitor and control the actions of ordinary citizens. Although networked computers had not yet come on to the scene, work on the ARPANET—the Internet's predecessor—began during this phase, in the 1960s.

In *Phase 2* (1970s and 1980s), computing machines and communications devices in the commercial sector began to converge. This convergence, in turn, introduced an era of computer/communications networks. Mainframe computers, minicomputers, microcomputers, and personal computers could now be linked together by way of one or more privately owned computer networks such as LANs and WANs (see section 1.1.1.), and information could readily be exchanged between and among databases accessible to networked computers. Ethical issues associated with this phase of computing involved personal privacy, intellectual property, and computer crime. Privacy concerns arose because electronic records containing personal and confidential information could easily be exchanged between two or more commercial databases, and concerns about intellectual property emerged because personal computers could be used to duplicate proprietary software programs. Concerns involving computer crime appeared during this phase because individuals could now use computing devices, including remote computer terminals, to break into and disrupt the computer systems of large organizations.

During *Phase 3* (1990–present), the Internet era, availability of Internet access to the general public has increased significantly. This was facilitated, in no small part, by the development and phenomenal growth of the World Wide Web. The proliferation of Internet- and Web-based technologies has contributed to additional ethical concerns involving computing technology; for example, issues of free speech, anonymity, jurisdiction, and trust have been hotly disputed during this phase. Ethical and social concerns involving disputes over the public vs. private character of personal information easily available on the Internet have been introduced during Phase 3.

Presently we are on the threshold of *Phase 4,* a point at which we have begun to experience an unprecedented level of convergence of technologies. We have already witnessed technological convergence in Phase 2, where we saw the convergence of computing and communications devices, resulting in privately owned networked systems. And in Phase 3, the Internet era, we saw the integration of text, video, and sound technologies on the Web. The computer was now beginning to be viewed much more as a new kind of medium than as a conventional type of machine.

At Phase 3, both the metaphor for the interface used to interact with computer technology and the metaphor for understanding that technology were still much the same as in Phases 1 and 2. A computer was still essentially a box, a CPU, with one or more peripheral devices, such as video screen, keyboard, or mouse serving as an interface to that box. And computers were still viewed as devices essentially external to humans, as things or objects "out there."

But now we appear to be on the cusp of a new and arguably even more significant era of convergence, for computers are becoming more and more a part of who and what we are as human beings. Consider the recent convergence of cybertechnology with biotechnology developments and genome research, and the ethical issues it raises. Also consider the ethical implications of developments in the field of nanotechnology (described in Chapter 11) will likely have. Already we have electronic (artificial) agents that are capable of making decisions for us. Additionally, the implications of the recent introduction of biochip implant technology has led some to predict that computing devices will soon be a regular part of our clothing and even of our bodies. In the future, it may become difficult for us to separate certain aspects of our biology from our technology. Computing devices would then no longer be thought of as things or objects that are "out there," external to humans.

However, we will not speculate any further about either the future of cybertechnology or the future of cyberethics. Our brief description of the evolution of cybertechnology and cyberethics and our speculations about the future have only provided a historical context for understanding the root of some of the ethical concerns involving cybertechnology.

Table 1-1 summarizes key aspect of each phase in the development of cyberethics as a field of applied ethics.

TABLE 1-1   **Summary of Four Phases of Cyberethics**

Phase	Time Period	Technological Features	Associated Issues
1	1950s–1960s	Stand-alone machines (large mainframe computers)	Artificial intelligence (AI), database privacy ("Big Brother")
2	1970s–1980s	Minicomputers and PCs interconnected via privately owned networks	Issues from Phase 1 plus concerns involving intellectual property and software piracy, computer crime, privacy, and the exchange of records
3	1990s–present	Internet and World Wide Web	Issues from Phases 1 and 2 plus concerns about free speech, anonymity, legal jurisdiction, virtual communities, etc.
4	Present to near future	Convergence of information and communication technologies with nanotechnology research and genetic and genomic research, etc.	Issues from Phases 1–3 plus concerns about artificial electronic agents ("bots") with decision-making capabilities, biochip implants, nano-computing research, genomic research, etc.

▶ 1.3 ARE CYBERETHICS ISSUES UNIQUE?

Few would dispute the claim that the use of cybertechnology has had a significant impact on our moral, legal, and social systems. Some also believe, however, that cybertechnology has introduced new and unique moral problems. Are any of these problems genuinely unique moral issues? There are two schools of thought regarding this question.

Consider once again the Amy Boyer cyberstalking case. Has it introduced any new ethical issues, or has it merely exacerbated existing ones? One could argue that there is nothing really new or unique in the stalking case that led to Boyer's death, because in the final analysis "crime is crime" and "murder is murder." According to this line of reasoning, whether a murderer happens to use a computer to assist in carrying out a particular homicide is irrelevant. One might further argue that there is nothing special about cyberstalking incidents in general, regardless of whether or not they result in a victim's death. Proponents of this position could point to the fact that stalking activities are hardly new, since these kinds of activities have been carried out in the off-line world for quite some time. The use of computer and Internet technology might be seen simply as the latest in a series of tools or techniques that are now available to aid stalkers in carrying out criminal activities.

Alternatively, some argue that forms of behavior made possible by cybertechnology have indeed raised either new or special ethical problems. Using the example of cyberstalking to support their view, they point out the relative ease with which stalking activities can now be carried out: Simply by using a computing device with Internet access, one can stalk persons without having to leave the comfort of his or her home. A stalker can, as Liam Youens did, easily acquire personal information about his or her victim because such information is readily accessible to on-line search requests. Furthermore, a stalker can roam the Internet either anonymously or under the cloak of an alias, or pseudo-name. The fact that a user can navigate the Web with relative anonymity makes it much more difficult for law enforcement agents to track down a stalker, either before or after that stalker has caused physical harm to the victim(s) (Grodzinsky and Tavani 2002).

Also consider issues having to do with *scope* and *scale*: An Internet user can stalk multiple victims simultaneously via the use of multiple "windows" on his or her computer screen. The stalker can also stalk victims who happen to live in states and nations that are geographically distant from the stalker. Stalking activities can now occur on a scale or order of magnitude that could not have been realized in the pre-Internet era. More individuals can now engage in stalking behavior because cybertechnology has made it easy, and, as a result, significantly more people can now become the victims of stalkers.

But do these factors support the claim that cybertechnology has introduced any new and unique ethical issues? Walter Maner (1996) argues that computer use has generated a series of ethical issues that (a) did not exist before the advent of computing, and (b) could not have existed if computer technology had not been invented. But is there any evidence to support Maner's claim? Next we consider two scenarios that, initially at least, might suggest that some new ethical issues have been generated by the use of cybertechnology.

▶ **SCENARIO I:** Designing a Controversial Computer System

One might argue that certain ethical issues involving design decisions facing computer professionals are unique because they never would have arisen had it not been for the invention of computer technology. For example, a software engineer might find herself in a situation where she must decide whether or not to participate in the design of a computer system that will likely be used to launch nuclear or chemical weapons. Is the ethical issue facing the engineer in this particular case one that is new because it is peculiar to computer technology? In one sense, it is true that moral concerns having to do with whether or not one should participate in the design of a certain kind of computer system did not exist before the advent of computing technology. However, it is true only in a trivial sense. Clearly, since long before computing technologies were available, engineers have been faced with ethical choices involving whether or not to participate in the design and development of certain kinds of controversial technological systems. Prior to the computer era, they had to make decisions involving the design of aircraft intended to deliver conventional as well as nuclear bombs. So, is the fact that certain technological systems happen to include the use of computer software or computer hardware components morally relevant in this case? Have any *new* or unique ethical issues, in a nontrivial sense of *unique*, been generated in this particular case? Based on our discussion of this scenario, there does not seem to be sufficient evidence to substantiate the claim that a new ethical issue has been introduced.

▶ **SCENARIO II:** Software Piracy

It might also be argued that ethical issues surrounding software piracy are new and thus unique to cybertechnology, because the art of pirating software programs would not have been possible if computer technology had not been invented in the first place. Once again, this claim would be true only in a trivial sense. The issue of piracy itself as a moral concern existed before the widespread use of computer technology. For example, people were able to pirate audiotapes simply by using two or more analog tape recorders to make unauthorized copies of proprietary material. The important point to note here is that moral issues surrounding the pirating of cassette tapes are, at bottom, the same issues underlying the pirating of computer software. They arise in each case because, fundamentally, the behavior associated with piracy raises moral concerns about property, fairness, rights, and so forth. So, as in Scenario I, there seems to be insufficient evidence to suggest that the ethical issues associated with software piracy are either new or unique in some nontrivial sense.

1.3.1 Distinguishing between Unique Technological Features and Unique Ethical Issues

Based on our analysis of these two preceding scenarios, we might conclude that there is nothing new or special about the kinds of moral issues associated with cybertechnology. In fact, some philosophers have argued that we have the same old ethical issues reappearing in a new guise. But is such a view accurate?

If we focus primarily on the moral issues themselves *as moral issues*, it would seem that perhaps there is nothing new. Cyberrelated concerns involving privacy, property, free speech, etc., can be understood as specific expressions of core (traditional) moral notions, such as autonomy, fairness, justice, responsibility, and respect for persons. However, if instead we focus more closely on cybertechnology itself, we see that there are some interesting and possibly unique features that distinguish this technology from earlier technologies. Walter Maner (1996) has argued that computing technology is "uniquely fast," "uniquely complex," and "uniquely coded." But even if cybertechnology has these unique features, does it necessarily follow that any of the moral questions associated with them must also be unique? As we will see in Chapter 3, one would commit a logical fallacy if he or she concluded that cyberethics issues must be unique simply because certain features or aspects of cybertechnology are unique. Characteristics that apply to technology itself need not apply to ethical issues associated with that technology.

1.3.2 An Alternative Strategy for Analyzing the Question about Uniqueness

Although it may be difficult to prove conclusively whether or not cybertechnology has generated any new or unique ethical issues, we must not rule out the possibility that many of the controversies associated with this technology might warrant special consideration from an ethical perspective. But what exactly is so different about issues involving cybertechnology that makes them deserving of special moral consideration? James Moor (1985) points out that computer technology, unlike most previous technologies, is "logically malleable"; it can be shaped and molded to perform a variety of functions. Because noncomputer technologies are typically designed to perform some particular function or task, they lack the universal or general-purpose characteristics that computing technologies possess. For example, microwave ovens and videocassette recorders are technological devices that have been designed to perform specific tasks. Microwave ovens cannot be used to view videotapes, and videocassette recorders cannot be used to cook or warm food. However, a computer, depending on the software used, can perform a range of diverse tasks: It can be instructed to behave as a video game, a word processor, a spreadsheet, a medium to send and receive e-mail messages, or an interface to Web sites. Hence, cybertechnology is extremely malleable.

Moor points out that because of its logical malleability, cybertechnology can generate "new possibilities for human action" that appear to be limitless. Some of these possibilities for action generate what Moor calls "policy vacuums," because we have no explicit policies or laws to guide new choices made possible by computer technology. These vacuums, in turn, need to be filled with either new or revised policies. But what exactly does Moor mean by "policy"? Moor (1999) defines policies as "rules of conduct," ranging from formal laws to "informal, implicit guidelines for actions." Viewing computer-ethics issues in terms of policies is useful, Moor believes, because policies have the right level of generality to consider when we evaluate the morality of conduct. As noted, policies can range from formal laws to informal guidelines. Moor also notes that policies can have "justified exemptions" because they are not absolute; yet policies usually imply a certain "level of obligation" within their contexts.

What action is required when one or more policy vacuums are discovered? A solution to this problem might seem quite simple and straightforward. We might assume that all we need to do is identify the vacuums that have been generated and then fill them with policies and laws. However, this will not always work, because sometimes the new possibilities for human action generated by cybertechnology also introduce "conceptual vacuums," or what Moor calls "conceptual muddles." In these cases, we must first eliminate the muddles by clearing up certain conceptual confusions before we can frame coherent policies and laws.

▶ **CASE ILLUSTRATION OF A POLICY VACUUM:** Duplicating Computer Software

One significant policy vacuum, which also involved a conceptual muddle, emerged with the advent of personal desktop computers (henceforth referred to generically as PCs). The particular vacuum arose because of the controversy surrounding the copying of software. When PCs became commercially available, many users discovered that they could easily duplicate software programs. They found that they could use their PCs to make copies of proprietary computer programs such as word processing programs, spreadsheets, and video games. Some users assumed that in making copies of these programs they were doing nothing wrong. At that time there were no explicit laws to regulate the subsequent use and distribution of software programs once they had been legally purchased by an individual or by an institution. Although it might be difficult to imagine today, at one time software was not clearly protected by either copyright law or the patent process.

Of course, there were clear laws and policies regarding the theft of physical property. Such laws and policies protected against the theft of personal computers as well as against the theft of a physical disk drive residing in a PC on which the proprietary software programs could easily be duplicated. However, this was not the case with laws and policies regarding the "theft," or unauthorized copying of software programs that resided on computers. Although there were intellectual property laws in place, it had not been determined that software was or should be protected by intellectual property (IP) law: It was unclear whether software should be understood as an idea (which is not protected by IP law), as a form of writing protected by copyright law, or as a set of machine instructions protected by patents. Consequently, many entrepreneurs who designed and manufactured software programs argued for explicit legal protection for their products. A policy vacuum arose with respect to duplicating software: Could a user make a backup copy of a program for herself? Could she share it with a friend? Could she give the original program to a friend? A clear policy was needed to fill this vacuum.

Before we can fill the vacuum regarding software duplication with a coherent policy or law, we first have to resolve a certain conceptual muddle by answering the question: What exactly is computer software? Until we can clarify the concept of software itself, we cannot frame a coherent policy as to whether or not we should allow the free duplication of software. Currently there is still much confusion, as well as considerable controversy, as to how laws concerning the exchange (and, in effect, duplication) of proprietary software over the Internet should be framed.

In Moor's scheme, how one resolves the conceptual muddle or decides the conceptual issue can have a significant effect on which kinds of policies are acceptable. Getting clear about the conceptual issues is an important first step, but it is not a sufficient condition for being able to formulate a policy. Finally, the justification of a policy requires much factual knowledge, as well as an understanding of normative and ethical principles.

Consider the recent controversy involving Napster. Proponents on both sides in the Napster dispute have experienced difficulties in making convincing arguments for their respective positions due, in no small part, to confusion regarding the nature and the status of information being downloaded and then exchanged between Internet users. Although cybertechnology has made it possible to exchange MP3 files, there is still debate, and arguably a great deal of confusion as well, about whether doing so clearly violates existing property laws. Until some of the conceptual confusions underlying the Napster case are resolved, it is difficult to imagine how a satisfactory policy regarding the exchange of MP3 files in peer-to-peer (P2P) transactions can be framed.

How exactly does Moor's insight that cyberethics issues need to be analyzed in terms of potential policy vacuums and conceptual muddles contribute to our earlier question as to whether there is anything unique or special about cyberethics? First, we should note that Moor takes no explicit stance on the question as to whether any cyberethics issues are unique. However, he does argue that cyberethics issues deserve special consideration because of the nature of cybertechnology itself, which is significantly different from alternative technologies in terms of the vast number of policy vacuums it generates (Moor 2001). So even though the ethical issues—that is, issues involving privacy, intellectual property, and so forth—might not be new or unique, they nonetheless can put significant pressure on our conceptual frameworks and normative reasoning to a degree not found in other areas of applied ethics. Thus it would seem to follow, on Moor's line of reasoning, that an independent field of applied ethics that focuses on ethical aspects of cybertechnology is indeed justified.

▶ 1.4 CYBERETHICS AS A BRANCH OF APPLIED ETHICS: THREE DISTINCT PERSPECTIVES

Cyberethics, as a field of study, can be understood as a branch of *applied ethics*. Applied ethics, as opposed to theoretical ethics, examines practical ethical issues. It does so by analyzing those issues from the vantage point of one or more ethical theories. Whereas ethical theory is concerned with establishing logically coherent and consistent criteria in the form of standards and rules for evaluating moral problems, the principal aim of applied ethics is to analyze specific moral problems themselves through the application of ethical theory. As such, those working in fields of applied ethics are not inclined to debate some of the finer points of individual ethical theories. Instead, their interest in ethical theory is primarily with how one or more theories can be successfully applied to the analysis of specific moral problems that they happen to be investigating.

For an example of a practical-ethics issue involving cybertechnology, consider again the Napster controversy (see Section 1.3.2). Recall that at the heart of this dispute is the question of whether the exchange of proprietary software, in a digital format known as MP3 files, over the Internet should be permitted. Those advocating the free exchange of MP3 files could appeal to one or more ethical theories to support their position. For example, they might appeal to utilitarianism, an ethical theory that is based on the principle that our policies and laws should be such that they produce the greatest good (happiness) for the greatest number of people. A utilitarian might argue that MP3 files should be distributed freely over the Internet because the consequences of allowing such a practice would make the majority of users happy and would thus contribute to the greatest good for the greatest number of persons affected.

Others might argue that allowing this proprietary material to be exchanged freely over the Internet would violate the rights of those who created, and who legally own, the material. Proponents of this view could appeal to a nonutilitarian principle or theory that is grounded in the notion of respecting the rights of individuals. According to this view, the concern is with protecting the rights of individuals who legally own the proprietary material in question, irrespective of the happiness that might or might not result for the majority of Internet users.

Notice that in the case involving the dispute over the exchange of MP3 files on the Internet, the application of two different ethical theories yields two very different answers to the question of which policy or course of action ought to be adopted. Sometimes, however, the application of different ethical theories to a particular problem will yield similar solutions. We will examine in detail some standard ethical theories, including utilitarianism, in Chapter 2. Our main concern in this textbook is with applied, or practical, ethics issues, and not with ethical theory per se. Wherever appropriate, however, ethical theory will be used to inform our analysis of moral issues involving cybertechnology.

Understanding cyberethics as a field of applied ethics that examines moral issues pertaining to cybertechnology is an important first step. But much more needs to be said about the perspectives that interdisciplinary researchers bring to their analysis of the issues that make up this relatively new field. Most scholars and professionals conducting research in this field of applied ethics have proceeded from one of three different perspectives—professional ethics, philosophical ethics, or descriptive ethics. Gaining a clearer understanding of what is meant by each of these perspectives is useful at this point.

1.4.1 Perspective # 1: Cyberethics as a Field of Professional Ethics

According to those who view cyberethics primarily as a branch of *professional ethics*, the field can best be understood as identifying and analyzing issues of ethical responsibility for computer professionals. Among the cyberethics issues considered from this perspective are those having to do with the computer professional's role in designing, developing, and maintaining computer hardware and software systems. Suppose a programmer discovers that a software product she has been working on is about to be released for sale to the public even though that product is unreliable because it contains "buggy" software. Should she blow the whistle?

Those who see cyberethics essentially as a branch of professional ethics would likely draw on analogies from other professional fields, such as medicine and law. They would point out that in medical ethics and legal ethics, the principle focus of analysis is on issues of moral responsibility that affect individuals as *members* of those professions. By analogy, they would go on to argue that the same rationale should apply to the field of cyberethics: The primary, and possibly even exclusive, focus of cyberethics should be on issues of moral responsibility that affect computer professionals.

Don Gotterbarn (1991), an advocate for the view that cyberethics is best understood as a field of professional ethics, has argued that the principal focus of computer ethics should be on issues of professional responsibility and not on the broader moral and social implications of that technology. The analogies used in his argument are instructive. Gotterbarn notes, for example, that in the past certain technologies have profoundly altered our lives, especially in the ways that many of us conduct our day-to-day affairs. Consider three such technologies: the printing press, the automobile, and the airplane. Despite the significant and perhaps revolutionary effects of each of these technologies, we do not have "printing press ethics," "automobile ethics," or "airplane ethics." So why, Gotterbarn asks, should we have a field of computer ethics apart from the study of those ethical issues that affect the professionals responsible for the design, development, and delivery of computer systems? In other words, Gotterbarn suggests that it is not the purview of computer ethics to examine any ethical issues other than those that affect computer professionals.

1.4.1.1 Professional Ethics and the Computer Science Practitioner

Gotterbarn's view about what the proper focus of computer ethics research and inquiry should be is shared by other practitioners in the discipline of computer science (see, for example, Baase 2003). However, some of those practitioners, as well as many philosophers and social scientists, believe that Gotterbarn's conception of computer ethics simply as a field of professional ethics is too narrow. In fact, some who identify themselves as computer professionals or as information professionals, and who are otherwise sympathetic to Gotterbarn's overall attention to professional ethics issues, believe that that a broader model is needed. Elizabeth Buchanan (2001), who also recognizes the important role of the analysis of ethical issues involving the "information professions," suggests that the study of cyberethics issues must include an examination of certain nonprofessional-ethics issues as well. In describing the field of information ethics as one that affects information professionals, Buchanan also suggests that the issues involving information ethics have a significant impact on non-information professionals (including ordinary computer users as well as individuals who have never used a computer).

Of course, Buchanan's category of "informational professional" is considerably broader in scope than Gotterbarn's notion of "computer professional." But the central point of her argument still holds, especially in the era of the Internet and the World Wide Web. In the computing era preceding the Web, Gotterbarn's conception of the field as one limited to ethical issues concerning computer professionals might have seemed more plausible than it does today. Now, computers are virtually everywhere, and the ethical issues generated by certain uses of computers and cybertechnology affect virtually everyone, professional and nonprofessional alike.

1.4.1.2 Applying the Professional Ethics Model to Cyberethics Issues

It is fairly easy to see how the professional-ethics model can be used to analyze issues involving professional responsibility that directly impact computer professionals. For example, issues concerned with the development and implementation of critical software would fit closely with the professional model. But can that model be extended to include cases that may only affect computer professionals indirectly?

Consider how some of the issues in the cyberstalking case involving Amy Boyer, described earlier in this chapter, might be analyzed from the perspective of professional ethics. From this vantage point, one might argue that cyberstalking in general and the murder of Amy Boyer in particular are not the kinds of concerns that are the proper business of computer ethics. We saw that someone like Gotterbarn might ask why a crime that happened to involve the use of a computer is the business of computer ethics. For example, he notes that a murder that happened to be committed with a surgeon's scalpel would not be considered the business of medical ethics. While murders involving the use of a computer, like all murders, are serious moral and legal problems, Gotterbarn suggests that they might not necessarily be examples of computer-ethics issues. Thus the ethical issues in the Amy Boyer case might not be genuine computer-ethics issues.

However, Gotterbarn and the advocates for his position are acutely aware that the software code developed by engineers can have implications that extend far beyond the computing profession itself. So, for example, engineers who develop code that can be used in applications to violate individual privacy may bear some of the responsibility for harms caused by that code. And Internet Service Providers who use the same code would also share some responsibility for privacy violations. Thus, someone approaching the Amy Boyer case from the perspective of professional ethics might ask the following kinds of questions: Was Boyer's right to privacy violated? If so, should the ISPs involved be held morally responsible or legally liable? And should the computer professionals who are employed by those ISPs, or who developed the software code that enabled Boyer's privacy to be violated, also be held responsible?

Many of the ethical issues discussed in this book have implications for computer professionals, either directly or indirectly. Issues which have a direct impact on computer professionals in general, and software engineers in particular, are examined in Chapter 4, which is dedicated to professional ethics. Computer science students and computer professionals will likely also want to assess some of the indirect implications that issues examined in Chapters 5 through 11 also have for the computing profession.

1.4.2   Perspective # 2: Cyberethics as a Field of Philosophical Ethics

What exactly is *philosophical ethics* and how is it different from professional ethics? Since philosophical methods and tools are also used to analyze issues involving professional ethics, any attempt to distinguish between the two might seem arbitrary, perhaps even odd. For our purposes, however, a useful distinction can be drawn between the two fields because of the approach each takes in addressing ethical issues. Whereas professional-ethics issues typically involve concerns of responsibility and obligation affecting individuals as members of a certain profession, philosophical ethics issues include broader concerns—social policies as well as individual behavior—that affect virtually everyone in society. Cybertechnology-related moral issues involving privacy, security, property, and free speech can affect everyone, including individuals who have never even used a computer.

To appreciate the perspective on cyberethics as a field of philosophical ethics, consider James Moor's classic definition of computer ethics (1985), which is virtually equivalent to what we mean by cyberethics. According to Moor, computer ethics is

> the analysis of the nature and social impact of computer technology and the corresponding formulation and justification of policies for the ethical use of such technology. [Italics added.]

Two points in Moor's definition are worth examining more closely. First, computer ethics (and, for that matter, cyberethics) is concerned with the social impact of cybertechnology in a broad sense, and not merely the impact of that technology for computer professionals. Secondly, this definition challenges us to reflect on the social impact of cybertechnology in a way that requires a justification for our social policies.

Why is cyberethics, as a field of philosophical ethics dedicated to the study of ethical issues involving cybertechnology, warranted when there aren't similar fields of applied ethics for other technologies? Recall our earlier discussion of Gotterbarn's observation that we do not have fields of applied ethics called "automobile ethics" or "airplane ethics," even though automobile and airplane technologies have significantly affected our day-to-day lives. Moor would disagree with Gotterbarn on this point, even though Moor does not deny that the professional-responsibility issues identified by Gotterbarn must also be taken into account. But how would Moor respond to Gotterbarn's central argument about the social impact of previous technologies and their connection (or lack of one) to ethics?

Moor notes that the introduction of automobile and airplane technologies did not affect our social policies and norms in the same kinds of fundamental ways that computer technology has. Of course, we have had to modify and significantly revise certain laws and policies to accommodate the implementation of new kinds of transportation technologies. In the case of automobile technology, we had to extend, and in some cases modify, certain policies and laws previously used to regulate the flow of horse-drawn modes of transportation. And clearly, automobile and airplane technologies have revolutionized transportation, resulting in our ability to travel faster and farther than was possible in previous eras.

What has made the impact of computer technology significantly different from that of other modern technologies? We have already seen that for Moor, three factors contribute to this impact: logical malleability, policy vacuums, and conceptual muddles. Because cybertechnology is logically malleable, its uses often generate policy vacuums and conceptual muddles. In Section 1.3.2 we saw how certain kinds of conceptual muddles contributed to some of the confusion surrounding software piracy issues in general, and the Napster controversy in particular. What implications do these factors have for the standard methodology used by philosophers in the analysis of applied-ethics issues?

1.4.2.1 Methodology and Philosophical Ethics

According to Philip Brey (2000), the standard methodology used by philosophers to conduct research in applied ethics has three distinct stages in that an ethicist must

1. identify a particular controversial practice as a moral problem,

2. describe and analyze the problem by clarifying concepts and examining the factual data associated with that problem,

3. apply moral theories and principles in the deliberative process in order to reach a position about the particular moral issue.

We have already noted how the first two stages in this methodology can be applied to an analysis of ethical issues associated with cyberpiracy. We saw that first, a practice involving the use of cybertechnology to pirate proprietary information was *identified* as morally controversial. At the second stage, the problem was *analyzed* in descriptive and contextual terms to clarify the practice and to situate it in a particular context. In the case of cyberpiracy, we saw that the concept of piracy could be analyzed in terms of moral issues involving theft and intellectual property theory. When we describe and analyze problems at this stage, we will want to be aware of and address any policy vacuums and conceptual muddles that are relevant.

At the third and final stage, the problem must be *deliberated* over in terms of moral principles (or theories) and logical arguments. Brey describes this stage in the method as the "deliberative process." Here, various arguments are used to justify the application of particular moral principles to the issue under consideration. For example, issues involving cyberpiracy can be deliberated upon in terms of one or more standard ethical theories, such as utilitarianism (defined in Chapter 2).

1.4.2.2 Applying the Method of Philosophical Ethics to the Amy Boyer Case

To see how the philosophical-ethics perspective of cyberethics can help us to analyze cyber-related moral issues other than digital piracy, we can revisit the cyberstalking case involving Amy Boyer. Our first task is to identify one or more moral issues associated with this particular case. We have already seen that the Boyer case raises several ethical issues. Recall that one of the ethical concerns we identified in that case of cyberstalking had to do with personal privacy; among the complaints in the wrongful death suit filed by Amy Boyer's stepfather was that his stepdaughter's privacy had been violated. We next ask whether the specific privacy concerns involving the Boyer case have generated any policy vacuums or conceptual muddles. Much of the personal information about Boyer that her stalker was able to retrieve from the Internet would likely be considered public information, since it was also accessible in public records. Of course, it is now much easier to access public records because of their on-line availability, in many instances, than it was in the pre-computer era, so we might now ask whether our existing privacy laws and policies regarding the access and flow of personal information are still adequate in the cyber era. In other words, does a policy vacuum exist here? The fact that personal information residing in public databases can now be accessed with relative ease through the use of Internet search facilities would seem to pose a challenge for our existing privacy policies. So, arguably, a policy vacuum has emerged here.

Next, we ask whether any conceptual vacuums or muddles have also been introduced. Consider criteria that we have traditionally used to distinguish between personal information that is essentially public and personal information that is considered private in nature. Is there also conceptual muddle here? That is, does the concept of personal information itself need to be re-examined in an age of cybertechnology? (We will address this particular question in Chapter 5, where we examine a set of privacy concerns that some now refer to as the "problem of privacy in public." We will see that our traditional conception of privacy, which has informed our current policies, may indeed need to be rethought in light of vacuums introduced by cybertechnology.) Once the policy vacuums and conceptual muddles have been resolved, we can then move on to the third and final stage, where we deliberate on how best to resolve the privacy issue involving the Boyer case. In our discussion of ethical theory in Chapter 2, we will see how this is done.

1.4.3 Perspective #3: Cyberethics as a Field of Descriptive Ethics

We have examined two perspectives on cyberethics that can both be understood as *normative* inquiries into applied ethics issues. Normative inquiries or studies, which focus on evaluating and prescribing moral systems, can be contrasted with *descriptive* inquiries or studies. Descriptive ethics describes aspects of particular moral systems and reports how members of various groups and cultures view particular moral issues. Whereas descriptive investigations provide us with information about "what *is* the case," normative inquiries evaluate situations from the vantage point of questions having to do with "what *ought to be* the case."

Those who approach cyberethics from the perspective of descriptive ethics often describe sociological aspects of a particular moral issue, such as the social impact of a certain technology on a certain community. For example, one way of analyzing moral issues surrounding the "digital divide" (examined in Chapter 10) is first to describe the problem in terms of its impact on various sociodemographic groups involving social class, race, and gender. We can investigate whether, in fact, fewer poor people, nonwhites, and women have access to cybertechnology than wealthy and middle-class persons, whites, and men. In this case, the investigation is one that is basically descriptive in character. If we were then to inquire whether the lack of access to technology for some groups relative to others was unfair, we would be engaging in a normative inquiry. For example, a normative investigation of this issue would question whether certain groups *should* have more access to cybertechnology than they currently have. The following scenario illustrates an approach to a particular cyberethics issue via the perspective of descriptive ethics.

▶ **SCENARIO III:** Describing the Impact of a Technology on a Community's Workforce

Imagine that a major employer in a certain community decides to implement a new kind of computer/information technology in the workplace. Further imagine that the implementation of this new technology has significant social implications for the community. If we analyze the impact that this new technology has with respect to the number of jobs that are gained or lost in that community, our investigation is essentially descriptive in nature. For example, imagine that since the introduction of Technology X, 8,000 workers in Community Y have lost their jobs. In reporting this phenomenon, we are simply describing an impact that the introduction of Technology X has for Community Y.

This inquiry and analysis of the issue in Community Y involves nothing more than simply describing what *is* the case. If, however, we argue that those workers *ought not* to have been displaced, then we make a claim that is normative. For example, one might argue that the workers should not have been displaced because of certain contractual obligations between the employer and its employees. Or we might argue that certain additional factors should have been taken into consideration when determining which workers would lose their jobs. Suppose that in the process of eliminating jobs, older workers and minority employees were disproportionately affected. Would that have affected the way we view the situation?

Our first account of the social impact of the new technology on workers in Community Y simply reported to us some information about the number of jobs lost to workers in that community. In the latter account, however, we did much more than merely describe what the impact was. There, we were also evaluating certain aspects of that impact for Community Y in terms of what we believed *ought* to have been done. In doing so, we shifted from an analysis of a social impact in terms of claims that were merely descriptive to an analysis in which the claims were essentially normative.

1.4.3.1 Descriptive vs. Normative Claims

To further illustrate the differences between claims that are normative and those that are descriptive, consider the following three assertions involving Bill Gates:

1. Bill Gates served as the Chief Executive Officer of Microsoft Corporation for many years.

2. Bill Gates should expand Microsoft's product offerings.

3. Bill Gates should engage in business practices that are fair to competitors.

As you might already have inferred, one of the claims is descriptive and two are normative. A person asserting (1) has made a descriptive claim about Gates. Someone asserting either (2) or (3), however, makes a normative claim. Assertions (2) and (3) are normative because they contain evaluative terms such as "should" and "ought." As such, these two assertions do more than merely report something about Gates in purely descriptive terms.

It is important to point out that not every normative claim is also a moral claim. For example, the normative assertions expressed in (2) and (3) are different in at least one very significant respect. Even though both assertions are normative, only (3) is also a moral assertion. We will consider the normative/descriptive distinction, as well as the distinction between moral and nonmoral normative claims, in greater detail in Chapter 2.

Figure 1-1 illustrates some differences between normative and descriptive assertions.

1.4.3.2 Some Benefits of Using the Descriptive Approach to Analyze Cyberethics Issues

How exactly is the examination of cyberethics issues from the perspective of descriptive ethics useful? For one thing, many sociologists and social scientists working in the field of cyberethics believe that focusing initially on descriptive aspects of these issues can help us to better understand certain normative features and implications. For example, Chuck Huff and Thomas Finholt (1994) have argued that when we understand the social effects of technology in its descriptive sense, the normative ethical questions become clearer. An analysis of the social impact of cybertechnology in descriptive terms can help to inform us in two important respects: First, approaching questions from the descriptive perspective can better

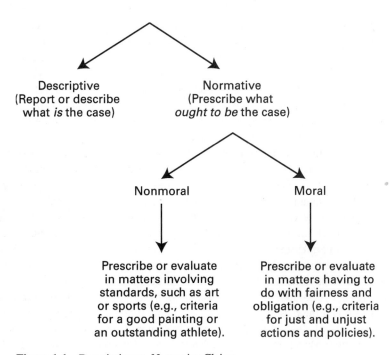

Figure 1-1   Descriptive vs. Normative Claims

prepare us for our subsequent analysis of practical ethical issues affecting our system of policies and laws. Second, the descriptive approach can help computer professionals in their attempts to design computer systems that might avoid social and ethical problems associated with earlier computer systems. So, using Huff and Finholt's model, we can see how the descriptive-ethics perspective can work in conjunction with the goals and objectives of both practical ethics and professional ethics.

We have already noted that virtually all of our social institutions, from work to education to government to finance, have been affected by cybertechnology. This technology has also had significant impacts on different sociodemographic sectors and segments of our population. The descriptive information that we gather about these groups can provide important information that, in turn, can inform legislators and policy makers who are drafting and revising laws in response to the effects of cybertechnology.

From the perspective of descriptive ethics, we can also better examine some of the impacts that cybertechnology has for our notions of community and democracy. We can ask, for instance, whether certain developments in virtual-reality technology have affected the way that we conceive traditional notions such as "community" and "neighbor." Is a community essentially a group of individuals with similar interests and perhaps a similar ideology, irrespective of geographical limitations? Is national identity something that is, or may soon become, anachronistic? While these kinds of questions and issues in and of themselves are more correctly conceived as descriptive rather than normative, they could have significant implications for our moral and legal systems as well. Much more will be said about the relationship between descriptive and normative approaches to ethical issues in Chapters 10 and 11.

1.4.3.3 Applying the Descriptive Ethics Approach to the Amy Boyer Case

Consider how someone approaching cyberethics issues from the perspective of descriptive ethics might analyze the cyberstalking case involving Amy Boyer. For one thing, she might inquire into whether there has been an increase in the number of stalking and stalking-related criminal activities. And if the answer to this question is "yes," she might next question whether such an increase is linked to the widespread availability of cybertechnology. Also, she might consider whether certain groups in the population are now more at risk than others with respect to being stalked in cyberspace. She could inquire whether there are any statistical patterns to suggest that celebrities and certain high-profile individuals, such as politicians and corporate leaders, are more likely to be stalked via cybertechnology than are ordinary individuals. She could ask if women are generally more vulnerable to the kinds of threats posed by cyberstalking than men. And, if they are, are younger, single women more likely to be stalked in cyberspace than women in other subgroups?

Also, a researcher approaching the Boyer case from the descriptive perspective might set out to determine whether a profile for a typical cyberstalker can be established. The researcher might pursue answers to the following kinds of questions: Is a typical cyberstalker someone who is young, white, and male? Is it likely that individuals who never would have thought of physically stalking a victim in geographical space might now be inclined to engage in cyberstalking, perhaps because of the relative ease of doing so with cybertechnology? Or is it the case that some of those same individuals might now be tempted to do so because they believe that they will not likely get caught? Also, has the fact that a potential cyberstalker realizes that he or she can stalk a victim on the Internet under the cloak of rela-

TABLE 1-2   Summary of Cyberethics Perspectives

Type of Perspective	Associated Disciplines	Issues Examined
Professional	Computer Science Engineering Library/Information Science	Professional responsibility System reliability/safety Codes of conduct
Philosophical	Philosophy Law	Privacy and anonymity Intellectual property Free speech
Descriptive	Sociology Behavioral Sciences	Impact of cybertechnology on governmental/financial/educational institutions and sociodemographic groups

tive anonymity contributed to the increase in stalking-related activities? These are a few of the questions that could be examined from the descriptive perspective of cyberethics.

Table 1-2 summarizes some key characteristics that differentiate the three main perspectives for approaching cyberethics issues.

In Chapters 4 through 11, we examine specific cyberethics questions from the vantage points of three perspectives: Issues considered from the perspective of professional ethics are examined in Chapter 4. Cyberethics issues considered from the perspective of philosophical ethics, such as those involving privacy, security, and intellectual property and free speech, are examined in Chapters 5 through 9. And issues considered from the perspective of descriptive ethics are examined in Chapters 10 and 11.

▶ 1.5 A COMPREHENSIVE CYBERETHICS METHODOLOGY

The three different perspectives of cyberethics described in the preceding section might suggest that three different kinds of methodologies are needed to analyze the range of issues examined in this textbook. The goal of this section, however, is to show that a single, comprehensive method can be constructed, and that this method will be adequate in guiding us in our analysis of cyberethics issues.

Recall the standard model used in applied ethics, which we briefly examined in Section 1.4.2.1. There we saw that the standard model includes three stages in which a researcher must (1) identify an ethical problem, (2) describe and analyze the problem in conceptual and factual terms, and (3) apply ethical theories and principles in the deliberative process. We also saw that James Moor argued that the conventional model was not adequate for an analysis of at least some cyberethics issues. Moor believed that additional steps, which addressed questions involving policy vacuums and conceptual muddles, are sometimes needed before we can move from the second to the third stage of the methodological scheme. We must now consider whether the standard model, with Moor's additional steps included, is complete. Philip Brey (2000) suggests that it is not.

Brey believes that while the (revised) standard model might work well in many fields of applied ethics, such as medical ethics, business ethics, and bioethics, it does not always fare well in cyberethics. Brey argues that the standard method, when used to identify ethical aspects of cybertechnology, tends to focus almost exclusively on the *uses* of that technology. As such, the standard method fails to pay sufficient attention to certain features that may be embedded in the technology itself, such as design features that may also have moral implications.

We might be inclined to assume that technology itself is neutral and that only the uses to which a particular technology is put are morally controversial. However, Brey and others believe that is a mistake to conceive of technology, independent of its uses, as something that is value-free, or unbiased. Instead, they argue, moral values are often embedded or implicit in features built into technologies at the design stage. For example, some feminist critics have pointed out that in the past the ergonomic systems designed for drivers of automobiles were biased toward men and gave virtually no consideration to women. That is, considerations having to do with the average height and typical body dimensions of men were implicitly built into the design specification. These critics also note that decisions about how the ergonomic systems would be designed were all made by men, which likely accounts for the bias embedded in that particular technological system.

1.5.1 Is Cybertechnology Neutral?

As noted in the preceding section, Brey believes that cybertechnology has certain built-in values and biases that are not always obvious or easy to detect. He worries that these biases can easily go unnoticed by computer ethics researchers. An example of how difficult it can be to detect relevant biases and values can be found in a case involving non-cybertechnology, such as, gun technology. You have probably heard the expression, "Guns don't kill people; people kill people." An assumption underlying this slogan is that guns, independent of their applications or uses, are neutral. That is, guns in and of themselves are neither good nor bad. It would seem that there is an element of truth in this claim—after all, guns in and of themselves do not kill people. And until some person actually handles the gun, no one typically dies as a result of that gun. However, some critics note that the above slogan can be misleading if it is used to convey the claim that guns are neutral in the sense that they are no different from any other technologies or tools when it comes to violence.

Corlann Gee Bush (1997) has argued that gun technology, like all technologies, is biased in certain directions. She argues that certain features inherent in gun technology cause guns to be biased towards violence. To illustrate this bias, Bush appeals to an analogy from physics in which an atom that either loses or gains electrons through ionization becomes charged, or "valenced" in a certain direction. She notes that all technologies, including guns, are similarly valenced in that they tend to favor certain directions rather than others.

Bush concedes that devices other than guns can be used effectively to kill people. For example, a hammer, an ice pick, or even a certain kind of computer hardware device could each be used to kill someone. She argues, however, that guns are "valenced toward violence" in a way that other tools and technologies that could also be used to kill people are not. She points out that the mere presence of a gun in a particular situation raises the level of violence. Of course, an assailant could bludgeon someone to death by using a certain kind of computer hardware device. The assailant could also use a hammer to strike several blows to a person's head causing that person's death, or he could even stab someone to death with an ice pick. Although ice picks, hammers, and computer hardware devices *can* each be used to kill people, these objects are less likely to result in the unplanned or accidental death of an individual than would the presence of a gun in a similar situation. They are less likely to result in someone's death because of the respective purposes and functions of ice picks, hammers, and computing devices.

Note that in cases involving the presence of a computer device, an ice pick, or a hammer, an assailant must make physical contact with his victim and must then apply some measure of physical force to carry out the murder. In the case involving a gun, on the other hand, the assailant is not required to make any physical contact at all. But perhaps more importantly, computer hardware devices, hammers, and ice picks are not charged or valenced toward killing someone in the same way guns are. The function of gun technology is such that it lends itself to violence and killing, by virtue of its intended purpose and design, even if a resultant death is not intended. So, if Bush is correct, technology is not neutral.

At this point, you might ask what exactly the preceding discussion about technologies being valenced has to do with our concern that computer technology might have embedded biases. Our purpose has been to show that all technologies, and by implication, computer technology, have embedded values and biases. Locating biases in software is important, and in Chapter 10 we examine some specific cases that illustrate gender bias in educational software and video games. Because Brey worries that many computer-ethics researchers assume computer technology is inherently neutral, he proposes a method that causes us to question such an assumption. To employ his method, we need to locate what Brey calls "embedded normative values" in computer technology. Exposing such values inherent in various computer technologies is the first step of Brey's "disclosive" method of computer ethics.

1.5.2 A "Disclosive" Method for Cyberethics

As noted earlier, Brey believes that the standard, or what he calls "mainstream," applied-ethics methodology is not always adequate for identifying moral issues involving cybertechnology. Brey worries that using the standard model we might fail to notice certain features embedded in the design of cybertechnology. He also worries about the standard method of applied ethics because it tends to focus on known moral controversies, and it fails to identify certain practices involving the use of cybertechnology that have moral import but that are not yet known. Brey refers to such practices as having "morally opaque" (or "morally nontransparent") features, which he contrasts with "morally transparent" features.

According to Brey, morally controversial features that are transparent tend to be easily recognized as morally problematic. For example, many people are aware that the practice of placing closed circuit video surveillance cameras in undisclosed locations is controversial from a moral point of view. Brey notes that it is, however, generally much more difficult to discern morally opaque features in technology. These features can be morally opaque for one of two reasons: either they are unknown or they are known but perceived to be morally neutral.

Consider an example of each type of morally opaque (or morally nontransparent) feature. Computerized practices involving data mining (defined in Chapter 5) would be unknown to those who have never heard of the concept of data mining and who are unfamiliar with data-mining technology. However, this technology should not be assumed to be morally neutral merely because data-mining techniques are unknown to nontechnical people, including many ethicists. Even if such techniques are opaque to many users, data-mining practices raise certain moral issues pertaining to personal privacy.

Next consider an example of a morally opaque feature in which a technology is well known. Most Internet users are familiar with search-engine technology. What users might fail to recognize, however, is that certain uses of search engines can be morally controversial with respect to personal privacy. Consequently, one of the features of search-engine technology can be morally controversial in a sense that it is not obvious or transparent to many people, including those who are very familiar with and who use search-engine technology. So while a well-known technology, like search-engine programs, might appear to be morally neutral, a closer analysis of practices involving this technology will disclose that it has moral implications.

Figure 1-2 illustrates some differences between morally opaque and morally transparent features.

Brey argues that an adequate methodology for computer ethics must first identify, or "disclose," features that, without proper probing and analysis, would go unnoticed as having moral implications. Thus, an extremely important first step in Brey's "disclosive" method is to reveal moral values embedded in the various features and practices associated with cybertechnology itself.

1.5.3 An Interdisciplinary and Multilevel Method for Analyzing Cyberethics Issues

Brey's disclosive model is both *interdisciplinary* and *multilevel*. It is interdisciplinary because it requires the collaboration of computer scientists, philosophers, and social scientists. And it is multilevel because the method for conducting computer-ethics research requires three levels of analysis:

- Disclosure level
- Theoretical level
- Application level

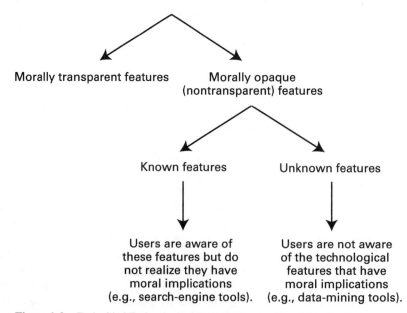

Figure 1-2 Embedded Technological Features Having Moral Implications

At the disclosure level, embedded moral values in the design of computer systems need to be disclosed. At this level, the technical expertise provided by computer scientists is critical, because this group of experts understands the details and nuances of computer technology in ways that philosophers and social scientists generally do not. Research at the disclosure level also often requires input from social scientists, however, who can evaluate aspects of system design from the perspective of human-interface requirements and expectations. After the embedded moral values have been disclosed, philosophers analyze the situation to determine whether the newly disclosed moral issues can be tested via existing ethical theories or whether additional theoretical analysis will be required. At the theoretical level, philosophers are capable of carrying out much of the required research. Finally, at the applications level, cooperation is needed among computer scientists, philosophers, and social scientists to complete the methodological process by applying ethical theory in deliberations about particular moral issues under consideration.

Table 1-3 describes the academic disciplines and the corresponding tasks and functions involved in Brey's disclosive model.

It is in the interdisciplinary spirit of the disclosive methodology proposed by Brey that we will examine the range of cyberethics issues described in Chapters 4 through 11.

1.5.4 A Strategy for Approaching Cyberethics Issues

The following methodological scheme, which expands on the original three-step scheme introduced in Section 1.4.2.1, is intended as a strategy to assist you in identifying and analyzing the specific cyberethics issues examined in this book. Note, however, that this procedure is not intended as a precise algorithm for resolving those issues in some definitive manner. Rather, its purpose is to guide you in the identification, analysis, and deliberation processes.

Step 1. *Identify* a practice involving cybertechnology or a feature in that technology that is controversial from a moral perspective.

    1a. Disclose any hidden (or opaque) features or issues that have moral implications.

    1b. If the issue is descriptive, assess the sociological implications for relevant social institutions and sociodemographic groups

    1c. If there are no ethical/normative issues, stop.

    1d. If the ethical issue is professional in nature, assess it in terms of existing codes of conduct/ethics for relevant professional associations (see Chapter 4).

TABLE 1-3 Brey's Disclosive Model

Level	Disciplines Involved	Task/Function
Disclosure	Computer Science Social Science (optional)	Disclose embedded features in computer technology that have moral import
Theoretical	Philosophy	Test newly disclosed features against standard ethical theories
Application	Computer Science Philosophy Social Science	Apply standard or newly revised/formulated ethical theories to the issues

1e. If one or more ethical issues remain, go to Step 2.

Step 2. *Analyze* the ethical issue by clarifying concepts and situating it in a context.

2a. If a policy vacuums exists, go to Step 2b; otherwise go to Step 3.

2b. Clear up any conceptual muddles involving the policy vacuum and go to Step 3.

Step 3. *Deliberate* on the ethical issue. The deliberation process requires two stages:

3a. Apply one or more ethical theories (see Chapter 2) to the analysis of the moral issue, and then go to Step 3b.

3b. Justify the position you reached by evaluating it against the rules of logic/critical thinking (see Chapter 3).

Note that you are now in a position to carry out much of the work required in the first two steps of this methodological scheme. In order to satisfy the requirements in Step 1e, a step that is followed only in cases involving professional-ethics issues, you will need to consult the relevant sections of Chapter 4. Upon completing Chapter 2, you will be able to execute Step 3a; and after completing Chapter 3, you will be able to satisfy the requirements for Step 3b.

▶ 1.6 CHAPTER SUMMARY

In this introductory chapter, we defined several key terms, including *cyberethics* and *cybertechnology*, that are used throughout this textbook. We also briefly described four evolutionary phases of cyberethics, from its origins as a loosely configured and informal field concerned with ethical and social issues involving stand-alone (mainframe) computers to a more fully developed field that is currently concerned with ethical aspects of ubiquitous, networked computers. We then briefly considered whether any cyberethics issues are unique or special in a nontrivial sense. We next examined three different perspectives on cyberethics, showing how computer scientists, philosophers, and social scientists each tend to view the field and approach the issues that comprise it. Within that discussion, we also examined some ways in which embedded values and biases involving cybertechnology can be disclosed. Finally, we introduced a comprehensive methodological scheme that incorporates the expertise of computer scientists, philosophers, and social scientists who work in the field of cyberethics.

▶ REVIEW QUESTIONS

1. What exactly is *cyberethics*? How is it different from and similar to "computer ethics" and "Internet ethics?"

2. What is meant by the term *cybertechnology*?

3. How can the Amy Boyer case of cyberstalking be used to illustrate many of the ethical issues raised by cybertechnology?

4. List some key aspects of each of the four phases in the evolution of cyberethics as a field of applied ethics.

5. Are cyberethics issues unique or special in any philosophically interesting, or nontrivial, sense?

6. Why does James Moor believe that cybertechnology poses special problems for identifying and analyzing ethical issues? Explain what Moor means by the expressions "logical malleability," "policy vacuum," and "conceptual muddle."

7. Summarize the principal aspects of the three main perspectives on cyberethics that we examined.

8. What is the difference between assertions or claims that are descriptive in nature and those that are normative? Provide an example of each.

9. Which criteria are used to distinguish normative inquiries from those that are essentially descriptive?

10. What are the three elements of the standard, or "mainstream," method for conducting applied-ethics research?

11. How is Philip Brey's "disclosive" method of computer ethics different from mainstream computer ethics?

12. How can Corlann Gee Bush's arguments about the nonneutrality of technology be used to support Brey's point about embedded values in cybertechnology?

13. What does Brey mean by "morally opaque" or "morally nontransparent" features embedded in computer technology?

14. In which ways is Brey's "disclosive" method both multilevel and interdisciplinary?

▶ DISCUSSION QUESTIONS

1. Analyze Don Gotterbarn's arguments for the claim that computer ethics is, at bottom, a field of applied ethics whose primary concern should be moral responsibility issues for computer professionals. Are his arguments convincing, or is his definition of the field too narrow, as some critics claim? How would you assess the impact of professional ethics issues in the overall scheme of cyberethics?

2. We briefly considered the question as to whether cyberethics issues are unique or special in any way. Luciano Floridi (1999) has argued that certain issues raised by cybertechnology stretch and strain our ethical concepts in such a way that our traditional categories of ethics are no longer sufficient to handle these issues. And Han Jonas (1984) has argued that modern technology has introduced ethical issues of such dramatic scale that our traditional framework of ethics must be replaced with a new moral system. Assess Floridi's and Jonas's concerns, based on what we have seen thus far about the kinds of moral issues generated by cybertechnology. Do we need a brand new framework of ethics?

3. Think of a controversial practice involving cybertechnology that has not yet been identified as an ethical issue, but which might eventually be recognized as one that has moral implications. Apply the first two steps of the three-step strategy that we developed in the concluding section of this chapter to your analysis of the issue/practice. Describe the conclusions you reached about this particular issue.

4. We identified three main perspectives from which cyberethics issues can be examined. Can you think of any additional perspectives from which cyberethics issues might also be analyzed? In addition to the Amy Boyer case, can you think of other cases involving cyberethics issues that would benefit from being analyzed from all three perspectives considered in Chapter 1? Explain.

▶ REFERENCES

Baase, Sara (2003). *A Gift of Fire: Social, Legal, and Ethical Issues in Computing*. 2d ed. Upper Saddle River, NJ: Prentice Hall.

Baird, Robert M., Reagan Ramsower, & Stuart E. Rosenbaum, eds. (2000). *Cyberethics: Social and Moral Issues in the Computer Age*. Amherst, NY: Prometheus Books.

Brey, Philip (2000). "Disclosive Computer Ethics," *Computers and Society*, Vol. 30, No. 4, December, pp. 10–16.

Buchanan, Elizabeth A. (2001). "Ethical Considerations for the Information Professions." R. A. Spinello and H. T. Tavani, eds. In *Readings in CyberEthics*. Sudbury, MA: Jones and Bartlett Publishers, pp. 523–534.

Bush, Corlann Gee (1997). "Women and the Assessment of Technology." In A. H. Teich, ed. *Technology and the Future*. 7th ed. New York: St. Martin's Press, pp. 157–159.

Bynum, Terrell Ward (1999). "The Development of Computer Ethics as a Philosophical Field of Study," *The Australian Journal of Professional and Applied Ethics*, Vol. 1, No. 1, pp. 1–29.

Floridi, Luciano (1999). "Information Ethics: On the Philosophical Foundation of Computer Ethics," *Ethics and Information Technology*, Vol. 1, No. 1, pp. 37–56.

Gotterbarn, Don (1991). "Computer Ethics: Responsibility Regained," *National Forum: The Phi Kappa Phi Journal*, Vol. 73, No. 3, pp. 26–31.

Grodzinsky, Francis S., and Herman T. Tavani (2002). "Some Ethical Reflections on Cyberstalking," *Computers and Society*, Vol. 32, No. 1, pp. 28–38.

Halbert, Terry, and Elaine Inguilli (2002). *Cyberethics*. Belmont, CA: Southwestern Thompson Learning.

Huff, Chuck, and Thomas Finholt, eds. (1994). *Social Issues in Computing: Putting Computing in its Place*. New York: McGraw–Hill.

Jonas, Hans. (1984). *The Imperative of Responsibility: In Search of an Ethics for the Technological Age*. Chicago, IL: University of Chicago Press.

Johnson, Deborah G. (2001). *Computer Ethics*. 3d ed. Upper Saddle River, New Jersey: Prentice Hall.

Langford, Duncan, ed. (2000). *Internet Ethics*. New York: St. Martin's Press.

Maner, Walter (1996). "Unique Ethical Problems in Information Technology," *Science and Engineering Ethics*, Vol. 2, No. 2, pp. 137–154.

Moor, James H. (1985). "What is Computer Ethics?" *Metaphilosophy*, Vol. 16, No. 4, October, pp. 266–275.

Moor, James H. (1999). "Just Consequentialism and Computing," *Ethics and Information Technology*, Vol. 1, No. 1, 1999, pp. 65–69.

Moor, James H. (2001). "The Future of Computer Ethics: You Ain't Seen Nothing Yet," *Ethics and Information Technology*, Vol. 3, No. 2, pp. 89–91.

Spinello, Richard A. (2003). *CyberEthics: Morality and Law in Cyberspace*. 2d ed. Sudbury, MA: Jones and Bartlett Publishers.

Spinello, Richard A., and Herman T. Tavani, eds. (2001). *Readings in CyberEthics*. Sudbury, MA: Jones and Bartlett Publishers.

Tavani, Herman T. (2001). "The Current State of Computer Ethics as a Philosophical Field of Inquiry," *Ethics and Information Technology*, Vol. 3, No. 2, pp. 97–108.

Willard, Nancy E. (1997). *The Cyberethics Reader*. New York: McGraw-Hill.

▶ FURTHER READINGS

Bynum, Terrell Ward (2001). "Ethics and the Information Revolution." In R. A. Spinello and H. T. Tavani, eds. *Readings in CyberEthics*. Sudbury, MA: Jones and Bartlett Publishers, pp. 9–25.

Edgar, Stacey L. (2003). *Morality and Machines: Perspectives on Computer Ethics*. 2d ed. Sudbury, MA: Jones and Bartlett Publishers.

Epstein, Richard E. (1997). *The Case of the Killer Robot: Stories about the Professional, Ethical, and Societal Dimensions of Computing*. New York: John Wiley and Sons.

Ermann, M. David, Mary B. Williams, and Michael S. Schauf, eds. (1997). *Computers, Ethics, and Society*. New York: Oxford University Press.

Friedman, Batya, ed. (1997). *Human Values and the Design of Computer Technology*. New York: Cambridge University Press.

Gorniak-Kocikowska, Krystyna. (1996). "The Computer Revolution and the Problem of Global Ethics," *Science and Engineering Ethics*, Vol. 2, No. 2, pp. 177–190.

Hester, D. Micah, and Paul J. Ford, eds. (2001). *Computers and Ethics in the Cyberage*. Upper Saddle River, NJ: Prentice Hall.

Johnson, Deborah G., and Helen Nissenbaum, eds. (1995). *Computing, Ethics and Social Values*. Englewood Cliffs, New Jersey: Prentice Hall.

Kling, Rob, ed. (1996). *Computerization and Controversy*. 2d ed. San Diego, CA: Academic Press.

Moor, James H. (1998). "Reason, Relativity, and Responsibility in Computer Ethics," *Computers and Society*, Vol. 28, No. 1, March, pp. 14–21.

Rosenberg, Richard S. (1997). *The Social Impact of Computing*. 2d ed. San Diego, CA: Academic Press.

Schneiderman, Ben (1997). *Designing the User Interface: Strategies for Effective Human-Computer Interaction*. New York: ACM Press.

Spinello, Richard A. (2003). *Case Studies in Computer and Information Ethics*. 2d ed. Upper Saddle River, New Jersey: Prentice Hall.

Spinello, Richard A, and Herman T. Tavani (2001). "The Internet, Ethical Values, and Conceptual Frameworks," *Computers and Society*, Vol. 31, No. 1, pp. 5–8.

Tavani, Herman T. (2002). "The Uniqueness Debate in Computer Ethics: What Exactly Is at Issue, and Why Does it Matter?" *Ethics and Information Technology*, Vol. 4, No. 1, pp. 37–54.

van den Hoven, Jeroen (1997). "Computer Ethics and Moral Methodology," *Metaphilosophy*, Vol. 28, No. 3, pp. 234–238.

Weckert, John, and Douglas Adeney (1997). *Computer and Information Ethics*. Westport, CT: Greenwood Press.

▶ ON-LINE RESOURCES

Bibliography on Computing, Ethics, and Social Responsibility. http://cyberethics.cbi.msstate.edu/biblio/.

Developing Online Computer Ethics (Dolce). http://csethics.uis.edu/dolce/.

Heuristic Methods for Computer Ethics. http://csweb.cs.bgsu.edu/maner/heuristics/maner.pdf.

Research Center for Computing and Society. http://www.southernct.edu/organizations/rccs/.

2

ETHICAL CONCEPTS AND ETHICAL THEORIES: ESTABLISHING AND JUSTIFYING A MORAL SYSTEM

In Chapter 1, we defined cyberethics as the study of moral issues involving cybertechnology. However, we have not yet defined what is meant by *ethics*, *morality*, and *the study of moral issues*. In Chapter 2 we define these terms as well as other foundational concepts, and we examine a set of ethical theories that will guide us in our deliberation on the specific cyberethics issues we confront in Chapters 4–11. To accomplish the objectives of Chapter 2, we provide answers to the following questions:

- What exactly is ethics, and how is it different from morality or a moral system?
- What are the elements that make up a moral system?
- Where do the rules in a moral system come from, and how are they justified?
- How is a philosophical study of morality different from studying morality from the perspectives of religion and law?
- Is morality essentially a personal, or private matter, or is it a public phenomenon?
- Is morality simply relative to particular cultures and thus culturally determined?
- How is meaningful dialogue about cyberethics issues that are global in scope possible in a world with diverse cultures and belief systems?
- What roles do classic and contemporary ethical theories play in the analysis of moral issues involving cybertechnology?
- Are traditional ethical theories adequate in the era of cybertechnology?

▶ 2.1 ETHICS AND MORALITY

Ethics is derived from the Greek *ethos,* and the term *morality* has its roots in the Latin *mores.* Both the Greek and Latin terms refer to notions of custom, habit, behavior, and character. Although "ethics" and "morality" are often used interchangeably in everyday discourse, we draw some important distinctions between the two terms as we will use them in this textbook. First, we define ethics as the study of morality. This definition, of course, raises two further questions:

a. What is *morality*?

b. What is *the study of morality*?

We have begun to answer question (b) in Chapter 1, where we described three approaches to cyberethics issues. You may want to review Section 1.4, which describes how moral issues can be studied from the perspectives of professional ethics, philosophical ethics, and descriptive ethics. We will say more about the study of morality from a philosophical perspective in Section 2.1.2.3. Now we begin by answering question (a).

2.1.1 What Is Morality?

There is no universally agreed upon definition of "morality" among ethicists and philosophers. For our purposes, however, *morality* can be defined as a system of rules for guiding human conduct, and principles for evaluating those rules. Note that (i) morality is a *system*; and (ii) it is a system comprised of moral *rules* and *principles*. Moral rules can be understood as rules of conduct, which are very similar to the notion of "policies," described in Chapter 1. There, policies were defined as rules of conduct that have a wide range of application. According to James Moor (1999), policies range from formal laws to "informal, implicit guidelines for actions."

There are two kinds of rules of conduct:

1. *Directives* that guide our conduct as individuals (at the microlevel)

2. *Social policies* framed at the macrolevel

Directives are rules that guide our individual actions and direct us in our moral choices at the "microethical" level (i.e., the level of individual behavior). "Do not steal" and "Do not harm others" are examples of directives. Other kinds of rules guide our conduct at the macrolevel (i.e., at the level of social policies and social norms).

Rules of conduct that operate at the "macroethical" level guide us in both framing and adhering to social policies. For example, rules such as "Proprietary software should not be duplicated without proper authorization," or "Software that can be used to invade the privacy of users should not be developed," are instances of social policies. Notice the correlation between the directive "Do not steal" (a rule of conduct at the microlevel), and the social policy "Unauthorized duplication of software should not be allowed" (a rule of conduct at the macrolevel). In Section 2.1.2 we will see that both types of rules of conduct are derived from a set of "core values" in a moral system.

The rules of conduct in a moral system are evaluated against standards called *principles.* For example, the principle of social utility, which is concerned with promoting the greatest good for the greatest number, can be used as the litmus test for determining whether

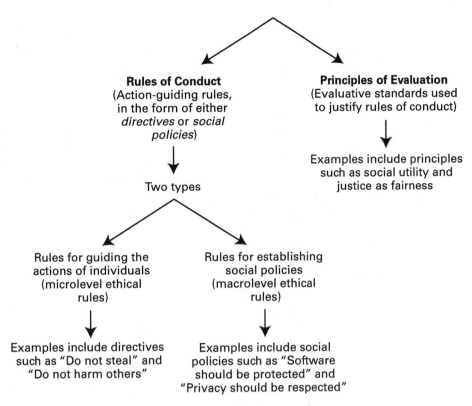

Figure 2-1   Basic Components of a Moral System

the policy "Proprietary software should not be copied without permission" can be justified on moral grounds. In this case, the policy in question can be justified by showing that not allowing the unauthorized copying of software will produce more overall social good than will a policy that permits software to be duplicated freely.

Similarly, the policy "Users should not have their privacy violated," might be justified by appealing to the same principle of social utility. Or a different principle such as "respect for persons" or possibly a principle based on the notion of fairness might be used to justify the social policy in question. Figure 2-1 illustrates the different kinds of rules and principles that comprise a moral system.

2.1.1.1 What Kind of a System Is a Moral System?

According to Bernard Gert (1998), morality is a "system whose purpose is to prevent harm and evils." Other ethicists, such as Louis Pojman (2001), have suggested that a moral system, in addition to preventing harm, should promote human flourishing. Although there is some disagreement regarding the extent to which the promotion of human flourishing is required of a moral system, virtually all ethicists believe that, at minimum, the fundamental purpose of a moral system is to prevent or alleviate harm and suffering. We have already seen that at the heart of a moral system are rules of conduct and principles of evaluation. We next consider some other characteristics that define a moral system.

Gert describes a moral system as one that is both public and informal. The system is *public,* he claims, because everyone must know what the rules are that define it. Gert uses the analogy of a game, which has a goal and a corresponding set of rules. The rules are understood by all of the players, and the players use the rules to guide their behavior in legitimately achieving the goal of the game. The players can also use the rules to evaluate or judge the behavior of other players in the game. However, there is one important difference between a moral system and a game: Not everyone is required to participate in a game, but we are all obligated to participate in a moral system.

Morality is also *informal* because, Gert points out, a moral system has no formal authoritative judges presiding over it. Unlike games in professional sports that have rules enforced by referees in a manner that approaches a legal system, morality is less formal. A moral system is more like a game of cards or like a pickup game in baseball or basketball. Here the players are aware of the rules, but even in the absence of a formal official or referee to enforce the game's rules, players generally adhere to them.

Gert's model of a moral system includes two additional features: *rationality* and *impartiality.* A moral system is rational in that it is based on principles of logical reason accessible to ordinary persons. Morality cannot involve special knowledge that can only be understood by privileged individuals or groups. The rules in a moral system must be available to all rational persons who, in turn, are *moral agents*, bound by the system of moral rules. We do not hold nonmoral agents (such as pets, young children, and mentally challenged persons) morally responsible for their own actions, but moral agents often have responsibilities to certain nonmoral agents.

A moral system is *impartial* in the sense that the moral rules are ideally designed to apply equitably to all participants in the system. In an ideal moral system, all rational persons are willing to accept the rules of the system, even if they do not know in advance what their particular place in that system will be. To ensure that impartiality will be built into a moral system, and that is members will be treated as fairly as possible, Gert (1998) invokes the "blindfold of justice" principle. Imagine that you are blindfolded while deciding what the rules of a moral system will be. Since you do not know in advance what position you will occupy in that system, it is in your own best interest to design a system in which everyone will be treated fairly. As an impartial observer who is also rational, you will want to ensure against the prospect of ending up in a group that is treated unfairly.

Table 2-1 summarizes four key features in Gert's model of a moral system.

TABLE 2-1   Four Features of Gert's Moral System

Public	Informal	Rational	Impartial
The rules are known to all of the members.	The rules are informal, not like formal laws in a legal system.	The system is based on principles of logical reason accessible to all its members.	The system is not partial to any one group or individual.

2.1.2   Deriving and Justifying the Rules of a Moral System

Thus far, we have defined morality as a system that is public, informal, rational, and impartial. We have also seen that the heart of a moral system are rules for guiding the conduct of the members of the system. But where exactly do these rules come from? And what criteria can be used to ground or justify these rules? On the one hand, rules of conduct involving individual directives and social policies are justified by the system's evaluative standards, or principles. But how are those principles in turn justified?

Basically, rules of conduct for guiding action in the moral system, whether individual directives or social policies, are ultimately derived from certain core *values*. Principles for evaluating rules of conduct, on the other hand, are typically grounded in one of three systems or sources: religion, law, or (philosophical) ethics. Figure 2-2 illustrates how the rules and principles that comprise a moral system are derived and grounded.

We next describe the core values in a society from which the rules of conduct are derived.

2.1.2.1 Core Values and Their Role in a Moral System

The term *value* comes from the Latin *valere*, which means having worth or being of worth. Values are objects of our desires or interests; examples include happiness, love, and freedom. Pojman suggests that moral principles are ultimately derived from a society's system of values.

Philosophers often distinguish between two types of values, *intrinsic* and *instrumental*. Any value that serves some further end or good is called an instrumental value because it is tied to some external standard. Automobiles, computers, and money are examples of goods that have instrumental value. Values such as life and happiness, on the other hand, are *intrinsic* because they are valued for their own sake. Later in this chapter, we will see that utilitarians

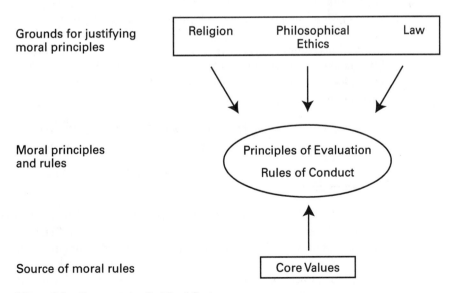

Figure 2-2   Components of a Moral System

argue that happiness is an intrinsic value. And in Chapter 5, we will see that some ethicists believe personal privacy is a value that has both intrinsic and instrumental attributes.

Another approach to cataloguing values is to distinguish *core values*, some of which may or may not also be intrinsic values, from other kinds of values. James Moor (1998), for example, believes that life, happiness, and autonomy are core values because they are basic to a society's thriving and perhaps even to its survival. Autonomy, Moor argues, is essentially a cluster of values that includes ability, security, knowledge, freedom, opportunity, and resources. Although core values might be basic to a society's flourishing, and possibly to that society's survival, it does not follow that each core value is also a moral value.

Sometimes descriptions of morals and values suggest that morals are identical to values. Values, however, can be either moral or nonmoral, and moral values need to be distinguished from the broader set of nonmoral values. Consider again the roles that rationality and impartiality play in a moral system. Rationality informs us that it is in our interest to promote values consistent with our own survival, happiness, and flourishing as individuals. When used to further only our own self-interests, these values are not necessarily moral values. Once we bring in the notion of impartiality, however, we begin to take the moral point of view. When we frame the rules of conduct in a moral system, we articulate one or more core moral values, such as autonomy, fairness, and justice. For example, the rule of a conduct "Treat people fairly" is derived from the moral value of fairness. And our moral values are, in turn derived from certain core nonmoral values (see Figure 2-3).

2.1.2.2 Three Approaches for Grounding the Principles in a Moral System

We have seen how the rules of conduct in a moral system are derived from a society's core values. Now we will consider how the principles that are used to justify the rules of conduct are grounded. As we suggested in Section 2.1.2, the principles are grounded in one of three sources: religion, law, and philosophical ethics. We now consider how a particular moral principle can be justified from the vantage point of each scheme. As an illustration, we can use the rule of conduct "Do not steal," since it underpins many cyberethics controversies involving software piracy and intellectual property. Virtually every moral system includes at least one rule that explicitly condemns stealing. But why exactly is stealing morally wrong? This particular rule of conduct is evaluated against one or more principles such as "We should respect persons" or "We should not cause harm to others," but how are these principles, in turn, justified? The answer depends on whether we take the religious, the legal, or the ethical (philosophical) point of view.

Approach #1: Grounding Moral Principles in a Religious System

Consider the following rationale for why stealing is morally wrong:

> Stealing is wrong because it offends God or because it violates one of God's Ten Commandments.

Here the "moral wrongness" in the act of stealing is grounded in religion; stealing, in the Judeo-Christian tradition, is explicitly forbidden by one of the Ten Commandments. From the point of view of these particular institutionalized religions, then, stealing is wrong because it offends God or because it violates the commands of a divine authority. Furthermore, Christians generally believe that those who steal will be punished in the next life even if they are not caught and punished for their sins in the present life.

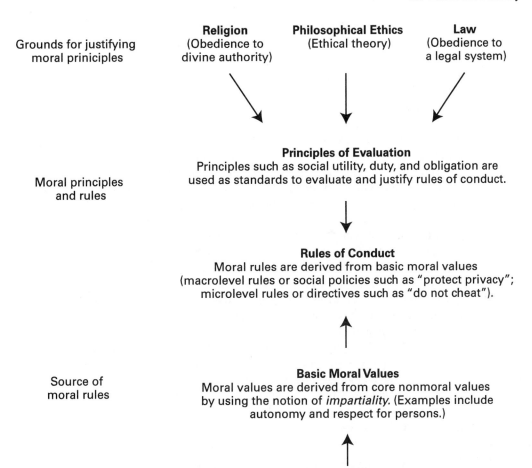

Figure 2-3 Components of a Moral System—An Expanded View

One difficulty in applying this rationale in the United States is that American society is pluralistic. While the United States was once a relatively homogeneous culture with roots in the Judeo-Christian tradition, American culture has in recent years become increasingly heterogeneous. People with different religious beliefs or with no religious beliefs at all can disagree with those whose moral beliefs are grounded solely on religious convictions. Because of these differences, many argue that we need to ground the rules and principles of a moral system in criteria other than those provided by organized religions. Some suggest that civil law can provide the foundation needed for a moral system to work.

Approach #2: Grounding Moral Principles in a Legal System

An alternative rationale to the one proposed in the preceding section is:

> Stealing is wrong because it violates the law.

One advantage of using law instead of religion as the ground for determining why stealing is wrong is that it eliminates certain kinds of disputes between religious and nonreligious persons and groups. If stealing violates the law of a particular jurisdiction, then the act of stealing can be declared wrong independent of any religious beliefs or disbeliefs—Christian, Muslim, or even agnostic or atheist. And since legal enforcement of rules can be carried out independent of religious beliefs there is a pragmatic advantage to grounding moral principles (and their corresponding rules) in law rather than in religion: those breaking a civil law can be punished, for example, by either a fine or imprisonment, or both.

But laws are not uniform across political boundaries: Laws vary from nation to nation and state to state within a given nation. In the United States, the unauthorized copying and distribution of proprietary software is explicitly illegal. However, in certain Asian countries, the practice of copying proprietary software is not considered criminal (or even if it is technically viewed as a crime, actual cases of piracy may not be criminally prosecuted). So there can be a diversity of legal systems just as there are a diversity of religious systems.

Perhaps a more serious flaw in using a legal approach is that history has shown that certain laws, although widely accepted, institutionalized, and practiced within a society, have nonetheless been morally wrong. For example, slavery was legally valid in the United States until 1865. And in South Africa, apartheid was legally valid until 1991. So if we attempt to ground moral principles in law, we are still faced with serious challenges. Also , we can ask whether is is possible, or even desirable, to institutionalize morality such that we require specific laws for every possible moral issue?

Approach #3: Grounding Moral Principles in a Philosophical System of Ethics

A third way to approach the problem of how to ground moral systems is to say:

> Stealing is wrong because it is wrong.

Notice what this statement implies. The moral rightness or wrongness of stealing is not grounded in any external authority, theological or legal. So regardless of whether God condemns stealing or whether stealing violates existing civil laws, stealing is held to be wrong in itself. On what grounds can such a claim be made? Many philosophers and ethicists argue that reason alone is sufficient to show that stealing is wrong—reason informs us that there is something either in the very act of stealing or in the consequences of the act that makes stealing morally wrong.

In the case of both religion and law, sanctions in the form of punishments can be applied to deter individuals from stealing. In the first case, punishment for immoral behavior is relegated to the afterlife. And in the second case, punishment can be meted out here and now. In the case of philosophical ethics, sanctions take the form of social disapprobation (disapproval) and, possibly, social ostracism, but there is no punishment in a formal sense.

According to the system of philosophical ethics, stealing is morally wrong by criteria that reason alone is sufficient to determine. Of course, we need to specify what these criteria are; we will do this in Sections 2.4–2.7, where we discuss four kinds of ethical theories. Figure 2-3 summarizes the main elements and features of the moral system that we have examined in this section and expands the key features of Figure 2-2.

In Figure 2-3, arrows from both directions ultimately lead to "Rules of Conduct." Using the rules of conduct as our reference point, we see that they are derived from basic moral values, which in turn are derived from a set of core nonmoral values. With the rules of conduct still serving as our point of reference but moving in the opposite direction, we see that these rules are evaluated and justified by a set of moral principles. These moral principles, in turn, are grounded in criteria that are either legal, religious, or philosophical, or some combination of the three.

2.1.2.3 The Method of Philosophical Ethics: Logical Argumentation and Ethical Theory

In Chapter 1, we briefly described the philosophical method and saw how it could be used to analyze cyberethics issues. We also saw that the method philosophers use to analyze moral issues is normative, in contrast to the descriptive method that is used by social scientists. We saw that sociological and anthropological studies are descriptive because they describe or report how people in various cultures and groups behave with respect to the rules of a moral system. For example, a sociologist might report that people who live in nations along the Pacific Rim believe that it is morally permissible to make copies of proprietary software for personal use. However, it is one thing simply to report or describe what the members of a particular culture believe about a practice such as duplicating proprietary software, and it is something altogether different to say that people ought to be permitted to make copies of that proprietary material. When we inquire into moral issues from the latter perspective, we engage in a normative investigation.

In Section 2.1.2.2., we saw that normative analyses of morality can involve religion and law as well as philosophy. We also saw, however, that what separated philosophy from the other two perspectives of normative analysis was the methodology used to study the moral issues. To approach these issues from the perspective of philosophical ethics is, in effect, to engage in a philosophical study of morality.

If you are taking a course in ethics for the first time, you might wonder what is meant by the phrase "philosophical study." We have already described what is meant by a descriptive study, which is essentially a type of scientific study. Philosophical studies and scientific studies are similar in that they both require that a consistent methodological scheme be used to verify hypotheses and theories; and these verification schemes must satisfy criteria of rationality and impartiality. But philosophical studies differ from scientific studies in that whereas scientists typically conduct experiments in a laboratory to confirm or refute one or more hypotheses, philosophers have no physical laboratory to test ethical theories and claims. Instead philosophers confirm or reject the plausibility of a certain claim or thesis by testing it against the rules of logical argumentation (which we will examine in Chapter 3); these rules are both rational and impartial. Another important feature that distinguishes a philosophical study of morality from other kinds of normative investigation into morality is the use of ethical theory in the analysis and deliberation of the issues.

Ethicists vs. Moralists

We note that ethicists who study morality from the perspective of philosophical methodology, and who thus appeal to logical arguments to justify claims and positions involving morality, are very different from moralists. Moralists often claim to have all of the answers regarding moral questions and issues. Many moralists have been described as "preachy" and "judgmental." And some moralists may have a particular moral agenda to advance. Ethicists, on the other hand, use the philosophical method in analyzing and attempting to resolve moral issues; they must remain open to different sides of a dispute, and their primary focus is on the study of morality and the application of moral theories. As such, they approach moral issues and controversies by way of standards that are both rational (based on logic) and impartial (open to others to verify).

▶ 2.2 DISCUSSION STOPPERS AS ROADBLOCKS TO MORAL DISCOURSE

We have suggested that impartial and objective standards, such as those provided by ethical theory and logical argumentation, can be used in our analysis of moral issues. However, many people might be surprised that tests and standards of any kind can be applied to disputes about morality and moral issues. So before beginning our examination of ethical theory, perhaps we should first acknowledge and try to address some concerns that many people frequently encounter when either they willingly engage in, or find themselves involuntarily drawn into, discussions involving moral issues. We will see why these concerns are often based on some conceptual confusions about the nature of morality itself.

Have you ever been engaged in a serious conversation about a moral issue when, all of a sudden, one party in the discussion interjects with a remark to the effect, "But who's to say what is right or wrong anyway?" Or perhaps someone might interject, "Who are we to impose our values and ideas on others?" Such clichés are just two examples of the kinds of simplistic or nonreflective questions that we are likely to hear in discussions involving moral issues. I call remarks of this type "discussion stoppers" because often they close down prematurely what otherwise might be a useful discussion. These stoppers can take many different forms, and some are more common than others, but we can articulate them as four questions:

1. People disagree about morality, so how can we reach agreement on moral issues?
2. Who am I/who are we to judge others and to impose my/our values on them?
3. Isn't morality simply a private matter?
4. Isn't morality simply a matter that different cultures and groups should determine for themselves?

2.2.1 Discussion Stopper # 1: People Disagree on Solutions to Moral Issues

Because different people often have different beliefs as to the correct answer to many moral questions, some infer that there is no hope of reaching any kind of agreement on answers to *any* moral question. And from this inference, some conclude that any meaningful discourse about morality is impossible. Three crucial points that people who draw these and similar inferences about morality fail to recognize, however, are as follows:

   i. Experts in other fields of study, such as science and mathematics, also disagree
       as to the correct answers to certain questions.
  ii. There is common agreement as to answers to some moral questions.
 iii. People do not always distinguish between disagreements about general princi-
       ples and disagreements about factual matters in disputes involving morality.

We briefly examine each of these points.

2.2.1.1 Experts in Many Fields Disagree on Fundamental Issues

First, we should note that morality is not the only area in which intelligent people have disagreements. Scientists and mathematicians disagree among themselves about core issues in
their disciplines, yet we do not dismiss the possibility of meaningful discourse in science
and mathematics merely because there is some disagreement among experts in those fields.
Consider also that computer scientists disagree among themselves whether open source
code is better than proprietary code, whether Linux is a better operating system than
Windows NT, or whether C++ is a better programming language than Java.

One example of how natural scientists can disagree among themselves is apparent in
the contemporary debate in physics regarding the nature of light. Some physicists argue that
light is ultimately composed of particles, whereas others claim that light is essentially composed of waves. Because physicists can disagree with each other, should we conclude that
physics itself must be a totally arbitrary enterprise? Or, alternatively, is it not possible that
certain kinds of disagreements among scientists might indeed be healthy for science? The
debate about the nature of light has actually contributed to moving the field of physics forward in ways that it otherwise would not progress. In this sense, then, a certain level of disagreement and dispute among scientists is a positive and constructive function in the overall
enterprise of scientific discovery. Similarly, why not assume that certain kinds of disagreements in ethics—that is, those that are based on points aimed at achieving constructive
resolutions—actually contribute to progress in the field of ethics?

Also note that disagreement exists among contemporary mathematicians as to whether
or not there is a greatest prime number. Because mathematicians disagree as to the validity
of certain mathematical claims, does it follow that the field of mathematics itself is arbitrary? Does it also follow that we should give up any hope of eventually reaching agreement
about basic truths in mathematics? And should we dismiss as arbitrary the theories of mathematics as well as the theories of physics, simply because there is some level of disagreement among scholars in both academic fields? Would it be reasonable to do so? If not, then
why should ethics be dismissed merely because there is some disagreement among ethicists
and among ordinary persons as to the correct answers to some moral issues?

Note that certain conditions (parameters, rules, etc.) must be satisfied in order for a particular claim or a particular theory to qualify as acceptable in debates among scientists and
among mathematicians. We will see that certain rules and parameters must also be satisfied
in order for a particular claim or theory to qualify as acceptable in debates among ethicists.
Just as there are claims and theories in physics and in mathematics that are not considered
plausible by the scientific and mathematical communities, similarly, not every claim or theory involving morality is considered reasonable by ethicists. Like mathematicians and scientists, ethicists continue to disagree with one another; for example, they will likely continue
to debate about which ethical theories should be applied in the case of cloning and genomic

research. But like scientists and mathematicians, ethicists will continue to work within the constraints of certain acceptable rules and parameters in advancing their various theories.

2.2.1.2 Common Agreement on Some Moral Issues

We can now turn to our second point: People have demonstrated considerable agreement on answers to some moral questions, at least with respect to moral principles. We might be inclined to overlook the significant level of agreement regarding ethical principles, however, because we tend to associate moral issues with highly controversial concerns such as the death penalty, euthanasia, abortion, and cloning, all involving life and death decisions. We tend to forget that there are also many basic moral principles on which we do agree, for instance, nearly everyone believes that people should tell the truth, keep promises, respect their parents, and refrain from activities involving stealing and cheating. And most people agree that "Murder is wrong." It would be prudent for us to pay closer attention to our beliefs regarding these core moral principles in order to find out why there is such agreement.

So if we agree on many basic moral principles, such as our commonly held belief that murder is wrong and stealing is wrong, then why are moral issues generally considered to be so controversial and why is the study of morality believed to be so difficult? Beliefs and assumptions regarding morality may be based on certain conceptual confusions, and one source of confusion may be our failure to distinguish between the alleged factual matters and the general principles that constitute moral issues. This brings us to our third point.

2.2.1.3 Disagreements about Principles vs. Disagreements about Facts

Richard De George (1999) has pointed out that in analyzing moral issues we need to be very careful to distinguish our disagreements about moral principles from our disagreements about certain facts, or empirical data, associated with a particular moral issue. For example, in the current debate over intellectual property rights in cyberspace, the dispute is not so much about whether we should accept the moral principle that stealing is wrong, for parties on both sides of the debate would acknowledge that stealing is indeed morally wrong. What they disagree about is whether an activity that involves either the unauthorized copying of proprietary software or the unauthorized exchange of proprietary information over a computer network is itself a form of stealing. In other words, the debate is not about a moral principle, but rather has to do with certain empirical matters, or factual claims.

Recall our discussion of the Napster controversy in Chapter 1. It might turn out this particular controversy is not a moral dispute but rather a debate over factual claims. And once the factual questions are resolved, the Napster controversy might be understood as one that is, at bottom, nonmoral in nature. Being able to recognize these distinctions will help us to eliminate some of the confusion surrounding issues that initially are perceived to be moral but ultimately may turn out to be nonmoral, or descriptive.

2.2.2   Discussion Stopper # 2: Who Am I to Judge Others?

People are often uncomfortable with the prospect of having to evaluate the moral beliefs and practices of others. We generally feel that it is appropriate to *describe* the different moral beliefs that others have but that it is inappropriate to make *judgments* about the moral beliefs held by others. This assumption is problematic on two levels: First, as a matter of descriptive fact, we constantly judge others in the sense that we make certain evaluations about them.

And second, from a normative perspective, in certain cases we *should* make
uations) about the beliefs and actions of others. We briefly examine both p

2.2.2.1 Persons Making Judgments vs. Persons Being Judgmental

First, we need to make an important distinction between making a judgmer
or something and being a judgmental person. Because someone makes a ju
uation, about X, it does not follow that he or she is also necessarily being a judgmental person. For example, a person can make the judgment "Linux is a better operating system than
Windows NT" and yet not be a judgmental person. One can also judge that "Mary is a better computer programmer than Harry" without necessarily being judgmental about either
Mary or Harry. Being judgmental is a behavioral trait exhibited by those who are strongly
opinionated or who tend to speak disparagingly of anyone who holds a position on some
topic that is different from their own. "Judging" in the sense "evaluating something," however, does not require that the person making the judgment be a judgmental person.

We routinely judge, or evaluate, others. We judge others whenever we decide who we
will pursue as friends, as lovers, or as colleagues. Judging is an integral part of social interaction. Without judgment at this level, we would not be able to form close friendships, as
opposed to mere acquaintances. And we would not be able to choose a spouse or to choose
where we wish to live, work, recreate, and so forth.

2.2.2.2 Judgments Involving Condemnations vs. Judgments Involving Evaluations

Why do we tend to be so uncomfortable with the notion of judging others? Part of our discomfort may have to do with how we currently understand the term "judge." As we saw
above, we need to be careful to separate the cognitive act of judging (i.e., making judgments
about someone or something) from the behavioral trait of "being judgmental." Consider the
biblical injunction that instructs individuals to refrain from judging others in the sense of
condemning them. In that sense of "judge" there would seem to be much truth in the biblical injunction.

However, there is also another sense of "judge" that means "evaluate," which is something we are often required to do in our everyday lives. Consider some of the routine judgments, or evaluations, you make when deciding between competing options available to
you in your day-to-day life. When you change jobs or purchase a house or an automobile,
you make a judgment about which job, house, or automobile you believe best for your purposes. When you chose the particular college or university that you are attending, you evaluated that particular institution relative to others.

There are also people employed in professions that require them to make judgments.
For example, professional sporting associations employ referees and field judges who make
decisions or judgments concerning controversial plays. Judges evaluate contest entries to
determine which entries are better than others. Think, for example, about the judging that
typically occurs in selecting the winning photographs in a camera club contest. Or consider
that when a supervisor writes a performance review for an employee, she is making a judgment about the employee's performance

2.2.2.3 Are We Ever Required to Make Judgments about Others?

It could be argued that just because we happen to make judgments about others, it doesn't
necessarily follow that we ought to judge persons. However, there are certain occasions

when we are not only justified in making judgments about others, but we are also morally obligated to do so. Consider, for instance, that in many societies an individual selects the person that he or she will marry, judging (evaluating) whether the person he or she is considering will be a suitable lifelong partner in terms of plans, goals, aspirations, etc. In this case, failing to make such judgment would be not only imprudent but also, arguably, immoral. It would be immoral because, in failing to make the appropriate judgments, one would not be granting his or her prospective spouse the kind of consideration that he or she deserves.

Next consider an example involving child abuse. If you see an adult physically abusing a child in a public place by repeatedly kicking the child, can you not at least judge that the adult's behavior is morally wrong even if you are uncomfortable with making a negative judgment about that particular adult?

Also consider a basic human-rights violation. If you witness members of a community being denied basic human rights, should you not judge that community's practice as morally wrong? For example, if women in Afghanistan are denied education, medical treatment, and jobs solely on the grounds that they are women, is it wrong to make the judgment that such practices, as well as the system that permits those practices, are immoral?

So it would seem that some serious confusions exist with respect to two distinct situations: (1) someone making a judgment about X, and (2) someone being a judgmental person. With that distinction in mind, we can avoid being judgmental and yet still make moral judgments when appropriate, and especially when we are obligated to do so.

2.2.3 Discussion Stopper # 3: Morality Is Simply a Private Matter

Many people assume that morality is essentially personal in nature and must therefore be simply a private matter. Initially, such a view might seem reasonable, but it is actually both confused and problematic. In fact, "private morality" is essentially an oxymoron, or contradictory notion. For one thing, morality is a *public* phenomenon—recall our discussion of Gert's account of morality as a "public system" in Section 2.1.1, where we saw that a moral system includes a set of public rules that apply to all of the members of that system. Thus morality cannot be reduced to something that is simply private or personal.

We have already seen that morality is a system of normative rules and standards whose content is studied by ethicists in the same way that mathematicians study the content of the field of mathematics. Would it make sense to speak of personal mathematics, personal chemistry, or personal biology? Such notions sound absurd because each discipline has a content area and a set of standards and criteria, all of which are open and available to all to examine. Since public rules make up the content of a moral system, which itself can be studied, we can reasonably ask how it would make sense to speak of private morality.

If morality were simply a private matter, then it would follow that a study of morality could be reduced to a series of descriptive reports about the personal preferences or personal tastes of individuals and groups. But is such an account of morality adequate? Are the moral choices that we make nothing more than mere personal choices? If you happen to prefer chocolate ice cream and I prefer vanilla, or if you prefer to own a laptop computer and I prefer to own a desktop computer, we will probably not choose to debate these preferences. You may have strong personal beliefs as to why chocolate ice cream is better than vanilla and why laptop computers are superior to desktop computers; however, you will most likely respect my preferences for vanilla ice cream and desktop computers, and, in turn, I will respect your preferences.

Do moral choices fit this same kind of model? Suppose you happen to believe that stealing is morally wrong, but I believe that stealing is okay (i.e., morally permissible). One day, I decide to steal your laptop computer. Do you have a right to complain? You would not, if morality is simply a private matter that reflects an individual's personal choices. Your personal preference may be not to steal, whereas my personal preference is for stealing. If morality is grounded simply in terms of the preferences that individuals happen to have, then it would follow that stealing *is* morally permissible for me but *is not* for you. But why stop with stealing? What if I happen to believe that killing human beings is okay?

You can probably see the dangerous implications for a system in which moral rules and standards are reducible to personal preferences and personal beliefs. The view that morality is private and personal can quickly lead to a position that some ethicists describe as *moral subjectivism.* According to this position, what is morally right or wrong can be determined by individuals themselves, so that morality would seem to be in the "eye of the beholder." Moral subjectivism makes pointless any attempt to engage in meaningful ethical dialogue.

2.2.4 Discussion Stopper # 4: Morality Is Simply a Matter for Individual Cultures to Decide

Some might assume that morality can best be understood not so much as a private or a personal matter but as something for groups or cultures to determine. According to this view, a moral system is dependent on, or relative to, a particular culture or group. Again, this view might initially seem quite reasonable; it is a position that many social scientists have found attractive. To understand some of the serious problems inherent in this position, it is useful to distinguish between *cultural relativism* and *moral relativism.*

2.2.4.1 Cultural Relativism

Cultures play a crucial role in the transmission of the values and principles that constitute a moral system. It is through culture that initial beliefs involving morality are transmitted to an individual. In this sense cultures provide their members with what ethicists often refer to as "customary morality," or conventional morality, where one's moral beliefs are typically nonreflective (or perhaps prereflective). For example, if asked whether you believe that acts such as pirating software or invading someone's privacy are wrong, you might simply reply that both kinds of behavior are wrong because your society taught you that they are wrong. However, is it sufficient for one to believe that these actions are morally wrong merely *because* his or her culture says they are wrong? Imagine, for example, a culture in which the principle "Murder is wrong" is not transmitted to its members. Does it follow that murdering people would be morally permissible for the members of that culture?

The belief that morality is simply a matter for individual cultures to decide is widespread in our contemporary popular culture. This view is often referred to as *cultural relativism,* and at its base is the following assumption:

    A   Different cultures have different beliefs about what constitutes morally right and wrong behavior.

Note that this assumption is essentially descriptive in nature. Although it is generally accepted that different groups have different conceptions about what is morally right and morally wrong behavior, this position has been challenged by social scientists who argue that the reported differences between cultures are greatly exaggerated. Other social scientists suggest that all cultures may possess certain universal core moral values. However, let us assume that claim (A) is true. Would it logically imply the following?

> **B** What is morally right or wrong for members of a culture or group can be determined only by that culture or group.

Note that (B), unlike (A), is a normative claim. Also note that to move from (A) to (B) is to move from cultural relativism to *moral relativism*.

2.2.4.2 Moral Relativism

What are the differences between the two forms of relativism? Moral relativism asserts that no universal standard of morality is possible, because different people have different beliefs about what is right and wrong. From this inference, relativists further suggest that, in matters of morality, anything goes. But this reasoning is problematic because it is essentially incoherent and inconsistent. For example, does it follow that individuals who reside outside a particular culture can never make any judgments about the behavior of those who live within that culture? In many cultures and tribes in West Africa a ritual of female circumcision is still practiced. Although this practice has been a tradition for generations, some females living in tribes that still perform it on teenage girls have objected. Let us assume, however, that the majority of members of cultures that practice female circumcision approve it. Would it be inappropriate for those who lived outside of West Africa to claim that the treatment of young women in those tribes is morally wrong? And if so, is it inappropriate (perhaps even morally wrong) to question the practice simply because the persons raising such questions are not members of the particular culture? If we embrace that line of reasoning, does it follow that a culture can devise any moral scheme it wishes as long as the majority of its members approve it? Is moral relativism a plausible thesis? It is even coherent? Perhaps the following scenario can help us to see the flawed reasoning in relativism.

▶ **SCENARIO:** Moral Relativism

Imagine that there are two cultures, Culture A and Culture B, that adjoin each other geographically. The members of Culture A are fairly peaceful people, tolerant of the diverse beliefs found in all other cultures. And they believe that cultures should essentially mind their own business when it comes to matters involving morality. Those in Culture B, on the other hand, dislike and are hostile to those outside their culture. Further imagine that the leaders of Culture B have developed a new computer system for delivering chemical weapons that will be used in military attacks on other cultures, including Culture A. What recourse does Culture A have in this case?

Since Culture A has taken a relativist position, it must be tolerant of all of Culture B's actions, as it would in the case of all cultures. Furthermore, Culture A cannot condemn the actions of Culture B, since on the relativist's view, moral judgments about Culture B can only be made by those who reside in that particular culture. So, Culture A cannot say that Culture B's actions are morally wrong.

TABLE 2-2 Summary of Logical Flaws in the Discussion Stoppers

Stopper #1	Stopper #2	Stopper #3	Stopper #4
People disagree on solutions to moral issues.	*Who am I to judge others?*	*.Ethics is simply a private matter*	*Morality is simply a matter for individual cultures to decide.*
1. Fails to recognize that experts in many areas disagree on key issues in their fields.	1. Fails to distinguish between the act of judging and being a judgmental person.	1. Fails to recognize that morality is essentially a public system.	1. Fails to distinguish between descriptive and normative claims about morality.
2. Fails to recognize that there are many moral issues on which people agree.	2. Fails to distinguish between judging as condemning and judging as evaluating.	2. Fails to note that personally-based morality can cause major harm to others.	2. Assumes that people can never reach common agreement on some moral principles.
3. Fails to distinguish between disagreements about principles and disagreements about facts.	3. Fails to recognize that sometimes we are required to make judgments.	3. Confuses moral choices with individual or personal preferences.	3. Assumes that a system is moral because a majority in a culture decides it is moral.

Moral relativists can say only that Cultures A and B are different. They cannot say that one is better than another, or that one is morally right while the other is morally wrong. Consider that while the systems for treating Jews used by the Nazis and by the British in the 1940s were clearly different, relativists could not say, with any sense of logical consistency, that one system was better than another. In the same way, Culture B cannot be judged by Culture A to be morally wrong even though Culture B wishes to destroy A and to kill all of its members. Perhaps you can see that there is a price to pay for being a moral relativist. Is that price worth paying?

Although moral relativism might initially seem attractive as an ethical position, we can now see why it is conceptually flawed. To debate moral issues, we need a conceptual and methodological framework that can provide us with impartial and objective criteria to guide us in our deliberations. Otherwise, ethical debate might quickly reduce to a shouting match in which those with the loudest voices or, perhaps worse yet, those with the biggest sticks win the day. Fortunately, ethical theory will provide us criteria that we can use to avoid the problems introduced by moral relativism. Before proceeding directly to our discussion of ethical theories, however, it would be useful to summarize some of the key points in our analysis of the four discussion stoppers. Table 2-2 summarizes these points.

► 2.3 WHY DO WE NEED ETHICAL THEORIES?

In our analysis of the four discussion stoppers, we saw some of the obstacles that we encounter when we debate moral issues. Fortunately, there are ethical theories that can guide us in our analysis of moral issues involving cybertechnology. But why do we need something as formal as ethical theory? Perhaps there are simpler, alternative schemes that we can use in our moral deliberations. For example, why not simply follow the Golden Rule or one's own conscience? Both of these rules of thumb seem like reasonable alternatives to having to construct, defend, and apply elaborate ethical theories. However, Louis Pojman points out some ways that both the Golden Rule and following one's conscience can seriously limit moral deliberation. Building on his insight, we next see why.

2.3.1 Some Problems in Following the Golden Rule and in Following One's Conscience

It is difficult to imagine that anyone would ever object to the spirit of the Golden Rule: "Do unto others as you would have them do unto you." However, this rule assumes that whatever I would be willing to accept that you do unto me, you would also be willing to accept that I do unto you. Suppose that I am a computer programmer, willing to give away my software programs for free. Because I am willing to do that for others, does it follow that I should expect others to do the same for me? Is it reasonable for me to expect that all programmers should freely share their programs with me? Unfortunately the Golden Rule, despite its virtues, is not a sufficiently comprehensive principle to guide us in all of our moral reasoning.

Another simple rule of thumb that initially might seem plausible is the principle: "Follow your conscience." On the face of it, following one's conscience seems like a reasonable maxim. It is, however, a dangerous rule in which to ground one's choices for acting morally. Consider that the terrorists who hijacked and deliberately crashed airplanes into the World Trade Center towers on September 11, 2001, might have been following their individual consciences. Conscience, it turns out, is subjective and thus cannot provide grounds for moral deliberation that are both rational and impartial.

2.3.2 The Structure of Ethical Theories

An essential feature of theory in general is that it guides us in our investigations and analyses. Science uses theory to provide us with general principles and structures with which we can analyze our data. Ethical theory, like scientific theory, provides us with a framework for analyzing moral issues via a scheme that is internally coherent and consistent as well as comprehensive and systematic. To be coherent, a theory's individual elements must fit together to form a unified whole. To be consistent, a theory's component parts cannot contradict each other. To be comprehensive, a theory must be able to be applied broadly to a wide range of actions. And to be systematic, a theory cannot simply address individual symptoms peculiar to specific cases while ignoring general principles that would apply in similar cases.

To see how a theory might satisfy or fail these criteria, we will look at an analogy involving the way Congress sometimes drafts and enacts a piece of legislation into law. In certain situations, lawmakers respond to a highly publicized and controversial incident by formulating and passing legislation that provides a "Band Aid" fix to a crisis but fails to address the central or core issue of a problem for which it was written. Consider in the following case illustration the kind of reasoning that the members of Congress used in passing the Video Protection Act (also known as the Bork Bill) in 1988. (In Chapter 5 we will consider the implications of this particular case for personal privacy. Our focus here, however, is on the reasoning process used in debating and passing that bill.)

▶ **CASE ILLUSTRATION:** The Bork Bill

Following Judge Robert Bork's nomination to the Supreme Court, Congress and the media engaged in an investigative process that preceded the formal confirmation hearings. One news reporter went to the video rental store where Bork rented videos and requested a list of movies that Bork had rented. The reporter intended to make some observations about the kinds of movies Bork preferred to view, including whether or not Bork had rented any adult movies or pornographic films. Not surprisingly, many in Congress were appalled when they learned that a reporter could so easily collect this kind of information about Judge Bork. In their hasty response to this incident, Congress passed the Video Protection Act in order to prevent reporters and other interested parties from finding out which movies individuals rent at video stores.

While some might praise Congress's action as a quick and timely response, others pointed out that this legislation was piecemeal rather than systematic. Was the real issue in this case a matter of keeping others from finding out which videotapes that Bork (or anyone else) happens to rent, or was it a much larger question? Even after the Bork Bill was passed into law, a reporter could still theoretically find out which kinds of books Bork purchased or which kinds of audiocassette tapes and compact discs he bought. So, rather than being a comprehensive and systematic piece of legislation, the Video Protection Act was yet one more piece of patchwork legislation that was incoherent, unsystematic, and noncomprehensive. An ideal law is not merely reactive to a particular incident, nor is it one that is hastily passed because it happens to involve a prominent person rather than ordinary citizens.

How does the analogy of framing the Bork Bill inform us as to how ethical theories might best be framed? Recall that one of the characteristics of a good theory is that it is general enough to guide us in the examination of more than one case. The Bork Bill is so specific that it fails to serve as a piece of general legislation to protect privacy rights of individuals in analogous cases. Of course, there is a vast difference between laws passed by Congress and the kinds of ethical theories that guide us in moral deliberation. Perhaps we can now see why a good theory will need to be comprehensive, systematic, and internally coherent and logically consistent. We next examine four different kinds of ethical theories: consequence-based, duty-based, contract-based, and character-based. As we examine each theory, see if it meets the criteria that we have determined essential for a successful ethical theory.

▶ 2.4 CONSEQUENCE-BASED ETHICAL THEORIES

Some have argued that the primary goal of a moral system is to produce desirable consequences or outcomes for its members. For these ethicists, the consequences (i.e., the ends achieved) of actions and policies provide the ultimate standard against which moral decisions must be evaluated. So if one must choose between two courses of action—that is, either Act A or Act B—the morally correct action will be the one that produces the most desirable outcome. Of course, we can ask the question, outcome for whom? Utilitarians argue that the consequences for the greatest number of individuals, or the majority, in a given society deserve consideration in moral deliberation. According to the utilitarian theory,

An individual act (X) or a social policy (Y) is morally permissible if the consequences that result from (X) or (Y) produce the greatest amount of good for the greatest number of persons affected by the act or policy.

Jeremy Bentham (1748–1832) was among the first philosophers to formulate utilitarian ethical theory in a systematic manner. Essentially, utilitarians draw on two principles in defending their theory:

i. The principle of social utility

ii. The belief that social utility can be measured by the amount of happiness produced

According to (i), the moral value of actions and policies ought to be measured in terms of their social usefulness. The more utility that specific actions and policies have, the more they can be defended as morally permissible actions and policies. In other words, if Policy Y encourages the development of a certain kind of computer software, which in turn would produce more jobs and higher incomes for those living in Community X, then Policy Y would be considered more socially useful and thus the morally correct policy. But how do we measure overall social utility? That is, which criterion can we use to determine the social usefulness of an act or a policy? The answer to this question can be found in principle (ii), which has to do with happiness.

Bentham argued that nature has placed us under two masters, or sovereigns: pleasure and pain. We naturally desire to avoid pain and to seek pleasure or happiness. However, Bentham believed that it is not the maximization of individual pleasure or happiness that is important, but rather generating the greatest amount of happiness for society in general. Since it is assumed that all humans, as individuals, desire happiness, it would follow on utilitarian grounds that those actions and policies that generate the most happiness for the most people are most desirable. Of course, this reasoning assumes:

a. All people desire happiness.

b. Happiness is an intrinsic good that is desired for its own sake.

We can ask utilitarians what proof they have for either (a) or (b). John Stuart Mill (1806–1873) offered the following argument for (a):

The only possible proof showing that something is audible is that people actually hear it; the only possible proof that something is visible is that people actually see it; and the only possible proof that something is desirable is that people actually desire it.

From the fact that people desire happiness, Mill inferred that happiness ought to be the criterion for morality. Unlike other goods that humans desire as means to one or more ends, Mill argued that people desire happiness for its own sake. Thus, he concluded that happiness is an intrinsic good. (Recall our earlier discussion of intrinsic values in Section 2.1.2.1.)

You might consider applying Mill's line of reasoning to some of your own goals and desires. For example, if someone asked why you are taking a particular college course (such as a course in cyberethics), you might respond that you wish to satisfy so many credit hours of course work in your major field of study or in your general education requirements. If you were then asked you why you wish to satisfy those course hours, you might respond that you wish to earn a college degree. If next someone asks you why you wish to graduate from college, you might reply that you wish to get a good-paying job. If you are then asked why you want a good-paying job, your response might be that you wish to purchase a home and that you would like to be able to save some money. If asked why again, you might reply that saving money would contribute to your financial and emotional security. And if further asked why you want to be financially and emotionally secure, you might respond that ultimately you want to be happy. So, following this line of reasoning, utilitarians conclude that happiness is an intrinsic good—that is, something that is good in and of itself, for its own sake, and not merely a means to some further end or ends.

2.4.1 Act Utilitarianism

We noted above that utilitarians look to the expected consequences of an act to determine whether or not that act is morally permissible. However, some critics point out that because utilitarianism tends to focus simply on the roles that individual acts and policies play in producing the overall social good (the greatest good for the greatest number), it is conceptually flawed. Consider a hypothetical scenario in which a new controversial policy is being enforced.

▶ **SCENARIO:** Act Utilitarianism

Suppose that 1 percent of the population in the United States are now forced to work as slaves in a manufacturing facility used by computer companies to produce chips. Further suppose that this practices results in lower prices for desktop computers for consumers in the United States. Arguably, such a practice might result in more overall happiness for American citizens because the remaining 99 percent of the population, who are not enslaved, can now purchase personal computers at a much lower price. Hence, 99 percent of the population benefit at the expense of the remaining 1 percent. The practice clearly seems consistent with the principle of producing the greatest good for the greatest number, yet, intuitively, such a practice also seems immoral.

The above scenario illustrates a major flaw in at least one version of utilitarianism, viz., *act utilitarianism*. According to act utilitarians:

An act, X, is morally permissible if the consequences produced by doing X result in the greatest good for the greatest number of persons affected by X.

All things being equal, actions that produce the greatest good (happiness) for the greatest number of people seem desirable. However, policies and practices based solely on this principle can also have significant negative implications for those who are not in the majority (i.e., the greatest number). Consider the plight of the unfortunate few who are enslaved in the computer chip processing plant. Because of the possibility that such bizarre cases could occur, some critics who embrace the goals of utilitarianism in general, reject act utilitarianism.

Critics who reject the emphasis on the consequence of individual acts point out that in our day-to-day activities we tend not to deliberate on each individual action as if that action were unique. Rather, we are inclined to deliberate on the basis of certain principles or general rules that guide our behavior. For example, consider some principles that may guide your behavior as a consumer. Each time that you enter a computer store, do you ask yourself, "Shall I steal this particular software game in this particular store at this particular time?" Or have you already formulated certain general principles that guide your individual actions, such as: "It is never morally permissible to steal"? In the latter case, you are operating at the level of a rule or principle rather than deliberating at the level of individual actions.

2.4.2 Rule Utilitarianism

Some utilitarians argue that the consequences that result from following *rules* or principles, not the consequences of individual acts, ultimately matter in determining whether or not a certain practice is morally permissible. This version of utilitarian theory, called *rule utilitarianism*, can be formulated in the following way:

> An act, X, is morally permissible if the consequences of following the general rule Y, of which act X is an instance, would bring about the greatest good for the greatest number.

Note that here we are looking at the consequences that result from following certain kinds of rules as opposed to consequences resulting from performing individual acts. Rule utilitarianism eliminates as morally permissible those cases in which 1 percent of the population is enslaved so that that the majority (the remaining 99 percent) can prosper. Rule utilitarians believe that policies that permit the unjust exploitation of the minority by the majority will have overall negative social consequences and thus will not be consistent with the principle criterion of utilitarian ethical theory.

Rule utilitarianism would seem to be a more plausible ethical theory than act utilitarianism. However, some critics reject all versions of utilitarianism because they believe that no matter how this theory is expressed, utilitarianism is fundamentally flawed. These critics tend to attack one or both of the following aspects of utilitarian theory:

I. Morality is ultimately tied to happiness or pleasure.

II. Morality can ultimately be determined by consequences (of either acts or policies).

Critics of utilitarianism argue that morality can be grounded neither in consequences nor in happiness. Hence, they argue that some alternative criterion or standard is needed.

► 2.5 DUTY-BASED ETHICAL THEORIES

Immanuel Kant (1724–1804) argued that morality must ultimately be grounded in the concept of duty, or obligations that humans have to one another, and never in the consequences of human actions. As such, morality has nothing to do with the promotion of happiness or the achievement of desirable consequences. Thus Kant rejects utilitarianism in particular, and all consequentialist ethical theories in general. He points out that, in some instances, performing our duties may result in our being unhappy and may not necessarily lead to consequences that are considered desirable. Theories in which the notion of duty, or obligation, serves as the foundation for morality are called *deontological* theories because they derive their meaning from the Greek root *deon*, which means duty. How can a deontological theory avoid the problems that plague consequentialist theories such as utilitarianism? Kant provides two answers to this question, one based on our nature as rational creatures, and the other based on the notion that human beings are ends-in-themselves. We briefly consider each of Kant's arguments.

What does Kant mean when he says that humans have a rational nature? Kant argues that what separates us from other kinds of creatures, what binds us morally, is our rational capacity. Unlike animals who may be motivated only by sensory pleasure, humans have an ability to reason and deliberate. So Kant reasons that if our primary nature were such that we merely seek happiness or pleasure, as utilitarians suggest, then we would not be distinguishable from other creatures in morally relevant ways. But because we have a rational capacity, we are able to reflect upon situations and make moral choices in a way that other kinds of (nonrational) creatures cannot. Kant argues that our rational nature reveals to us that we have certain duties or obligations to each other as a rational beings in a moral community.

We can next examine Kant's second argument, which concerns the roles of human beings as ends-in-themselves. We have seen that in focusing on criteria involving the happiness of the majority, utilitarians allow, even if unintentionally, that some humans can be sacrificed for the ends of the greatest number. Kant argues that a genuinely moral system would never permit some humans to be treated as means to the ends of others. He also believes that if we are willing to use a standard based on consequences (such as social utility) to ground our moral system, then that system will ultimately fail to be a moral system. Kant also argues that each individual, regardless of his or her wealth, intelligence, privilege, or circumstance, has the same moral worth. From this, Kant infers that each individual, therefore, is an end in him- or herself and thus should never be treated merely as a means to some end. Thus we have a duty to treat fellow humans as ends.

2.5.1 Rule Deontology

Is there a rule or principle that can be used in an objective and impartial way to determine the basis for our moral obligations? For Kant, there is such a standard or objective test, which can be formulated in a principle that he calls the *categorical imperative*. Kant's imperative has a number of variations, and we will briefly examine two of them. One variation of his imperative directs us to:

> Act always on that maxim or principle (or rule) that ensures that all individuals will be treated as ends-in-themselves and never merely as a means to an end.

Another variation of the categorical imperative can be paraphrased in the following way:

> Act always on that maxim or principle (or rule) that can be universally binding, without exception, for all human beings.

Kant believed that if everyone followed the categorical imperative, we would have a genuinely moral system. It would be a system based on two essential principles: universality and impartiality. In such as system, every individual would be treated fairly since the same rules would apply universally to all persons. And because Kant's imperative observes the principle of impartiality, it does not allow for one individual or group to be privileged or favored over another. In other words, if it is morally wrong for you to engage in a certain action, then it is also morally wrong for all persons like you—that is, all rational creatures (or moral agents)—to engage in that action. And if you are obligated to perform a certain action, then every moral agent is likewise obligated to perform that action.

▶ **SCENARIO:** Kant's Principles of Universality and Impartiality

To illustrate Kant's points about the role that universal principles play in a moral system, consider the following story. A student once approached me after class to turn in a paper that was past due. I informed the student that his paper was late and that I was not sure that I would accept it. He then replied that he was actually doing me a favor by turning in the paper late. He reasoned that if he had turned in the paper when it was due, I would have been swamped with papers. Now, however, I would be able to read his paper in a much more leisurely manner, without having the stress of so many papers to grade at once. I then told the student that I appreciated his concern for me, but I asked him to reflect on his reasoning for a moment. Specifically, I asked him to imagine a case in which every student, fearing that I would be overwhelmed with papers arriving at the same time, decided to turn their papers in one week late. He soon saw the problem that would arise if everyone used his rationale.

On Kantian grounds, the student can only make an exception for himself if everyone else had the right to make exceptions for themselves, as well. But if everyone did that, then what would happen to the very notion of following rules in a society? It is not that negative consequences would result from this that bothers Kant. Rather, if everyone decided that he or she could make an exception for him- or herself whenever it was convenient to do so, we couldn't even have practices such as promise keeping and truth telling. For those practices to work, they must be universalizable (apply to all persons equally). When we make exceptions for ourselves, we break the principle of impartiality, and we treat others as means to our ends

In Kant's deontological scheme, we do not consider the potential consequences of a certain action or of a certain rule to determine whether that act is morally permissible. Rather, the objective rule to be followed—that is, the litmus test for determining when an action will have moral worth—is whether the act complies with the categorical imperative.

For a deontologist like Kant, enslaving humans would always be immoral, regardless of whether the practice of having slaves might result in greater social utility (e.g., cheaper personal computers) than the practice of not allowing slavery. The practice of slavery is immoral, not because it might have negative social consequences in the long term, but because

a. it allows some humans to be used only as a means to an end, and

b. a practice like slavery could not be consistently applied in an objective, impartial, and universally binding way.

Kant would ask, for example, whether we could consistently impose a universal maxim that would allow slavery. He believed that we could not consistently (in a logically coherent sense) formulate such a principle that would apply to all humans, since we would have to allow that we also be willing to be subject to slavery. If we allow for the practice that some individuals can be enslaved but not others, then we would be allowing for exceptions to the moral rule. We would also be allowing some individuals to be used only as a means to the ends of others rather than as ends-in-themselves.

Although Kant's version of deontological ethics avoids many of the difficulties of utilitarianism, it too has been criticized as an inadequate ethical theory. Critics point out, for example, that even if Kant's categorical imperative provides us with as the ultimate test for determining when some particular course of action is our duty, it will not help us in cases where we have two or more conflicting duties. Consider that in Kant's system, we have duties to both keep promises and tell the truth. Thus, acts such as telling a lie or breaking a promise can never be morally permissible. However, Kant's critics point out that sometimes we encounter situations in which we are required *either* to tell the truth and break a promise *or* to keep a promise and tell a lie. In these cases, we encounter genuine moral dilemmas. Kant's deontological theory does not provide us with a mechanism for resolving such conflicts.

2.5.2 Act Deontology

Although Kant's version of deontology has at least one significant flaw, some philosophers believe that a deontological account of morality is nonetheless the correct kind of ethical theory. They also believe that a deontological ethical theory can be formulated in a way that avoids the charges of Kant's critics. One attempt at reformulating this theory was made by David Ross (1930). Ross rejects utilitarianism for many of the same reasons that Kant does. However, Ross also believes that Kant's version of deontology is not fully adequate.

Ross argues that when two or more moral duties clash, we have to look at individual situations in order to determine which duty will override another. Like act utilitarians, then, Ross stresses the importance of analyzing individual situations to determine the morally appropriate course of action to take. Unlike utilitarians, however, Ross believes that we must not consider the consequences of those actions in deliberating over which course of action morally trumps, or outweighs, another. Like Kant, Ross believes that the notion of duty is the ultimate criterion for determining morality. But unlike Kant, Ross does not believe that blind adherence to certain maxims or rules can work in every case for determining which duties we must ultimately carry out.

Ross believes that we have certain *prima facie* (or self-evident) *duties* which, all things being equal, we must follow. He provides a list of prima facie duties such as honesty, benevolence, justice, and so forth. For example, each of us has a prima facie duty not to lie and a prima facie duty to keep a promise. And if there are no conflicts in a given situation, then each prima facie duty is also what he calls an *actual duty*. But how are we to determine our actual duty is in situations where two or more prima facie duties conflict with one another? Ross also believes that our ability to determine what our actual duty will be in a particular situation is made possible through a process of "rational intuitionism" (similar to one used in mathematics).

We saw that for Kant, every prima facie duty is, in effect, an absolute duty because it applies to every human being without exception. We also saw that Kant's scheme provides no procedure for deciding what we must do when two or more duties conflict. However, Ross believes that we can determine what our overriding duty is in a particular situation by using a deliberative process that requires two steps:

a. Reflect on the competing prima facie duties.

b. Weigh the evidence at hand to determine which course of action would be required in a particular circumstance.

The following scenario illustrates how Ross's procedure can be carried out.

▶ **HYPOTHETICAL SCENARIO:** A Dilemma That Involves Conflicting Duties

Imagine that you made a promise to meet a classmate at 7:00 in the library to study together for a midterm exam for a computer science course you are taking. All things being equal, you have a moral obligation to keep your promise to your friend. Here, Kant and Ross are both in agreement. Now suppose on your way to meet your friend you receive a call on your cell phone informing you that your grandmother has been taken to the hospital and that you should go immediately to the hospital. Also suppose that you are unable to reach your friend to inform her about what has happened. What should you do in this case?

For a rule deontologist like Kant, the answer is unclear since you have two absolute duties: one to visit your grandmother in the hospital, and another to keep your promise to a friend. For Ross, however, the following procedure for deliberation is used. You would have to weigh between the two prima facie duties in question to determine which will be your actual duty in this particular circumstance. In weighing between the two conflicting duties, your actual duty in this situation would be to visit your grandmother, which means of course that you would have to break your promise to your friend. However, in a different kind of situation involving a conflict of the same two duties, your actual duty might be to keep the promise made to your friend and not visit your grandmother in the hospital.

Notice that in cases of weighing between conflicting duties, Ross places the emphasis of deliberation on certain aspects of the particular situation or context, rather than on mere deliberation about the general rules themselves. Unlike utilitarians, however, Ross does not appeal to the consequences of either actions or rules in determining whether a particular course of action is morally acceptable.

One difficulty for Ross's position is that, as noted above, it uses a process called "rational intuitionism." Appealing to the intuitive process used in mathematics to justify certain basic mathematical concepts and axioms, Ross believes that the same process can be used in morality. However, his position on moral intuitionism is controversial and has not been widely accepted by contemporary ethicists. And since intuitionism is in an important component in Ross's theory of act deontology, many ethicists who otherwise might be inclined to adopt Ross's theory have been skeptical of it. However, variations of that theory have been adopted by contemporary deontologists.

To see how some deontological and utilitarian arguments can be applied specifically in the controversy involving the use of electronic spam, see Section 9.5.

Figure 2-4 summarizes key features that differentiate act and rule utilitarianism and act and rule deontology.

▶ 2.6 CONTRACT-BASED ETHICAL THEORIES

During the past two centuries, consequence-based and duty-based ethical theories have tended to receive the most attention from philosophers and ethicists. However, other kinds of ethical theories, such as those that emphasize criteria involving social contracts and individual rights have recently begun to receive some serious attention as well.

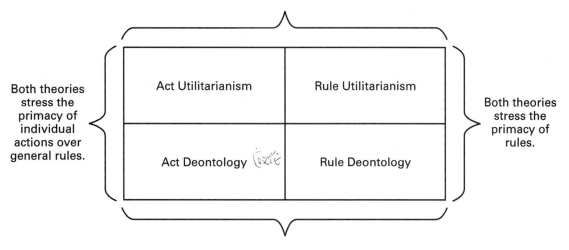

Both theories emphasize the importance of consequences.

Both theories stress the primacy of individual actions over general rules.

Act Utilitarianism | Rule Utilitarianism

Act Deontology | Rule Deontology

Both theories stress the primacy of rules.

Both theories emphasize the importance of duty or obligation.

Figure 2-4   Acts vs. Rules and Consequences vs. Duties

From the perspective of social-contract theory, a moral system comes into being by virtue of certain contractual agreements between individuals. One of the earliest formal versions of a contract-based ethical theory can be found in the writings of Thomas Hobbes (1588–1679). In his classic work *Leviathan*, Hobbes describes an original "premoral" state that he calls the "state of nature." It is premoral because there are no moral (or legal) rules yet in existence. In this state, each individual is free to act in ways that satisfy his or her own natural desires. According to Hobbes, our natural (or physical) constitution is such that in the state of nature we act in ways that will enable us to satisfy our desires (or appetites) and to avoid what Hobbes calls our "aversions." While there is a sense of freedom in this natural state, the condition of our day-to-day existence is hardly ideal. In this state, each person must continually fend for herself; and, as a result, each must also avoid the constant threats of others, who are inclined to pursue their own interests and desires.

Hobbes describes this state of nature as one in which life is "solitary, poor, nasty, brutish, and short." Because we are rational creatures, and because we see that it would be in our best interests to band together, Hobbes notes that we eventually establish a formal legal code. In doing this, Hobbes believes that we are willing to surrender some of our "absolute" freedoms to a sovereign. In return, we receive many benefits, including a system of rules and laws that are designed and enforced to protect individuals from being harmed by other members of the system.

One virtue of the social-contract model of ethics is that it gives us a motivation for being moral. We see that it is in our individual self-interest to develop a moral system with rules. This type of motivation for establishing a moral system is conspicuously absent in both the utilitarian or deontological theories. So a contract-based ethical theory might seem to have one advantage over them.

2.6.1 Some Criticisms of Social-Contract Theory

Some critics point out that social-contract theory provides the foundation for only a minimalist morality. It is minimalist in the sense that we are obligated to behave morally only where an explicit or formal contract exists. So if I have no express contract with you, or if a country like the United States has no explicit contract with a developing nation, there is no moral obligation for me to help you or for the United States to come to the aid of that developing nation. Of course, we can think of many situations involving morality where there are no express contracts or explicit laws describing our obligations to each other. Yet we also tend to believe that in at least some of these cases we are morally obligated to help others when it is in our power to do so.

Consider the case of Kitty Genovese who was murdered outside her apartment building in New York in 1967, as thirty-eight neighbors in her apartment building watched. During the incident, none of Genovese's neighbors came to her rescue or called the police. When interviewed after the fact, some of her neighbors responded that they did nothing wrong. In one sense, they were correct, since there was no explicit law requiring that they do anything at all. So technically, these neighbors were correct, at least from a legal perspective. But we can certainly ask whether her neighbors had a moral obligation to do something rather than simply be indifferent. It is in this sense, then that social-contract theory can be seen as being minimalist and legalistic, and not a robust theory of morality.

Another way to think about minimalist morality is to think of the difference between two principles: (a) doing no harm, and (b) doing good. A minimalist morality would insist merely that we do not harm others. As such, it does not require that we come to the aid of others. But is that an adequate view of morality? Should we accept such a moral system as complete? If you happen to see a child drowning in water that is four feet deep, and it is in your power to rescue the child, are you not morally obligated to do so? Are you under no moral obligation to assist simply because you may have no explicit legal contract requiring you to rescue that particular child?

According to a minimalist account of morality, you are not *required* to make any effort to save the child. All that is required is that you not actively harm the child (or anyone else). But some argue that a moral system demands much more of us than simply doing no harm. That is, it may also obligate us to do good when it is in our power to do so. According to the latter view of morality, then, if we could rescue the child without any inconvenience to ourselves, we would be morally obligated to do so (even if we have no explicit contract).

2.6.2 Rights-based Contract Theories

Closely associated with social-contract ethical theories are rights-based theories of morality. Some philosophers have argued that independent of whether individuals happen to have any legal rights, all humans have certain moral rights or natural rights. Philosophers such as Thomas Aquinas (1225–1274), as well as several of the founders of the United States, believed that humans possess some natural rights. In the United States Constitution, for example, the framers asserted that all humans are entitled to life, liberty, and the pursuit of happiness because these rights are "inalienable" and "self-evident."

Of course, it is one thing for philosophers and legal scholars to assert that humans are endowed with natural or moral rights; and it is something altogether different to ensure that such rights are guaranteed and are protected by the state. Hence, the need for explicit legal rights identified in a governing charter or constitution. Legal rights are grounded in "positive law," or civil law, whereas moral rights or natural rights are not. However, some argue that moral rights are derived from natural law; and because of this, they further argue that these rights exist independently of any legal rights that might happen to be granted to citizens of a certain nation via that nation's system of positive laws.

Philosophers and legal scholars often differentiate between two kinds of legal rights: *positive rights* and *negative rights*. Having a negative right to something means simply that one has the right not to be interfered with in carrying out the privileges associated with that right. For example, your right to vote and your right to own a computer are both negative rights. They are negative rights in the sense that as a holder of those rights, you have the right (and the expectation) not to be interfered with in exercising your right to go to polls to cast your vote in a particular election or your right to purchase a computer. However, as holder of a negative right, you cannot demand (or even expect) that others must either physically transport you to the voting polls if you are unable to travel there on your own, or provide you with a computer if you cannot afford to purchase one.

Positive rights, it turns out, are very rare. And since those rights tend to be far more controversial than negative rights, philosophers and legal scholars have had a much more difficult time justifying them. In the United States, one's right to receive an education is a positive right. All American citizens are entitled to such an education; and thus they must be provided with a free public education through the twelfth grade. An interesting question, for our purposes, is, what would happen in the event that our formal education process requires that each student own a computer and that he or she has access at home to the Internet? In that case, would students also have to be provided with a home computer and free Internet access? (We take up the question of universal access issues and the "digital divide" in Chapter 10.)

Some would argue that access to adequate health care should also be a positive right as well, because they believe health care is something that citizens have a right to be provided (even if they cannot afford to pay for it). In many European countries, universal access to health care is viewed as a positive right. In the United States, however, this is not the case, and the topic of national health care is presently a hotly disputed political issue.

Discussion about the nature of rights can be both confusing and controversial. In the United States, many conservative political and religious leaders believe that in recent years far too much emphasis has been placed on individual rights. As a result, they believe that we have not paid enough attention to corresponding responsibilities that individuals also have in virtue of possessing those rights. However, we will not pursue that line of controversy here.

▶ 2.7 CHARACTER-BASED ETHICAL THEORIES

A fourth type of ethical theory that must be considered, especially in light of the recent attention it has received, is *virtue ethics* (also sometimes described as "character ethics"). This ethical theory ignores the special roles that consequences, duties, and social contracts play in moral systems, especially with respect to determining the appropriate standard for evaluating moral behavior. Rather, it focuses on criteria having to do with the character development of individuals and their acquisition of good character traits from the kinds of habits they develop. The fundamental principles of virtue ethics were introduced in the writings of Plato and Aristotle nearly 2,500 years ago. In more recent times, virtue ethics has gained respect among ethicists as a viable contemporary ethical theory, in large part, through the influential work of Alasdair MacIntyre (1981).

2.7.1 Being a Moral Person vs. Following Moral Rules

Aristotle believed that ethics was something not merely to be studied, but rather to be lived or practiced. In fact, Aristotle thought of ethics as a "practical science," like politics. To become an ethical person, in Aristotle's view, one is required to do more than simply memorize and deliberate on certain kinds of rules. What is also needed, Aristotle argued, is that people develop certain *virtues*. The Greek word for virtue is *arete*, which means excellence. Aristotle believed that to be a moral person, one had to acquire the right virtues (strengths or excellences). Through the proper training and acquisition of good habits and character traits, Aristotle believed that one could achieve moral virtues such as temperance and courage that are needed to "live well."

Because virtue ethics focuses primarily on character development and moral education, it does not need to rely on a system of formal rules. Consider that both utilitarians and deontologists depend on having a system of rules when they ask a question such as, What should we do in such and such a case or situation? For utilitarians, the answer could be found by measuring the anticipated outcomes of following a general rule or principle. And for deontologists the answer can be determined by using a formal rule such as the categorical imperative as a principle for determining which duties you have. For contract theorists, questions involving moral obligation ultimately rest on the principle or rule, What is the nature of my contract, if any, in this particular situation? Virtue ethicists take a very different tack. Instead of asking, What should I *do* in such and such a situation? a virtue ethicist asks, What kind of person should I *be*? Hence the emphasis on *being* a moral person, and not simply understanding what moral rules are and how they apply in certain situations. Whereas deontological and utilitarian theories are action-oriented and rule-oriented, virtue ethics is agent-oriented because it is centered on the agent herself.

Virtue ethicists believe that a moral person is one who is necessarily disposed to do the right thing. They correctly point out that when we engage in routine acts in our daily lives, including many of our nonnormative actions, we do not deliberate by asking ourselves, What ought I to do in such and such a case? In our earlier criticism of act utilitarianism, we considered a situation in which an individual would be required to deliberate over whether or not to steal an item each time he or she entered a computer store. A virtue ethicist would point out that if that person had developed the right kind of moral character (through the acquisition of the correct moral habits), he or she would not be in a position that required such deliberation. That is, the moral person is already disposed not to steal items from department stores because of the kinds of character traits that he or she has previously developed. And in the example involving the drowning child, considered in the section on contract-based ethical theory, a virtue ethicist would also likely point out that a moral person would not have to deliberate. Regardless of whether someone had an explicit legal contract to help rescue the child, a moral person is predisposed to attempt to rescue the child if it were in his or her power to do so.

2.7.2 Acquiring the Correct Habits

Consider the following illustration of a disposition to behave in a certain way. When you woke up this morning and began to prepare for your day's events, did you ask yourself the question, Should I brush my teeth today? Chances are likely that this question never crossed your mind. Why not? The answer, of course, is that you have already developed certain habits such that you are disposed to brush your teeth in the morning without having to question it or even think about it. Of course, the act of brushing one's teeth is not an act that has any moral significance. But it is the process of character formation, especially the development of moral habits, that is crucial to becoming a fully moral person, from the perspective of virtue ethics.

As noted above, Aristotle believed that ethics was something to be lived and practiced, not simply studied. Thus some philosophers and ethicists believe that to teach ethics, one must first be an ethical person. The teacher who instructs students on the virtues but who himself lacks them would be a poor model for aspiring students. James Moor (2002) suggests that virtue ethics instruction is the "first level" in teaching (computer) ethics. He believes that building habits of character such as kindness, truthfulness, honesty, trustworthiness, helpfulness, generosity, and justice are important prerequisites in preparing for the second level of instruction. Once students have mastered the virtues, they can then move to the second level where they learn the established rules of a moral system.

Some ethics instructors have argued that students are better able to relate to ethics instruction examples that involve virtue ethics than other traditional theories. For this reason, Frances Grodzinsky (1999) has suggested that aspects of virtue ethics should be incorporated into the ethics training for computing professionals. Grodzinsky believes that aspiring computer professionals who wish to develop a sensitivity to ethical aspects of their profession often find the principles of virtue ethics far more useful than the kinds of rigid rules required in ethical theories such as utilitarianism and deontology. She notes that action-guiding rules associated with utilitarian and deontological theories often tend to be perceived by students as too abstract and formal. However, those students are able to grasp what it means to develop certain character traits and thus become (or be) a certain kind of person.

It would seem that the re-emergence of virtue ethics, despite the fact that its origins can be traced back to classical Greece, has provided ethicists with some fresh insights. However, we should also note that virtue ethics is not without its critics. One of the chief drawbacks of taking virtue ethics as a complete theory of ethics is that it neither helps resolve conflicts among virtues nor encourages examination of consequences. Some critics point out that a virtue- or character-based ethics would seem to have a better chance of taking hold in a society that is homogeneous rather than in one that is heterogeneous or pluralistic. The ancient Greek society could be considered fairly homogeneous in the sense that the world that Plato and Aristotle inhabited included a consensus as to what the ideal values, including the moral education of the young, were. In contemporary America, which is much more heterogeneous than classical Greek society, we have a diversity of views about which ideals and values are most important.

It is also worth pointing out that character-based ethical systems would tend to flourish in cultures where the emphasis placed on community life is stronger than that accorded to the role of individuals themselves. Beginning with the Enlightenment in the West,

TABLE 2-3   **Four Types of Ethical Theory**

Type of Theory	Advantages	Disadvantages
Consequence-based (Utilitarian)	Stresses promotion of happiness and utility	Ignores concerns of justice for the minority population
Duty-based (Deontology)	Stresses the role of duty and respect for persons	Underestimates the importance of happiness and social utility
Contract-based (Rights)	Provides a motivation for morality	Offers only a minimal morality
Character-based (Virtue)	Stresses moral development and moral education	Depends on homogeneous community standards for morality

considerable emphasis has been placed on the importance of individual autonomy and individual rights. As you might already have suspected, aspects of utilitarianism, deontological ethics, and contractualism ethics are strongly tied to the notions of individual rights and responsibilities. In the ancient Greek world of Aristotle's time, the notion of community was paramount. Thus virtues ethics faces certain challenges in contemporary Western society that it would not have had to endure in the classical Greek *polis,* or city-state.

▶ 2.8 INTEGRATING ASPECTS OF CLASSICAL ETHICAL THEORIES INTO A SINGLE COMPREHENSIVE THEORY

We have completed our examination of the four main types of ethical theories, and we have noted some of the strengths and weaknesses of each theory. While virtue ethics stresses the development of character on the part of individuals, it also has the disadvantage of being bound by the limitations of homogeneous community standards. In this sense, virtue ethics does not likely have the universal requirements needed for an adequate ethical theory. Contract theory seems useful in that it provides a motivation for being moral and it enables us to articulate which explicit moral obligations we have and do not have, both as individuals and as a society. However, the weakness of the social-contract view is that it provides us with only a minimalist theory of morality. Consequentialist theories such as utilitarianism are useful because they aim at promoting happiness and the social good. Yet, we also saw that utilitarians tend to ignore the importance of justice and fairness in their preoccupation with promoting social utility. Deontologists, on the other hand, stress the importance of obligation and respect for persons, and thus emphasize the principles of fairness and justice. However, we saw that deontologists fail to pay sufficient attention to the promotion of happiness and the social good. Thus each theory has its weakness, despite its strengths.

Recognizing the strengths of individual ethical theories, some philosophers have suggested ways in which elements of two or more theories might be integrated into a single, more comprehensive framework. For example, John Rawls (1971) in his seminal book *A Theory of Justice* outlines some ways in which aspects of deontology and utilitarianism could be combined into an overarching ethical theory. More recently, James Moor (1999) has proposed a scheme that integrates aspects of utilitarian and deontological theory into a framework he calls "just consequentialism." We briefly examine key aspects of this theory in the following section.

2.8.1 Moor's Just-Consequentialist Theory

Moor believes that only an ethical approach that combines considerations of consequences of action with more traditional deontological considerations of duties, rights, and justice can provide us with a defensible ethical theory that yields a useful framework for applied ethics. He calls his approach, which is influenced by Gert and others, "just consequentialism." Moor begins by considering what kind of conduct we want ethics to regulate. He believes first and foremost everyone wants to be protected against suffering unnecessary harms. We don't want to be killed or suffer great pain or have our freedoms taken away. Human nature is such that people value the same kind of basic goods (life, happiness, abilities, security, knowledge, freedom, opportunities, and resources). The specifics of these may be manifest somewhat differently in different cultures (some kinds of freedoms may be more important in some cultures than others, for example) but the general set of goods, which Moor calls "core values" (see Section 2.1.2.1), is shared by all. Losing any of these goods counts as harm, and all of us want ethics to protect us from others causing us harm. This point is captured by the familiar ethical maxim "Do no harm," described earlier. Stealing someone's computer causes a loss of resources to that person, and lying about software bugs undermines the purchaser's knowledge. Thus it is not surprising that we regard stealing and lying as unethical activities in light of their harmful consequences.

Another desirable objective of ethics, according to Moor, is to support justice, rights, and duties. We want others to keep their promises and agreements, to obey the law, and to fulfill their duties in whatever roles they play. These specific obligations are generated within societies, and to the extent that they spring from just agreements, laws, and social situations, we justifiably expect others to fulfill their duties toward us. For example, we want a software engineer to produce reliable software. We believe it is her duty as a professional to develop effective and safe software and that we have a right to expect good quality when we buy it. Another familiar maxim of ethics is "Do your duty," where "duty" here designates specific duties people acquire by their roles in society such as a signer of contract, a citizen, a parent, an employer or an employee. Violating one's just duty, such as knowingly designing defective software for later production and sales, in the absence of contravening considerations is clearly unethical.

Moor believes that, if all we had to do to be ethical were to do no harm and perform our duties, then ethics would be challenging but at least easy to understand. But, as Moor argues, the ethical life is not nearly so simple. Often actions involve a mixture of goods and evils as well as conflicts among duties. Sometimes we need to make exceptions to our general policies for action. How do we decide what to do? His approach to the decision is executed in two steps: the deliberation stage and the selection stage. First, at the deliberation stage, we should consider the various possible policies for action from an impartial point of view. "Impartial" does not mean that everyone is treated the same but that the policy is regarded as a rule governing the situation without consideration to the particular individuals who happen to be involved. This is what Bernard Gert has in mind by his "blindfold of justice" (see Section 2.1.1.2) or what John Rawls suggests with his "veil of ignorance." This is a technique to establish the justice of a policy—it will not be just if one will not accept the policy as a general rule of conduct, not knowing who plays which roles in the situation.

For example, consider the illustration of cyberstalking discussed in Chapter 1, in which Liam Youens stalked Amy Boyer on the Internet and eventually murdered her. Let us assume that Youens was obsessed with his victim and got significant gratification out of his deeds. If we consider a policy for doing such action impartially, we will clearly reject it. We will not endorse a policy of allowing someone to stalk and kill us even if such murderers get significant pleasure from it. It is easy to reject such a policy as unjust and unethical when considered from an impartial point of view.

However, many policies will pass the impartiality test, and we will still need to consider whether we should adopt them. We need to move to the second step in the decision-making process, the selection stage, and weigh carefully the good consequences and the bad consequences of the remaining policies. In this second step it may be less of a choice between ethical vs. unethical policies than between better vs. worse policies. Although we may be able to at least partially rank policies, legitimate disagreements about the rankings often exist.

For instance, consider the controversial issues as to whether we should adjust or even have a policy of intellectual property protection. For many years in many places there were no laws protecting intellectual property. It is far from clear that this situation was unjust or even bad. A culture might maintain that sharing information and invention is more valuable to the society's members' welfare and the society's cohesiveness than trying to protect intellectual property. Witness the rationale given for the open source movement today. Others might maintain that having intellectual-property protection laws is important to protect creators and to produce innovative products for everyone's benefit.

According to Moor, it is important to keep in mind that although we may disagree about the merits of various policies and how to rank them, rational discussion of the relevant policies is very possible and highly desirable. People may overlook values embedded in a situation and may change their rankings once informed. People may not be fully aware of the consequences of various policies. Moor does not believe that complete agreement on controversial policies can or necessarily should be reached, as people may ultimately rank benefits and harms differently. Nevertheless, considerable consensus about some policies being better than others can often be generated. Moor points out that frequently much of the disagreement hinges on differences about the facts of the case than on value differences. (Recall our early analysis of differences involving "disagreements about principles" and "disagreements about facts" in Section 2.2.1.3, in our discussion of discussion stoppers in ethics.) It would radically change much of the debate about the need for protecting MP3s, for example, if it could be demonstrated that *as a matter of fact* downloading MP3s to preview them dramatically increases sales or if it could be demonstrated that *as a matter of fact* downloading MP3s to preview them dramatically decreased the quality of music that was produced.

2.8.2 Applying the Just-Consequentialist Framework to Cybertechnology

Perhaps Moor's ethical framework of just consequentialism can be summarized in terms of a strategy that includes the following steps:

1. *Deliberate* over various policies from an impartial point of view to determine whether they meet the criteria for being ethical policies. A policy is ethical, if it

   a. does not cause any unnecessary harms to individuals and groups, and

   b. supports individual rights, the fulfilling of duties, etc.

2. *Select* the best policy from the set of just policies arrived at in the deliberation stage by ranking ethical policies in terms of benefits and (justifiable) harms. In doing this, be sure to

   a. weigh carefully between the good consequences and bad consequences in the ethical policies, and

   b. distinguish between disagreements about facts and disagreements about principles and values, when deciding which particular ethical policy should be adopted. (Knowledge about the facts surrounding a particular case should inform the decision-making process.)

We apply the above strategy, wherever appropriate, in suggesting policies in response to moral issues that arise from specific cyberethics issues examined in Chapters 4–11 of this textbook.

▶ 2.9 CHAPTER SUMMARY

In this chapter, we defined ethics as the study of morality. In elaborating on that definition, we drew some useful distinctions between morality (as a system of rules and principles) and ethics (as the study of that system). Acknowledging the distinction between normative and descriptive studies of morality, we saw that normative investigations into morality can be conducted from the perspectives of religion and law as well as from philosophy. We also noted that only philosophical ethics offers a method to analyze moral issues based exclusively on the application of ethical theory and logical argumentation. We also examined the roles that ethical theories ideally play in guiding us in our moral deliberations about cyberethics issues. We saw that consequence-based, duty-based, contract-based, and character-based theories each had certain strengths and weaknesses. Finally, we examined James Moor's proposal for a framework that incorporates aspects of consequence-based and duty-based theories into one unified, comprehensive theory, called "just consequentialism." We summarized Moor's framework into a two-step process that we will use, wherever possible, in our analysis of the cyberethics issues examined in this textbook.

▶ REVIEW QUESTIONS

1. What is *ethics*, and how can it be distinguished from *morality*?

2. What is meant by a *moral system*? What are some of the key differences between the "rules of conduct" and the "principles of evaluation" that comprise a moral system?

3. What does Bernard Gert mean when he describes morality in terms of an "informal, public system?" How is a moral system both similar to, and different from, a game for Gert?

4. Describe how the ideals of "rationality" and "impartiality" are used in a moral context. What is meant by the expression "moral agent?"

5. What are some of the key differences between *moral values* and nonmoral values?

6. How do religion, law, and philosophy each provide different grounds for justifying a moral principle?

7. Why are sociological and anthropological studies of morality descriptive studies?

8. What exactly is meant by the expression "philosophical study?" How is a philosophical study applied to an analysis of moral issues?

9. Describe four different kinds of "discussion stoppers" in ethical discourse.

10. Why are these "discussion stoppers" problematic for the advancement of ethical dialogue and debate?

11. What is ethical relativism? Describe some of the distinctions that can be drawn between cultural relativism and ethical relativism.

12. What is ethical theory, and what important functions do ethical theories play in the analysis of moral issues?

13. What are the distinguishing features of consequence-based ethical theories?

16. Describe some of the key differences between act utilitarianism and rule utilitarianism.

17. Which features distinguish duty-based ethical theories from alternative types of theories?

18. Describe some of the main differences between act deontology and rule deontology.

19. What is meant by the expression "contract-based" ethical theories?

20. What is meant by the expression "character-based" (or "virtue-based") ethical theories?

▶ DISCUSSION QUESTIONS

1. Consider once again the four types of "discussion stoppers" that we examined in this chapter. Is that collection of "stoppers" complete? Can you think of any additional discussion stoppers that might also block or shut down moral discourse? Why is it so easy to fall victim to one or more of those stoppers when discussing moral issues in general, as well as moral issues involving the use of cybertechnology in particular?

2. Consider the following situation. You have just been appointed to the board of directors of XYZ.com. Unfortunately, the dot.com company has been experiencing some difficult financial times, resulting in revenue losses in three of the last four quarters. As you assume your new position, you discover that two proposals are on the table. Each proposal has been put forth as a means for dealing with XYZ's immediate financial problems. Proposal #1 recommends all employees be retained, but that an immediate wage freeze for all employees be imposed for the next six months. (Employees may even be asked to take a 5 percent cut in pay if things do not improve by the end of that period.) Proposal #2 recommends that wages not be frozen, but that 5 percent of the XYZ's work force be laid off. (One piece of reasoning behind this proposal is that taking more drastic measures will "protect" 95 percent of XYZ's workers and will send a message to Wall Street and local investors that XYZ is serious about improving its financial position and that it will soon be a stable company once again.) The board is evenly split, seven members favoring proposal# 1 and seven favoring proposal #2. Yours will be the tie-breaking vote. In your deliberation, describe how an *act utilitarian*, a *rule utilitarian*, a *rule deontologist*, and an *act deontologist* would reach each a solution to this dilemma. Which solution seems most plausible?

3. Consider a case in which the United States government, with the approval of the majority of Americans, decides to round up all Arab-Americans and relocate them into internment camps. Imagine that you have a friend who is an American citizen of Arab descent. She asks you to protect her from the authorities. You have known this person all of your life, and you are convinced that she is a loyal American. So you agree to hide her in the third floor of your house. Next imagine that a United States federal agent knocks on your door and asks if you know the whereabouts of the person you are hiding. How would you respond to that agent? You now face a gen-

uine moral dilemma because you cannot both keep your promise to your friend and tell the truth to the federal agent. Initially, your gut reaction might suggest that the solution to your dilemma is really quite simple. For example, you might believe that a far greater good will be served by lying to the federal agent than by breaking your promise to your friend. However, to embrace the moral principle inherent in that line of reasoning is to fall back into utilitarianism. And we have already seen some of the difficulties that can result from trying to be a consistent and thoroughgoing utilitarian. Furthermore, could you consistently universalize a moral principle that states: "Whenever you must choose between telling the truth to authorities and breaking a promise to a friend, always honor your promise." Will that principle work in every case? Will Ross's theory help in this situation? Explain.

4. Are any of the four traditional ethical theories we examined adequate to handle moral issues that arise as a result of cybertechnology? Is a brand new ethical theory needed, as some have argued, for the Internet age; or can a comprehensive, integrated theory, such as the one proposed by James Moor (i.e., his theory of "just consequentialism") be used successfully to resolve moral issues involving cybertechnology? Explain.

▶ REFERENCES

Aristotle (1962). *Nicomachean Ethics*. Trans. M. Oswald. New York: Bobbs-Merrill.

Bentham, Jeremy (1948). *Introduction to the Principles of Morals and Legislation*. W. Harrison, ed. London: Oxford University Press.

De George, Richard T. (1999). *Business Ethics*. 5th ed. Upper Saddle River, NJ: Prentice Hall.

Gert, Bernard (1998). *Morality: Its Nature and Justification*. New York: Oxford University Press.

Grodzinsky, Frances S. (1999). "The Practitioner From Within: Revisiting the Virtues," *Computers and Society*, Vol. 29, No. 1, pp. 9–15.

Hobbes, Thomas (1962). *Leviathan*. New York: Collier Books.

Kant, Immanuel (1965). *Fundamental Principles of the Metaphysics of Morals*. Trans. T. K. Abbott. London: Longman's.

MacIntyre, Alasdair (1981). *After Virtue*. South Bend: University of Notre Dame Press.

Mill, John Stuart (1965). *Utilitarianism*. New York: Bobbs-Merrill, 1965.

Moor, James H. (1999). "Just Consequentialism and Computing," *Ethics and Information Technology*, Vol. 1, No. 1, 1999, pp. 65–69.

Moor, James H. (2002). "The Importance of Virtue in Teaching Computer Ethics." In Mitsugu Ochi et al., Eds. *Proceedings of the Foundations of Information Ethics (FINE 2001)*. Hiroshima, Japan: Hiroshima University Press, pp. 29–38

Pojman, Louis P. (2001). *Ethics: Discovering Right and Wrong*. 4th ed. Belmont, CA: Wadsworth Publishing Co.

Rawls, John (1971). *A Theory of Justice*. Cambridge, MA: Harvard University Press.

Ross, W. D. (1930). *The Right and the Good*. London: Oxford University Press.

▶ FURTHER READINGS

Arthur, John, ed. (1996). *Morality and Moral Controversies*. 4th ed. Upper Saddle River, NJ: Prentice Hall.

Birsh, Douglas. (1998). *Ethical Insights: A Brief Introduction*. Mountain View, CA: Mayfield Publishing.

Cahn, Steven and Joram Haber, eds. (1995). *Twentieth-Century Ethical Theory*. Englewood Cliffs, NJ: Prentice Hall.

Crisp, Roger and Michael Slote, eds. (1997) *Virtue Ethics*. New York: Oxford University Press.

DeMarco, Joseph (1996) *Moral Theory: A Contemporary Overview*. Sudbury, MA: Jones and Bartlett Publishers.

Edel, Abraham (1994). *Method in Ethical Theory*. New Brunswick, NJ: Transaction Publishers.

Gert, Bernard (1999). "Common Morality and Computing," *Ethics and Information Technology*, Vol. 1, No. 1, pp. 57–64.

Gowans, Christopher W., ed. (2000). *Moral Disagreements: Classic and Contemporary Readings*. New York: Routledge.

Harris, C. E. (1997). *Applying Moral Theories*. 3d ed. Belmont, CA: Wadsworth Publishing.

Hinman, Lawrence, M. ed. (1996). *Contemporary Moral Issues: Diversity and Consensus*. Upper Saddle River, NJ: Prentice Hall.

Johnson, Mark (1993). *Moral Imagination: Implications of Cognitive Science for Ethics*. Chicago: University of Chicago Press.

Jonas, Hans. (1984). *The Imperative of Responsibility: In Search of an Ethics for the Technological Age*. Chicago: University of Chicago Press.

Ladd, John, ed. (1973). *Ethical Relativism*. Belmont, CA: Wadsworth Publishing.

Moor, James H. (1998). "Reason, Relativity, and Responsibility in Computer Ethics," *Computers and Society*, Vol. 28, No. 1, pp. 14–21.

Moser, Paul K., and Thomas L. Carson, eds. (2000). *Moral Relativism: A Reader*. New York: Oxford University Press.

Pritchard, Michael S. (1998). "Professional Responsibility: Focusing on the Exemplary," *Science and Engineering Ethics*, Vol. 4, No. 2, pp. 215–234.

Rachels, James. (1998). *The Elements of Moral Philosophy*. 3d ed. New York: McGraw-Hill.

Singer, Peter. (1993). *Practical Ethics*. 2nd ed. New York: Cambridge University Press.

Sterba, James. (1997). *Morality in Practice*. 5th ed. Belmont, CA: Wadsworth Publishing.

Triplett, Timm (2002). "Bernard Gert's *Morality* and Its Application to Computer Ethics," *Ethics and Information Technology*, Vol. 4, No. 1, pp. 79–92.

Weston, Anthony. (2000). *A 21st-Century Ethical Toolbox*. New York: Oxford University Press.

3

CRITICAL THINKING SKILLS AND LOGICAL ARGUMENTS: TOOLS FOR EVALUATING CYBERETHICS ISSUES

You may wonder why a chapter dedicated to critical thinking skills and logical argumentation tools is included in a book on cyberethics. To appreciate the important role that these skills and tools play in our examination of cyberethics issues, recall the methodological framework that we developed in Chapter 1. There, we saw that the final step of that methodology requires that we be able to defend or justify our position by evaluating it against the rules of logical argumentation. In Chapter 3 we examine some basic critical thinking concepts we need to do this. To accomplish these objectives, we

- define *argument* and show how logical arguments are used in disputes involving ethical aspects of cybertechnology;
- identify some common logical fallacies that occur in everyday reasoning and show how they apply to arguments involving cyberethics issues;
- propose a strategy for identifying "fallacy types" that may emerge in future disputes; and
- present a seven-step strategy for distinguishing between arguments that are valid and invalid, sound and unsound, inductive and fallacious.

Additional material on critical thinking skills is included in Appendix E, available at www.wiley.com/college/Tavani.

▶ 3.1 LOGICAL ARGUMENTS

We begin by asking what exactly is meant by the expressions *critical thinking* and *logical argument*. The term "critical thinking" is now widely used in higher education contexts to refer to a range of analytical skills, such as those used to distinguish alleged factual claims from opinions and value judgements(Tavani 1994) and analyze the accuracy of claims made in advertising and marketing. Brook Moore and Richard Parker (1999) define critical thinking as "simply the careful deliberate determination of whether we should accept, reject, or suspend judgment about a claim." Claims, a logical argument, or simply statements, in turn, are often used in a form of reasoning called an *argument*. For our purposes, an argument can be defined as a form of reasoning that attempts to establish the truth of one claim (called a *conclusion*) based on the assumed truth of the evidence in other claims (called *premises*) provided to support the conclusion. Note that an argument has three important characteristics in that it

i. is a form of reasoning;

ii. is comprised of claims (1.e., statements or assertions); and

iii. aims at establishing a conclusion (i.e., one claim) based on evidence provided by one or more other claims, called premises.

3.1.1 The Role of Logical Arguments and Their Application in Cybertechnology Contexts

Consider a hypothetical dispute about whether a controversial and powerful new computer chip—code-named Chip X—is being developed in Japan. This new chip is alleged to be so powerful in speed and performance that it will eclipse any computer chips that manufacturers in the United States, such as Intel or AMD, will be capable of producing during the next several years. Chip X will also enable the manufacturer to monitor certain activities of those users whose computers contain the chip in ways that pose serious threats to personal privacy.

Suppose I claim that Chip X is currently under development by Mishito Corporation. Let us further suppose that you are skeptical about my claim. There are a number of ways I could attempt to convince you: I could persuade you to accompany me on a trip to Japan to see first-hand whether or not Chip X is being developed there. In this case, we could obtain direct evidence about my claim. But if you are unable or are unwilling to accompany me to Japan, I might instead show you a copy of the design specifications for Chip X, extracted from a confidential Mishito Corporation document that I happened to acquire. Or perhaps I could ask a mutual colleague of ours who recently studied as an exchange student at the University of Hiroshima, where the field testing for this new chip is being carried out, to corroborate my claim. Both of these methods would provide us with indirect evidence so that, ultimately, we should be able to resolve the disputed claim about Chip X either directly or indirectly.

I can put together the evidence to construct a *logical argument* that supports my claim. We can then debate the strength of my argument without going to Japan to verify my claim directly. But before we debate, we must first understand some essential features of an argument's *structure*.

3.1.2 The Structure of a Logical Argument

We noted in Section 3.1 that an argument consists of two or more claims; one of which is called the conclusion, and the others are called the premises. The standard form for representing an argument is to list the premises first and then state the conclusion. The following structure represents an argument's standard form:

PREMISE 1
PREMISE 2 (optional)
PREMISE 3 (optional)

.

.

.

PREMISE *n* (optional)

CONCLUSION

To support my claim that Chip X is currently being developed in Japan, the conclusion of my argument, I would need to list the evidence in the form of one or more premises. For example, I could use the following argument form:

PREMISE 1. When I recently visited the Computer Science Department at the University of Hiroshima in Japan I noticed that graduate students and professors there were field-testing a new computer chip, whose code name is Chip X.

PREMISE 2. I have a copy of the design specifications for Chip X, which shows that it will be several times faster than any chip currently available in the United States.

PREMISE 3. Lee Smith, a mutual colleague of ours who was recently an exchange student in the computer science program at the University of Hiroshima and who participated in the field-testing of Chip X, will corroborate my claim.

CONCLUSION. Chip X is currently being developed in Japan.

This particular argument includes three premises and a conclusion; additional premises could be added. However, an argument requires at least one premise along with a conclusion. In this section, we are concerned only with argument structure and not with how strong the argument might be. An argument, however weak, still qualifies as an argument if it has one or more premises and a conclusion.

You might have observed that the claim expressed in the conclusion to our argument about Chip X could also be verified (i.e., determined to be either true or false) independent of the evidence provided in the argument's premises. Since the conclusion contains a statement that is descriptive, or empirical (i.e., capable of being observed through experience), the truth or falsity of the conclusion could be resolved in this case simply by going to Japan to see whether such a chip was actually being developed there.

However, not all arguments have empirical or descriptive statements as their conclusions. Suppose that I want to convince you that people should be able to include information on their Web sites about how to build bombs. Further suppose that my reason for holding this view is based on the principle that people are allowed to write books on how to build bombs, and authors of Web sites should have the same rights and freedoms as authors of books. And suppose I base my reasoning for this claim on the right of authors to express themselves as guaranteed in the First Amendment of the United States Constitution. My argument could be constructed as follows:

PREMISE 1. An author's freedom to write a book on how to build a bomb is one that is protected by the First Amendment.

PREMISE 2. Authoring a book is similar to constructing a Web site.

CONCLUSION. Constructing a Web site on how to build a bomb ought to be protected by the First Amendment.

Notice how this argument differs from the preceding one. For one thing, we can't simply go to Japan to determine whether the conclusion is true or false. For another, the conclusion contains a normative statement (one that includes "ought"). Unlike the previous argument, which contained a descriptive statement in its conclusion that could be verified independently of the argument, we depend on the *form of reasoning* alone to help us determine whether the conclusion is true. In doing this, we will *assume* that the premises in this argument are true and then ask whether the conclusion would logically follow from them.

Initially, the reasoning in this argument might seem plausible: the author cleverly uses an analogy involving a legal right that applies in physical space. So we might assume that any rights that apply to individuals in physical space should automatically be extended to cyberspace.

In this argument, we are also asked to consider certain features or characteristics that are common to both (printed) books and Web sites. Clearly, we can draw a number of analogies here. For example, both books and Web sites can communicate and disseminate information to readers; each is authored by one or more persons; and so forth. However, there is a danger in pushing some of these analogies too far: Whereas books are tangible items existing in physical space, Web sites are neither. And the scope of a Web site allows it to be accessed by members of the international community, some of whom may have no access to books or may lack sufficient funds to purchase books. We begin to see many dissimilarities between books and Web sites, so we must be cautious about drawing conclusions when reasoning by analogy. Later in this chapter, we will see why arguments of this kind are not valid.

Next, consider a case in which someone tries to convince you that Internet users should not expect to retain their privacy when they engage in on-line activities, because the Internet is essentially a public forum or public space. Notice that, as stated, the conclusion of the argument precedes the premise. However, we can convert the argument into standard form as follows:

PREMISE: The Internet is in public space.

CONCLUSION: Those who use the Internet should not expect to retain any personal privacy.

Is the argument convincing? Before we evaluate this argument's reasoning, we should point out that a key term in the premise is unclear or imprecise: we first need to understand what is meant by "public space." We also need to consider whether the Internet can indeed be considered a public space or, for that matter, any kind of space at all. (In Chapter 9, we consider arguments as to whether the Internet is best conceived of as a place, like a bookstore, or as a broadcast medium, like television and radio.)

But let us assume that the premise in this argument is true. Does it follow that Internet users should have no expectations about retaining their personal privacy? Consider, for example, that while public rest rooms and pubic telephone booths both reside in public space, people expect to retain some privacy while using those facilities. (We will consider issues involving personal privacy in public space in our discussion of privacy and cyberspace in Chapter 5.)

So the argument does not appear to be very convincing; the conclusion would not likely follow from the premise, even when the premise is assumed true. In fact, the argument is fallacious, and in Section 3.8, we will see why—that is, we will identify which rules it breaks. In the next section, however, we will see that there is also a much simpler technique we can use to identify fallacious argument forms that frequently appear in everyday discourse.

▶ 3.2 CRITICAL THINKING SKILLS FOR IDENTIFYING LOGICAL FALLACIES IN EVERYDAY REASONING

Contrary to what many people assume, "fallacy" does not mean false statement, rather, it means *faulty reasoning*. It is possible for an argument to contain all true statements and still be fallacious. (Later in this chapter we will also see that an argument can contain all false statements and still technically be deductive or valid.)

At this point, you might be unsure about your ability to recognize a fallacious argument. Fortunately, there is an informal method for identifying one that does not require knowledge of some of the more sophisticated rules that comprise formal systems of logic. Because so many fallacies appear in everyday reasoning, logicians have categorized them in ways that are convenient for us to recognize. We refer to these kinds of fallacious arguments as *informal logical fallacies*.

The following ten informal fallacies, or "fallacy types," each illustrated with one or more examples involving computers and cybertechnology, are typical of argument forms that surface time and again in ordinary everyday discourse.

3.2.1 *Ad Hominem* Argument

In the *ad hominem* argument, an attack is directed to the person rather than to the substance of the person's argument. For example, imagine that Senator Ted Kennedy has opposed a bill before Congress that supports the construction of a new controversial national missile defense system (we will construct an argument for this issue in Section 3.3). Further suppose that Kennedy opposes the bill even though its passage would mean thousands of new jobs for computer professionals in Massachusetts. Now imagine that a proponent of this legislation, Senator Y, offers the following objection to Kennedy's position:

> How can we take seriously a position regarding the future of our national defense that has been proposed by a senator who has been arrested for drunken driving and who has been involved in extramarital affairs?

What is wrong with Senator Y's attack, and why does the reasoning used in it commit a logical fallacy? Note that Senator Y did not attack the merits or weaknesses of Kennedy's position on the national missile defense system, rather he attacked the personal character of the senator. Even if Kennedy's personal character is questionable, that point is irrelevant to whether the bill he has opposed should be passed or defeated, or whether it is a well-conceived piece of legislation or one that is ill-founded. Unfortunately, the debate over the merits or deficiencies of the bill is cut short, or at least temporarily derailed, because of the *ad hominem* attack.

One might object that if Kennedy's character were attacked because of allegations that he had sold secrets to foreign governments, then the personal attack would be justified and thus not a fallacy. Although national-security related allegations might have greater relevance in the argument as to why Kennedy's position on the missile-defense-system debate should not be taken seriously, the argument would still be fallacious because the attack fails to focus on the merits of the issues being debated; instead it focuses on personal character.

3.2.2 Slippery Slope Argument

The slippery slope argument is also sometimes called the "edge of the wedge" argument. It has the form "X could possibly be abused; therefore, we should not allow X." For example, one might argue:

> We should not allow Microsoft to bundle its Web browser, Internet Explorer (IE), as part of the Windows operating system. If we allow IE to be bundled, then Microsoft will next bundle Word, its proprietary word-processing system. And if we allow Microsoft to do that, it will next bundle its entire suite of office applications with the Windows operating system. And if that is allowed to happen, then all of Microsoft's competitors will go out of business and Microsoft will become a true monopoly. If it is not already a *de facto* monopoly, Microsoft is already well on its way to becoming one. So we must stop Microsoft now by not permitting it to bundle IE with Windows.

It should be fairly easy to spot the fallacy here: The author assumes that allowing Microsoft to bundle IE inevitably leads to an abusive slippery slope that logically implies that Microsoft's competitors will all be forced out of business and that Microsoft will become a true monopoly. It may well be that Microsoft will become a monopoly, and that it is already a *de facto* monopoly. However, that claim cannot be substantiated merely in terms of the evidence provided in the above argument.

3.2.3 Fallacy of Appeal to Authority

Arguments that conform to the fallacy of authority (*argumentum ad vericundiam*) have the following form:

PREMISE 1. X is an authority in field Y.

PREMISE 2. X said Z.

CONCLUSION. Z.

As an example, imagine that Tim Berners-Lee, who designed the HTTP protocol that became the standard for the World Wide Web, has agreed to do an advertisement for AOL. Further imagine that someone draws the following inference from the ad:

> Tim Berners-Lee has said publicly that AOL is a highly reliable ISP for home use. And Berners-Lee is clearly an expert on matters involving the Web and the Internet. So AOL must be a reliable ISP.

Can you spot the fallacy here? It is true that Berners-Lee is an expert on Web design; and it is also true that AOL is a fairly reliable ISP. However, is the argument's conclusion that AOL is a reliable ISP, even if true, warranted by the premises? Simply because Berners-Lee wrote the code that became the standard for the World Wide Web, and thus is an expert on some matters involving the Web, does that make him an authority on ISPs and their reliability?

3.2.4 False Cause Fallacy

The false cause argument (*post hoc ergo propter hoc*—after this, therefore because of this) reasons from the fact that event X preceded event Y to the conclusion that event X is necessarily the cause of event Y. Consider the following argument about the Netscape Navigator Web browser vis-à-vis Microsoft's Windows 98 operating system:

> Shortly after the release of Windows 98, Netscape's stock plummeted severely. Hence, there is no doubt that the release of Windows 98 is responsible for the decline in Netscape's fortunes in the stock market.

Can you identify the fallacy in the above argument? Even though it might be tempting to attribute Netscape's decline to the release of Microsoft's Windows 98, the person making this argument has overlooked the possibility of other factors that might have caused Netscape's decline in the stock market.

3.2.5 Begging the Question

An argument commits the fallacy of begging the question when its premise(s) presuppose the truth of the conclusion it is trying to establish. In such a case, the reasoning is circular. Consider the following argument:

> Object-oriented programming languages are superior to non-structured programming languages because the former type of programming languages are structured.

Why is this reasoning fallacious? Here the author of the argument has reasoned in a circle—instead of establishing that object-oriented programming languages are superior, the authors assumes that to be the case, that is, the truth of the premise presupposes the truth of the conclusion, rather than supplying evidence for the conclusion.

3.2.6 Fallacy of Composition/Fallacy of Division

The fallacy of composition confuses the characteristics that apply to the parts of a whole, or to the individual members of a group, with the characteristics of the whole itself. For example, consider the following form of reasoning:

> The new XYZ Desktop Computer is the best system on the market. XYZ has the fastest processor currently available on any PC; it comes with twice the amount of RAM than any of its competitors; and it comes equipped with a suite of office applications that are superior to those on any currently available system. Also, its monitor offers the best resolution and graphic display currently available on any commercial desktop computer.

Here the fallacy should be obvious. Each of the component parts of this desktop computer is the best that is currently available. However, it clearly does not follow that the system will necessarily be the best one available. The connections between the various parts of this system might not be well designed; we are not told how reliable the computer system is vis-à-vis its competitors. These kinds of flaws are apparent in all argument forms that commit the fallacy of composition. A film that has the best cast (Tom Hanks, Julia Roberts), one of the best directors (Steven Spielberg), and one of the best soundtrack composers (John Williams) might still be a flop. The quality of the individual parts does not necessarily guarantee the same quality in the overall product.

Next consider the flip side of this fallacy: the fallacy of division. The fallacy of division mistakenly infers that the same attributes or characteristics that apply to the whole or to the group must also apply to every part of the whole or to every member of the group. See if you can spot the fallacy in the following argument:

Harvard University is the number one ranked university in the country. Thus, Harvard must have nation's top computer science department.

Does the conclusion to the above argument follow from its premise? Clearly not! Harvard might be ranked first overall among universities in the United States, but the possibility remains that MIT, Stanford University, or some other institution has the nation's top-ranked computer science department.

3.2.7 Fallacy of Ambiguity

Fallacious reasoning can occur whenever one or more terms are used ambiguously; ambiguous terms have more than one interpretation, and it is not always clear which interpretation the author intends. Consider the following argument:

Humans can think, and computers can think; therefore, computers are human.

In this case, it is possible that both premises are true in the actual world. However, the sense in which computers are said to think is not necessarily the same sense in which humans, in fact, think. Here, the term "think" is used ambiguously. So even if it is true that computers can think in one sense of that term, it doesn't necessarily follow that computers can think in the same sense that humans do. Even if computers and humans could both think in the same sense, it doesn't follow that computers must be human. Consider that animals do many things in ways that are similar to humans, yet we do not infer that animals are humans. (One might object to the above argument being called a fallacy by noting that if thinking is defined as something that only humans could do, then, by definition, computers would have to be human. While this kind of move might avoid the fallacy of ambiguity, it introduces other problems since the premise "computers can think" would now be questionable.)

Another variation of the fallacy of ambiguity can be found in the following argument:

Computers have memory. Having memory enables us to recall experiences from our childhood. Therefore, computers can recall experiences from their childhood.

Notice that "memory" is used in two different senses in the above argument.

Although both examples of the fallacy of ambiguity illustrate exaggerated cases, many arguments used in everyday language commit variations of this fallacy.

3.2.8 Appeal to the People (*Argumentum ad Populum*)

Sometimes people appeal to the notion that there is strength in numbers. I remember once seeing a jacket to a record album that contained the following expression: "Fifty million Elvis fans can't be wrong." Is that true? Does it follow that because Elvis Presley had fifty million fans, that those numbers alone were sufficient to prove that Elvis was a great recording artist. Do sheer numbers count? Suppose that 150 million Americans believed that slavery was okay. Would that mean that slavery must be okay? The fallacy of the appeal to the people assumes that because X is popular, or because the majority of people agree with X, then X must be an acceptable standard. The following argument commits the fallacy of popular appeal.

> The majority of Americans believe that it is perfectly acceptable to share music over the Internet. So, despite the objections of greedy entrepreneurs in the recording industry, Napster (along with Gnutella and KaZaA) should be allowed to serve the wishes of the American people.

You should be able to spot the fallacy in this argument quite easily. Perhaps there are good reasons for why Napster should be allowed to continue to operate. However, those reasons have not been well articulated in this argument. What if the majority of Americans believed that all software should be distributed free of charge, does it follow that it should? The appeal to popular opinion has been an effective strategy, and in a democracy there are cases where such an appeal is clearly warranted and appropriate. The fallacy, of course, is to assume that every kind of issue—especially those concerning moral questions—can be decided in terms of a popular referendum.

3.2.9 The Many/Any Fallacy

This fallacy assumes that because many things of a certain kind have a feature, anything of that kind has that feature. It has the following form:

PREMISE. Many items of a certain kind, A, have property B.

CONCLUSION. Any item of the kind A has B.

Clearly, many items of a certain kind can have a property B without all of them having B. Note that many intellectual property protections policies could be justifiable, but does it follow that any intellectual property policy is justifiable? Similarly, does it follow from the fact that many sorting algorithms are efficient that any sorting algorithm is efficient? In his description of this fallacy, James Moor (1998) made the point that there are many acceptable ways to travel from Boston to Madrid, but it doesn't follow that any way of traveling between these cities is acceptable. For example, traveling from Boston to Madrid via Pluto or even by way of Bangkok, Thailand, would not be acceptable, at least for most travelers.

Consider how a variation on this fallacy could arise in a discussion involving the use of programming languages to write a particular kind of software application. Theoretically, there are many programming languages—Basic, Fortran, Ada, Cobol, Java, C++, and so forth—that *could* be used to write the code for a particular kind of software application, but it doesn't follow that any programming language can be used to write the code *efficiently*. While there might be legitimate disputes as to whether C++ or Java is better for writing a particular Internet application, most programmers would agree that for Internet applications either of these two languages is superior to Fortran or Cobol.

3.2.10 The Virtuality Fallacy

Recently coined by James Moor (2001), the virtuality fallacy has the following form:

PREMISE 1. X exists in cyberspace

PREMISE 2. Cyberspace is virtual.

CONCLUSION. X (or the effect of X) is not real.

Those who defend questionable forms of on-line behavior, such as launching viruses and engaging in unauthorized entries into computer systems, sometimes suggest that these activities cause no real harm to people. Some reason that because these activities are virtual activities carried out in the virtual world, their effects are only virtual and thus not real. You should be able to spot the fallacy in this line of reasoning. Imagine that someone has posted an insulting remark about you to a bulletin board in an on-line forum. Arguably, the locus of offense is in cyberspace or virtual space as opposed to real (physical) space. Does it follow that the harm is not real, or that the particular harm caused to you is any less real than it would have been had it occurred in a physical setting?

▶ 3.3 CONSTRUCTING AN ARGUMENT

Think of some situations in which arguments are used by those in powerful positions, as well as by ordinary persons. Lawyers, for example, use arguments to try to persuade juries; and politicians often use arguments to convey their positions to their constituencies. All of us use arguments when we try to convince a friend, a spouse, or a boss about some point or other. Ultimately, arguments will succeed or not succeed depending on how well they are constructed and how strong the reasoning mechanisms they use are. We refer to those features as "argument strength" and we examine that concept in Section 3.4. In this section, we focus on how arguments are constructed.

Arguments often appear as editorials in newspapers and periodicals where they are sometimes expressed in prose forms that can obscure the argument, making it difficult to isolate and analyze. When this happens we must locate the arguments concealed in the text before we can analyze them. Consider the current debate over the need for a new national missile defense (NMD) system, which has been controversial from both a domestic and an international perspective. A fairly straightforward argument in favor of NMD in the editorial section of a newspaper might look something like the following:

> We must build a national missile defense system because without such a system we are vulnerable to nuclear attacks from rogue nations that might arise in the future. Engineers and computer scientists have testified that they can design a computer-guided missile defense system that is effective, safe, and reliable. It is our obligation as Americans to take whatever measures we can to protect the safety of our citizens.

Before we analyze this argument, however, it is perhaps worth making a few parenthetical remarks about certain events leading up to NMD. The current debate in Congress over NMD can be viewed as an updated version of the earlier "Star Wars" debate, officially known as the Strategic Defense Initiative (or SDI). That debate, which took place in the early 1980s, is significant for cyberethics because it was one of the first ethical controversies to catch the attention of a group of computer ethics "pioneers." More recently, arguments surrounding the classic SDI controversy, as well as current arguments for and against NMD, are examined in detail in both Bowyer (2001, 2002) and Yurcik and Doss (2002). We will examine some specific ethical issues pertaining to Star Wars and NMD of interest to computer professionals in Chapter 4. Our primary purpose in this chapter, however, is to consider the NMD controversy only insofar as it illustrates how logical arguments can be constructed and analyzed.

There is strong support for NMD among many conservative politicians, including the current Bush administration. As suggested above, a proponent of the NMD system could construct an argument for his or her case by first asserting that without such a new missile system, the United States is vulnerable to future attacks from potential "rogue nations" that might acquire nuclear weapons. The proponent might next want to assure us that there is sufficient and compelling evidence that such a missile defense system would be safe and reliable. Finally, the NMD supporter might assume the following principle: "We must do whatever is necessary to preserve the safety of America and its people." The structure of the proponent's argument can be represented as follows:

PREMISE 1. Without the new National Missile Defense System, the United States is vulnerable to nuclear attacks in the future from "rogue nations."

PREMISE 2. Computer scientists and engineers have testified before Congress that they can design a computer-guided missile defense system that is both safe and reliable.

PREMISE 3. The United States must do whatever is necessary to preserve the military defense of the nation and the safety of its citizens.

CONCLUSION. The United States should build the new National Missile Defense System.

Thus far, we have considered only the structure of this argument. That is, we have described its two basic components—its premises and conclusion—and we have represented it in standard logical form. Now we ask, is the reasoning used in the argument strong? Are there rules that will enable us to determine this? To answer these questions, we first need to understand the difference between valid and invalid arguments.

▶ 3.4 VALID AND INVALID ARGUMENTS

The first question we could ask about the sample argument described in the preceding section is whether its reasoning is strong or weak—that is, Is the argument's reasoning *valid* or is it *invalid*? "Valid" and "invalid" are technical terms in logic. Whereas claims are either true or false, arguments will be either valid or invalid; it is incorrect to refer to an argument as either true or false, and it is incorrect to refer to a claim as either valid or invalid.

How can we determine whether a particular argument is valid or invalid? In formal systems of argumentation, elaborate schemes that consist of symbols, rules, and tables have been constructed for determining when arguments are valid or invalid. But fortunately we can use an informal system developed by John Nolte (1984). Nolte's system does not require that we know anything about the *actual* truth or falsity of the claims in an argument's premise(s) in order to determine whether an argument is valid or invalid. Instead, we only need to determine whether the argument's conclusion would necessarily follow from its premises, when those premises are all *assumed* to be true. In other words, we ask

Is the relationship between the premises and the conclusion such that *if* all of the premises in the argument are assumed true, it would be impossible for the conclusion to be false?

The concern here is with the relationship of truth conditions *between* the premises and the conclusion. The premises and the conclusion could be true or false independent of each other, but that is not relevant for testing the argument's validity. We ask only whether the assumed truth of the premises is sufficient to guarantee the truth of the conclusion. If the answer is yes, then the argument is valid. If, however, it is logically possible for the argument's conclusion to be false at the same time that its premises are true, then the argument is invalid.

You can apply this test for validity to the argument for the new national missile defense system that we considered above. Imagine that all of the argument's premises are true statements. Is it possible—that is, could you conceive of a possible instance such that—when those premises are true, the conclusion could still be false? Of course, the premises could be imagined to be false, and the conclusion could be imagined to be false as well. But the relevant question here is: what happens when all of the premises are imagined to be true? Could the claim in the argument's conclusion (i.e., "the United States should build the new missile defense system") be false, even when Premises 1–3 are assumed true? The answer is yes. Hence, the argument is invalid.

To show an argument invalid, all that we need to do is to produce one *counterexample* to the argument. A counterexample is a logically possible case in which the argument's conclusion could be imagined to be false while (at the same time) the argument's premises are assumed true. In the NMD argument, we can coherently imagine a logically possible case where the conclusion "the United States should build the new national missile defense system" is false when the claims stated in Premises 1–3 are assumed true. For example, we can imagine a case in which all three premises are true but some alternative strategy not involving the development of a new missile defense system could provide for the safety of America. So a counterexample is possible; thus the argument is invalid.

Note, however, although this particular argument has been shown to be invalid, it does not follow that the argument's conclusion is, in fact, false. All that has been shown is that the argument is invalid because the form of reasoning employed in it does not succeed in guaranteeing that the conclusion must be true. It is still possible, of course, that the conclusion could be true. But a different argument would need to be constructed to show that the inference is valid.

Suppose we added a fourth premise, "The National Missile Defense system is necessary to preserve the defense and safety of the United States and its citizens," to the argument. The amended argument would be as follows:

PREMISE 1. Without the new National Missile Defense System, the United States is vulnerable to nuclear attacks in the future from "rogue nations."

PREMISE 2. Computer scientists and engineers have testified before Congress that they can design a computer-guided missile defense system that is both safe and reliable.

PREMISE 3. The United States must do whatever is necessary to preserve the military defense of the nation and the safety of its citizens.

PREMISE 4. The National Missile Defense system is necessary to preserve the defense and safety of the United States and its citizens.

CONCLUSION. The United States should build the new National Missile Defense System.

This argument would now be valid. If Premises 3 and 4 are both assumed true, then the conclusion cannot be false. Of course, we could next ask whether all of the premises on this argument are in fact true. Premises 1 and 2 are fairly uncontroversial claims, though Premise 2 might be challenged by programmers who believe that building a completely reliable computer system is not possible. However, both Premises 3 and 4 are controversial: Premise 4 can be shown to be false if it can be demonstrated that the United States could be adequately protected without the newly proposed missile defense system; Premise 3, which is a normative statement, can also be shown to be false if, for instance, we can provide an exception to the principle included in it. For one thing, we could ask both whether indeed the United States *must* do whatever is necessary to make the United States safe and what exactly we mean by the phrase "whatever is necessary?" For example, what if making the United States safe entailed closing down all systems of transportation, all government offices, and all schools, for an indefinite period of time that could go on for years? It might protect United States citizens but would it be an acceptable alternative? And United States citizens might be willing to make tradeoffs rather than shut down major institutions essential to their day-to-day lives. So Premise 3, as stated, is also false. However, even if all of the premises are eventually shown to be false, the argument itself is still valid because its conclusion follows from the premises if they are assumed true.

Figure 3-1 illustrates the basic distinction between valid and invalid arguments.

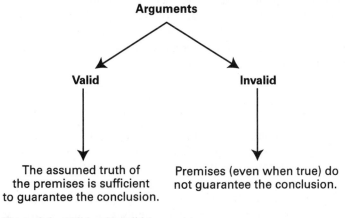

Figure 3-1 Valid and Invalid Arguments

Next consider the following argument.

PREMISE 1. People who own iMac computers are smarter than those who own PCs.

PREMISE 2. My roommate owns an iMac computer.

PREMISE 3. I own a PC.

CONCLUSION. My roommate is smarter than me.

This argument meets all of the criteria for validity: *If* all three of the premises in this argument are assumed true, then the conclusion (*my* roommate is smarter than me) must be true. In other words, no counterexample to this argument's reasoning form is possible. However, the argument's validity alone is not sufficient to establish that the argument succeeds in the final analysis (as we will see in the following sections). It shows only that when all of the premises are assumed true, the conclusion is also necessarily true.

This argument, like all valid arguments, is valid in virtue of its *logical form*; an argument's logical form, not its content, determines its validity and invalidity. An example of a valid logical form is as follows:

PREMISE 1. All *A* are *B*.

PREMISE 2. *C* is *A*.

CONCLUSION. *C* is *B*.

Any argument that has this form is valid, regardless of the content represented by *A*, *B*, or *C*. As long as the premises "All *A* are *B*" and "*C* is *A*" are both assumed true, there is no way that the conclusion "*C* is *B*" could be coherently conceived to be false. Even if the two premises in this particular argument turn out to be false in the actual world, the argument continues to be valid by virtue of its logical form.

We can now see that it is important to separate two distinct questions:

   i. What is the strength of reasoning of the argument (i.e., is it valid or invalid)?

  ii. Are the argument's premises true in the actual world?

To say that an argument is valid does not necessarily mean that its premises are true in the actual world. An argument can be valid in terms of its logical form and yet still be unsound. One more step is required for an argument to qualify as a *sound argument*. To be sound, all of the premises (included in the valid argument) must be true in the real world, and not merely assumed true as in the case of the test for validity. For how to determine whether a statement is true or false, see Appendix E, available at www.wiley.com/college/Tavani.

▶ 3.5 SOUND ARGUMENTS

To assume that the premises of an argument are true is an important first step in the process of evaluating arguments, because doing so enables us to determine the logical relationship between the argument's premise(s) and conclusion and thus determine that argument's strength of reasoning. The reasoning strength will be one of either validity or invalidity. If we can produce one counterexample by showing a possible case where the argument's conclusion can be false even when all of its premises are assumed true, we have shown the argument to be invalid. If the argument is shown to be invalid, we can stop here for the time being. To show that the argument was valid, all that we had to do was to show that no counterexample was possible. And to do that, we considered the hypothetical or assumed truth of the argument's premises vis-à-vis the argument's conclusion. If the argument is valid, then we must determine if it is sound by going on to the next step, where we test the premises to see whether they are true or false in the actual world.

Consider again the two arguments in the preceding section: one involving a NMD system, and the other involving the intelligence of iMac users. Both arguments were shown to be valid. (The argument defending the need for a NMD system had to be modified; but once we modified it, it met the criteria for validity.) We can now further examine each argument to see if it is also sound. An argument will be sound if (a) the argument is valid and (b) all of the premises are actually true (and not merely assumed to be true).

First consider the NMD system. If one or more of Premises 1–4 are false, then the argument will be unsound. Premise 3, "The United States must do whatever is necessary to preserve the military defense of the nation and the safety of its citizens," is clearly questionable. Surely, the goal of national defense is one of the highest priorities of a political administration. But we have already seen that the phrase "whatever is necessary" is problematic. For example, would such a principle give the United States government the right to use *any* means that it happened to deem necessary to bring about some desired end?

Suppose some government officials believed that it was necessary to put all non-United States citizens under house arrest? Or suppose that some of those officials believed that all United States citizens should be subject to constant search and seizure, both within and outside their homes? Would these measures be acceptable? Perhaps under the most severe and dire circumstances some proposals of this type might seem plausible. But it is still not exactly clear that such drastic measures would be necessary. So Premise 3 in the missile defense argument cannot be confirmed to be true, even if Premises 1, 2, and 4 can. Thus this argument is not sound even though it is valid. Because it is unsound, the argument does not succeed. However, once again we should be careful to note that even when an argument is unsound, or even when it is invalid, it does not necessarily follow that the argument's conclusion is false. Rather, we can only infer that the evidence given, that is, the particular premises used to support the argument's conclusion are not adequate because (when used alone) they fail to meet certain logical requirements.

Returning to the argument involving claims about the intelligence of iMac users, we saw that when we assume the truth of all three premises of that argument, the conclusion can not be imagined to be false; hence the argument is valid. But is it also sound? We need to examine each premise in more detail. Premises 2 and 3—"My roommate owns an iMac computer" and "I own a PC," respectively—are relatively easy to verify because both are descriptive claims. To see if they are true or false, we simply go to the dormitory room or to the apartment where my roommate and I live and observe whether my roommate indeed owns an iMac computer and whether I own a PC.

Premise 1—"People who own iMac computers are smarter than those who own PCs"—however, is more controversial and hence more difficult to verify than the other premises. Clearly, more evidence would be needed to show that Premise 1 is true; in fact, it certainly seems suspect. So despite the fact that the argument is valid in virtue of its logical form, we cannot yet say that it is sound. Thus the argument would appear, at best, to be not sound, but inconclusive.

3.5.1   Strategy for Evaluating an Argument

The following four-step strategy is useful for evaluating an argument to determine whether it is sound or unsound.

Step 1.   Convert the argument into standard form. (List the premises, followed by the conclusion.)

Step 2.   Test the argument for its strength of reasoning to see whether it is valid or invalid. (Assume the premises to be true, and ask yourself whether the conclusion must also be true when those premises are assumed true. Is a counterexample to the argument possible?)

Step 3.   Is the argument valid?

If yes, go to Step 4.

If no, stop.

Step 4.   Is the (valid) argument also sound? That is, are the premises true in the actual world?

    a. If the argument is valid and if all of the premises are true in the actual world, then the argument is also sound. (To determine a statement's truth-conditions, see Appendix E, at www.wiley.com/college/Tavani.)

    b. If the argument is valid but one or more premises can be shown to be false, then the argument is unsound. (Until questionable premises can be verified, i.e., determined to be either true or false, then the overall argument is inconclusive.)

As you might suspect, sound arguments are not very common; and often they are about matters that are either trivial or uncontroversial. Consider the following argument.

PREMISE 1.   CEOs of major computer corporations are high-school graduates.

PREMISE 2.   Bill Gates was the CEO of a major computer corporation.

CONCLUSION.   Bill Gates is a high-school graduate.

This argument is clearly valid because no counterexample can be constructed; that is, there is no possible case where Premises 1 and 2 could both be (assumed) true and the conclusion be false at the same time. As it turns out, the premises are also true in the actual world, so this argument is sound; however, it is also not terribly informative. Perhaps you can now see why there are so few sound arguments that are also informative: Relatively few valid arguments are sound, and relatively few sound arguments are informative or nontrivial.

Figure 3-2 illustrates the basic differences between valid arguments that are sound and those that are unsound.

At this point, you might ask, What good is a valid argument if it contains false premises? You might also wonder whether certain types of invalid arguments whose premises are true in the actual world are better than valid arguments that contain one or more false premises.

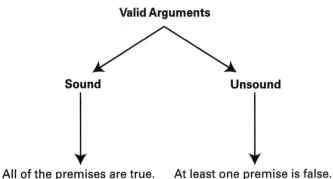

Figure 3-2 Sound and Unsound Valid Arguments

▶ 3.6 INVALID ARGUMENTS

Consider the following argument:

PREMISE 1. All CEOs of major United States computer corporations have been United States citizens.

PREMISE 2. Bill Gates is a United States citizen.

CONCLUSION. Bill Gates has been a CEO of a major computer corporation in the United States.

Even though all three of the claims included in this argument (i.e., the two premises and the conclusion) are true in the actual world, we can show that this argument is invalid by producing at least one counterexample. We can imagine a possible case where the premises in this argument are both true, but the conclusion—that Bill Gates has been CEO of a major computer corporation—is false. For example, we can imagine him a consultant, or a programmer; or he could be employed outside the computer field. However, there is even a more serious flaw in this argument: If we substitute for "Bill Gates" the names Al Gore, Michael Jordan, Julia Roberts, or Rudolph Guliani, we see that although each of these persons is a United States citizen, none has been a CEO of a major computer corporation. Yet by the logic used in the argument, it would follow that if any of these people is a United States citizen, then he or she must also be or have been a CEO. We have shown that this argument is invalid. If you noticed that the reasoning in this argument was weak, now you know exactly why.

We next determine whether the following argument is valid or invalid:

PREMISE 1. Most CEOs of computer corporations are college graduates.

PREMISE 2. Larry Ellison is the CEO of Oracle, a computer corporation.

CONCLUSION. Larry Ellison is a college graduate.

Notice that all of the statements included in this argument happen to be true in the real world. But is the reasoning valid? Clearly not. All we need is one counterexample to show why. If we substitute the name "Bill Gates" for "Larry Ellison," the premises of the argument remain true but the conclusion is false. The argument is invalid; but because the premises are true, this particular invalid argument is stronger overall than either of the two arguments we considered that were valid but unsound. Overall argument strength, as opposed to an argument's strength of reasoning, takes into account the actual truth condition of the argument's premises. We saw that an argument's strength of reasoning is concerned only with the hypothetical or assumed truth of those premises.

▶ 3.7 INDUCTIVE ARGUMENTS

Not all invalid arguments are necessarily weak arguments; in fact, some are quite strong. Hence, we should not automatically discard every invalid argument simply because it is not valid. Some invalid arguments are *inductive*. Although inductive arguments do not necessarily guarantee the truth of their conclusions in the way that valid arguments do, inductive arguments nonetheless provide a high degree of probability for their conclusions. Those invalid arguments that are not inductive are fallacious arguments; we will discuss them in the next section. In this section, we describe the criteria that must be satisfied for an argument to be inductive.

Let's determine the strength of reasoning of the following argument:

PREMISE 1. 75 percent of people who currently own iMac computers previously owned Apple IIe computers.

PREMISE 2. My roommate currently owns an iMac computer.

CONCLUSION. My roommate previously owned an Apple IIe computer.

Based on the technique discussed earlier in this chapter, we can see that this argument is not valid: A counterexample to the argument is possible. For instance, my roommate is among the 25% of people who currently own an iMac desktop computer, and my roommate previously owned a PC, then both premises are true, but the conclusion "My roommate previously owned an Apple IIe computer" is false. So clearly the argument is invalid.

This argument and the argument in the preceding section designed to show that Bill Gates is the CEO of a major computer corporation are both invalid, but they are different in their strength of reasoning. The argument that tried to show that Gates must be or have been a CEO because "Gates is a United States citizen" and "all CEOs of major computer corporations have been United States citizens" has weak reasoning. On the other hand, the form of reasoning used in the argument to show that "my roommate owned an Apple IIe computer at one time" is much stronger. When we assume truth of the claims "My roommate currently owns an iMac computer" and "75 percent of iMac owners previously owned Apple IIe computer," the conclusion ("My roommate previously owned an iMac computer") is *very likely* also to be true. Hence this (invalid) argument is also inductive.

As suggested above, some inductive arguments, although invalid, can be stronger overall than some valid arguments. But how is that possible? We have seen examples of valid arguments that contained premises that were false in the actual world. Inductive arguments consisting of premises that are all true in the actual world are generally stronger than unsound arguments. As you consider the various arguments involving privacy, free speech, security, etc., in Chapters 4 through 9, determine which ones meet the criteria of being inductive with all true premises. Such arguments will be much more successful in estab-

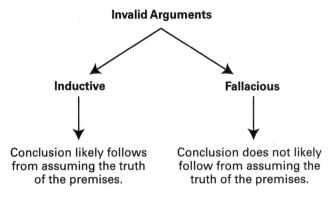

Figure 3-3   Inductive and Fallacious Invalid Arguments

lishing their positions (i.e., they will be much stronger) than will deductive arguments that contain one or more false premises.

Figure 3-3 illustrates the basic differences between invalid arguments that are inductive and invalid arguments that are fallacious.

▶ 3.8 FALLACIOUS ARGUMENTS

In Section 3.2, we examined some "fallacy types," informal logical fallacies that tend to recur in everyday reasoning. We also learned certain techniques for spotting some of the more common fallacies or fallacious arguments. In this section, we examine a different technique for determining when an argument is fallacious. Recall the argument that we considered in Section 3.6 to show that Bill Gates has been the CEO of a major computer corporation. All of the statements or claims in that particular argument were true in the actual world, so the argument might have seemed fairly strong. Yet, because we could produce a counterexample (and in fact, we saw that we could easily produce several counterexamples), clearly the argument was invalid.

We next ask whether the argument is inductive or fallacious. That is, how likely is it that the argument's conclusion, "Gates has been the CEO of a major computer corporation," would be true based simply on the assumed truth of the argument's premises? Even though the conclusion could be true—and even though it is, in fact, true—the truth or falsity would have to be established on grounds other than those given in the premises used to support the conclusion that Gates has been a CEO. Hence this argument is *fallacious*.

Note that an argument's being fallacious has nothing to with the actual truth or falsity of its premises, so you have probably noticed a certain irony with respect to an argument's strength of reasoning. We have seen that an argument can be valid and yet contain one or more false premises and a false conclusion; and conversely, an argument can be fallacious despite the fact that all of its premises as well as its conclusion could be true.

Recall an argument that we examined in Section 3.1.2:

PREMISE. The Internet is in public space.

CONCLUSION. Those who use the Internet should not expect to retain any personal privacy.

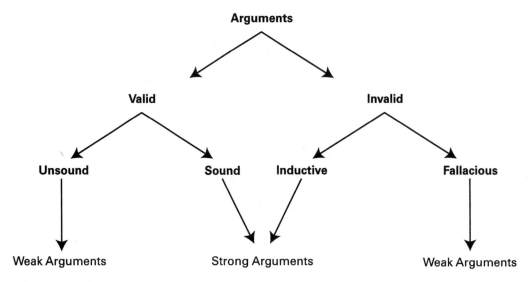

Figure 3-4 Comprehensive View of Arguments

We noted earlier that this argument is fallacious, and we can now better understand the reason why. When we evaluate the argument's strength of reasoning, that is, whether it is valid or invalid, we first ask whether a counterexample can be produced. Let us assume that the premise—The Internet is in public space—is true. Is it possible for that statement to be true, and the conclusion (Internet users cannot expect to retain their privacy) to be false, at the same time? The answer would appear to be "yes." So a counterexample can be produced, and the argument is invalid. We can next ask whether the argument is inductive or fallacious. In the argument's current form, the conclusion does not likely follow from the premise, even when that premise is assumed true. So the argument is fallacious.

Figure 3-4 presents an overview of the different kinds of argument forms that we have examined in this chapter:

3.8.1 Strategy for Evaluating an Argument II: Expanded Version

The following strategy, which consists of seven steps, expands on the four-step strategy described earlier in Section 3.5:

Step 1. Convert the argument into standard form. (List the premises, followed by the conclusion.)

Step 2. Test the argument for its strength of reasoning to see whether it valid or invalid. (Assume the premises to be true, and ask yourself whether the conclusion must also be true when those premises are assumed true. Is a counterexample to the argument possible?)

Step 3. Is the argument valid?

If yes, go to Step 4.

If no, go to Step 5.

Step 4. Is the (valid) argument also sound? That is, are the premises true in the actual world?

    a. If the argument is valid and if all of the premises are true in the actual world, then the argument is also sound. (To determine a statement's truth-condition, see Appendix E, at www.wiley.com/college/Tavani.)

    b. If the argument is valid but one or more premises can be shown to be false, then the argument is unsound. (Until questionable premises can be verified, i.e., determined to be either true or false, then the overall argument is inconclusive.)

Step 5. Is the (invalid) argument inductive or fallacious? (How likely will the conclusion be true when the premises are assumed true?)

    a. If the conclusion will likely be true when the premises are assumed true, the argument is inductive.

    b. If the conclusion would not likely be true even when the premises are assumed true, the argument is fallacious. (Keep in mind that a fallacious argument can be made up of individual claims that are themselves true in the actual world.)

Step 6. Determine whether the premises in your argument are either true or false.

Step 7. Make an overall assessment of the argument. That is, describe the argument's strength of reasoning in conjunction with the truth conditions of the argument's premises. (For example, is the argument inductive with all true premises? Is it inductive with some false premises? Is it fallacious with a mixture of true and false premises, and so forth? Remember that an inductive argument with premises that are all true is stronger than a valid argument with one or more false premises.)

▶ 3.9 CHAPTER SUMMARY

In this chapter, we examined key elements of logical arguments. We introduced some techniques for spotting informal logical fallacies that occur in everyday reasoning. We also considered some strategies for differentiating among arguments that were valid, inductive, and fallacious. In the remaining chapters of this textbook, we will see how the critical thinking skills introduced in Chapter 3 can be used to evaluate arguments involved in many of the cyberethics disputes that we examine.

▶ REVIEW QUESTIONS

1. What is a logical argument? What are the two main components of an argument?
2. What is the purpose or function of a logical argument?
3. Identify five common logical fallacies that can be found in everyday discourse, and provide one example for each that involves cybertechnology.
4. What is the difference between argument strength and argument structure?
5. What is the essential difference between an argument that is valid and one that is invalid?
6. What is a counterexample, and how can it be used to show that an argument is invalid?

7. How is it possible for an argument to be valid but not successful?

8. What is required for an argument to be sound?

9. What is the main difference between invalid arguments that are inductive and invalid arguments that are fallacious?

10. Describe the essential features of the seven-step strategy we constructed for distinguishing between arguments that are valid, inductive, and fallacious.

▶ DISCUSSION QUESTIONS

1. Based on what you have learned in this chapter, construct an argument to support or refute the view that all undergraduate students should be required to take a course in cyberethics. Next, analyze your argument to see if it is either valid or invalid. If it is valid, determine whether it is also sound. If it is invalid, determine whether it is inductive or fallacious.

2. Locate a recent article that describes some moral, legal, or social issue involving cybertechnology. How many invalid arguments can you find in that article? How many of these invalid arguments are also fallacious? Can you identify in that article any of the common fallacy types that we described in this chapter?

3. Identify some of the arguments that have been made on both sides in the Napster debate. Evaluate the arguments in terms of their strength of reasoning. Can you find any valid arguments? Can you find any inductive arguments?

4. Construct an argument for or against the view that privacy protection should be improved in e-commerce transactions. Next evaluate your arguments against the rules for valid, inductive, and fallacious arguments. Does your argument contain any of the common or "informal" fallacies discussed in Section 3.2?

▶ REFERENCES

Artz, John M. (1998). "Narrative vs. Logical Reasoning in Computer Ethics," *Computers and Society*, Vol. 28, No. 4, pp. 3–5.

Bowyer, Kevin W. (2001). "Critical Thinking Skills." Chapter 2 in *Ethics and Computing: Living in a Computerized World*. 2d ed. New York: IEEE Press.

Bowyer, Kevin W.(2002). "Star Wars Revisited: Ethics and Safety Critical Software," *IEEE Technology and Society*, Vol. 21, No. 1, pp. 13–26.

Moor, James H. (1998). "Reason, Relativity, and Responsibility in Computer Ethics," *Computers and Society*, Vol. 28, No. 1, pp. 14–21.

Moor, James H. (2001). "Just Consequentialism and Computing." Presented at the Humanities Lecture Series, Rivier College, Nashua, NH.

Moore, Brooke Noel, and Richard Parker (1995). *Critical Thinking*. 4th ed. Mountain View, CA: Mayfield Publishing.

Nolte, John E. (1984). *Informal Logic: Possible Worlds and Imagination*. New York: McGraw Hill.

Tavani, Herman T. (1994). "Facts, Opinions, and Value Judgments," *InSight*, Vol. 2, No. 1, pp. 153–166.

Yurcik, William, and David Doss (2002). "Software Technology Issues for a U.S. National Missile Defense System," *IEEE Technology and Society*, Vol. 21, No. 2, pp. 36–46.

▶ FURTHER READINGS

Artz, John M. (2000). "The Role of Emotion in Reason," *Computers and Society*, Vol. 30, No. 1, pp. 14–16.

Epstein, Richard L. (1999). *Critical Thinking*. Belmont, CA: Wadsworth Publishing.

Johnson, Robert M. (1999). *A Logic Book: Fundamentals of Reasoning*. Belmont, CA: Wadsworth Publishing.

Kahane, Howard, and Nancy Cavender (1998*). Logic and Contemporary Rhetoric: The Use of Reason in Everyday Life*. 8th ed. Belmont, CA: Wadsworth Publishing.

Mulen, John D. (1995). *Hard Thinking: The Reintroduction of Logic into Everyday Life*. Lanham, MD: Rowman and Littlefield.

Munsen, Ronald A., and David A. Conway (2001). *Basics of Reasoning*. Belmont, CA: Wadsworth Publishing.

Ruggerio, Vincent R. (1997). *Thinking Critically About Ethical Issues*. 4th ed. Mountain View, CA: Mayfield Publishing.

4

PROFESSIONAL ETHICS, CODES OF CONDUCT, AND MORAL RESPONSIBILITY

In July 1988, the USS *Vincennes*, a United States Navy shipped equipped with the Aegis Radar System, accidentally shot down an Iranian passenger airliner, killing 230 people. A poorly designed user interface to the computerized radar system contributed significantly to this accident. Between June 1985 and January 1987, a series of malfunctions involving the Therac-25, a computerized radiation therapy machine, resulted in six serious accidents and three deaths. The problem was eventually traced to a bug in a software program that, in certain instances, caused massive overdoses of radiation to be administered to patients.

Both the Therac-25 and the Aegis incidents are examined in detail in this chapter, in Sections 4.5.2 and 4.6, respectively. Accidents of this type are sometimes categorized as "computer error" or "computer malfunction." But who, exactly, is responsible for these computer errors and malfunctions? It would seem reasonable to hold the manufacturers of unreliable computer systems legally liable for harms caused by faulty design interfaces or by "buggy" software. But we must also ask to what extent the computer professionals, especially the software engineers who design and develop "safety-critical" and life-critical applications, bear responsibility for the harmful consequences that result from unreliable computer systems.

In this chapter, we examine a range of issues often categorized under the general heading "professional ethics." More specifically, we analyze the following questions:

- What do we mean by "professional ethics" in a computing context?
- Do computer professionals have any special moral responsibilities?
- What are professional codes of ethics, and what important functions do they serve in the computing profession?

- What is "whistle-blowing," and when is it permissible or perhaps even required by computer professionals?

- Which standards of moral responsibility, legal liability, and accountability should apply in cases of computer malfunctions, especially in safety-critical computer systems?

- Which conditions must be satisfied in order to have an adequate model of risk analysis for the development of software, especially for safety-critical and life-critical systems?

Issues involving software reliability and risk are also examined from the perspective of computer security in Chapter 6, where concerns about the vulnerability and reliability of computer systems are considered from the vantage point of attacks on computer systems from external sources, such as hackers. In this chapter, our concern with unreliable computer systems centers primarily on issues that arise as a result of malfunctions and errors generated from internal sources; that is, we are concerned with reliability and safety issues that can be traced to the coding and testing of software and to the manufacturing of hardware components used in computer systems.

A principal objective of this chapter is to determine the extent to which computer professionals should be held accountable for malfunctions involving computer systems. We have already briefly alluded to concerns about responsibility for safety-critical and life-critical systems such as Aegis and Therac. Note, however, that our analysis of responsibility and reliability issues in Chapter 4 is not limited to safety-critical and life-critical systems; we will also be concerned with reliability failures and malfunctions of computer systems, which might not be "safety-critical," but which can cause businesses and ordinary users to lose work, time, and money. For example, the computerized baggage system at the new Denver airport, while not a safety-critical system, nonetheless caused both damage to luggage and routing problems, costing the airport millions of dollars. Before examining specific cases involving unreliable computer systems, however, we first briefly consider some foundational issues in professional ethics.

▶ 4.1 PROFESSIONAL ETHICS

Recall that in Chapter 1 we described professional ethics as one of the three main perspectives through which computer ethics issues can be identified and analyzed. We saw that, when applied to computing, professional ethics is a field of applied ethics concerned with moral issues that impact computer professionals. You may also recall in Chapter 1 that Don Gotterbarn (1991) argued that professional ethics is the principal, perhaps even exclusive, perspective through which ethical issues involving the computing field should be examined. Although this claim is controversial and will not be further considered here, we have dedicated this chapter to an analysis of computer ethics issues from the vantage point of professional ethics.

We begin by recalling that the phrase "professional ethics" could suggest that professionals have their own system of ethics, separate from ordinary ethics. Of course, one could reasonably argue that independent of whether a particular moral issue happens to arise in either a professional or a nonprofessional context, ethics is ethics; the same ethical rules involving honesty, fairness, and so forth should apply to professionals as well as to ordinary individuals, so that if it is wrong for ordinary people to steal, cheat, and lie, then it is wrong for professionals as well. Thus one might conclude that a separate field of study called "professional ethics" is not really needed. However, many ethicists argue that the kinds of moral issues affecting professionals are sufficiently distinct and specialized to warrant a separate field of study. Some also argue that, at least in certain cases, professionals do have special moral obligations, which exceed those of ordinary individuals. To grasp the essential points in the arguments advanced by these ethicists, it is useful first to understand what is meant by "profession" and "professional."

4.1.1 What Is a Profession?

According to Allan Firmage (1991), a *profession* can be understood in terms of the attributes and requirements of a professional practice. Firmage points out that the American Society of Civil Engineers (ASCE) defines a profession as a "calling in which special knowledge and skill are used in . . . the service of mankind." So "having a calling," "possessing special knowledge and skill," and "providing a service" are examples of attributes that would distinguish a profession from many ordinary occupations.

Ernest Greenwood (1991) believes that professions are occupational fields that can be distinguished in terms of five characteristics: (i) systematic theory, (ii) authority, (iii) community sanction, (iv) ethical codes, and (v) culture. For the most part, these five characteristics apply to the computing profession as well. Consider that the field of computing has a systematic theory of knowledge (computer science); a number of professional societies with ethical codes (see Section 4.3); and an emerging culture (sometimes referred to as a "high-tech culture"). The computing profession differs from traditional professions such as medicine and law, however, with respect to individual autonomy for its members. While many doctors and lawyers work in private practice, most computer professionals are not self-employed; even though some work as independent consultants, most are employed by corporations.

4.1.2 Who Is a Professional?

Professionals who comprise a given profession also tend to have certain defining attributes and requirements. According to the Engineers' Council for Professional Development (ECPD), a *professional* is one who "recognizes his or her obligation to society by living up to established and accepted codes of conduct." In Section 4.3, we examine professional codes of conduct that apply to the computer profession in general, and software engineering in particular.

Medical doctors, lawyers, accountants, and other professionals often find themselves in situations in which their decisions and actions can have significant social effects; for example, medical doctors can prescribe the use of certain drugs for their patients, who otherwise would have no legal access to them, and lawyers are bound by special obligations such as client confidentiality that would not apply if they were acting as ordinary citizens. In these cases, a professional's roles and responsibilities can exceed those of ordinary individuals. Sometimes these roles and responsibilities are said to *differentiate* professionals from nonprofessional persons.

Elizabeth Buchanan (2001) believes that the roles and responsibilities of professionals are differentiated from ordinary individuals because "professionals are experts in a field, which provides them an advantage over the lay person and that professional's work has the potential to impact—either positively or negatively—the general public at large."

Buchanan goes on to note that computer professionals (or what she calls "information professionals") have the potential to adversely affect an "increasingly large and diverse clientele by failing to act responsibly, fairly, timely, and appropriately." Arguably, these roles and responsibilities differentiate at least certain kinds of computer professionals from ordinary individuals. The extent to which a computer professional's roles and responsibilities are highly differentiated, however, is a matter of some dispute. To understand why this is so, it would first help to understand what exactly is meant by the expression "computer professional."

4.1.3 Who Is a Computer Professional?

Broadly speaking, a *computer professional* is anyone employed in the computer, information-technology (IT), or information/communications fields, from specialists such as support personnel, network administrators, and computer-repair technicians, to professionals who are responsible for providing unfettered access to electronic information in libraries (Buchanan suggests that an "information professional" can be conceived of along these lines.) Computer professionals might also include faculty and instructors who teach in departments as diverse as information management, library science, and communications, as well as computer science.

Or a computer professional might be thought of in more narrow terms, in which case only software engineers would be included. Of course, there are various gradients in between the two ends of this spectrum. A computer professional could be defined in a way that would exclude professionals in communications and library science, yet still include professionals whose computer-specific job descriptions extend beyond software engineering per se, such as software technical writers, software quality analysts, and software managers and supervisors who play key roles in the software-development process and make up a *software engineering team*. Gotterbarn, Miller, and Rogerson (1999) suggest that a software engineering team can be thought of as those who contribute by direct participation to "the analysis, specification, design, development, certification, maintenance and testing of software systems."

For purposes of this chapter, we will consider "computer professionals" to include software engineers and software engineering teams, as well as computer-science instructors in colleges, universities, and in industry settings—those who are responsible for educating and training the members of software engineering teams. We will not include IT professionals in end-user support roles (e.g., network administrators and computer sales and support personnel) in our definition of computer professionals, nor will we include lawyers, accountants, nurses, or other professionals who are either employed by computer companies or who work closely with computers as part of their regular employment.

▶ 4.2 DO COMPUTER PROFESSIONALS HAVE ANY SPECIAL MORAL RESPONSIBILITIES?

Some ethicists believe that all professionals, regardless of their practice, have special moral obligations. For example, Michael Bayles (1989) argues that professionals have a special obligation to their clients—to be worthy of a client's trust; and this, Bayles further suggests, leads to obligations of honesty, candor, competence, diligence, loyalty, and discretion. In Bayles's scheme, all professionals who happen to work in the computing field would be bound to similar standards of obligations to their clients, whether these professionals are engineers, IT support personnel, or corporate accountants. But are there also specific moral obligations that apply to computer professionals in the more narrow sense in which we have defined the term?

As noted above, we are restricting "computer professional" to software engineers and the members of software engineering teams. Thus an important question for us to ask is, Does this group of professionals have any special moral obligations that differentiate them from other professionals who work in the computing field? Don Gotterbarn (1999) believes that because software engineers and their teams are responsible for developing safety-critical systems, they have significant opportunities to: (i) do good or cause harm, (ii) enable others to do good or cause harm, and (iii) influence others to do good or cause harm. Thus Gotterbarn suggests that the roles and responsibilities involved in the development of safety-critical systems is a differentiating factor.

4.2.1 Safety-Critical Software

What exactly is safety-critical software? Kevin Bowyer (2001) points out that the phrase "safety-critical system" is often used to refer to computer systems that can have a "direct life-threatening impact." Under this definition, examples of safety-critical software applications typically include

- aircraft and air traffic control systems,
- mass transportation systems,
- nuclear reactors,
- missile systems,
- medical treatment systems.

However, Bowyers believes that an understanding of safety-critical systems that includes only these examples is too narrow. He suggests that a broader definition be adopted in which safety-critical systems are also understood as software applications used in the design of physical systems and structures whose failures can also have an impact that is life-threatening. Here, the range of safety-critical applications can be expanded to include software used in the

- design of bridges and buildings,
- selection of water disposal sites,
- development of analytical models for medical treatment.

We use the expanded sense of "safety-critical software" in this chapter. And we examine two important cases of computer malfunctions involving safety-critical software in our discussions of moral accountability and risk assessment issues in Sections 5.5 and 5.6, respectively.

▶ 4.3 PROFESSIONAL CODES OF ETHICS AND CODES OF CONDUCT

Many professions have established professional societies, which in turn have adopted codes of conduct. For example, the medical profession established the AMA (American Medical Association), and the legal profession established the ABA (American Bar Association). Both associations have formal codes of ethics/conduct for their members. The computing profession has also established a number of professional societies, the largest of which are the Association for Computing Machinery (ACM) and the Institute for Electrical and Electronics Engineers-Computer Society (IEEE-CS). Both organizations have adopted professional codes of ethics, and the full texts of these two codes are included in Appendixes A and B.

Both the ACM and the IEEE codes contain general statements about what is expected, and in some cases what is required, to be a member in good standing. The IEEE Code of Ethics contains ten general directives; the first four instruct members

1. to accept responsibility in making engineering decisions consistent with the safety, health, and welfare of the public . . . ;
2. to avoid real or perceived conflicts of interest wherever possible . . . ;
3. to be honest . . . ;
4. to reject bribery in all its forms; . . . .

The ACM Code of Ethics and Professional Conduct, on the other hand, is more complex. It contains twenty-four imperatives, formulated as statements of personal responsibility. Like the IEEE Code, the ACM Code also lists general moral imperatives:

as an ACM member I will

1.1 contribute to society and human well-being,

1.2 avoid harm to others,

1.3 be honest and trustworthy,

1.4 be fair and take action not to discriminate,

1.5 honor property copyrights and patents,

1.6 give proper credit for intellectual property,

1.7 respect the privacy of others,

1.8 honor confidentiality.

From these general imperatives, a list of more specific professional responsibilities follows. These include the directives:

2.1 Strive to achieve the highest quality . . . in . . . work.

2.2 Acquire and maintain professional competence.

These directives are then followed by six "organizational leadership imperatives," which include:

3.1 Articulate social responsibilities of members . . . .

3.2 Manage personnel and resources to design and build information that enhance the quality of working life.

The fourth component of the ACM Code stresses "compliance with the code," and consists of two imperatives:

4.1 Uphold and promote the principles of this code.

4.2 Treat violations of this code as inconsistent with membership of the ACM.

4.3.1 The Purpose of Professional Codes

Professional codes of ethics are often designed to motivate members of an association to behave in certain ways; they *inspire*, *guide*, *educate*, and *discipline* the members. Codes inspire by providing a positive stimulus for ethical conduct (Martin and Schinzinger, 1995). They also provide helpful guidance and advice for individual members when they confront situations that are morally complex. Codes educate by informing the members of a profession about their ethical responsibilities. And codes have a disciplinary or penal function when they specify grounds for punishing members.

In addition to these four primary functions, codes can have secondary roles. They can alert prospective clients and employers to what they may or may not expect by way of service from a member of the profession (Ladd, 1995); they can sensitize, that is, raise the consciousness of, a professional society's members by alerting individuals to ethical aspects of their jobs that otherwise might have been overlooked; and they can, by informing the public about the profession, enhance its status.

To be effective, a professional code must be broad, yet specific. Bruce Perlman and Roli Varma (2002) point out that a code must be broad enough to cover the ethical conflicts and concerns likely to arise in its professional field (such as computing), but, at the same time, a code cannot be so broad that it reaches to extraneous incidents. It must also be sufficiently specific to serve as a guide to making sound decisions for practical action in actual circumstances that are likely to arise in the computing field. To accomplish the first objective, Perlman and Varma believe that a code needs to encompass the principles that guide professions in general, and ethics in particular. And to satisfy the second objective, a code is measured by the degree to which its rules serve as effective guides for computer professionals and practitioners. Perlman and Varma also note that in engineering contexts professional codes face a special challenge because the practice of engineering often dictates secrecy, whereas the ethics of engineering requires transparency, or openness.

4.3.2 Some Criticisms of Professional Codes

Initially, it might seem surprising that anyone would be critical of professional codes in general or of specific codes developed for computer professionals. However, critics of professional codes of ethics have pointed out that the ethical codes adopted by professional computer societies have no "teeth." For example, violations of the ACM or the IEEE Codes, unlike violations of professional codes in the fields of medicine and law, do not necessarily threaten the employment of those who violate them. Also, computer professionals are not usually required to be members of either the ACM or the IEEE to be employed in the computing field or to practice as computer professionals.

Michael Davis (1995) has pointed out that professional codes are often dismissed on grounds that they are too vague, self serving, inconsistent, unrealistic, and unnecessary. To

Davis's list, we could add one more characteristic—professional codes also tend to be incomplete. Ben Fairweather (2001) believes that codes of conduct for computing professionals have been influenced by a conception of computer and information ethics that is limited to four traditional areas of concern: privacy, accuracy, property, and accessibility. He argues that a professional code built on a foundation that includes such a narrow range of ethical concerns can provide certain loopholes for unethical behavior in an organization: An incomplete code might unintentionally provide an organization with an easy way to avoid a specific ethical issue that is not easily categorized under the four traditional criteria. Fairweather also worries that authors of incomplete codes might, by virtue of what they have left out of a specific code, be indirectly responsible for sanctioning employees' behavior that, in the final analysis, turns out to be immoral.

John Ladd (1995) has criticized ethical codes on slightly different grounds, arguing that these codes rest on a series of confusions that are both intellectual and moral. His complex arguments can be summarized in three main points. First, Ladd notes that ethics is basically an "open-ended, reflective, and critical intellectual activity." Because ethics is a field of study that consists of issues to be examined, explored, discussed, deliberated, and argued, it requires a process of deliberation and argumentation. (Recall our definition of ethics in Chapter 2.) Directives listed in a professional code may give an employee the mistaken notion that all he or she needs to do is to locate a directive and then blindly follow it. More importantly, however, Ladd notes that individuals are not told what to do in a situation where two or more of a code's principles or directives conflict with one another. Here the individual needs to deliberate; yet professional codes do not typically provide any hierarchy of principles or any mechanism for choosing one directive over another.

Second, Ladd is critical of codes because of the confusions they introduce with respect to responsibilities involving microethics vs. macroethics issues (i.e., confusions about which responsibilities apply to individual professionals and which responsibilities apply to the profession itself). Recall that we briefly discussed the microethical/macroethical distinction in Chapter 2. In the context of professional ethics, microethical issues apply to personal relationships between individual professionals and other individuals, such as clients. Macroethical issues, on the other hand, apply to social problems that confront members of a profession collectively, or as a group. As such, most microethical issues involve the application of ordinary moral notions (such as honesty and civility) that would also hold when dealing with other individuals in nonprofessional contexts. Macroethical issues, however, are more complex, since they involve the formulation of policies at the level of social organizations. Ladd believes that we need to distinguish between questions such as "Which responsibilities do I, as a computer professional, have in such-and-such a situation?" and "Which responsibilities does the computing profession, as a profession, have in such-and-such a situation?" He concludes that professional codes of ethics cannot help us to make this important distinction.

Third, Ladd believes that attaching disciplinary procedures and sanctions to codes effectively turns them into legal rules or authoritative rules of conduct rather than ethical rules. The role of ethics in general, he argues, is to appraise, criticize, and even defend the principles, rules, and regulations, but it is not to dictate or to punish. Also, when individuals are compelled to obey directives, they are deprived of their autonomy, that is, their ability to choose, which is crucial in moral deliberation. So Ladd argues that professional codes rest on confusions about both the nature and purpose of morality, which ultimately result in a series of contradictions.

4.3.3 In Defense of Professional Codes

It is very important to point out at this stage of our discussion of professional codes that not everyone has been critical of them. In fact, even some critics who have identified specific limitations or weaknesses in professional codes have also defended and praised them. For example, Michael Davis (1995), whose criticisms of professional codes were described in the previous section, has argued that codes are extremely important for engineering professionals because they are central to advising individual engineers how to conduct themselves. Since an engineer cannot always rely on his or her own private conscience when making moral decisions, Davis believes that codes play an essential role in helping engineers evaluate their conduct against external standards. He also believes that codes can help individual engineers to better understand engineering as a profession.

Heinz Luegenbiel (1983) believes that we can better appreciate the importance of codes of ethics if we recognize them for what they really are—guides. He suggests that we substitute the expression "guides for ethical engineering decision making" for the phrase "codes of ethics." Luegenbiel also suggests that, rather than laying out actual rules of normative behavior, the elements of a professional code should describe areas of concern for practicing engineers. He proposes a strategy that would place increased emphasis on educating engineers about the important roles that professional codes play in their profession.

Don Gotterbarn (2000) has suggested that some of the criticism leveled against professional codes might be eliminated if we think of them as serving three important, but distinct, functions; that is,

- Codes of ethics
- Codes of conduct
- Codes of practice

Gotterbarn describes *codes of ethics* as "aspirational," because they often serve as mission statements for the profession and can thus provide vision and objectives. *Codes of conduct*, on the other hand, address the professional and the professional's attitude and behavior. Finally, *codes of practice* relate to operational activities within a profession. Gotterbarn points out that the degree of enforcement possible with respect to specific violations of a professional code is dependent on the type of code violated. For example, he notes that violations involving codes of ethics, which are primarily aspirational, are often considered no more than "light concerns." Consequently, violations of these codes may not have any serious consequences for individuals. Violations involving codes of conduct, on the other hand, can range from warnings given to an individual to the possibility of exclusion from practicing in a profession. Violations of codes of practice go one step further, however, in that they may also lead to legal action.

Gotterbarn notes that the hierarchy in the three types of codes parallels the three levels of obligation owed by professionals. The first level includes a set of ethical values, such as integrity and justice, which professionals share with other humans by virtue of a shared humanity. The second level of responsibility is shared by all professionals, regardless of their fields of specialization. The third (and deeper) level comprises several obligations that derive directly from elements unique to a particular professional practice, such as software engineering. This threefold distinction is incorporated in a professional code recently developed by a joint task force of the IEEE-CS/ACM, which we examine in the next section.

Table 4-1 lists some of the strengths and weaknesses of professional codes.

TABLE 4-1   Some Strengths and Weaknesses of Professional Codes

Strengths	Weaknesses
Codes inspire the members of a profession to behave ethically.	Directives included in many codes tend to be too general and too vague.
Codes guide the members of a profession in ethical choices.	Codes are not always helpful when two or more directives conflict.
Codes educate the members of a profession about their professional obligations.	A professional code's directives are never complete or exhaustive.
Codes discipline members when they violate one or more of the code's directives.	Codes are ineffective (have no "teeth") in disciplinary matters.
Codes "sensitize" members of a profession to ethical issues and alert them to ethical aspects they otherwise might overlook.	Codes do not help us distinguish between microethics issues and macroethics issues.
Codes inform the public about the nature and roles of the profession.	Directives in codes are sometimes inconsistent with one another.
Codes enhance the profession in the eyes of the public.	Codes can be self-serving for the profession.

4.3.4   The IEEE-CS/ACM Software Engineering Code of Ethics and Professional Practice

Recently, both the ACM and IEEE approved a joint code of ethics for software engineers: the *IEEE-CS/ACM Software Engineering Code of Ethics and Professional Practice* (SECEPP). Don Gotterbarn (1999) believes that as a code for computer professionals SECEPP is unique for two reasons: First, it is intended as *the* code for the software engineering profession, unlike the individual codes (such as those of the ACM and IEEE) designed for particular professional societies within the computing profession. Second, Gotterbarn believes that SECEPP is distinctive in that it has been adopted by two international computing societies: ACM and IEEE-CS.

SECEPP is organized into two main parts: a short version and a longer, or full, version. Each version has its own preamble, and the full text for each version is included in Appendix C. SECEPP comprises eight core principles:

1. **PUBLIC**—Software engineers shall act consistently with the public interest.

2. **CLIENT AND EMPLOYER**—Software engineers shall act in a manner that is in the best interests of their client and employer, consistent with the public interest.

3. **PRODUCT**—Software engineers shall ensure that their products and related modifications meet the highest professional standards possible.

4. **JUDGMENT**—Software engineers shall maintain integrity and independence in their professional judgment.

5. **MANAGEMENT**—Software engineering managers and leaders shall subscribe to and promote an ethical approach to the management of software development and maintenance.

6. PROFESSION—Software engineers shall advance the integrity and reputation of the profession consistent with the public interest.

7. COLLEAGUES—Software engineers shall be fair to and supportive of their colleagues.

8. SELF—Software engineers shall participate in lifelong learning regarding the practice of their profession and shall promote an ethical approach to the practice of the profession.

4.3.4.1 Does SECEPP Provide an Appropriate Balance between Generality and Specificity?

We noted above that professional codes are often criticized for being too vague and too general to be useful, yet there is also the danger of being too specific. If a professional code is too specific, it might fail to instruct members about general principles regarding ethical behavior and ethical decision making. SECEPP does include some very specific language, but it also has general prescriptions found in most professional codes. And, at the general level, SECEPP emphasizes the profession's obligation to the public at large, including concern for the public's health, safety, and welfare. For example, in the preamble to the full version of the code, software engineers are encouraged to

- consider broadly who is affected by their work,
- examine if they and their colleagues are treating other human beings with due respect,
- consider how the public, if reasonably well informed, would view their decisions,
- analyze how the least empowered will be affected by their decisions.

The preamble to the short version of SECEPP summarizes aspirations at a high level of abstraction. The specific clauses included in the full version, on the other hand, give examples of how these aspirations change the way software engineering professionals act *as* professionals. The code's principal authors (Gotterbarn, Miller, and Rogerson, 1999) note that "without the aspirations, the details can become legalistic and tedious; without the details, the aspirations can become high sounding but empty; together, the aspirations and the details form a cohesive code." SECEPP's supporters believe that this code achieves an ideal balance between the general and the specific.

4.3.4.2 Does SECEPP Avoid Criticisms of Earlier Professional Codes?

One criticism often directed at professional codes is that they are incomplete; recall Ben Fairweather's argument in Section 4.3.2. Another criticism notes that most codes provide no mechanism for choosing between principles when two or more of them conflict; recall John Ladd's critique, also included in Section 4.3.2. Don Gotterbarn (2000) believes that SECEPP has overcome both difficulties.

Regarding the charge of incompleteness, Gotterbarn is willing to concede that the principles included in SECEPP are not intended to be exhaustive. He also acknowledges that no code could reasonably anticipate every possible moral controversy that can arise. However, he believes that SECEPP addresses the problem of completeness by providing "general guidance for ethical decision making." Gotterbarn argues that ethical tensions that arise can best be addressed by "thoughtful consideration of fundamental principles, rather than blind reliance on detailed regulations." He also points out that SECEPP should not be viewed as a simple algorithm that generates ethical decisions. And Gotterbarn notes that the individual principles that comprise SECEPP are not intended to be used in isolation from one another.

With respect to the second major criticism of professional codes, Gotterbarn points out that SECEPP has a "hierarchy of principles." This hierarchy enables engineers to prioritize their roles and responsibilities and to determine which ones are overriding when two or more conflict. Recall the list of eight principles that make up SECEPP: the ordering of these principles is intended to offer some guidance in cases where two or more rules conflict. SECEPP's hierarchy of principles states that concern for the health, safety, and welfare of the public is primary in all ethical judgments.

4.3.4.3 The Role of SECEPP in Certification/Licensing Issues for Software Engineers

A recently debated issue that we have not yet considered is whether software engineers should be required to become certified or licensed before they are allowed to practice. The Association for Computing Machinery (ACM) distinguishes between licensing and certification by noting that certification is a "statement by a recognized authority that a person is competent in an area." Licensing, on the other hand, is regulated in the United States by legislation at the state level (White and Simons, 2002). Many of those in favor of licensing and certification requirements for software engineers point out that lawyers must pass a bar exam in order to practice law, and accountants must pass an exam to be certified as public accountants. Some have also pointed out that even hairdressers and barbers, who are not always thought of as professionals, must be certified by a state agency in order to practice. On the other hand, we could point out that college professors, who are typically thought of as professionals, can teach courses (at least in certain disciplines) at universities without having to pass a state's certification requirements. So there appears to be an anomaly, or at least an inconsistency, with respect to professional occupations and their roles vis-à-vis state certification and licensing requirements.

Some computer specialists are certified by recognized agencies to perform particular kinds of tasks; for example, network administrators have been certified by organizations such as Microsoft or Novell. For the most part, however, professionals working in the computer field have not been certified or licensed. That may soon change for software engineers: Texas has passed a law that requires software engineers who wish to practice in that state to be licensed. Similar legislation for licensing software engineers is pending in many state legislatures.

Some analysts worry that without a universal code such as SECEPP in place for software engineers, individual states can certify software engineers without defining a standard of practice. According to Gotterbarn (2000), this oversight is dangerous for two reasons:

i. Licensed software engineers will obey the law, but laws provide inadequate guidance in many critical situations.

ii. The failure to connect specific ethical standards to licensing encourages the mistaken view that there is little agreement among software engineers about their professional and moral obligations.

Gotterbarn believes that SECEPP's role in licensing is significant, because the code provides a mechanism for helping engineering practitioners make ethical judgments in those situations where the law is silent.

Thus far, ACM has not endorsed any proposals for licensing software engineers. For one thing, ACM points out, a software engineering license could be interpreted as an authoritative statement that the licensed engineer is capable of producing software systems of "consistent reliability, dependability, and usability." According to ACM, the current "state of knowledge and practice" in the field of software engineering is "too immature" to give assurances of this type (White and Simons, 2002). However, ACM has made it clear that it is very concerned with the role software engineers play in designing computer systems that affect public health and safety. John Knight and Nancy Leveson (2002) sum up ACM's position on the licensing of software engineers *vis-à-vis* the challenge of protecting the public interest:

> Licensing software engineers who work on safety-critical systems . . . would be neither practical nor effective in achieving the goal of public interest, and it could even have serious negative ramifications. The real issue, however, is not licensing per se but determining how best to protect the public without unduly affecting engineering progress, the economy, the engineering and computing professions, or individual rights.

Knight and Leveson also suggest that approaches other than licensing and certification might be more effective and that those approaches need to be evaluated.

4.3.5 Educating Computer Professionals about the Existence of Codes of Ethics

How are future computer professionals supposed to discover that codes of ethics are available for them? Of course, the same question applies to professionals already working in the field who are not members of the ACM or the IEEE and who do not hold undergraduate degrees in computer science. We consider each question separately.

With respect to future computer professionals, a formal process is already in place to instruct undergraduate students about professional computing codes. A joint IEEE-CS task force on curriculum recently issued a report titled *IEEE-CS/ACM Computing Curricula 2001*. This report recommends that sixteen core hours of instruction on social, ethical, and professional topics be included in the curriculum for undergraduate computer science students. Ethics instruction is organized into ten units (see Appendix D at www.wiley.com/college/Tavani for detailed information about the content for each unit). One unit (SP5) specifically addresses the question of professional codes, stating that explicit instruction be given on "professional and ethical responsibilities (the nature of professionalism, codes of ethics, ethical dissent and whistleblowing)."

We next consider the second question regarding education about codes of conduct— how should those already employed in the computer field learn about the professional codes that apply to them? In Section 4.3.3, we saw that Heinz Leugenbiehl proposed a strategy for educating engineers, including those already practicing in the field, about the important roles that professional codes play in the engineering profession. Implementing some of the themes in Leugenbiehl's proposal, Perlman and Varma (2002) suggest that instruction about ethical codes could be integrated into training programs in the workplace. Newly hired engineers could be assigned mentors, who themselves have been trained in ethical awareness in the engineering profession. Consider that some companies, such as Lockheed Martin, have had-official ethics officers who can assist in implementing such training programs.

4.3.6 Some Concluding Thoughts on Professional Codes

You can examine the full texts of the IEEE Code, the ACM Code, and SECEPP in Appendixes A, B, and C, respectively. You can then decide for yourself whether these codes are too general and too vague, as some critics suggest, or whether they are too narrow in scope, as other critics have argued. You can also determine whether SECEPP is sufficiently robust in terms of its breadth and depth to withstand the criticisms of earlier professional codes.

In defense of professional codes, it would be unfair to ask too much of them; for example, there are certain kinds of professional decisions that codes of ethics cannot help us make. If you are entering the computing profession, you might ask yourself a number of questions along the following lines. Should I work for a software company that has contracts with the United States Department of Defense? Should I accept a position with a software company that designs computer systems that could be used in warfare? Should I work for a large corporation like Microsoft, which has been sued by the United States Government for violating antitrust laws? Should I work on software projects that will advance computing and global communication in developing countries? Professional codes were never designed or intended to answer these kinds of questions.

So professional codes clearly have some limitations, especially if one looks to them for advice in how to make professional career choices. However, we should be careful not underestimate the important contributions that well-developed professional codes, such as SECEPP, have made to the relatively new computing profession (Spinello and Tavani, 2001). Critics may be correct in pointing out that following the directives of a professional code can never be a substitute for the kind of careful moral deliberation that is needed in certain controversial cases. Nevertheless, well-developed codes of conduct provide professionals with an important first step in the overall ethical deliberation process.

▶ 4.4 CONFLICTS OF PROFESSIONAL RESPONSIBILITY: EMPLOYEE LOYALTY AND WHISTLE-BLOWING

What exactly is employee loyalty? Do employees and employers have a special obligation of loyalty to each other? Should loyalty to one's employer ever preclude an employee's "blowing the whistle" in critical situations? In which cases can whistle-blowing be justified? Each of these questions is examined in this section.

4.4.1 Do Employees Have an Obligation of Loyalty to Employers?

Many ethicists believe that while loyalty may not be an obligation that is absolute, we nonetheless have a prima facie obligation of loyalty in employment contexts. In other words, all things being equal, an employee should be loyal to his or her employer and vice versa. What is the origin of the concept of employee loyalty in an engineering context? Carl Mitcham (1997) points out that historically, engineers believed that they had a basic obligation to be loyal to institutional authority. Originally, an engineer was a soldier who designed military fortifications or operated engines of war, such as catapults. Mitcham notes that early civil engineering could be viewed as peacetime military engineering in which engineers were duty-bound to obey their employer, which was often some branch of the government. So it may well be the case that this historical precedent has contributed to the sense of loyalty many engineers currently have for their institutions and employers.

Does employee loyalty still make sense in the context of a large computer corporation? Ronald Duska (1991) argues that in employment contexts, loyalty only arises in special relationships that are based on a notion he calls "mutual enrichment." So in relationships in which parties are pursuing their self-interests, the notion of loyalty does not apply. Duska believes that employer-employee relationships—at least where corporations are concerned—are based on self-interest and not on mutual enrichment; from this, Duska concludes that employees do not necessarily have an obligation of loyalty to their corporate employers. He notes that corporations would like their employees to believe that employees do have such an obligation, since the belief serves the interests of the corporation.

John Ladd (1991) also believes that for corporations, loyalty can only be in one direction. He argues that a corporation cannot be loyal to an employee in the same sense that employees are supposed to be loyal to the corporation, because the corporation's goals must be competitively linked to the benefits employees bring to the corporation. A corporation can be good to employees only because it is good for business, that is, it is in the company's own self-interest. So, like Duska, Ladd cites corporate self-interest as an obstacle to the balanced employer-employee relationship required for mutual loyalty.

In one sense, Duska's and Ladd's arguments seem plausible. Consider, for instance, that corporations often go through downsizing phases in which loyal employees who have served a company faithfully for several years are dismissed as part of restructuring plans. On the other hand, some employers have shown what would certainly appear to be a strong sense of loyalty to employees. For example, consider a case in which an employer continues to keep an employee on the payroll even though that employee has a chronic illness that causes her to miss several months of work. Or consider a case in which several employees are kept on by a company despite the fact that their medical conditions have caused the corporation's health insurance costs to increase significantly, thereby reducing the company's overall earnings. Also consider a recent case involving the owner of Malden Mills, whose physical plant in Massachusetts was destroyed by fire. The mill's proprietor, Aaron Feurestein, could have been excused from any future obligations to his employees, and he could have chosen to rebuild his facility in a different state or country where employees would work for lower wages. Instead, Feurestein continued to pay and provide benefits for his employees while a new facility was being built in Massachusetts. So there have been instances in which employers have been very loyal to their employees.

How should the notion of employee loyalty apply in computing contexts? Do computer professionals necessarily have an obligation to be loyal to their employers? A thorough examination of the arguments on both sides of this issue, unfortunately, would take us beyond the scope of this chapter, so we will assume that, all things being equal, computer professionals should be loyal to their employers.

However, sometimes an employee's obligation of loyalty can come into conflict with other obligations, such as those to society in general, especially where health and safety considerations are at stake. How are computer professionals supposed to balance their obligation of loyalty to an employer against their obligations of loyalty that lie elsewhere? For one thing, loyalty should not viewed as something that an employee must give exclusively or blindly to one's employer. Instead, loyalty should be seen as an obligation that individuals have to society as a whole, especially where safety and health issues are at stake. Divided loyalties, of course, can result in serious conflicts for employees, and in certain cases the moral dilemmas they generate are so profound that an employee must determine whether to blow the whistle.

4.4.2 Whistle-blowing

What exactly is whistle-blowing? Consider two definitions: Norman Bowie (1982) defines whistle-blowing as "the act of an employee informing the public on the immoral or illegal behavior of an employee or supervisor." And Sisela Bok (1997) defines whistle-blowing as an act in which one "makes revelations meant to call attention to negligence, abuses, or dangers that threaten the public interest." From these two definitions, we see that whistle-blowing situations can arise not only in cases of overt wrongdoing (involving specific acts that are either illegal or immoral), but also in instances of negligence where one or more individuals have failed to act.

4.4.2.1 Determining When to Blow the Whistle

When should an employee blow the whistle? Consider a recent whistle-blowing incident in which Colleen Rowley, an FBI employee, came forth to describe how critical messages had failed to be sent up the Federal Bureau's chain of command in the days immediately preceding the tragic events of September 11, 2001. Was it appropriate for her to blow the whistle on her supervisor? Was she disloyal to her supervisor and her fellow employees in doing so?

Should individuals in positions of authority in corporations such as Enron and WorldCom have blown the corporate whistle about their illegal accounting practices, which were discovered in early 2002? One could argue that failing to blow the whistle in the Enron case resulted in thousands of people losing their retirement savings and, in some cases, their entire life savings.

There are, no doubt, cases where a decision to blow the whistle might have saved human lives. Consider, for example, the Space Shuttle *Challenger* disaster in January 1986, which resulted in the deaths of the seven crew members. Engineers who designed the space shuttle were aware of the safety risks in launching the shuttle in cooler temperatures. In fact, some engineers, when learning the *Challenger* was scheduled for launch on a cool January morning, went to their supervisors to express their concerns. However, a decision was made to stick with the original launch date. Having received no support from their supervisors, should those engineers have gone directly to the press? Would whistle-blowing at that level have saved the lives of the *Challenger's* crew?

You may have heard of a now classic case involving the Ford Pinto (automobile), which had a gas tank that was unsafe. (The trial concluded in 1980.) The faulty design of the Pinto's gas tank caused the car to catch on fire when involved in certain collisions, even at lower speeds. In some cases these fires caused the deaths of Pinto drivers and passengers. Many of the engineers who worked on the Pinto's design were aware that its gas tank was unsafe, and they strongly recommended that the design be changed. However, a management decision was made at Ford to go ahead and produce Pintos with unsafe gas tanks. Should the engineers involved have gone public? This particular incident has since sparked considerable debate about when it is appropriate for an employee to blow the whistle.

In cases such as the *Challenger* and the Pinto, many believe that the engineers involved had a responsibility to blow the whistle on management. We next briefly examine two classic cases of whistle-blowing in a computing/engineering context: one that that occurred in the late 1960s/early 1970s, and another in the early 1980s.

▶ **WHISTLE-BLOWING CASE ILLUSTRATION I:** BART

A now classic whistle-blowing incident that received considerable attention in the media in the early 1970s involved BART (Bay Area Rapid Transit) in California. Under development at BART was a new, computerized mass transit system, which was behind schedule, over budget, and arguably unsafe. Three engineers working on the project were concerned about the safety of the transit system's ATC (automatic train control) system. First, they went to their managers to express their concerns; getting no satisfaction at that level, the three engineers next took their concerns to the organization's board of directors; And, finally, after receiving no support from the board, the engineers decided to go to the press with their story. Shortly afterwards, they were fired.

Since the BART incident, whistle-blowing laws at both the federal and state levels have been passed. In addition to the federal Whistle-blower Protection Act of 1989, many states, such as Florida, have passed their own laws to protect whistle-blowers. However, not all states have done this; and the level of protection granted to whistle-blowers in states where legislation has been enacted varies considerably; many individuals feel that it is still too risky to go public with their concerns.

▶ **WHISTLE-BLOWING CASE ILLUSTRATION II:** SDI

A United States military proposal called the Strategic Defense Initiative (SDI) was hotly debated during the early 1980s. SDI, which was also referred to as "Star Wars," was a missile defense system intended to provide a defense shield against incoming ballistic missiles. The Star Wars initiative, originally proposed by the Reagan administration, was controversial from the outset. Supporters of this initiative argued that SDI was necessary for national defense purposes. Critics, however, argued that the system was unreliable and posed a safety hazard.

David Parnas, a consultant on the Star Wars project, was paid $1,000 per day for his expertise. However, shortly after he joined the SDI project team, Parnas became convinced that it was not possible to construct SDI software that could confidently be expected to work when needed. His argument for the inadequacy of SDI (Parnas, 1987) was based on three reasons:

1. The specifications for the software could not be known with any confidence.
2. The software could not undergo realistic testing.
3. There would not be sufficient time during an attack to repair and reinstall failing software (no "real-time" debugging).

Parnas concluded that SDI could not be trusted, and he eventually went public with his position. Supporters of SDI accused Parnas of disloyalty and of acting out of his own self-interest. Parnas's defenders pointed out that Parnas walked away from a lucrative consulting contract. Did Parnas do the right thing? It is interesting to note that William Yurcik and David Doss (2002) believe that the arguments used by Parnas in the case of SDI also apply in the controversy involving the most recent national missile defense proposal put forth by the current Bush administration. Recent arguments advanced for and against NMD were briefly examined in Chapter 3.

4.4.2.2 Can Professional Codes Guide Engineers in Whistle-blowing Decisions?

As noted above, legislation has been enacted at both the federal and state levels to protect employees who go public with certain kinds of information. We also noted that individual state laws vary considerably with the amount and kind of protection offered to whistle-blowers. It would seem appropriate to ask what measures the engineering and computing professions themselves have taken to protect whistle-blowers. Perhaps a more fundamental question is, What kind of guidance do the ethical codes adopted by engineering and computing professions provide members when they are confronted with specific dilemmas that could lead to a whistle-blowing decision? Sections 6.12 and 6.13 of SECEPP state that an engineer is obligated to

- express concerns to the people involved when significant violations of this Code are detected unless this is impossible, counterproductive, or dangerous,
- report significant violations of this Code to appropriate authorities when it is clear that consultation with people involved in these significant violations is impossible, counterproductive or dangerous.

Although guidelines such as these are useful, many believe that they are still too vague. It would be helpful if engineers had more straightforward criteria for determining when they are permitted, or perhaps even required, to blow the whistle.

4.4.2.3 When Is One Permitted/Required to Blow the Whistle?

Richard De George (1981) has offered some specific conditions for when an engineer is (a) *permitted* to blow the whistle, and (b) *obligated* to do so. De George believes that engineers and other workers are permitted to go public with information about the safety of a product if the following conditions are met:

1. The harm that will be done by the product to the public is serious and considerable.
2. The engineers (or employees) have made their concerns known to their superiors.
3. The engineers (or employees) have received no satisfaction from their immediate supervisors and they have exhausted the channels available within the corporation, including going to the board of directors.

Although De George argues that one is permitted to blow the whistle when conditions 1 through 3 are satisfied, he does not believe that a person is yet required to do so. To have a strict moral obligation to blow the whistle, De George believes that two additional conditions must be satisfied:

4. The engineers (or employees) have documented evidence that would convince a reasonable, impartial observer that his/her view of the situation is correct and the company policy wrong.
5. There is strong evidence that making the information public will in fact prevent the threatened serious harm.

4.4.2.4 Evaluating De George's Criteria

Are De George's criteria for whistle-blowing reasonable? Gene James (1991) believes that De George's conditions that require one to blow the whistle are too lenient; James suggests that an individual has a moral obligation to blow the whistle when only DeGeorge's first three conditions are met. James argues that we have a prima facie obligation to "disclose organizational wrongdoing" that we are unable to prevent, and this can occur when De George's first three conditions are satisfied. According to James, the degree of the obligation depends on the extent to which we can foresee the severity and consequences of the wrongdoing.

James also worries that De George's model leaves us with no guidance when we are confronted with cases involving sexual harassment, violations of privacy, industrial espionage, and so forth. According to James, a key problem in De George's model is that "harm" is not adequately defined. For example, James suggests that harm can result in cases where violations of human rights, such as privacy and property, occur as well as in life-critical and safety-critical situations.

Kenneth Alpern (1991) also argues that De George's model lets engineers off too easily from their obligation to blow the whistle. However, Alpern bases his criticism of De George's model on different grounds from James's. Alpern believes that engineers must be willing to make greater sacrifices than others because engineers are in a greater position to do certain kinds of social harm. He believes that these obligations come from a fundamental principle of "ordinary morality"—viz., we must *do no harm*. So Alpern suggests that because engineers have a much greater obligation to society than ordinary individuals do to prevent harm, engineers can be required to blow the whistle in cases that other individuals would not.

It is important to note at this point that De George also has defenders who believe that whistle-blowing should only be required in extraordinary cases. John Ladd (1991), for example, believes that requiring engineers to blow the whistle in nonextraordinary cases (such as those described in De George's conditions 1–3) can be undesirable from an ethical point of view because it demands that these individuals be "moral heroes." Ladd agrees with De George that engineers should not have to be heroes or saints. Interestingly, De George has pointed out that just when one engineering myth—viz., ethics has no place in engineering—has finally been displaced, a new myth has surfaced: Engineers must be moral heroes.

4.4.3 An Alternative Strategy for Understanding Professional Responsibility

De George and Ladd seem correct in claiming that engineers should not be required to be moral heroes or saints. Yet, James and Alpern also seem to be correct in noting that engineers, because of the positions of responsibility they hold, should be expected to make greater sacrifices. Michael McFarland (1991) offers an interesting position in this debate; McFarland's position can be viewed as an alternative strategy and perhaps even as a compromise position. McFarland suggests that, collectively, engineers might be held to a higher standard of social responsibility than ordinary individuals, but that the onus of responsibility should not fall directly on engineers as individual engineers. Rather, it should be shouldered by engineers as members of the engineering profession.

McFarland's model is based on the assumption that, as moral agents, we have a prima facie obligation to come to the aid of others. In describing the nature of this obligation, he uses a nonengineering analogy involving the Kitty Genovese case. (We briefly examined this incident in Chapter 2.) Recall that Genovese was murdered in New York City in 1965 as thirty-eight people in and around her apartment building watched or listened. It has since been argued that if some of Genovese's neighbors had banded together to come to her aid, she would have survived. The analogy for engineers that McFarland wishes to draw is that when no other sources of help are available, engineers should take responsibility by banding together. McFarland recognizes that if engineers act as individuals, they might not always have the ability to help. If they act collectively, however, they might be able to accomplish goals that would otherwise not be possible. Consider that if Genovese's neighbors had acted individually to intervene in her behalf, they might have put themselves at great risk. However, if they had acted collectively as a group, the neighbors could have overcome Genovese's assailant.

McFarland believes that unless an engineer's work is seen in a wider social context, that is, in its relation to society, an adequate account of the moral responsibility of engineers cannot be given. He also believes that unless engineers work collaboratively on ethical matters, they will not be able to meet all of their responsibilities. Thus McFarland's model encourages engineers to shift their thinking about responsibility issues from the level of individual responsibility (the microethical level), to responsibility at the broader level of the profession itself (the macroethical level).

▶ 4.5 MORAL RESPONSIBILITY, LEGAL LIABILITY, AND ACCOUNTABILITY

Thus far, our examination of issues involving the moral responsibility of computing professionals has focused mainly on questions concerning employee loyalty and whistle-blowing. We have seen that some of these questions have focused on the responsibilities of computing professionals as individuals, while others have dealt with responsibilities facing the computing profession itself. We have also noted that these questions illustrate essential differences between issues of responsibility involving microethics and macroethics. However, we have not yet fully considered the concept of moral responsibility itself.

Philosophers often describe the concept of responsibility in terms of certain conditions that must be satisfied. Two such conditions are *causality* and *intent*. In other words, some agent, X, is held morally responsible for an act, Y, if X caused Y. Here, a person could be held responsible even if he or she did not intend the outcome. Consider that Robert Morris, the Cornell graduate student who launched the "Internet worm" in 1988, claimed that he did not intend that the Internet be brought to a standstill. Nonetheless, Morris was held responsible for the outcome *caused* by his unleashing the computer worm. Agents can also be held responsible when they *intend* for something to happen, even if they ultimately fail to cause (or bring about) the intended outcome. For example, consider a scenario in which a disgruntled student intends to blow up a college's computer lab, but at the last minute is discovered and prevented from doing so. Even though the student failed to carry out his objective—cause the bomb to detonate in the computer lab—we hold the student morally culpable because of his intentions.

The term "responsibility" is often used in nonmoral contexts; for example, we speak of a power surge as responsible for the crash of a computer system. But we do not attribute blame to the storm that caused the power surge, which in turn caused the computer to crash. The storm and the power surge are responsible only in the nonmoral sense. By considering whether we can blame an agent for an action, we can determine if we can hold the agent morally responsible—the sense of "responsible" that concerns us in this chapter.

4.5.1 Distinguishing Responsibility from Liability and Accountability

It would be helpful at this point to distinguish responsibility from the related notions of liability and accountability. Responsibility differs from liability in that *liability* is a legal concept, sometimes used in the narrow sense of "strict liability." To be strictly liable for harm is to be liable to compensate for it even though one did not necessarily bring it about through faulty action. Here, the moral notion of blame may be left out. A property owner may be legally liable for an injury to a guest who falls in the property owner's house, but it does not necessarily follow that the property owner was also morally responsible for any resulting injury. (We elaborate on the notion of liability in Section 4.5.4, where we examine the legal liability of producers of defective computer software.)

Helen Nissenbaum (1995) distinguishes between responsibility and accountability by suggesting that responsibility is only part of what is covered by the "robust and intuitive notion of accountability." In Nissenbaum's scheme, *accountability* is a broader concept than responsibility, and means that someone, or some group of individuals, or perhaps even an entire organization is *answerable*. In a computing context, she notes that accountability means

> there will be someone, or several people *to answer* not only for malfunctions in life-critical systems that cause or risk grave injuries and cause infrastructure and large monetary losses, but even for the malfunctions that cause individual losses of time, convenience, and contentment. [Italics added]

Table 4-2 summarizes the elements we have used to differentiate moral responsibility, legal liability, and accountability.

Nissenbaum believes that the notion of accountability has been "systematically undermined" in the computer era, despite the fact that we are increasingly dependent on safety-critical and life-critical systems controlled by computers. In Section 4.2, we saw that safety-critical applications included software used in aircraft and air traffic control systems, in nuclear reactors, in missile systems, and in medical treatment systems, as well as in the selection of water disposal sites and in the design of bridges and buildings. Nissenbaum argues that a major barrier to attributing accountability to the developers of safety-critical software is the problem of "many hands."

TABLE 4-2   Responsibility, Legal Liability, and Accountability

Moral Responsibility	Legal Liability	Accountability
Attributes blame (or praise) to individuals.	Does not attribute blame or fault to those held liable.	Does not necessarily attribute blame (in a moral sense).
Usually attributed to individuals rather than collectivities or groups.	Typically applies to corporations and property owners.	Can apply to individuals, groups of individuals, and corporations.
Notions of guilt and shame apply, but no legal punishment or compensation need result.	Compensation can be required even when responsibility in a formal sense is not admitted	Someone or some group is answerable (i.e., it goes beyond mere liability).

4.5.2 Accountability and the Problem of Many Hands

Computer systems are typically developed in large organizational settings. Because these systems are the products of engineering teams or of corporations, as opposed to the products of a single programmer working in isolation, many hands are involved in their development. Thus it is very likely that no single individual grasps all of the code used in developing a particular safety-critical system. As a result, it is difficult to determine who exactly is accountable whenever one of these safety-critical systems results in personal injury or harm to individuals; it is not always clear whether the manufacturer of the system hardware (the machine) or the engineering teams that developed the system's software, or both, should be held accountable.

When thinking about the problem of many hands from the perspective of strict moral responsibility, as opposed to accountability, two difficulties arise: first, we tend to attribute moral responsibility for an accident to an individual, but not to groups or collectivities. Thus we sometimes encounter difficulties when we try to attribute blame to an organization. Philosophers such as John Ladd (1991) have argued that we should distinguish between individual responsibility and collective responsibility. Nissenbaum suggests that by using "accountability" we can avoid the tendency to think only at the level of individuals in matters typically associated with assigning moral responsibility.

The second difficulty arises because the concept of moral responsibility is often thought of as exclusionary, as John Ladd (1995) points out. In other words, if we can show that *A* is responsible for *C*, then we might infer that *B* cannot be held responsible for *C*. Ladd believes that moral responsibility should be viewed as nonexclusionary. Again, Nissenbaum seems to suggest that if we use "accountability" instead of "responsibility," we can circumvent this difficulty: Holding Sally accountable for making unauthorized copies of proprietary software does not necessarily preclude holding Harry accountable as well, as when Harry pays Sally for making copies of the pirated software.

So Nissenbaum believes that holding one individual accountable for some harm need not necessarily let others off the hook, because several individuals may be accountable. Nor does it mean letting organizations off the hook, because they too may be accountable. As Nissenbaum puts the matter, "We should hold each fully accountable because many hands ought not necessarily lighten the burden of accountability." The following case illustrates some of the problems in determining accountability when many hands are involved in the development of a safety-critical system.

▶ **CASE ILLUSTRATION:** Therac-25

The case of the Therac-25, discussed briefly in the opening of this chapter, illustrates how many hands can obscure accountability. The Therac machines, including the Therac-25 model, are computer-controlled radiation treatment machines that were built by Atomic Energy of Canada Limited (AECL). During the two-year period 1985–1987, the Therac-25 massively overdosed patients in six known incidents. The overdoses caused severe radiation burns, which in turn resulted in the deaths of three individuals and irreversible injuries (one minor and two very serious) to three others.

Eventually the Therac-25 malfunction was traced not to a single source but to numerous faults, including two significant software-coding errors ("bugs") and a faulty microswitch. One bug involved radiation-dosage errors: If a subsequent request to change a previously entered radiation dosage was entered in a certain sequence through the user interface, a software bug caused the new entry to be ignored, and the entry instructing the original dosage was used. Instead of receiving 200 RADs, one radiation patient received 20,000 RADs; this patient died shortly afterwards from excessive radiation (Levinson and Turner, 1993).

A number of interesting questions regarding the locus of responsibility were raised in the wake of the Therac-25 accidents. Who exactly should be held accountable for the deaths and injuries that resulted from the computer malfunction? Is the hospital, which may be found legally liable, also accountable in a larger sense? Should the company that manufactured and sold the Therac system to the hospital be held accountable? Were the engineers and programmers who worked on the design and development of this system ultimately responsible for the injuries and deaths caused to the radiation patients? Should they be held liable?

When engineers design physical structures such as bridges and airplanes, certain levels of redundancy and tolerance are built into those systems. For example, one missed detail in the construction of a bridge will not cause it to collapse; nor will one missed detail in the assembly of one of the physical components of an airplane's subsystems necessarily cause the plane to crash. However, one errant line of software code can cause a program to crash, and in a safety-critical software application, one errant line of code can result in deaths, as well as in serious injuries. (Of course, this problem is compounded when computers are networked together because software bugs in one computer system can be propagated across a network.)

4.5.3 Could an Industry-wide Standard Help Resolve the Many-Hands Problem

Because of the severity of the malfunctions that can arise in life-critical and safety-critical systems, some have proposed that an industry-wide standard be adopted to help ensure the development of more reliable computer systems. Robert Steele (2000), who has called for a "standard of due diligence" for the computing profession, points out that consumers would not purchase automobiles if they believed that the tires would fall off while they are driving. Yet, he notes, consumers are expected to purchase computer systems that are often unreliable. We elaborate on Steele's arguments in Chapter 6, where we consider whether a standard that he proposes would help reduce security problems in the computer networks that underpin our critical infrastructure.

Helen Nissenbaum (1995) argues that a "substantive standard" for the computing profession is not only needed, it should be "clarified and vigorously promoted." According to Nissenbaum, guidelines for producing safer and more reliable computers should include a standard that incorporates

- a formal analysis of system modules as well as of the entire system,
- meaningful quality assurance and independent auditing, and
- built-in redundancy.

Nissenbaum believes that a standard of care comprising these criteria would provide a nonarbitrary means for determining accountability; it would offer a tool for distinguishing between malfunctions due to inadequate practices and those that occur in spite of a programmer or designer's best efforts. Nissenbaum also suggests that if such standard of care had existed at the time Therac-25 was produced, the software developers of the system could have been held accountable for the deaths and injuries that resulted.

4.5.4 Legal Liability and Moral Accountability

In Section 4.5.1, we saw that legal liability can be distinguished from both moral responsibility and accountability. Nissenbaum believes that in computer contexts, it is important to keep "accountability" distinct from "liability to compensate." She concedes that liability offers a partial solution to problems resulting from computer malfunctions, because at least it addresses the needs of the victims; however, she also notes that accepting liability as a substitute for accountability can further obscure the process of determining who is accountable for computer malfunctions.

Is it reasonable to hold computer corporations legally liable for products they sell that are either unreliable or defective? Supporters of liability law believe that holding owners legally liable makes sense because owners are typically in the best position to directly control their property. Nissenbaum believes that because ownership implies a "bundle of rights," it should also imply responsibilities such as being liable. Software owners (who are also usually the software's producers) are in the best position to directly affect the quality of the software they release to the public. Yet, ironically, the trend in the software industry, Nissenbaum points out, is to "demand maximal property protection while denying, to the extent possible, accountability." Software manufacturers frequently include disclaimers of liability on their products such as "This software is sold as is."

Nissenbaum also suggests that strict liability would shift the accountability to the producers of defective software, thereby addressing an anomaly (perhaps even a paradox) with respect to our current understanding of overall accountability: While liability laws protect the public against potential harm, most producers of software deny accountability for software errors. Producers sometimes base their argument on the notion that software is prone to error in ways that surpass other technologies. Nissenbaum concludes that strict liability laws can send a message cautioning software producers to take extraordinary care to produce safe and reliable systems. Strict liability laws may also cause manufacturers to reassess the level of risk tolerated in the process of developing software.

▶ 4.6 ASSESSING RISK IN THE SOFTWARE-DEVELOPMENT PROCESS

Some analysts have suggested that in order to reduce software failures, we must first address issues involving the level of risk currently associated with the development of computer systems. Don Gotterbarn (2001) argues that ethical risks associated with the entire "software development life cycle" must also be taken into consideration. For Gotterbarn, the life cycle of software includes the maintenance phase as well as the design and development stages.

Bruce Schneir (2000) notes that in the context of computer security, risk-assessment models can be used to make informed decisions about the most cost-effective controls in order to limit risks to one's assets. Gotterbarn worries that while much attention has been paid to cost-effectiveness, very little thought has been given to ethical considerations in the models of risk used in the software development process. In these models, risk has typically been understood in terms of either scheduling, budgeting, or specification requirements. Gotterbarn argues that software can satisfy all three conditions and still fail to meet an acceptable standard of risk assessment. To see how this is possible, we examine a case involving the Aegis Radar System that we discussed in the opening section of this chapter.

▶ **CASE ILLUSTRATION:** The Aegis Radar System

The Aegis Radar System was developed by the United States Navy to allow ships to monitor space around them. In July 1988, the USS *Vincennes*, equipped with the Aegis system, accidentally shot down an Iranian passenger aircraft, killing 230 people. Many believe that a contributing element to—and arguably the key reason for—the accident was the poor design of the Aegis system's user interface. In response to the *Vincennes* incident, some computer ethicists have argued that system designers need to realize the importance of building features that affect human abilities and limitations into the interfaces of safety-critical systems.

Some analysts believe that accidents like the one involving the Aegis system on the *Vincennes* are inevitable because they result from the mathematical errors in calculation. Critics of this interpretation, however, believe that the Aegis accident was an error of engineering judgment, that is, an error not reducible to engineering science or to mathematics. They also believe that similar errors could be better understood if an adequate model of risk assessment were used.

The Aegis Radar System met all the requirements that the developer and customer had set for it; in fact, it satisfied the three conditions specified above: it was on schedule, it was within budget, and it satisfied design specification requirements. Yet the use of the Aegis system resulted in the deaths of more than 200 airline passengers. Are risks involving accidents of this magnitude acceptable in schemes for the development of software?

Don Gotterbarn suggests that software failures like the one involving the Aegis system are the result of two defects in current models of risk assessment for software development:

1. an overly narrow conception of risk, and
2. a limited notion of "system stakeholders."

With respect to (1), Gotterbarn argues that a model of risk assessment based solely on cost-effectiveness and using only criteria such as budget and schedule, is overly narrow. He suggests the model-assessment be enlarged to include social, political, and ethical issues. Regarding (2), Gotterbarn notes that the only stakeholders typically given consideration in risk-assessment models for software development are the software developers and customers, and he argues that this limited notion of "system stakeholders" leads to the development of systems that have unanticipated negative effects. Gotterbarn concludes that unless an adequate risk model for software development is framed, we may be doomed to experiencing future computer malfunctions like the Aegis system on the *Vincennes*.

We will discuss software risk, reliability, and vulnerability in detail in Chapter 6, which examines computer security issues. In Chapter 6 we focus on intrusions into computer systems from external sources such as hackers. A model for assessing and managing risk, especially as it applies to securing our computer network-dependent infrastructure, is also included in that chapter.

▶ 4.7 CHAPTER SUMMARY

In this chapter, we examined some ethical problems that confront computer professionals, and we focused on the kinds of issues and challenges that software engineers and their team members sometimes face in the development of safety-critical software. We saw that professional codes of ethics/conduct are useful insofar as they inspire and educate professionals entering and working in the field of computing. We also saw, however, that many professional codes have serious limitations. We noted that the IEEE-CS/ACM Software Engineering Code of Ethics and Professional Practice (SECEPP) was designed to avoid many of the shortcomings of earlier professional codes of ethics.

We also saw how the role of accountability has been undermined in the computer era, for both individual computer professionals and the profession as a whole. We saw that because accountability is diffused by the problem of many hands, it is not always easy to determine where accountability and responsibility for computer malfunctions and errors in safety-critical software systems ultimately lie. Finally, we considered a proposal for revising the conventional models of risk assessment used in developing software for safety-critical systems.

▶ REVIEW QUESTIONS

1. What is professional ethics?

2. Who is a computer professional?

3. Do computer professionals have special moral responsibilities that ordinary computer users do not have? If so, what are some of those special responsibilities?

4. Why was it useful to limit our discussion of moral issues affecting computer professionals to issues affecting software engineers and engineering teams?

5. How do Gotterbarn, Miller, and Rogerson propose that we define the profession of software engineering? Who is included in a software engineering team?

6. What are professional codes of ethics, and what functions do these codes serve?

7. List some of the benefits of professional code of ethics. Describe some of the criticisms of these professional codes.

8. Why does John Ladd believe that professional codes rest on a series of errors that are both intellectual and moral? Describe the arguments he uses to support his position.

9. Describe Don Gotterbarn's threefold distinction: codes of ethics, codes of conduct, and codes of practice. Does Gotterbarn's distinction eliminate any of the criticisms that have been raised against professional codes? Explain.

10. How does the IEEE-CS/ACM Software Engineering Code of Ethics and Professional Practice avoid some of the difficulties found in earlier professional codes?

11. Do computer professionals have a presumed, or prima facie, obligation of loyalty to their employers? Explain.

12. Describe the arguments by Ronal Duska and John Ladd regarding employee loyalty.

13. What exactly is whistle-blowing?

14. Describe Richard De George's criteria for determining when one is required to blow the whistle as opposed to when one is permitted to do so. Are De George's criteria useful in making this distinction? Explain.

15. In which ways do Gene James and Kenneth Alpern disagree with De George's model for whistle-blowing?

16. Describe John Ladd's argument in defense of De George's position on whistle-blowing.

17. Why Does Helen Nissenbaum believe that the notion of accountability has been systematically undermined in the computer age? How does she distinguish between accountability and responsibility?

18. What does Nissenbaum mean by "the problem of many hands" in a computing context?

19. Why does Nissenbaum believe that it is important to distinguish between moral accountability and legal liability?

20. According to Don Gotterbarn, what is required for a model of risk analysis to be adequate in the software development process for safety-critical systems?

▶ DISCUSSION QUESTIONS

1. Describe some virtues of the ethical codes of conduct adopted by professional societies such as the ACM and IEEE-CS, and list some shortcomings of these professional codes as well. In the final analysis, do the advantages of having a code outweigh the prospects of not having one? Use either an actual or a hypothetical case to establish the main points in your answer.

2. Do you believe that a coherent and comprehensive code of conduct for computer professionals is possible? If so, which of the codes mentioned in this chapter best approximates such a code? Before answering this question, consult the full descriptions of the professional codes included in Appendixes A, B, and C.

3. You have been working for the XYZ Computer Corporation as an entry-level software engineer since you graduated from college last May. You have done very well so far; you are respected by management, well liked by your fellow employees, and have been assigned to a team of engineers that has consistently worked on the most critical and valued projects and contracts that XYZ Corp. has secured. Their most recent contract is for a United States defense project involving the missile defense system, and again, you have been assigned to the team that will develop software for this project. However, you are staunchly opposed to the project objectives, so you ask to be reassigned. Your supervisor and coworkers, as well as upper management, are disappointed to learn of your strong feelings about this project. You are asked to reconsider your views, and you are promised a bonus and a substantial pay increase if you agree to work on this project during the next year. You also discover from a colleague that refusing to work on this project would greatly diminish your career advancement at XYZ and may even make you vulnerable to future layoffs. To compound matters, you and your spouse are expecting your first child in about three months and you recently purchased a home. What would you do? Describe the process of ethical deliberation that you would undertake in trying to resolve this dilemma.

4. For the past six months you have worked on a project to develop a transportation software program for the city of Agropolis, which has been designed to make some much-needed improvements to Agropolis's system of public transportation. You and your team of programmers have worked very hard on this project, but you have encountered difficulties that could not possibly have been anticipated in the original design plan; these difficulties have put your project significantly behind schedule. The city transportation planners are nervous, because they depend on the software from your company to get the new transportation system up and running. And the management at your company is very uncomfortable because they signed a contract to deliver the required software on time. Although the software is not yet foolproof, testing thus far reveals that it works about 99 percent of the time. The few glitches that remain apply only to the transportation system's backup code, which arguably would be needed in only the most severe emergencies. Residents of the city are also eager to have the new transportation system in place.

> A decision is made by the management of your company and by the managers of the city transportation system to go ahead and implement the software as it is. They base their decision on the probability that a backup system would not be needed for several months (at which time the remaining bugs should be fixed). A decision was also made by management on both sides not to announce publicly that the software still has a few

bugs. You and a few of your coworkers believe that the bugs are more dangerous than management is willing to admit. What would you do in this case? Would you be willing to blow the whistle? Defend your position.

5. Recall the various arguments that we examined as to when it is appropriate, and sometimes mandatory, for software engineers and IT professionals to blow the whistle. The criteria for whistle-blowing, as least for those working in some federal government agencies, may have changed recently. In November 2002, the Homeland Security Act passed in both Houses of Congress and was signed into law by President Bush. On one interpretation of the new law, whistle-blowing acts similar to that of Colleen Rowley—who blew the whistle on her FBI superiors who failed to act on information in the days preceding September 11—would be illegal and thus a punishable offense. What implications could this have for software engineers and other computer professionals whose employment comes under the auspices of the Homeland Security Department? In this case, what set of rules should computer professionals follow?

▶ REFERENCES

Alpern, Kenneth (1991). "Moral Responsibility for Engineers." In D. G. Johnson, ed. *Ethical Issues in Engineering*. Englewood Cliffs, NJ: Prentice Hall, pp. 187–195.

Bayles, Michael D. (1989). *Professional Ethics*. 2d ed. Belmont, CA: Wadsworth Publishers.

Bowie, Norman (1982). *Business Ethics*. Englewood Cliffs, NJ: Prentice Hall.

Bok, Sissela (1997). "The Morality of Whistle-blowing." In M. D. Ermann, M. B. Williams, and M. S. Schauf, eds. *Computers, Ethics, and Society*. 2d ed. New York: Oxford University Press, pp. 271–278.

Bowyer, Kevin, ed. (2001). *Ethics and Computing: Living Responsibly in a Computerized World*. 2d ed. New York: IEEE Press.

Buchanan, Elizabeth A. (2001). "Ethical Considerations for the Information Professions." In R. A. Spinello and H. T. Tavani, eds. *Readings in CyberEthics*. Sudbury, MA: Jones and Bartlett Publishers, pp. 523–534.

Davis, Michael (1995). "Thinking Like an Engineer." In D. G. Johnson and H. Nissenbaum, eds. *Computing Ethics & Social Values*. Englewood Cliffs, NJ, pp. 586–597.

De George, Richard T. (1981). "Ethical Responsibilities of Engineering in Large Organizations: The Pinto Case," *Business and Professional Ethics Journal*, Vol. 1, No. 1, pp. 1–14.

Duska, Ronald (1991). "Whistle-blowing and Employee Loyalty." In D. G. Johnson, ed. *Ethical Issues in Engineering*. Englewood Cliffs, NJ: Prentice Hall, pp. 241–247.

Fairweather, N. Ben (2001). "No PAPA: Why Incomplete Codes of Ethics are Worse Than None at All." In R. A. Spinello and H. T. Tavani, eds. *Readings in CyberEthics*. Sudbury, MA: Jones and Bartlett Publishers, pp. 545–556.

Firmage, D. Allan (1991). "The Definition of a Profession." In D. G. Johnson, ed. *Ethical Issues in Engineering*. Englewood Cliffs, NJ: Prentice Hall, pp. 63–66.

Gotterbarn, Don (1991) "Computer Ethics: Responsibility Regained," *National Forum: The Phi Kappa Phi Journal,* Vol. 71, No. 3, pp. 26–31.

Gotterbarn, Don (1999). "The Ethical Software Engineer," *IEEE Institute*, February. Reprinted in K. W. Bowyer, ed. (2001). *Ethics and Computing: Living Responsibly in a Computerized World*. 2d ed. New York: IEEE Press, p. 67.

Gotterbarn, Don (2000). "Computer Professionals and YOUR Responsibilities." In D. Langford, ed. *Internet Ethics*. New York: St. Martin's Press, pp. 200–219.

Gotterbarn, Don (2001). "Reducing Software Failures: Addressing the Ethical Risks of the Software Development Cycle." In T. W. Bynum et al., eds. *Proceedings of Ethicomp 2001: The Fifth International Conference on the Social and Ethical Impacts of Information and Communication Technology*. Vol. 2. Gdansk, Poland: Wydawnictwo Mikom, pp. 9–21.

Gotterbarn, Don Keith Miller, and Simon Rogerson (1999). "Software Engineering Code of Ethics Approved," *Communications of the ACM*, Vol. 42, No. 10, pp. 102–107.

Greenwood, Ernest (1991). "Attributes of a Profession." In D. G. Johnson, ed., *Ethical Issues in Engineering*. Englewood Cliffs, NJ: Prentice Hall, pp. 67–77.

James, Gene (1991). "Whistle-blowing: Its Moral Justification." In D. G. Johnson, ed. *Ethical Issues in Engineering*. Englewood Cliffs, NJ: Prentice Hall, pp. 263–278.

Knight, John C., and Nancy G. Leveson (2002). "Should Software Engineers Be Licensed?" *Communications of the ACM*, Vol. 45, No. 11, pp. 87–90.

Ladd, John (1991). "Collective and Individual Moral Responsibility in Engineering: Some Questions." In D. G. Johnson, ed. *Ethical Issues in Engineering*. Englewood Cliffs, NJ: Prentice Hall, pp. 26–39.

Ladd, John (1995). "The Quest for a Code of Professional Ethics: An Intellectual and Moral Confusion." In D. G. Johnson and H. Nissenbaum, eds. *Computers, Ethics and Social Values*. Englewood Cliffs, NJ: Prentice Hall, pp. 580–585.

Luegenbiehl, Heinz C. (1983). "Codes of Ethics and the Moral Education of Engineers," *Business and Professional Ethics Journal*, Vol. 2, No. 4, pp. 41–61.

Levinson, Nancy G., and Clark S. Turner (1993). "An Investigation of the Therac-25 Accidents," *IEEE Computer*, Vol. 26, No. 7, pp. 18–41.

Martin, Michael, and Roland Schinzinger (1995). "Codes of Ethics." In D. G. Johnson and H. Nissenbaum, eds. *Computers, Ethics and Social Values*. Englewood Cliffs, NJ: Prentice Hall, pp. 576–580.

McFarland, Michael C. (1991). "The Public Health, Safety, and Welfare: An Analysis of the Social Responsibility of Engineers." In D. G. Johnson, ed. *Ethical Issues in Engineering*. Englewood Cliffs, NJ: Prentice Hall, pp. 159–174.

Mitcham, Carl (1997). "Engineering Design Research and Social Responsibility." In K. Schrader-Frechette and L. Westra, eds. *Technology and Values*. Lanham, MD: Rowman and Littlefield, pp. 261–278.

Nissenbaum, Helen (1995). "Computing and Accountability." In D. G. Johnson and H. Nissenbaum, eds. *Computing, Ethics, & Social Values*. Englewood Cliffs, NJ: Prentice Hall, pp. 526–538.

Parnas, David Lorge (1987). "Professional Responsibility to Blow the Whistle on SDI," *Abacus*, Winter, pp. 46–52.

Perlman, Bruce, and Roli Varma (2002). "Improving Engineering Practice," *IEEE Technology and Society*, Vol. 21, No. 1, pp. 40–47.

Schneir, Bruce (2000). *Secrets and Lies: Digital Security in a Networked World*. New York: John Wiley & Sons.

Spinello, Richard A., and Herman T. Tavani (2001). "Professional Ethics and Codes of Conduct." In R. A. Spinello and H. T. Tavani, eds. *Readings in CyberEthics*. Sudbury, MA: Jones and Bartlett Publishers, pp. 515–522.

Steele, Robert (2000). Interview conducted in the PBS Television series *Frontline* special, "Hackers."

White, John, and Barbara Simons (2002). "ACM's Position on the Licensing of Software Engineers," *Communications of the ACM*, Vol. 45, No. 11, p. 93.

Yurcik, William, and David Doss (2002). "Software Technology Issues for a U.S. National Missile Defense System," *IEEE Technology and Society*, Vol. 21, No. 2, pp. 36–46.

▶ FURTHER READINGS

Anderson, Ronald, Deborah G. Johnson, Don Gotterbarn, and Judith Perrolle (1993). "Using the New ACM Code of Ethics in Decision Making," *Communications of the ACM*, Vol., 36, No. 2, pp. 98–107.

Baase, Sara (2003). "Professional Ethics and Responsibilities." Chapter 10 in *A Gift of Fire: Social, Legal, and Ethical Issues for Computers and the Internet*. 2d ed. Upper Saddle River, NJ: Prentice Hall.

Bagart, Donald (2002). "Texas Licensing of Software Engineers: All's Quiet for Now," *Communications of the ACM*, Vol. 45, No. 11, pp. 92–93.

Baron, Marcia (1991). "The Moral Status of Loyalty." In D. G. Johnson, ed. *Ethical Issues in Engineering*. Englewood Cliffs, NJ: Prentice Hall, pp. 225–240.

Borning, Alan (1987). "Computer System Reliability and Nuclear War," *Communications of the ACM*, Vol. 30, No. 2, pp. 112–131.

Bowyer, Kevin (2002). "Star Wars Revisited: Ethics and Safety Critical Software," *IEEE Technology and Society*, Vol. 21, No. 1, pp. 13–26.

Edgar, Stacey L. (2003). "Responsibility, Liability, Law, and Professional Ethics. Chapter 10 in *Morality and Machines*. 2d ed. Sudbury, MA: Jones and Bartlett Publishers.

Epstein, Richard G. (1997). "The Wheel," *Computers and Society*, Vol. 27, No. 2, pp. 8–13.

Gotterbarn, Don (1999). "How the New Software Engineering Code of Ethics Affects You," *IEEE Software*, November/December, pp. 58–64.

Grodzinsky, Frances S. (1999). "The Practitioner From Within: Revisiting the Virtues," *Computers and Society*, Vol. 29, No. 1, pp. 9–15.

Hodges, Michael (2001). "Does Professional Ethics Include Computer Professionals? Two Models for Understanding." In D. M. Hester and P. J. Ford, eds. *Computing and Ethics in the CyberAge*. Upper Saddle River, NJ: Prentice Hall, pp. 195–203.

Jacky, Jonathan (1991). "Safety Critical Computing: Hazards, Practices, Standards and Regulations." In C. Dunlop and R. Kling, eds. *Computerization and Controversy: Value Conflicts and Social Choices*. San Diego, CA: Academic Press, pp. 612–631.

Johnson, Deborah G. (2001). "Professional Ethics." Chapter 3 in *Computer Ethics*. 3d ed. Upper Saddle River, NJ: Prentice Hall.

Littlewood, Bev, and Lorenzo Stringi (1995). "The Risks of Software." In D. G. Johnson and H. Nissenbaum, eds. *Computing, Ethics, & Social Values*. Englewood Cliffs, NJ: Prentice Hall, pp. 432–437.

Luegenbiehl, Heinz C. (1992). "Computer Professionals, Moral Autonomy, and a Code of Ethics," *Journal of System Software*, Vol. 17, pp. 61–68.

Martin, Michael, and Roland Schinzinger (1999). *Introduction to Engineering Ethics*. New York: McGraw-Hill.

May, Larry, and S. Hoffman (1991). *Collective Responsibility*. New York: Rowman and Littlefield.

McFarland, Michael C. (1990). "Urgency of Ethical Standards Intensifies in Computer Community," *IEEE Computer*, Vol. 23, No. 3, pp. 77–81.

Moor, James H. (1998). "If Aristotle Were a Computing Professional," *Computers and Society*, Vol. 28, No. 3, pp. 13–16.

Neuman, Peter G. (1988). "Are Risks in Computing Systems Different from Those in Other Technologies?" *Software Engineering Notes*, Vol. 1, No. 2.

Parnas, David L., A. John van Schouwen, and Shu Po Kwan (1990). "Evaluation of Safety-Critical Software," *Communications of the ACM*, Vol. 33, No. 6, pp. 639–647.

Snapper, John (1985). "Responsibility for Computer-based Errors," *Metaphilosophy*, Vol. 16, pp. 289–295.

Unger, Steven H. (1994). *Controlling Technology: Ethics and the Responsible Engineer*. New York: John Wiley & Sons.

5

PRIVACY AND CYBERSPACE

Of all the ethical issues associated with the use of cybertechnology, perhaps none has received more media attention than concern about the loss of personal privacy in the Internet era. In this chapter, we examine issues involving personal privacy and cybertechnology by asking the following questions:

- How are privacy concerns generated by the use of cybertechnology different from privacy issues raised by earlier technologies?
- What exactly is personal privacy, and why is it valued?
- How do computerized techniques used to gather and collect information, such as Internet "cookies," raise concerns for personal privacy?
- How do the transfer and exchange of personal information across and between databases, carried out in computerized merging and matching operations, threaten personal privacy?
- How do tools used to mine personal data from large "data warehouses" exacerbate existing privacy concerns involving cybertechnology?
- How do Internet searches and on-line public records contribute to the problem of "privacy in public?"
- Do privacy-enhancing tools currently available on the Internet provide users with adequate on-line privacy protection?
- Are existing privacy laws and data-protection schemes adequate in the Internet era?

We begin by looking at some ways to distinguish current issues associated with cybertechnology from privacy concerns involving earlier technologies.

▶ 5.1 ARE PRIVACY CONCERNS ASSOCIATED WITH CYBERTECHNOLOGY UNIQUE OR SPECIAL?

Concerns about personal privacy existed long before the advent of computers and cybertechnology. Prior to the information era, for example, the camera and the telephone presented challenges for privacy, so we can ask, What, if anything, is special about the privacy concerns that are associated with cybertechnology? Consider the impact that changes in technology have had on privacy with respect to

- the *amount* of personal information that can be gathered,
- the *speed* at which personal information can be transmitted,
- the *duration* of time that the information can be retained,
- the *kind* of information that can be transferred.

Cybertechnology makes it possible to collect and store much more information about individuals than was possible in the precomputer era. The *amount* of personal information that could be collected in the precomputer era was determined by practical considerations, such as the physical space required to store the data and the time and difficulty involved in collecting the data. Today, of course, digitized information that can be stored electronically in computer databases takes up very little storage space and can be collected with relative ease.

Consider the speed at which information is exchanged and transferred between databases. At one time, records had to be physically transported between filing destinations; the time it took to move them depended upon the transportation systems—e.g., motor vehicles, trains, airplanes, and so forth—that carried the records. Now, of course, records can be transferred between electronic databases in milliseconds through high-speed cable lines or even ordinary telephone lines.

With so much information being collected and transferred so rapidly, many have expressed concerns about its accuracy as well as the difficulties in tracking down and correcting any inaccuracies that might have been transferred. In an interview conducted for the BBC TV series *The Machine That Changed the World* (1990), Harvard law professor Arthur Miller points out that trying to correct such information is like chasing a greased pig—you may get your hands on the pig, but it is very difficult to keep the pig firmly in your grip. Although issues concerning the accuracy of personal information are clearly distinguishable from those concerning privacy per se, accuracy issues are frequently associated with privacy issues, and both are impacted by information technology.

Also consider the *duration* of information—that is, how long information can be kept. Before the information era, information was manually recorded and stored in file cabinets and then in large physical repositories; it is unlikely that report cards my parents received as a eighth-graders still exist somewhere as physical records in file cabinets, for at that time, report cards were not computerized but instead existed, literally, as ink marks on paper. But now my daughter, currently an eighth-grader, receives report cards that are both generated and stored using computer technology. As an electronic record, her report card can be kept indefinitely; and the grades she receives as an eighth-grader can follow her throughout her life.

In the past, practices involving the retention of personal data were perhaps more forgiving. Because of practical limitations, such as physical storage space, that affected how long personal data could be kept on file, much of the personal information collected and stored had to be destroyed after a certain number of years. Since information could not be archived indefinitely, people with blemished records sometimes had the opportunity to start over again—deleting records from the past provided a kind of frontier from which one could "go West" and begin again. Today, of course, one's electronic dossier would follow on the trip west, precluding the possibility of starting over with a clean slate. We can argue whether the current means of data retention is a good thing, but it is difficult to dispute the claim that now, because of cybertechnology, each of us has what Arthur Miller describes as a "womb-to-tomb dossier."

Cybertechnology has also generated privacy concerns because of the *kind* of personal information that can now be collected. For example, every time you engage in an electronic transaction, such as making a purchase with a credit card or withdrawing money from an ATM, transactional information is collected and stored in several computer databases; this information can then be transferred electronically across commercial networks to agencies that request it. Personal information, retrieved from transactional information that is stored in computer databases, has been used to construct electronic dossiers, containing detailed information about an individual's commercial transactions, including purchases made and places traveled—information that can reveal patterns in a person's preferences and habits.

Although the privacy concerns that we now associate with cybertechnology may not be totally new, or even different in kind, from those we associate with earlier technologies, few would dispute the claim that cybertechnology has exacerbated them. In Sections 5.4 through 5.7, we examine specific uses of cybertechnology that raise concerns for personal privacy. First, however, we examine the concept of personal privacy to better understand what privacy is and why we value it.

▶ 5.2 WHAT IS PERSONAL PRIVACY?

Privacy is neither clearly understood nor easily defined. We often hear that one's privacy has been "lost," "diminished," "intruded upon," "invaded," "violated," "breached," and so forth. Privacy is sometimes viewed as an "all-or-nothing" concept—something that one either has (totally) or does not have at all. At other times, privacy is viewed as something that can be diminished, for example, as a repository of personal information that can be eroded gradually. Some conceptions of privacy use a spatial metaphor, such as a zone that can be intruded upon or invaded by individuals and organizations. And sometimes privacy is thought of in terms of confidentiality that can be violated, or trust that can be breached. Because of these different conceptions, it is useful to distinguish between having privacy (in a descriptive sense) and having a right to privacy (a normative notion). We will say more about this distinction in Section 5.2.4.

Privacy analysts have pointed out that in the United States, the meaning of privacy has evolved during the past two centuries. Initially, privacy was understood in terms of freedom from (physical) intrusion. Later it became associated with freedom from interference into one's personal affairs. Most recently, privacy has come to involve access to and control of personal information. Although the main emphasis in this chapter is on informational privacy, we also briefly examine the other two views.

5.2.1 Accessibility Privacy: Freedom from Unwarranted Intrusion

In a seminal paper on privacy, Samuel Warren and Louis Brandeis suggested that privacy could be understood as "being let alone" or "being free from intrusion." Appearing in the *Harvard Law Review* in 1890, the Warren and Brandeis article made the first explicit reference to privacy as a legal right in the United States. Many Americans are astonished to find out that there is no explicit mention of privacy in either the Constitution or its first ten amendments, the Bill of Rights. However, some legal scholars believe that a right to privacy can be inferred from the Fourth Amendment, which protects citizens against unreasonable searches and seizures of personal affects (i.e., papers, artifacts, etc.) by the government. Many legal scholars believe that the Fourth Amendment also provides legal grounds for a right to privacy protection from nongovernmental intrusion as well.

Warren and Brandeis also suggested that our legal right to privacy is grounded in our "right to inviolate personality." In part, they were responding to a certain use of a new technology—not the computer, of course, but rather the camera—which had begun to threaten individual privacy in new ways. Photographs of people began to appear in newspapers, for example, in gossip columns, along with stories that were defamatory and sometimes even false. Warren and Brandeis believed that individuals have a (legal) right not be intruded upon in this manner. Because this definition of privacy as freedom from unwarranted intrusion focuses on the harm that can be caused through physical access to a person or to a person's possessions, Judith DeCew (1997) and others have described this view as *accessibility privacy*.

5.2.2 Decisional Privacy: Freedom from Interference in One's Personal Affairs

Privacy is also sometimes conceived of as freedom from interference in one's personal choices, plans, and decisions; some refer to this view as *decisional privacy*. This kind of privacy has also been associated with reproductive technologies having to do with contraception. In *Griswold v. Connecticut*, 1965, the court ruled that a person's right to get counseling about contraceptive techniques could not be denied by state laws. The view of privacy as freedom from external interference into one's personal affairs has since been appealed to in legal arguments in a series of controversial court cases, such as those involving abortion and euthanasia. For example, this view of privacy was appealed to in the landmark Supreme Court decision on abortion (*Roe v. Wade*, 1973), as well as in a state court's decision involving Karen Ann Quinlan's right to be removed from life-support systems and thus her "right to die." Because it focuses on one's right not to be interfered with decisional privacy can be distinguished from both accessibility privacy and informational privacy.

5.2.3 Informational Privacy: Control over the Flow of Personal Information

Because of the increasing use of technology to gather and store personal information, many contemporary analysts view privacy as one's ability to restrict access to and control the flow of one's personal information. Privacy concerns are now often framed in terms of questions such as: Who should have access to one's personal information? To what extent can individuals control the ways in which information about them can be gathered, stored, mined, combined, recombined, exchanged, and sold? These are our concerns in this chapter, where we focus on *informational privacy*.

Table 5-1 summarizes the three views of privacy.

TABLE 5-1   Three Views of Privacy

Accessibility Privacy	Privacy is defined as one's physically being let alone, or freedom from intrusion into one's physical space.
Decisional Privacy	Privacy is defined as freedom from interference in one's choices and decisions.
Informational Privacy	Privacy is defined as control over the flow of one's personal information, including the transfer and exchange of that information.

5.2.4   A Comprehensive Account of Privacy

James Moor (1997) has introduced an account of privacy that incorporates important elements of the nonintrusion, noninterference, and informational views of privacy. According to Moor, "an individual has privacy *in a situation* if in that particular situation the individual is *protected from intrusion, interference, and information access* by others" [italics Added]. Important in this definition is Moor's notion of "situation." He leaves the definition deliberately broad so that it can apply to a range of contexts, or "zones," that can be "declared private" in a normative sense. For example, a situation can be an "activity" or a "relationship," or it can be the "storage and access of information" in a computer.

Central to Moor's theory is a distinction between *naturally private* and *normatively private* situations, enabling us to differentiate between the conditions required for (a) having privacy, and (b) having a right to privacy. This distinction, in turn, enables us to differentiate between a loss of privacy and a violation of privacy. In a naturally private situation, individuals are protected from access and interference from others by natural means, for example, physical boundaries that one enjoys while hiking alone in the woods. In this case, privacy can be *lost* but not *violated*, because there are no norms—conventional, legal, or ethical—according to which one has a *right,* or even an expectation, to be protected. In a normatively private situation, on the other hand, individuals are protected by conventional norms (laws and policies) because they are situated in zones or contexts formally or informally established to merit normative protection. The following two scenarios will help us to differentiate between normative and natural (or descriptive) privacy.

▶ TWO SCENARIOS

First, consider a case in which you are logged on to the Internet in the computer lab at your university late one night, when no one else is around to notice. Here, you have privacy in the descriptive, or natural, sense because no one is physically observing you. If later a person happens to walk into the lab and notice you, then you have lost natural privacy. However, your privacy has not been invaded or violated because a computer lab is not a zone that has been declared normatively private, so you are not normatively protected from being seen there by others.

Next, consider a case in which you are logged on to the Internet while in your dormitory room or apartment. Someone peeps through a keyhole in the door and observes you at your computer. In this case, you have lost not only natural privacy but normative privacy as well, because dormitories and apartment buildings are examples of zones or "situations" that we, as a society, have declared normatively private.

▶ 5.3 WHY IS PRIVACY IMPORTANT?

Of what value is privacy? Is privacy universally valued? Or is it valued mainly in Western, industrialized societies where greater importance is placed on the individual? Is privacy something that is valued for its own sake—that is, does it have intrinsic value? Or is it valued as a means to an end, in which case it has only instrumental worth?

5.3.1   Is Privacy a Universal Value?

It has been argued that some non-Western nations and cultures do not value individual privacy as much as we do in the West. Alan Westin (1967) believes that countries with strong democratic political institutions consider privacy more important than do less democratic ones. Nations such as Singapore and the People's Republic of China seem to place less importance on individual privacy and greater significance on broader social values, which are perceived to benefit the state's community objectives. Even in countries such as Israel, with strong democratic systems but an even stronger priority for national security, individual privacy may not be as important a value as it is in most democratic nations. Even though privacy has at least some universal appeal, it is not valued to the same degree in all nations and cultures. As a result, it may be difficult to get universal agreement on privacy laws and policies in cyberspace.

5.3.2   Is Privacy an Intrinsic Value?

Recall our discussion of intrinsic and instrumental values in Chapter 2. There we saw that happiness has intrinsic value because it is desired for its own sake. Money, on the other hand, has instrumental value since it is desired as a means to some further end or ends.

While few would argue that privacy is an intrinsic value, desired for its own sake, others, including Charles Fried (1990) argue that while privacy is instrumental, it is not merely instrumental. Fried suggests that unlike most instrumental values that are simply one means among others, privacy is also essential, necessary to achieve important human ends, such as trust and friendship. We tend to associate intrinsic values with necessary conditions and instrumental values with contingent, or non-necessary conditions; so while privacy is instrumental in that it is a means to certain human ends, Fried shows us that it is also a necessary condition for achieving those ends.

Perhaps an analogy involving human biology can help to illustrate the central point of Fried's argument: A human heart and a human appendix each have instrumental worth, but neither is valued intrinsically. Yet while the appendix has mere instrumental or contingent worth and can be removed without serious consequences to the biological survival of a human being, having a heart—whether one's own natural heart, a transplanted heart, or even an artificial heart—is essential, or necessary, for one's biological survival. Note that we do not value our heart merely because it is a means to some end, viz., our having a biological life; instead, we value it because our biological life would be inconceivable without our heart. Similarly, Fried believes that we value privacy not simply because it serves as a means to human ends such as trust and friendship; rather, having those human ends would be inconceivable without privacy.

Although agreeing with Fried's claim that privacy is more than merely an instrumental value, James Moor (1998) takes a different approach to illustrate this point. Like Fried,

Moor argues that privacy itself is not an intrinsic value. Moor believes that privacy is the articulation, or "expression," of the "core value" *security*, which in turn is essential across cultures, for human flourishing. (We examine the concept of security as it relates to privacy in Chapter 6). And like Fried, Moor shows why privacy is necessary to achieve certain ends. Moor further suggests that as information technology insinuates itself more and more into our everyday lives, privacy becomes increasingly important for articulating, or expressing, the core value security.

Others have argued that privacy is valuable because it is essential for individual autonomy. James Rachels (1995) believes that having privacy enables us to control how much personal information we wish to disclose and how much we choose to retain. Thus privacy enables us to form relationships with individuals, which can range from intimate to casual, depending on how much information about ourselves we share with others.

5.3.3 Privacy as a Social Value

Some argue that privacy should not be thought of as a value that simply benefits individuals; for example, Alan Westin (1967) suggests that privacy is also essential for democracy. Priscilla Regan (1995) points out that we often frame debates over privacy simply in terms of how to balance privacy interests as individual goods against interests involving the larger social good; in such debates, Regan believes, interests benefiting the social good will generally override concerns regarding individual privacy. If, however, privacy is understood as not solely concerned with individual good but as contributing to the broader social good, then in debates involving the balancing of competing values, individual privacy might have a greater chance of receiving equal consideration.

Since privacy can be of value for greater social goods, such as democracy, as well as for individual autonomy and choice it is worth protecting. In Sections 5.4 through 5.6, we examine how privacy is threatened by three different practices that use cybertechnology:

a. *Data-gathering* techniques used to collect and record personal information, often without the knowledge and consent of users

b. *Data-exchange* techniques used to transfer and exchange personal data across and between computer databases, typically without the knowledge and consent of users

c. *Data-mining* techniques used to search large databases in order to generate consumer profiles based on the behavioral patterns of certain groups

▶ 5.4 GATHERING PERSONAL DATA: COLLECTION AND RECORDING MECHANISMS

Collecting and recording data about people is hardly new. Since the Roman era, governments have collected and recorded census information. Not all data-gathering and data-recording practices have caused controversy about privacy. However, cybertechnology makes it possible to collect data about individuals without their knowledge. We next examine some controversial ways in which cybertechnology is used to monitor, collect, and record personal data.

5.4.1 "Dataveillance" Techniques

Some believe that the greatest threat posed to personal privacy by cybertechnology lies in its capacity for surveillance and monitoring. Others worry less about the monitoring per se and more about the vast amounts of transactional data recorded using cybertechnology. Roger Clarke (1988) has used the term *dataveillance* to capture both the surveillance (data-monitoring) and data-recording techniques made possible by computer technology. There are, then, two distinct controversies about dataveillance: one having to do with surveillance as a form of data monitoring, and one having to do with the processing of data. In this section, we examine both aspects beginning with surveillance and monitoring techniques.

First, we should note the obvious, but relevant, point that privacy threats associated with surveillance are by no means peculiar to cybertechnology. Long before the advent of cybertechnology, individuals (e.g., private investigators and stalkers) as well as organizations, including governmental agencies all over the world, have used both electronic and nonelectronic devices to monitor individuals and groups.

Telephone conversations have been subject to government surveillance by wiretapping, but phone conversations have also been monitored in the private sector as well; for example, telephone conversations between consumers and businesses are frequently monitored, sometimes without the knowledge and consent of the consumers who are party to them. Video cameras can monitor consumers' movements while they shop at certain stores, and scanning devices such as those used by the "intelligent highway vehicle systems" such as E-ZPass subject motorists to highway surveillance while they drive. So surveillance is by no means a recent concern, or, for that matter, is it associated solely or even mainly with the use of cybertechnology.

In the past, it was not uncommon for companies to hire individuals to monitor the performance of employees in the workplace. Now, however, there are "invisible supervisors," that is, computers, that can continuously monitor the activities of employees around the clock without failing to record a single activity of the employee. We will discuss workplace monitoring in greater detail, including recent arguments that have been used both to defend and denounce computerized monitoring (see Chapter 10, where we consider workplace issues involving cybertechnology). In the remainder of this section, we consider surveillance techniques that involve monitoring and recording personal data in on-line activities, including e-commerce activities on the Internet and the Web.

In the early days of information technology, computers were owned and operated mostly by large public agencies. During that period, many feared that a strong centralized government would be able to monitor the day-to-day activities of its citizens, so some countries enacted privacy legislation and data protection guidelines to protect citizens against government practices of gathering and recording personal data. Today, however, surveillance-related privacy threats come not only from governments and their agencies, but also from those businesses and corporations who use on-line data-gathering tools and techniques.

Although on-line users may not always realize that they are under surveillance, on-line businesses can now monitor users who visit their Web sites to determine how frequently these persons visit and to draw conclusions about the preferences they show while accessing their sites. Even the number of "clickstreams"—key strokes and mouse clicks—entered by a Web-site visitor can be monitored and recorded; consider, for example, the controversies associated with one type of on-line surveillance technology, "cookies."

5.4.2 Internet Cookies

Cookies are files that Web sites send to and retrieve from the computer systems of Web users, enabling Web site owners to collect information about an individual's on-line browsing preferences whenever a person visits a Web site. The use of cookies by Web site owners and operators has generated considerable controversy, in large part because of the novel way that information about Web users is collected and stored. Data recorded about the user is stored on a file placed on the hard drive of the user's computer system; this information can then be retrieved from the user's system and resubmitted to a Web site the next time the user accesses that site. No other data-gathering mechanism actually stores the data it collects about a particular user on that user's computer system. It is also important to note that the exchange of data between the user and Web site typically occurs without the user's knowledge and consent

Those who defend the use of cookies tend to be owners and operators of on-line businesses and Web sites. These entrepreneurs and business groups maintain that they are performing a service for repeat users of a Web site by customizing the user's means of information retrieval. They also point out that, because of cookies, they are able to provide a user with a list of preferences for future visits to that Web site. Privacy advocates, on the other hand, see the matter quite differently. They argue that activities involving the monitoring and recording of an individual's activities while visiting a Web site and the subsequent downloading of that information onto a user's computer (without informing the user), clearly cross the privacy line. Some privacy advocates also point out that information gathered about a user via cookies can eventually be acquired by on-line advertising agencies, who can then target that user for on-line ads.

Initially, you might feel a sense of relief in discovering that, generally, owners and operators of one Web site cannot access cookies-related information pertaining to a user's activities on another Web site. However, information about a user's activities on different Web sites can, under certain circumstances, be compiled and aggregated by on-line advertising agencies such as DoubleClick, that pay to place advertisements in the form of banners on Web sites. The ad banners include a link from a host's Web page to the advertising agency's URL (uniform resource locator), so when a user accesses a Web page that contains an advertisement from DoubleClick, cookies can be sent to the user's system not only from the Web site requested by the user but also from the on-line advertising agency operating on that site. The advertising agency can then retrieve the cookie from the user's system and use the information it acquires about that user in its marketing advertisements. DoubleClick can also acquire information about that user from data in cookies that it retrieves from other Web sites the user has visited and where DoubleClick also advertises. The information can then be combined and cross-referenced in ways that enable a marketing profile of that user's on-line activities to be constructed and used in more direct advertisements.

Some see DoubleClick's practices as especially worrisome because DoubleClick attempted to purchase a database company called Abacus; had the acquisition gone through, Doubleclick could have compiled personal information from the two unrelated databases. We will discuss some of the implications of such a practice for privacy in a later section of this chapter that focuses on techniques and practices involved in merging computerized records.

Several privacy advocates have argued that because cookies technology involves monitoring and recording a user's activities while visiting Web sites (without the user's knowledge and consent) as well as the subsequent downloading of that information onto a user's computer system, it violates the user's privacy. To assist Internet users in their concerns about cookies, a number of privacy-enhancing tools, which are discussed in detail in Section 5.8, have recently been made available. One such product from Pretty Good Privacy (PGP), called PGPcookie.cutter, enables users to identify and block cookies on a selective basis. In the newer versions of most Web browsers, users have an option to disable cookies, so that they can either opt-in or opt-out of cookies, assuming that they (i) are aware of cookies technology, and (ii) know how to enable/disable that technology on their Web browsers.

Many privacy advocates object to the fact that the default status for most Web browsers is such that cookies will automatically be accepted unless explicitly overridden by the user. As we noted above, cookies technology involves downloading the information it gathers about users onto the user's computer system, so that cookies technology raises concerns involving encroachment or intrusion into a user's physical space as well as privacy concerns regarding the clandestine method used to gather data about users who visit Web sites.

▶ 5.5 EXCHANGING PERSONAL DATA: MERGING AND MATCHING ELECTRONIC RECORDS

In the previous section we examined ways in which personal data could be gathered using on-line surveillance techniques and then recorded electronically in computer databases. Other tools have been devised to transfer and exchange those records across and between computer databases. Simply collecting and recording personal data, in itself, might not seem terribly controversial if, for example, the data were never used, transferred, exchanged, combined, or recombined. Some would argue, however, that the mere collection of personal data itself is problematic from a privacy perspective, assuming that if data is being collected, there must be some motive or purpose for its collection. Of course, the reason, as many now realize, is that transactions involving the sale and exchange of personal data are a growing business.

Much of the personal data that is gathered electronically by one organization is later exchanged with other organizations; indeed, the very existence of certain institutions depends on the exchange and sale of personal information. Many now believe that professional information-gathering organizations such as Equifax, Experion (formerly TRW), and Trans Union (credit reporting bureaus), as well as the MIB (Medical Information Bureau) violate the privacy of individuals because of the techniques they use to facilitate the exchange of personal information across and between databases. These techniques are known as computer merging and computer matching.

5.5.1 Merging Computerized Records

Few would dispute the claim that organizations, in both the public and private sectors, have a legitimate need for information about individuals in order to make intelligent decisions concerning those individuals. For example, if you are applying for a credit card, it would be reasonable for the credit company to request information about you. However, few would also disagree with the claim that individuals should have a right to keep some personal information private. A crucial question, then, is, What kind of control can an individual expect to retain over the personal information that individual has given to an organization?

Can, for example, an individual expect that personal information provided to an organization for legitimate use in a specific context will remain within that organization?

Computer merging is the technique of extracting information from two or more unrelated databases that contain information about some individual or group of individuals, and then integrating that information into a composite file. It occurs whenever two or more disparate pieces of information contained in separate databases are combined. Consider the following sequence of events in which you voluntarily give information about yourself to three different organizations: First, you give information about your income and credit history to a lending institution in order to secure a loan. You next give information about your age and medical history to an insurance company to purchase life insurance. You then give information about your views on certain social issues to a political organization you wish to join. Each of these organizations can be said to have a legitimate need for information to make certain decisions about you—insurance companies have a legitimate need to know about your age and medical history before agreeing to sell you life insurance and lending institutions have a legitimate need to know about your income and credit history before agreeing to lend you money to purchase a house or a car. And insofar as you voluntarily give these organizations the information requested, no breach of your privacy has occurred.

Now suppose that without your knowledge and consent, information about you that resides in the insurance company's database is transferred and merged with information about you that resides in the lending institution's database or in the political organization's database. Even though you voluntarily gave certain information about yourself to three different organizations, and even though you voluntarily authorized each organization to have the information, it does not follow that you authorized any one organization to have some combination of that information. When organizations merge information about you in a way that you did not specifically authorize, you lose control over the way in which that information about you is exchanged. Yet this is precisely what happens to much of the personal information that businesses and organizations gather and store electronically.

▶ **CASE ILLUSTRATION:** Merging Information Retrieved from DoubleClick's and Abacus' Databases

In our discussion of cookies technology in the previous section, we described how DoubleClick, an on-line advertising company, used cookies to compile data from multiple Web sites on which it placed DoubleClick ad banners. If, for example, DoubleClick advertised on 1,000 Web sites, it could retrieve cookie files from any user who visited any of those sites. Because DoubleClick was able to compile the cookies-related information it received from its advertisement banners that had been clicked on by users at multiple Web sites, DoubleClick was in a position to compile and cross-reference cookies-related information in ways that individual Web site owners and operators themselves cannot. As we noted earlier, DoubleClick's policy regarding the information it gathers from cookies has been criticized by many privacy advocates.

To compound the controversy surrounding DoubleClick's data-gathering practices, the on-line advertising company announced in November 1999 that it planned to purchase Abacus Direct Corporation, a database company. Abacus's databases contained not only records of consumer's catalogue purchases but also actual names and telephone numbers that had been collected by Abacus primarily from off-line transactions. DoubleClick was now putting itself in position to merge the Abacus database with its own database, which consisted of information gained primarily from Internet cookies files.

With its newly merged data, DoubleClick would have an information mosaic about individuals that included not merely anonymous and indirect information (such as IP addresses and ISP-related information) but also direct personal information. The Web profiles in DoubleClick's original database, gathered via cookies, included data about where users (each with an IP address) go on-line, how long they stay on-line, and so on. That information could now be compared to and combined with explicit personal information (gathered off-line and stored in Abacus's databases), including names, addresses, and phone numbers.

In January 2000, Double Click was sued by a woman who complained that her right to privacy had been violated. She claimed that DoubleClick's business practices were deceptive, because the company had quietly reversed an earlier policy by which it provided businesses with only anonymous data about Internet users (acquired from cookies files). Because of public pressure, DoubleClick backed off from its proposal to purchase Abacus, and many users were able to see for the first time the privacy threats that can result from merging electronic data.

5.5.2 Matching Computerized Records

Computer matching is a variation on the technology used to merge computerized records. It involves cross-checking information in two or more unrelated databases to produce matching records, or "hits." In federal and state government applications, this technique has been used by various agencies and departments for the express purpose of creating a new file containing a list of potential law violators, as well as individuals who have actually broken the law or who are suspected of having broken the law.

Consider a case in which you complete a series of forms for various federal and state government agencies, such as the Internal Revenue Service (IRS), your state government's motor vehicle registration department, or your local government's property tax assessment department. You supply the specific information requested and in addition, you include general information requested on each form, such as your social security number and driver's license number, which can be used as identifiers in matching records about you that reside in multiple databases. The information is then electronically stored in the agencies' respective databases, and routine checks (matches) can be made against information (records) contained in those databases. For example, your property tax records can be matched against your federal tax records to see whether you own an expensive house but declared only a small income. Records in an IRS database of divorced or single fathers can be matched against a database containing records of mothers receiving welfare payments to generate a list of potential deadbeat parents.

In filling out the various governmental forms, you agreed to give some information to each government agency. It is by no means clear, however, that you authorized information given to any one agency to be exchanged with other agencies. You had no say in the way information that you authorized for use in one context was subsequently used in another. Because of this contextual violation of personal information, some have argued that practices involving computerized matching of records containing personal data raises serious threats for personal privacy. The debate over computerized record matching has been hotly contested, and it has been denounced because of its implications for stereotyping and profiling certain classes or groups of individuals. Computerized record matching has also been criticized by civil-liberties groups who fear that such a practice might lead to a new form of social control.

Defenders of matching, of course, see the matter in a different light. At first glance, it might seem that matching computer records is a socially desirable practice because it enables us to track down deadbeat parents, welfare cheats, and the like. Whereas supporters of computerized matching such as Richard Kusserow (1995) have argued that computer matching is needed to "root out government waste and fraud," critics such as John Shattuck (1995) maintain that matching computerized records violates individual freedoms, including one's right to privacy. Although few would object to the ends that could be achieved, we can question whether the practice of computerized matching is compatible with individual privacy.

Even if computerized record matching does help to root out governmental waste, would that fact alone justify such a practice? Consider this counterexample: Suppose that 24-hour video surveillance and daily drug testing of government employees also help to root out government waste and fraud—would such means also be justifiable in order to reach the desired end? Proponents of computer matching might argue that 24-hour video surveillance and daily drug testing of government workers violate the privacy of workers in ways that matching computerized records does not.

Opponents have pointed out that computer matches have been made even when there was no suspicion that a particular individual or group of individuals had violated the law. For example, computer records of entire categories of individuals, such as government employees, have been matched against databases containing records of welfare recipients on the chance that a "hit" will identify one or more "welfare cheats." One popular line of reasoning frequently cited to defend computer matching is: If you have done nothing wrong, you have nothing to worry about. Critics, however, point out that such a defense misses an important point—one that is illustrated in the following scenario.

▶ **SCENARIO:** Using Matching Techniques to Monitor Mail Entering and Leaving Your Neighborhood

Imagine that local law enforcement authorities have heard rumors that members of an organized crime syndicate have been communicating via the United States Postal Service with someone living in your neighborhood. On the basis of these rumors, they are eager to investigate this matter but lack sufficient evidence to obtain a search warrant. Instead, the authorities decide to intercept the mail sent to and from homes in your neighborhood and then compare the information included in the return and destination addresses on the envelopes against a list of names and addressees of suspected mobsters. When you discover what the authorities are doing and you protest against it, you are told, "If you have nothing to hide, you have nothing to worry about." Of course, you could respond that even though you have nothing to hide, you believe that you still have quite a bit to worry about; that is, you have to worry about how to retain your privacy under such conditions.

Computer matching is like the cross-checking procedures in the above scenario. Although many citizens might be inclined to view the kind of electronic surveillance implicit in computer matching less intrusive, or at least less objectionable, than the physical surveillance techniques used in intercepting and cross checking the mail sent to and from a particular neighborhood, both practices raise serious privacy concerns.

Another line of argumentation sometimes used to defend a practice like computer matching is as follows:

Privacy is a legal right.

Legal rights are not absolute.

When one violates the law (i.e., commits a crime), one forfeits one's legal rights.

Therefore, criminals have forfeited their right to privacy.

Initially, this line of reasoning seems quite plausible, but does it apply in the case of computerized record matching? First of all, this argument assumes that we have an explicit legal right to privacy. Let us assume, for the sake of argument, that we have such a right and that all legal rights are (or ought to be) conditional only. Even with the addition of these two assumptions, problems remain: for example, those who maintain that a deadbeat parent has, in violating the law, given up his right to privacy accorded to individuals who have not broken the law seem at the same time to either disregard or ignore any right to provacy accorded to individuals who have not broken the law. For it was only by matching records of innocent individuals that a "hit," identifying one or more alleged criminals, was generated. So even if criminals do forfeit their right to privacy, the process of identifying these criminals requires that several non-criminals will forfeit that right as well.

▶ **CASE ILLUSTRATION:** Biometric Technology and Data Matching at Super Bowl XXXV

A computerized matching technique that involves the use of biometric identifiers has been used by some government agencies. At Super Bowl XXXV in January 2001, a facial-recognition technology scanned the faces of individuals entering the stadium. The digitized facial images were then instantly matched against images in a centralized database of suspected criminals and terrorists. At the time, this practice was criticized by civil-liberties proponents. (As might be suspected, however, the attitudes of many changed significantly later that year following the tragic events of September 11.)

We will examine this biometric technique in greater detail in Chapter 7, where we discuss cybercrime. However, it is useful at this point to discuss how this biometric-based matching technique differs from the computerized record-matching practice we considered in this section.

Initially, one might argue that the biometric-based matching technique used to scan and match faces of individuals at stadiums and airports, as well as other public places, is essentially no different from the computerized record-matching operations previously used to catch welfare cheats and deadbeat parents. But in traditional computerized record matching, all of the databases involved contain records of individuals who were (or should have been) assumed to be innocent. As we saw, records of government workers (presumed to be innocent) were matched against records of welfare recipients (also presumed to be innocent) to ferret out any persons who just happen to be in both groups. In the case of the face-recognition program used at Super Bowl XXXV, however, images of persons entering the football stadium were matched against a database of persons already known (or at least suspected) to be criminals and terrorists. So the objectives of the targeted matches at Super Bowl XXXV were much more specific than were those of the "fishing expeditions," the traditional computerized record-matching practices. Perhaps this is one reason why the biometric-based matching operations aimed at catching terrorists and dangerous criminals have been less controversial than traditional record-matching practices used by federal and state governments.

▶ 5.6 MINING PERSONAL DATA

A form of data analysis that uses techniques gained from research and development in artificial intelligence (AI) has been used to "mine" personal data. Formally referred to as Knowledge Discovery in Databases, or KDD, the process is now more commonly known as *data mining*. Essentially, data mining involves the indirect gathering of personal information through an analysis of implicit patterns discoverable in data. Data-mining activities can generate new and sometimes nonobvious classifications or categories; as a result, individuals whose data is mined can become identified with or linked to certain newly created groups that they might never have imagined to exist. This is further complicated by the fact that current privacy laws offer individuals no protection with respect to how information about them acquired through data-mining activities is subsequently used, even though important decisions can be made about those individuals based on the patterns found in the mined personal data. So data-mining technology raises special concerns for personal privacy.

5.6.1 How Does Data Mining Threaten Personal Privacy?

What is so special about the privacy concerns raised by data-mining techniques? For example, how do they differ from privacy issues introduced by more traditional data-retrieval techniques, such as computerized merging and matching operations that we examined in Section 5.5? For one thing, privacy laws as well as informal data-protection guidelines have been established for protecting personal data that is

- *explicit* in databases (in the form of specific electronic records),
- *confidential* in nature (e.g., data involving medical, financial, or academic records),
- *exchanged* between or across databases.

However, virtually no legal or normative protections apply to personal data manipulated in the data-mining process, where personal information is typically

- *implicit* in the data,
- *nonconfidential* in nature,
- *not exchanged* between databases.

Unlike personal data that resides in explicit records in databases, information acquired about persons via data mining is often derived from implicit patterns in the data. The patterns can suggest "new" facts, relationships, or associations about a person, placing that person in a newly "discovered" category or group. Also, because most personal data collected and used in data-mining applications is considered neither confidential nor intimate in nature, there is a tendency to presume that such data must by default be *public* data. And unlike the personal data that is often exchanged between or across two or more databases in traditional database-retrieval processes, in the data-mining process personal data is typically manipulated within a single database, or a *data warehouse*.

The following scenario (Tavani 1999)illustrates one way that data-mining techniques can threaten personal privacy. As you consider the privacy issues raised in this scenario, keep in mind an interesting assumption that Helen Nissenbaum (1997) has exposed on the part of those in the commercial sector:

An aggregate of information does not violate privacy if its parts, taken individually, do not.

Also consider the question raised by Joseph Fulda (1999):

"Is it possible for data that do not in themselves deserve legal protection to contain implicit patterns that deserve such protection?"

▶ **SCENARIO:** Data Mining at the XYZ Bank

Consider a hypothetical case involving Lee, a junior executive at the ABC Marketing Firm, who has recently applied for an automobile loan at the XYZ Bank. To secure the loan Lee agrees to complete the usual forms required by the bank for loan transactions. He indicates that he has been employed at the ABC Marketing Company for more than three years and that his current annual salary is $120,000. He also indicates that he has $10,000 in a separate savings account, which he intends to use as a down payment for a new BMW. On the loan form, Lee also indicates that he is currently repaying a $15,000 personal loan used to finance a family vacation to Europe the previous year.

Thus far, the transaction between Lee and the bank seems appropriate. To borrow money from XYZ Bank, Lee has authorized the bank to have the information about him, that is, his current employment, salary, savings, outstanding loans, etc., that it needs to make an informed decision as to whether or not to grant him the loan.

Lee has given the bank information about him for use in one context, viz., to make a decision about whether or not he should be granted a loan to purchase a new automobile. He is assured that the information given to the bank will not be exchanged with a third party without first getting Lee's explicit consent. So unlike cases involving the computerized merging and matching of records that we considered in Section 5.5, no information about Lee is to be either exchanged or cross referenced between databases. However, it is unclear whether the bank has agreed not to use the information it now has in its databases about Lee for certain in-house analyses.

Next, imagine that the bank's computing center runs a data-mining program on information in its customer databases and discovers a number of patterns. One reveals that executives earning more than $120,000 but less than $150,000 annually, who purchase luxury cars (such as BMWs), and who take expensive vacations often go into business for themselves within five years of employment. A second data-mining algorithm reveals that the majority of marketing entrepreneurs declare bankruptcy within one year of starting their own businesses. All of a sudden, Lee is a member of a group that neither he nor possibly even the loan officers at the bank had ever known to exist, *viz.*, the group of marketing executives likely to start a business and then declare bankruptcy within a year. With this new category and new information about Lee, the bank determines that Lee, and people that fit into Lee's group, are long-term credit risks.

5.6.2 Do Data-mining Practices Raise Special Privacy Concerns?

Why does the mining of data about Lee by the XYZ Bank raise concerns for privacy? Although Lee voluntarily gave the bank information about his annual salary, about previous vacation loans, and about the type of automobile he intended to purchase, he gave each piece of information for a specific purpose and use, in order that the bank could make a meaningful determination about Lee's request for an automobile loan. It is, however, by no means clear that Lee authorized the bank to use disparate pieces of that information for more general data-mining analyses that would reveal patterns involving Lee that neither he nor the bank could have anticipated at the outset.

Why is the mining of data in Lee's case controversial from a privacy perspective? First, the information that Lee is someone likely to start his own business, which would probably lead to his declaring personal bankruptcy, was not explicit in any of the data (records) about Lee; rather it was implicit in patterns of data about people similar to Lee in certain respects but vastly different from him in other respects. Second, the information about Lee was extracted from databases internal to the bank and was not transferred to or exchanged with any external databases. Third, at least some of the information about Lee, for example, that he took a vacation in Europe the previous year, can be considered public rather than private, or intimate, information about him. Finally, Lee's case illustrates how data-mining can generate new categories and groups such that the people whom the data-mining analysis identifies with those groups would very likely have no idea that they would be included as members. And we have seen that, in the case of Lee, certain decisions can be made about members of these newly generated groups simply by virtue of those individuals being identified as members. For example, it is doubtful that Lee would have known that he was a member of a group of professional individuals likely to start a business, and that he was a member of a group whose businesses were likely to end in bankruptcy. The "discovery" of such groups is, of course, a result of the use of data-mining tools.

Recall that no information about Lee was exchanged with databases outside the bank, so the bank, as agreed, did not transfer data about Lee to an external database without Lee's consent. However, the bank did use information about Lee internally in a way that he had not explicitly authorized. And it is in this sense—unauthorized internal use by data users—that data-mining raises serious concerns for personal privacy. Note also that even if Lee had been granted the loan for the automobile, the bank's data-mining practices would still have raised serious privacy concerns. Lee was merely one of many bank customers who had voluntarily given certain personal information about themselves to the bank for use in one context—in this example, a loan request—and subsequently had that information used in ways that they did not specifically authorize.

In Table 5-2, we summarize some of the differences in mining, matching, and merging techniques used to process personal information.

TABLE 5-2 Mining, Matching, and Merging Techniques for Manipulating Personal Data

Data **Merging**	A data-exchange process in which personal data from two or more sources is combined to create a "mosaic" of individuals that would not be discernable from the individual pieces of data alone.
Data **Matching**	A technique in which two or more unrelated pieces of personal information are cross-referenced and compared to generate a match, or "hit," that suggests a person's connection with two or more groups.
Data **Mining**	A technique for "unearthing" implicit patterns in large single databases, or "data warehouses," revealing statistical data that associates individuals with nonobvious groups; user profiles can be constructed from these patterns.

5.6.3 Data-mining on the Internet

Traditionally, the mining of personal data has depended on large commercial databases called data warehouses, which store the data, consisting primarily of transactional information. One chain of grocery stores in the Midwest discovered, through data-mining, that men who shopped for disposable diapers for infants during the evening hours also purchased beer. So the food chain decided to relocate its supply of beer next to the diapers. Clearly, this use of data-mining has more to do with optimizing the movement of inventory than with personal information about the men who purchased the diapers and beer. Nonetheless, we can see how one use of data-mining can easily lead to other uses that threaten privacy.

Data-mining techniques are now also used by commercial Web sites to analyze data about Internet users, which can then be sold to third parties. Unlike data mined from large data warehouses, which is in turn usually mined from data originally gained from consumer transactions, personal data mined from the Internet (from personal Web pages, as well as from noncommercial Web sites) need not be (and frequently is not) transactional. Because of Internet commerce, however, much transactional information now, of course, can also be gained from the Web as well.

While some users realize that data about their consumer transactions on the Internet are likely to be recorded and exchanged with other databases, few assume that data included on their own (noncommercial) Web pages would be analyzed by data-mining programs. For one thing, the amount of data on the Internet is so vast that one might assume it impossible to mine that data in ways that could be useful. However, because data-mining tools employ sophisticated and advanced AI technology, they can "comb" through massive amounts of data not possible to analyze with traditional information-retrieval techniques.

"Intelligent agents," or what some now describe as "softbots" (intelligent software robots or agents) that act on behalf of human beings, are able to sift through and analyze the mounds of data on the Internet. Both sophisticated search engines and *metasearch* engines "crawl" through the Web in order to uncover general patterns in information retrieved from their requests across multiple Web sites. In Section 5.7.1, we examine some specific ways in which the use of Internet search engines raise privacy concerns even though the kind of personal information retrieved from on-line search facilities might not seem to need explicit privacy protection. To see why such protection might indeed be needed in these cases, however, we first examine some questions underlying the problem of "privacy in public."

▶ 5.7 THE PROBLEM OF PROTECTING PERSONAL PRIVACY IN PUBLIC

Thus far, we have examined how cybertechnology can be used to gather, exchange, and mine personal information. With the exception of data-mining, which manipulates personal, but noneconfidential information, the kind of personal information gathered and exchanged was often confidential and intimate in nature. For example, we saw how financial and medical records could be exchanged between two or more databases using computerized merging and matching. This confidential and very personal information is referred to as Non-Public Personal Information (NPI). Privacy analysts are now concerned about a different kind of personal information—Public Personal Information (PPI), which is neither confidential nor intimate and which is also being gathered, exchanged, and mined using cybertechnology.

PPI includes information such as where you work or attend school or what kind of car you drive; it is information about you as a particular person. PPI has not enjoyed the privacy protection that has been granted to NPI.

Until recently, most concerns about personal information that was gathered and exchanged electronically were limited to NPI, and because of the attention it has received, privacy laws and policies were established to protect NPI. But now privacy advocates are extending their concern to PPI; they are arguing that PPI deserves greater legal and normative protection than it currently has. Helen Nissenbaum (1998) refers to this challenge as the "problem of protecting privacy in public."

Why should the collection of PPI generate concern about personal privacy? Suppose that I discover some information about you: You are a junior at Technical University, you frequently attend your university's football games, and you are actively involved in your university's computer science club. In one sense, the information that I have discovered about you is personal, because it is about *you* (as a person), but it is also public, because it pertains to things that you do in the public sphere. Should you be worried that this information about you is so easily available? Certainly in the past, the public availability of such seemingly harmless and uncontroversial information about you was no cause for concern. Imagine that eighty years ago a citizen petitioned his or her congressperson to draft legislation protecting the privacy of each citizen's movements in public places. It would have been difficult then to make a strong case for such legislation; no one would have seen any need to protect that kind of personal information. But now some are arguing that we need to protect privacy in public, that our earlier assumptions are no longer tenable. Helen Nissenbaum (1997) notes that many in the commercial sector proceed from an assumption that she believes is misleading, that "[t]here is a realm of public information about persons to which no privacy norms apply." Keep this assumption in mind as you consider the following scenario.

▶ **SCENARIO:** Shopping at SuperMart and Nile.com

Suppose that you decide to shop for groceries one day at SuperMart. If I see you enter or leave SuperMart, or if we are both shopping in this store at the same time, I now have information that you shop (or have at least, once, shopped) at SuperMart. This information could be considered "public" both in the sense that it was acquired in a public forum and in the sense that it is neither intimate nor confidential in nature. Although this information is about *you as a person,* it is not the kind of personal information to which, as a society, we would typically grant privacy protection.

If I also happen to pass by you in one of the aisles at SuperMart, I can observe the contents of your shopping basket; I may notice that you are purchasing several bottles of wine but relatively little food. Again, I have acquired this information about you by observing your activity in a public forum, so it would be considered public information, and as such, would not warrant any normative privacy protection. So what, then, exactly is the problem of privacy in public? Why should we be concerned about information that is gathered about what we do in public places?

Let us continue the shopping metaphor, but this time consider shopping that takes place in cyberspace. Suppose you log on to the Internet and decide to visit an on-line bookstore called Nile.com to locate a particular book that you are considering purchasing. On the one hand, you cannot be observed by people in physical space nor can you be seen by other on-line customers on the Nile.com Web site, for you are visiting this book store on a computer located in your own home. However, from the second that you log on to the Nile.com Web site, information about you is being intentionally gathered and carefully recorded: The cookies technology that we described in Section 5.4.2 records the exact time that you entered the Nile bookstore, and it will record the exact time that you leave. As you make contact with the Nile Web site, Nile requests a cookie file from your computer to determine whether you have previously visited this site. If you have visited this site before and clicked on items that interested you, Nile can find a record of these items. The information stored in that cookie file can be used by Nile to alert you to newly released books that it has determined might interest you, based on an analysis of the data Nile collected from your previous visits to its site. The information that Nile now has about you does not seem categorically different from the information that SuperMart might also have about you (assuming that you used the store's "courtesy card" in making your purchases). However, there are significant differences in the ways that information about you can be gathered, recorded, and then used as a result of your shopping at each store.

When you shopped in physical space at SuperMart, only your actual purchases could be recorded and stored in SuperMart's databases. Items that might have only caught your attention and items that you might also have picked up or even placed in your cart at one point while shopping but did not eventually purchase at the check-out register are not recorded by SuperMart's data-collection system. However, as you shop, or even browse, at Nile, there is a record of virtually every move you make—every book that you search, review, etc., as well as the one(s) you purchase. Yet, just like the information gathered about your shopping habits in physical space at SuperMart, this personal information that Nile has gathered about your browsing and shopping habits on-line is considered and treated as public information.

Now we can see why some people worry about having their movements in cyberspace tracked and recorded. The information Nile gathered about you is, in effect, *Nile's* information, even though it pertains to *you* as a person; Nile now owns that information about you, as well as the information it has about its other customers, and is, in principle at least, free to do with that information whatever it chooses. On the one hand, the information seems fairly innocuous—after all, who really cares which books you happen to browse or purchase? However, this information can be combined with other information about your on-line transactions at additional Web sites to create a consumer profile of you, which can then be sold to a third party.

One argument that on-line entrepreneurs might advance to defend these business practices is that if a user puts information about him- or herself into the public domain of the Internet, then that information is no longer private. Of course, one response to this line of reasoning could be to question whether users clearly understand the ways that data they submit might subsequently be used.

In the Nile scenario, Nile used information about you in ways that you neither authorized nor intended. Helen Nissenbaum (1998) believes that such practices violate "contextual integrity." We can also ask, Is it fair that businesses can "own" information about us and then do with that information whatever they please for as long as they want? Joseph Fulda (2001) questions whether the old legal rule which states, "Anything put by a person in the public domain can be viewed as public information," should still apply. He admits that such a rule may have served us well, but only before data was "mined" to produce profiles and other kinds of patterns about individuals.

5.7.1 Search Engines and the Retrieval of Personal Information from the Internet

Internet search engines are valuable for directing us to available on-line resources for academic research, commerce, recreation, and so forth, so it might be surprising to find that search-engine technology too can be controversial from the perspective of personal privacy. But Internet search engines can be used to locate personal information about individuals; in some cases that information resides in public records, many of which are available to Internet users. In other cases, it resides in commercial databases (such as docusearch.com) and is available to Internet users for a small fee. We shall see that other types of personal information about individuals is available because it has been placed on the Internet inadvertently, often without the knowledge and consent of those affected.

How can search-engine technology conflict with personal privacy? Consider that by entering someone's name in a search-engine program's entry box, users can potentially locate and retrieve information about that individual. Also consider that individuals may be unaware that their names are included on a Web site or in databases accessible to a search-engine. Consider that those who are not Internet users might be altogether unfamiliar with search-engine programs and their ability to retrieve personal information. Each of these considerations raises questions about search engines and personal privacy. Marie Wright and John Kakalik (1997) note that certain information about individuals that was once difficult to find and even more difficult to cross-reference is now readily accessible and collectible through on-line automated search facilities such as Internet search engines.

The fact that one can search the Internet for information about someone does not seem terribly controversial. After all, people regularly place information about themselves on Web sites (or perhaps authorize someone else to do it for them). But there is also personal information on some Web pages that individuals have neither included nor explicitly authorized. David Kotz (1998) points out that since many e-mail discussion lists (electronic mailing lists, or listservers) are stored and archived on Web pages, it is possible for a search engine to locate information that users have contributed to them. Search engines can also search through archives of news groups such as Usenet, where on-line users also post and retrieve information. One such group, *DejaNews*, was set up to save permanent copies of new postings; as such, it provides search engines with a comprehensive, searchable database. Because the various news groups contain links to information posted by a person, they can provide search-engine users with considerable insight into that person's interests and activities.

One might also assume that, by virtue of the fact that it is available to the public, information available on the Internet, including personal information is public information. But should such information be unprotected merely because it is available for viewing by the public? The following scenario (Tavani 1998) may cause us to question whether at least some personal information included on Web pages or in databases accessible to Internet users should not be viewed as public information.

▶ **SCENARIO:** Using an Internet Search Engine to Locate a Friend

Consider that an individual named Pat contributes to a cause sponsored by a gay/lesbian organization. Pat's contribution is later acknowledged in the organization's newsletter, a hardcopy publication that has a limited distribution. The organization's publications, including its newsletter, are subsequently converted to electronic format and posted on the organization's Web site. That Web site is then "discovered" by a search-engine program, and an entry with its address is recorded in the search engine's database. Assume that Pat has read the hardcopy newsletter that describes the various contributions members have made to the organization. It is possible that Pat has read the newsletter but still has no idea that it is also on the organization's Web site and that the existence of this Web site has been discovered by one or more search engines.

Now, further suppose that Pat is an acquaintance of yours from high school and that you have not seen Pat since you both graduated two years ago. You cross paths briefly at a sporting event and agree to get together for lunch to catch up on your lives since your high school days. Curious to learn what Pat has recently been up to, and to prepare yourself to discuss some of these activities with Pat when the two of you get together for lunch, you decide to inquire about Pat via the Internet. You access the Google.com search engine, type Pat's full name in the entry box, and Google returns a series of "hits" about Pat, one of which identifies Pat in connection with the gay/lesbian organization. What would you likely infer about Pat on the basis of this hit?

Until now, you had no reason to wonder about Pat's sexual orientation or preferences. Pat has never disclosed to you any information about sexual preferences, nor has Pat revealed through any public activities of which you had been aware any behavior traits associated with homosexuals. Yet as a result of a hit returned from the Google search engine, you start to question Pat's sexual orientation.

Perhaps Pat is, as a matter of fact, homosexual, and perhaps Pat is not. Pat's sexual orientation is not what is at issue here. (Of course, even if Pat is a homosexual, and even if Pat is not troubled that others are aware of it, it is still problematic, from a privacy perspective, that inferences about Pat's sexual orientation can be made in ways that Pat is unable to affect or influence.)

Since contributors to the gay/lesbian organization might have no idea that the organization's newsletter is publicly available on-line to anyone with Internet access, we can ask whether the use of search-engine technology in Pat's case has raised any legitimate privacy concerns. Has Pat's privacy been violated in any way? Or is the fact that the information about Pat was already in some sense public (it existed in printed material that was available to relatively few people) a relevant matter? Can't we make a reasonable case for normatively protecting that information in cyberspace?

We next consider a strategy to resolve disputes involving personal information that seems to span the private vs. public divide.

5.7.2 Accessing Public Records via the Internet

How can the use of on-line search facilities to access publicly documented personal information be so controversial from a privacy perspective? All of the personal information about Pat was already public in some sense, that is, it was PPI. Note that there is also another kind of personal information that can be considered public—viz., personal information in public records located in files in municipal buildings and accessible to the general public. Public records have been available to anyone willing to go to those municipal buildings and request hardcopy versions of them. Some municipalities charge a small fee to retrieve and copy the requested records.

Many of these public records have now been posted on government Web sites. Because this kind of information is now readily accessible on-line, has that changed anything? Perhaps an equally important question is: Why were such records made public in the first place? Were they made public so that companies could collect the information in them, mine it, combine it with other information, and then sell it for a profit? Pre-Internet entrepreneurs could have done this. But early "information entrepreneurs" without computer technology would have had to hire legions of clerks to collect the (publicly available) data, sort it according to some scheme, and then compile and print it for sale. The process would have been physically impractical and hardly profitable, given the labor it involved; it would probably never have occurred to anyone even to attempt it prior to the advent of sophisticated information technology. Clearly, records were not made public so that entrepreneurs could manipulate and sell information mined from them. So again, we can ask ourselves, *Why were* our public records made public in the first place?

For governmental agencies at all levels to operate efficiently, records, containing personal information, need to be accessible. For example, municipal governments need real estate information for tax-assessment purposes, state governments need information about motor vehicle owners and operators, and federal governments need social security and income tax information. Records have to be easily accessible to and transferable and exchangeable between governmental agencies at various levels. Since they contain information that is neither confidential nor intimate, they are, with good reason, "public records." It has been assumed that the availability of public records causes no harm to individuals, and that communities are better served because of the access and flow of those records for what seems like legitimate purposes. But information-gathering companies now access those public records, manipulate them to discover patterns useful to businesses, and then sell that information to third parties. Was *this* the original intent for making such information accessible to the public?

Some information entrepreneurs have inferred that because public records are, by definition, "public," they ought to be made available on the Internet, arguing:

Public records have always been available to the public.

Public records have always resided in public space.

The Internet is a public space.

Therefore, all of public records ought to be made available on the Internet.

Many in the commercial sector believe that offices responsible for maintaining public records now have a legal obligation to make *all* public records available on-line; Many information merchants are pleased by the number of public records that are, in fact, already on-line, but they believe that until all public records have been made available electronically, those responsible for overseeing these records have not gone far enough. The presumption here is that the government has no right to restrict or limit, in any way, information that has been deemed appropriate for public records. Is this a reasonable presumption? Consider two recent incidents, one involving public records at the city level and the other at the state level, that have outraged many citizens.

▶ **TWO CASE ILLUSTRATIONS:** Using the Internet to Access Public Records in the City of Merrimack, New Hampshire and in the State of Oregon

Merrimack, New Hampshire, made real estate records available on-line; with a networked computer, one could enter the address of any house in Merrimack and retrieve the current tax assessment for the house, the price paid by the most recent owner, and a description of the physical layout of the house, including the location of doors and windows. Many of Merrimack's citizens were outraged that this information was available over the Internet, although the same information had previously been available as public records, stored in physical file cabinets at City Hall. Some residents worried that prospective burglars could plan break-ins by accessing the detailed physical layouts of Merrimack homes, readily available on-line.

Oregon placed the state's motor vehicle records on the Internet. Michael Scanlan (2001) describes how an independent computer consultant used the means available to any private citizen to purchase data from Oregon's Department of Motor Vehicles, which was already available off-line to anyone willing to pay a small fee. Once he purchased the information and converted it to electronic format, the consultant set up a Web site where any Internet user could, for a small fee, enter an Oregon license plate number and obtain the name and address of the owner of the registered vehicle. Citizens of Oregon were outraged, and eventually, the state's governor intervened and persuaded the consultant to close down the Web site.

We ask again, What was the purpose of making such records public in the first place? Was it to facilitate commerce in the private sector? Of course, selling information, as the State of Oregon did, can now be a source of revenue for governments. But what are the ethical implications of a state selling public records that will be placed on-line?

Whether public records should be placed on the Internet could be debated by setting the public's right to know against the private rights of individuals, but this might not be the best way to frame the debate in the Internet age. A compromise solution to the problems raised by putting public records on-line might be to post them on password-protected Web sites with restrictions for access. Of course, this would not satisfy information merchants, who want unrestricted access to information in public records. Can cybertechnology itself provide us with solutions to some of our privacy concerns?

▶ 5.8 A TECHNOLOGICAL SOLUTION TO ON-LINE PRIVACY CONCERNS: PRIVACY-ENHANCING TOOLS (PETs)

We have seen how cybertechnology has exacerbated privacy concerns. Ironically, perhaps, cybertechnology also provides tools that can protect the privacy and personal information of users while they are engaged in on-line activities.

Although privacy advocates have typically argued for stronger laws to protect the privacy of individuals, the e-commerce sector has lobbied for voluntary controls and industry self-regulation as an alternative to more privacy legislation, and the solutions proposed by one camp have generally been unacceptable to the other. Now, some members of each camp appear ready to embrace a compromise: *privacy-enhancing tools* or *PETs,* which users can employ to either (a) protect their personal identity while interacting with the Web, or (b) protect the privacy of communications (such as e-mail) sent over the Internet. An example of (b) is encryption tools that encode and decode e-mail messages. We will examine them in Chapter 8. Here we consider whether PETs actually do protect users' identities in on-line activities.

Certain PETs enable users to navigate the Internet either anonymously or pseudonymously; some of the best-known anonymity tools are available from Anonymizer.com. It is important to note that although Anonymizer users enjoy anonymity while visiting Web sites, they are not anonymous to Anonymizer.com or to their own ISPs. A user's activities on a Web site can be recorded in server log files and can thus be traced back to a specific ISP and IP address. To enjoy complete anonymity on the Internet, on-line users need tools that do not require them to place their trust in a single "third party" (such as Anonymizer). Two anonymity programs that do not require such trust are Crowds and Onion Routing.

Crowds is an anonymity tool based on the idea that people can be anonymous when they blend into a crowd. Reiter and Rubin (1999) point out that when Crowds users submit an Internet request, such as the URL of a certain Web site, the request is sent from a "randomly selected member of their crowd." So neither the server at the end of the destination (e.g., a particular Web site) nor any member of the "crowd" can determine where the request originated. Although we could discuss PETs in more detail, in this chapter we are interested in determining whether PETs are adequate tools for protecting the privacy of users.

Although PETs enable users to roam the Web with relative anonymity or pseudo-nymity, they are not useful for e-commerce transactions in which users must reveal their identities to complete transactions. Some e-commerce sites provide a stated privacy policy that is backed by certified "trustmarks" or "trust seals" (discussed in more detail in Section 5.9.1). These trust agreements between users and e-commerce sites can be viewed as PETs in that they are intended to protect a user's privacy while engaging in on-line consumer transactions. But are they adequate to the task? To answer this question, we will analyze PETs relation to consumer education, informed consent, and social equity.

5.8.1 Educating Users about PETs

How are on-line users supposed to find out about the existence of PETs? Should users have to find out about these tools themselves? There is currently no requirement for on-line entrepreneurs to inform users about the existence of PETs or to make those tools available to them. Furthermore, on-line consumers must not only discover that PETs exist, but they must also learn how to use these tools. So at present, responsibility for learning about the existence of PETs is incumbent upon on-line consumers.

If PETs are not automatically bundled with either operating-system or application software, or if they are not provided as part of the Web interfaces of on-line vendors, who is responsible for distributing them? Should on-line entrepreneurs provide PETs, or should consumers be required to locate PETs and then install them on their systems? Is it reasonable and is it fair to expect users to be responsible for these tasks?

Consider PGP (Pretty Good Privacy), one of the more popular PETs. The PGP tool PGPcookie.cutter enabled users to avoid having cookie files sent to their computers. And fortunately for on-line users, PGP was available free of charge. However, the onus was on users, first to discover that PGP applications existed, and then to track down their location and download them on to their computers. Today, of course, the latest versions of most Web browsers allow users to reject cookies, but the default setting on many browsers automatically accepts cookies unless the user explicitly rejects them.

We could reasonably ask why the default setting should not be changed such that Web sites would have to get a user's permission to send a cookie file to that user's computer system. The Web site could inform, and possibly educate, the user about the existence of cookies, and then ask whether he or she is willing to accept them. Why not presume that users do not want cookie information recorded and stored on their computer systems, and then set the default conditions on Web browsers accordingly? And why not further presume that users do not want their personal data used in ways they did not explicitly authorize when they released it to a commercial Web site? We could appeal here to the view advocated by Judith DeCew (1997), who claims that we should "presume in favor of privacy" and then develop ways that would "allow individuals to determine for themselves how and when that presumption should be overridden." Independent of questions about where the presumption should reside—that is, in favor of the privacy of individuals or with the interests of on-line vendors—the widespread application and use of PETs will require a massive educational effort.

5.8.2   PETs and the Principle of Informed Consent

Even if the education-related issues involving PETs can be resolved, other ethical questions need to be asked. First, do PETs sufficiently assist on-line users in making *informed* decisions about the disclosure of their personal data in commercial transactions? Traditionally, the principle of informed consent has been the model, or standard, for disclosure involving personal data. But certain on-line commercial activities do not strictly adhere to the informed consent principle. For instance, users who willingly consent to provide information about themselves for one purpose (or in one on-line transaction) often have no idea how that information might have secondary uses. Although this problem is not unique to PETs or to e-commerce, e-commerce practices have exacerbated concerns about the secondary use of personal data.

There are two separate issues: first, the need to inform users that their personal data is being collected (even if it is used only in one particular context for one specified purpose), and second, the need for permission to use personal data in secondary applications. Although most commercial Web sites now collect personal information, not all actually disclose their information-gathering practices to consumers.

Some on-line entrepreneurs have advanced the argument that no one is forcing users to reveal personal data and that the disclosure of such data is done on a completely voluntary basis. Assume that a user has willingly consented to disclose personal data to an e-commerce vendor for use in a specific context (e.g., a business transaction). Has the user also granted the vendor permission to use that information for additional, "secondary" purposes? Does the on-line vendor now "own" that information, and is the vendor now free to do with it whatever he or she chooses? Recall our discussion in Section 5.6 about data-mining. We saw that specific information given by a consumer for use in one context, say in an application for an automobile loan, could be subsequently "mined" from internal databases to determine consumer patterns implicit in the data. We also saw that despite an impeccable credit history, an individual, as a result of this process, might be denied a consumer loan based solely on his or her identification with a newly created category or group, which the user could have had no idea even existed. Would that be fair?

Also we can ask, Can businesses that collect personal data possibly know in advance exactly how that data will be used in secondary and future applications? In cases of data mining, for example, it would seem that on-line businesses could *not* adequately inform users about exactly how their personal data might be used. What kind of *informed* choice, then, could users make in such a case? Can we—indeed should we—assume that most consumers understand the intricacies of data mining? Furthermore, it would be difficult to adequately explain such a technique as part of an on-line transaction without making the transaction cumbersome and perhaps "unfriendly," altogether discouraging e-commerce.

Some on-line entrepreneurs have responded to charges of privacy violations by pointing out that in most cases users are provided with the means to either "opt-in" or "opt-out" of having their personal data collected, as well as having that data made available for secondary use. But the default is such that if no option is specified by the user when he or she discloses personal data for use in one context, that disclosed personal data is also available for secondary use. Hence, the policy is "presumed consent," not informed consent. Is that presumption fair to on-line consumers? And is the ability simply to opt-in or opt-out of disclosing personal information fair to all on-line consumers, especially to those who are less affluent?

5.8.3   PETs and Issues of Social Equity

We saw in the preceding section that certain PETs now enable users to opt-in or opt-out of releasing their personal data when responding to queries in on-line commercial transactions. Judith DeCew (1997) has referred to flexibility in choice as the principle of "dynamic negotiation." According to this principle, users are empowered because they can *choose* whether to grant or withhold information about themselves in on-line transactions.

As an enticement to users to disclose personal data, some commercial Web sites offer discounts or rebates on their products in exchange for the right to use personal information for secondary uses such as data mining. Unfortunately, less affluent people might be more inclined to sell personal data about themselves. We can certainly ask, Is it fair that users in lower socioeconomic groups will, by virtue of their economic status, have less choice as to whether to sell (i.e., less control over) their personal data?

We can also ask whether certain groups of individuals having less control over their personal data than other groups do is acceptable from a human rights perspective. If privacy is indeed a fundamental human right—as some have maintained that it is—then we can reasonably ask whether individual privacy ought to be put up for sale as if it were a commodity. Of course, a critic might argue that having a legal right pertaining to *X* means that one also has a right to waive his or her right to *X*. According to this view, if one chooses to waive one's right to privacy by selling one's personal data, then that person's right has not been violated. But what if privacy is *not* simply a legal right but is also a moral right, or *human right*?

Issues involving human rights cannot be resolved simply. Consider, for instance, an analogy involving the sale of human organs, such as kidneys, especially by people in developing countries. Even though some people have, in one sense—that is, without external coercion—freely elected to sell one of their kidneys, we can ask whether they would have freely chosen to do so if they were not financially impoverished. Are those persons acting as fully autonomous agents? Is a social system that allows wealthy people to live longer than poor people merely because wealthy people can purchase vital human organs from poorer people just and moral?

Admittedly, it might appear a stretch—perhaps even a giant leap!—to move from the sale of one's personal data to the sale of one's vital human organs. However, the ability to act autonomously in matters involving human rights, in light of one's financial status, is similar in each case (assuming, of course, that privacy is a basic human right).

We have heard about the "technology haves" vs. "technology have-nots" and the "information poor" vs. the "information rich." Will there soon be classes of "privacy rich" and "privacy poor" as well? An ideal resolution to privacy issues involving e-commerce—whether that resolution turns out to be technological, legal, or both—would respect the rights of all, regardless of social class or economic status. PETs, at least in their current form, clearly do not provide such a solution, for even if PETs give on-line users control over their personal information in a formal or theoretical sense, there are larger issues involving fairness that militate against PETs as a solution.

Since PETs provide on-line users with ways of protecting their identity and also offer on-line consumers some choice in controlling the flow of their personal information, they are an empowering rather than a disabling technology. But PETs alone are insufficient for resolving the underlying ethical challenges—especially those involving education, informed consent, and social equity—for personal privacy in an information age (Tavani 2000).

▶ 5.9 PRIVACY LEGISLATION AND INDUSTRY SELF-REGULATION

We saw in the previous section that although PETs offer on-line users means to protect their identity in certain kinds of activities, they are not the "magic bullet" many of their staunchest supporters have suggested. Recognizing the limitations of PETs, some privacy advocates believe that stronger privacy laws will protect on-line consumers, while others in the commercial sector, for example, believe that additional privacy legislation is neither necessary nor desirable. Instead, they suggest strong industry controls regulated by standards applicable to various independent "platforms."

Generally, privacy advocates have been either skeptical or suspicious of voluntary controls, including industry standards for "self-regulation initiatives." Instead, they argue for stricter privacy legislation and data protection principles to protect the interests of on-line users, or "data subjects." We begin this section with a look at certain self-regulatory schemes for privacy protection that is provided to consumers by industry standards.

5.9.1 Industry Self-regulation Initiatives Regarding Privacy

Many industry advocates for the use of "voluntary controls" to address the privacy concerns of users admit that tools such as PETs might not be adequate to protect the privacy of consumers engaged in on-line e-commerce transactions. However, they also believe that alternatives to privacy legislation are possible. These advocates point to the establishment of industry standards that have already been accepted and implemented. These standards are similar to PETs in the sense that they are intended to protect a user's privacy, but unlike PETs in that they are not themselves tools.

To attract on-line consumers who avoid e-commerce activities because they worry about privacy, many on-line entrepreneurs have supported the need for Internet-wide privacy standards. The World Wide Web Consortium (W3C), an international industry consortium, was commissioned to provide these standards. In 1997, it announced its Platform for Privacy Preferences (P3P), through which Internet users could specify their own individualized Web privacy preferences. They could enter their privacy preferences into their Web browsers, choosing from a range of options and could change their privacy preferences each time they accessed a Web site. Adhering to the P3P standard, data exchange between a user and Web site would occur only when a user's indicated privacy preferences match that Web site's stated privacy policy. Although W3C was charged with establishing privacy standards on the Web, it was not set up to enforce the actual protection of personal data; additional measures are needed to assure users that any personal information that they release to a Web site will be used only in the ways they specify. "Negotiation agent" and "trust engine" technologies have been developed to assist users in this process.

An industry-backed privacy initiative called TRUSTe, which is self-regulatory, ensures that Web sites adhere to the privacy policies they advertise. TRUSTe uses a branded system of "trustmarks" (graphic symbols), which represent a Web site's privacy policy regarding personal information. Trustmarks provide consumers with the assurance that a Web site's privacy practices accurately reflect its stated policies. Through this PET-like feature, on-line users can file a complaint to TRUSTe if the Web site bearing its trust seal does not abide by the stated policies. Any Web site that bears the TRUSTe mark and wishes to retain that seal must satisfy several conditions: The Web site must clearly explain in advance its general information-collecting practices, including which personally identifiable data will be collected, what the information will be used for, and with whom the information will be shared. Also, the Web site must disclose whether the user will be able to correct and update personally identifiable information, and whether the user information will be removed from that Web site's database upon request (Wright and Kakalik, 1997). Web sites that bear a trust seal but do not conform to these conditions can have their seal revoked. And Web sites displaying trust seals, such as TRUSTe, are subject to periodic and unannounced audits of their sites.

Critics point out that the practical application of TRUSTe and similar tools may prove difficult: The amount of information users are required to provide may discourage some users from carefully reading and thus adequately understanding what is expected from them. Various warnings these tools display may appear unfriendly and thus work against the ideal of easy Web site access and use; "friendlier" trustmarks or graphic icons might result in on-line users being supplied with less direct information that is important to protecting their privacy. Advocates of tools such as TRUSTe argue that since on-line users will be better able to make informed choices regarding electronic purchasing and other types of on-line transactions, those users would clearly benefit from programs like TRUSTe.

Critics worry that such programs do not go far enough. Consider, for example, a recent case involving the e-commerce Web site Toysmart.com.

▶ **CASE ILLUSTRATION:** Toysmart.com

Online consumers who engaged in transactions with Toysmart were assured, via an on-line trust seal that their personal data would be protected. The vendor's policy stated that personal information disclosed to Toysmart would be used internally but would not be sold to or exchanged with external vendors. So users dealing with Toysmart could expect that their personal data would remain in Toysmart's databases and not be further disclosed or sold to a third party. In the spring of 2000, however, Toysmart was forced to file for bankruptcy.

Toysmart ceased operations in May 2000 and decided to solicit bids for its assets, which included its databases containing the names of customers. Parties interested in purchasing that information believed that they were under no obligation to adhere to the privacy policy that Toysmart had established with its clients. So whoever either took over Toysmart or purchased Toysmart's databases, would, in principle, be free to do whatever they wished with the personal information it had gathered, despite the fact that such information was given to Toysmart by clients under the belief that information about them would be protected indefinitely.

The Toysmart incident illustrates a case in which individuals exercised control over their personal information in one context—that is, in electing whether to disclose information about themselves to Toysmart in on-line transactions—based on specific conditions stated in Toysmart's privacy policy. However, it also turned out that these individuals were not guaranteed that the personal information they disclosed to Toysmart would be protected in the future. Thus it would seem that controls beyond those provided by trustmarks and e-commerce vendors are needed. Such controls, in the form of policies and laws, would ensure that a zone of privacy is established and enforced to protect individuals against subsequent (unauthorized) uses of the personal information they disclose in on-line activities.

5.9.2 Privacy Laws and Data-protection Principles

Many nations have recently passed or are currently in the process of seriously considering strong privacy legislation. The United States, however, has not taken the lead on legislation initiatives; some would argue that the United States is woefully behind the European nations in this regard. In fact, in the United States there is currently very little privacy protection in legal statutes. In 1974, Congress passed the Privacy Act, which has been criticized both for containing far too many loopholes and for lacking adequate provisions for enforcement. It applies only to records in federal agencies and thus is not applicable in the private sector. Subsequent privacy legislation in the United States has resulted in a "patchwork" of individual state and federal laws that are neither systematic nor coherent. (Recall our discussion of the "Bork Bill" in Chapter 2.)

Generally, the United States government has resisted requests from the public for stronger privacy laws, siding instead with business interests in the private sector who believe that such legislation would undermine economic efficiency and thus adversely impact the overall economy. Critics point out, however, that many of those businesses who have subsidiary companies or separate business operations in countries with strong privacy laws and regulations, such as nations in Western Europe, have found little difficulty in complying with the privacy laws of the host countries; profits for those American-owned companies have not suffered because of their compliance. In any event, there is now increased pressure on the United States government to enact stricter privacy laws and on American businesses to adopt stricter privacy polices and practices because of global e-commerce pressures, especially from Canada and the European Union (EU).

European nations have, through the implementation of strict data-protection principles, been far more aggressive than the United States in addressing privacy concerns of individuals. In 1980, most Western European nations signed on to the Organization for Economic Cooperation and Development (OECD) Principles, and in the early 1990s the European community began to consider synthesizing the data-protection laws of the individual European nations. The European Community has recently instituted a series of directives, including the EU Directive 95/46/EC of the European Parliament and of the Council of Europe of 24 October 1995, which is referred to as the EU Directive on Data Protection, designed to protect the personal data of its citizens by prohibiting the transborder flow of such data to countries that lack adequate protection of personal data.

Dag Elgesem (1999) has pointed out that the central concept of the European Directive is the *processing* and *flow* of personal data, unlike earlier privacy legislation in Europe that focused simply on the recording and the storage of that information. Several principles make up the European Directive; among them are the principles of Data Quality, Legitimate Purposes, Sensitive Data, and The Right to Be Informed. Whereas the Data Quality Principle is concerned with protecting the data subject's reasonable expectations concerning the processing of data about that subject, the Legitimate Purposes Principle lists the purposes for which the processing of personal data about the data subject are considered legitimate. What helps to ensure that each of these principles is enforced on behalf of data subjects is the presence of privacy protection commissions and boards in the various European nations. As in the case of Canada, which has also set up privacy oversight agencies with a Privacy Commissioner in each of its provinces, many European countries have their own data-protection agencies.

In this section, we have considered a number of proposed solutions to on-line privacy concerns. Some have called for stricter privacy laws on the part of governments and for the formation of privacy oversight commissions to enforce those laws. Others call for more serious self-regulatory measures by those in the commercial sector. And some proposals have suggested the need for technological solutions that empower on-line users by providing them with privacy-enhancing tools. Can these various proposals, or at least relevant aspects of them, be successfully combined or integrated into one comprehensive proposal?

5.9.3 Two Comprehensive Proposals for Resolving Privacy Issues

We have seen some of the strengths and limitations of privacy legislation and data-protection principles, of industry self-regulation initiatives, and of privacy-enhancing technologies. Each proposal has its advantages and inadequacies. Perhaps, then, some combination of these individual solutions can be integrated into a more comprehensive and robust privacy policy for the information era. Roger Clarke (1999) and Wang, Lee, and Wang (1998) have suggested ways of combining the individual pieces.

Arguing for a "co-regulatory" model, Clarke believes that a successful on-line privacy policy must include strong legislation, a privacy oversight commission, and industry self-regulation, and that these provisions must also be accompanied by privacy-enhancing technologies that individuals can use. He further believes that both a "privacy watchdog agency" and sanctions are needed for his privacy scheme to work.

Wang, Lee, and Wang also suggest that governments, businesses, and individuals each have a key role in any successful privacy policy. Government would promote strong privacy laws in both the public and private sectors, establish independent privacy commissions to oversee the implementation and enforcement of those laws, and educate the public about privacy issues. Businesses would be responsible for both promoting self-regulation for fair information practices and educating consumers about on-line-privacy policies, and individuals themselves would be responsible for using privacy-enhancing technologies and security tools. The authors admit, however, that developing and implementing an adequate privacy policy is "one of the most challenging public policy issues of the information age."

Because of the limitations in each of the three solutions that we have considered—technological tools (PETs), legislation, and industry self-regulation—a comprehensive policy is needed. Proposals similar to the models suggested by Clarke and by Wang, Lee, and Wang would better ensure adequate privacy protection in the age of cybertechnology.

▶ 5.10 CHAPTER SUMMARY

We have seen that privacy is an important value, essential for human ends such as friendship, autonomy, and democracy. We have also seen how nonpublic personal information

(NPI) is threatened by data-gathering and data-exchanging techniques, including computerized matching and merging of records. And we also saw how public personal information (PPI) is threatened by cybertechnology, by data-mining. We have suggested that a comprehensive privacy proposal is needed to resolve the current threats posed by cybertechnology.

▶ REVIEW QUESTIONS

1. What is personal privacy, and why is privacy difficult to define?

2. Why is privacy valued? Is privacy an intrinsic value or an instrumental value? Explain.

3. List some ways in which the privacy threats posed by cybertechnology differ from those posed by earlier technologies.

4. Describe some of the common data-gathering and surveillance techniques used on the Internet, and explain why those techniques are problematic for personal privacy.

5. What does Roger Clarke mean by "dataveillance?"

6. What are Internet cookies, and why are they considered controversial from the perspective of personal privacy?

7. Explain computerized merging. Why is it controversial from the perspective of personal privacy?

8. Describe the technique known as computerized matching? What problems does it raise for personal privacy?

9. What is data mining, and why is it considered controversial? How are privacy controversies surrounding data-mining practices exacerbated by the Internet?

10. What is meant by "privacy in public?" Describe the "problem of protecting personal privacy in public space."

11. How can the use of Internet search engines to locate personal information be controversial from a privacy perspective?

12. Why does on-line access to public records pose problems for personal privacy?

13. What are privacy-enhancing technologies (PETs), and how are they limited by (user) education, informed consent, and social equity?

14. Describe some of the voluntary controls and self-regulation initiatives that have been proposed by representatives from industry and e-commerce. Are they adequate solutions?

15. List some principles included in the European Union (EU) Directive on Data Protection. What are some of the strengths and weaknesses of those individual principles in particular, and of the EU Directive in general?

16. How could individual proposals for resolving privacy problems—that is, proposals involving technological solutions (such as PETs), industry self-regulation, and privacy laws—be combined into a comprehensive proposal for resolving privacy issues in the era of cybertechnology?

▶ DISCUSSION QUESTIONS

1. Consumer surveys have suggested that many Internet users are concerned about losing bits of their privacy when they are engaged in on-line activities. In fact, many Internet users identify privacy as their number one concern, ahead of concerns about ease of use, security, cost, spam, and so forth. Do only individuals who elect to use the Internet have reason to be concerned about losing their privacy? What about people who have never even used a computer—should they also worry? Explain.

2. Initially, privacy concerns involving computer technology arose because citizens feared that a strong centralized government could easily collect and store data about them. In the 1960s, for example, there was talk of constructing a national computerized database in the United States, and many were concerned that George Orwell's prediction of Big Brother in his classic book *1984* had finally arrived. The centralized database, however, never materialized. Now privacy advocates suggest that we have fewer reasons to be concerned about the federal government's role in privacy intrusions (Big Brother) than we do about privacy threats from the commercial sector (Big Bucks and Big Browser). Is that assessment accurate? Defend your answer.

3. Through the use of currently available on-line tools and techniques, ordinary users can easily acquire personal information about others. In fact, anyone who has Internet access can find information about us that we ourselves might have had no idea is publicly available there. Recall the cyberstalking case involving Amy Boyer, described in Chapter 1. One of the questions considered there was whether Boyer's privacy was violated while she was being stalked. We saw that Boyer's stalker was able to take advantage of Internet search facilities to acquire much of the information he needed to track down his victim. Is it true that individual privacy is threatened by the use of search engines? Explain.

4. In debates regarding access and control of personal information, it is sometimes argued that an appropriate balance needs to be struck between individuals and organizations: Individuals claim that they should be able to control who has access to their information, and organizations, including government and business groups, claim to need that information in order to make appropriate decisions. How can a reasonable resolution be reached that would satisfy both parties?

5. Surveys conducted by *Business Week*, Harris Associates, Equifax and others in the period preceding September 11, 2001, suggested that most Americans were either concerned or very concerned about their privacy. However, a Harris Interactive poll taken in late September 2001 presented a very different picture of how Americans had come to regard privacy. According to that poll, 86 percent favored the use of biometric technology (such as facial-recognition software) in public places, 68 percent favored the implementation of a national ID card, and 54 percent approved expanding government monitoring of cell phones and e-mail. In the post-September 11 world, we might ask ourselves why we should worry about protecting personal privacy. After all, some would say that we now inhabit a different world—that is, a world in a virtual state of war! It is said that in war, truth is the first causality; if so, then perhaps war's second casualty is privacy. Assuming that you care about personal privacy, is privacy still as important to you today as it was before September 11? Explain.

6. In the days and weeks immediately following the tragic events of September 11, 2001, some political leaders claimed that "extraordinary times call for extraordinary measures"; in times of war, basic civil liberties and freedoms, such as privacy, need to be severely restricted for the sake of national security and safety. Perhaps, as a nation, the value that we have traditionally attached to privacy has diminished significantly since then. Consider that the majority of American citizens strongly supported the USA (United and Strengthening America) PATRIOT (Provide Appropriate Tools Required to Intercept and Obstruct Terrorism) Act, which passed by an overwhelming margin in both houses of Congress and was enacted into law on October 21, 2001. Privacy advocates have since expressed their concerns about this act, noting that it might have gone too far in eroding basic civil liberties. Some critics also fear that certain provisions included in the act could easily be abused; for example, those in power could use those provisions to achieve controversial political ends under the convenient guise of national defense. Examine some of the details of USA PATRIOT Act (which can be viewed on the Web), and determine whether its measures are as extreme as its critics suggest. Are those measures consistent with the value of privacy, which Americans claim to embrace? Do privacy interests need to be reassessed, and possibly recalibrated, in light of recent attacks by and ongoing threats from terrorists?

▶ REFERENCES

Clarke, Roger (1988). "Information Technology and Dataveillance," *Communications of the ACM*, Vol. 35, No. 5, pp. 498–512.

Clarke, Roger (1999). "Internet Privacy Concerns Confirm the Case for Intervention," *Communications of the ACM*, Vol. 42, No. 2, February, pp. 60–67.

DeCew, Judith W. (1997). *In Pursuit of Privacy: Law, Ethics, and the Rise of Technology*. Ithaca, New York: Cornell University Press.

Elgesem, Dag (1999). "The Structure of Rights in Directive 95/46/EC on the Protection of Individuals with Regard to the Processing of Personal Data and the Free Movement of Such Data." *Ethics and Information Technology*, Vol. 1, No. 4, pp. 283–293.

Fried, Charles (1990). "Privacy: A Rational Context." In M. D. Ermann, M. B. Williams, and C. Gutierrez, eds. *Computers, Ethics, and Society*. New York: Oxford University Press, pp. 51–67.

Fulda, Joseph S. (1999). "A New Standard for Appropriation, with Some Remarks on Aggregation," *University of New Brunswick Law Journal*, Vol. 48, pp. 313–323.

Fulda, Joseph S. (2001). "Data Mining and Privacy." In R. A. Spinello and H. Tavani, eds. *Readings in CyberEthics*. Sudbury, MA: Jones and Bartlett Publishers, pp. 413–417.

Kotz, David (1998). "Technological Implications for Privacy." Paper presented at the Conference on The Tangled Web: Ethical Dilemmas of the Internet, Dartmouth College, August 7–9.

Kusserow, Richard P. (1995). "The Government Needs Computer Matching to Root Out Waste and Fraud." In D. G. Johnson and H. Nissenbaum, eds. *Computers, Ethics, & Social Values*. Englewood Cliffs, NJ: Prentice Hall, pp. 299–304.

Miller, Arthur (1990). Interviewed in the BBC/WGBH TV Series *The Machine That Changed the World*.

Moor, James H. (1997). "Towards a Theory of Privacy for the Information Age," *Computers and Society*, Vol. 27, No. 3, pp. 27–32.

Moor, James H. (1998). "Reason, Relativity, and Responsibility in Computer Ethics," *Computers and Society*, Vol. 28, No. 1, pp. 14–21.

Nissenbaum, Helen (1997). "Toward an Approach to Privacy in Public: Challenges of Information Technology," *Ethics and Behavior*, Vol. 7, No. 3, pp. 207–219

Nissenbaum, Helen. (1998). "Protecting Privacy in an Information Age," *Law and Philosophy*, Vol. 17, pp. 559–596.

Rachels, James. (1995). "Why Privacy Is Important." In D. G. Johnson and H. Nissenbaum, eds. *Computers, Ethics, & Social Values*. Englewood Cliffs, NJ: Prentice Hall, p. 351–357.

Regan, Priscilla M. (1995). *Legislating Privacy: Technology, Social Values, and Public Policy*. Chapel Hill: The University of North Carolina Press.

Reiter, Michael K., and Aviel D. Rubin (1999). "Anonymous Web Transactions with *Crowds*," *Communications of the ACM*, Vol. 42, No. 2, pp. 32–38.

Scanlan, Michael (2001). "Informational Privacy and Moral Values," *Ethics and Information Technology*, Vol. 3, No. 1, pp. 3–12.

Shattuck, John (a995). "Computer Matching is a Serious Threat to Individual Rights." In D. G. Johnson and H. Nissenbaum, Eds. *Computers, Ethics & Social Values*. Englewood Cliffs, NJ: Prentice Hall, pp. 310–314.

Tavani, Herman T. (1998). "Internet Search Engines and Personal Privacy." In *Proceedings of the Conference on Computer Ethics: Philosophical Enquiry: CEPE '97*, edited by M. J. van den Hoven. Rotterdam, The Netherlands: Erasmus University Press, pp. 214–223.

Tavani, Herman T. (1999). "Informational Privacy, Data Mining and the Internet." *Ethics and Information Technology*, Vol. 1, No. 2, pp. 137–145.

Tavani, Herman T. (2000). "Privacy-enhancing Technologies as a Panacea for Online Privacy Concerns: Some Ethical Considerations," *Journal of Information Ethics*, Vol. 9, No. 2, pp. 26–36.

Wang, Huaiqing, Matthew K. O. Lee, and Chen Wang (1998). "Consumer Privacy Concerns About Internet Marketing," *Communications of the ACM*, Vol. 41, No. 3, pp. 63–70.

Warren, Samuel, and Louis Brandeis. (1890). "The Right to Privacy," *Harvard Law Review*, Vol. 14, No. 5.

Westin, Alan F. (1967). *Privacy and Freedom*. New York: Atheneum Press.

Wright, Marie, and John Kakalik. (1997). "The Erosion of Privacy," *Computers and Society*, Vol. 27, No. 4, December, pp. 22–25.

▶ FURTHER READINGS

Agre, Philip, and Marc Rotenberg, eds. (1997). *Technology and Privacy: The New Landscape*. Cambridge, MA: MIT Press.

Bennett, Colin J. (2001). "Cookies, Web Bugs, Webcams, and Cue Cats: Patterns of Surveillance on the World Wide Web," *Ethics and Information Technology*, Vol. 3, No. 3, pp. 197–210.

Bennett, Colin J., and Rebecca Grant, eds. (1999). *Visions of Privacy: Policy Choices for the Digital Age*. Toronto: University of Toronto Press.

Chaum, David (1991). "Achieving Electronic Privacy," *Scientific American*, August, pp. 96–101.

Cranor, Lorrie Faith. (1999). "Internet Privacy," *Communications of the ACM*, Vol. 42, No. 2, February, pp. 28–31.

Elgesem, Dag. (1996). "Privacy, Respect for Persons, and Risk." In C. Ess, ed. *Philosophical Perspectives on Computer-mediated Communication*. New York: State University of New York Press.

Etzioni, Amatai (1999). *The Limits of Privacy*. New York: Basic Books.

Gandy, Oscar H. (1993). *The Panoptic Sort: A Political Economy of Personal Information*. Boulder, CO: Westview Press.

Gotterbarn, Don (1999). "Privacy Lost: The Net, Autonomous Agents, and 'Virtual Information,'" *Ethics and Information Technology*, Vol. 1, No. 2, pp. 147–154.

Introna, Lucas D. (1997). "Privacy and the Computer: Why We Need Privacy in the Information Society," *Metaphilosophy*, Vol. 28, No. 3, pp. 259–275.

Loudon, Kenneth C. (1986). *Dossier Society: Value Choices in the Design of a National Information System*. New York: Columbia University Press.

Marx, Gary (2001). "Murky Conceptual Waters: The Public and the Private," *Ethics and Information Technology*, Vol. 3, No. 3, pp. 157–169.

Pounder, C. N. M. (2000). "Internet Use and the Data Protection Act." In D. Langford, ed. *Internet Ethics*. London: Macmillan; New York: St. Martin's Press, pp. 243–266.

Spinello, Richard A. (1997) "The End of Privacy." In R. E. Long, ed. *Rights to Privacy*. New York: H. W. Wilson.

Tavani Herman T., and James H. Moor (2001). "Privacy Protection, Control Over Information, and Privacy-Enhancing Technologies," *Computers and Society*, Vol. 31, No. 1, pp. 6–11.

Vedder, Anton H. (2001). "KDD, Privacy, Individuality, and Fairness," In R. A. Spinello and H. Tavani, eds. *Readings in CyberEthics*. Sudbury, MA: Jones and Bartlett Publishers, pp. 404–412.

CHAPTER

▽

6

SECURITY IN CYBERSPACE

Can computer break-ins ever be justified on ethical grounds? This is one of many security-related issues that we will examine in Chapter 6. Other questions include:

- How are security issues different from privacy issues in a computer context?
- How are violations of computer security similar to and different from computer crime?
- What is the difference between computer system security and data security?
- What is meant by "hacking" and the "hacker ethic"
- Is there a difference between cyberterrorism and information warfare?
- Is total security in cyberspace a reasonable expectation and goal?
- How can risk-analysis models help us achieve greater security in cyberspace?

▶ 6.1 DEFINING COMPUTER SECURITY

What exactly do we mean by "computer security" and "security in cyberspace?" Like privacy, *security* has no universally agreed upon definition. Many of us might think that we have a clear understanding of what is meant by "security" until we are asked to define it. The expression *computer security* often conjures up notions like "reliability," "availability," "safety," "integrity," "confidentiality," and "privacy." In discussing cybertechnology, we can think of security as protection against

    i.   unauthorized access to computer systems,

    ii. alteration of data that resides in and is transmitted between computer systems,

    iii. disruption, vandalism, and sabotage of computer systems and networks.

A simple and straightforward definition of computer security has been offered by Simpson Garfinkel and Eugene Spafford (1996), who suggest that a computer is secure when two conditions are satisfied: You can depend on it and its software behaves as you expect. Joseph Kizza (1998), on the other hand, defines computer security in terms of three elements:

- Confidentiality
- Integrity
- Availability

Confidentiality protects against unauthorized disclosure of information to third parties; *integrity* prevents unauthorized modification of files; and *availability* prevents unauthorized withholding of information from those who need it when they need it.

Some security experts believe that *consistency* (ensuring that the data we see today will be the same data we see tomorrow) and *controlling access to resources* are also important for computer security (see Spafford et al., 1989). So perhaps we can think about computer security in terms of a cluster of concepts, ranging from confidentiality and integrity of data, to availability and reliability of systems to broader concerns involving access and control.

When computer security protects against mischief and vandalism in cyberspace, it can overlap with computer crime.

6.1.1 Computer Security and Computer Crime

Are violations of computer security the same as computer crime? Every violation of security involving cybertechnology is criminal, but not every crime in cyberspace necessarily involves a breach, or violation, of security. Consider some computer-related crimes that have no direct implications for computer security: An individual can use a personal computer to make unauthorized copies of proprietary software programs; a person can use the Internet to stalk a victim in cyberspace; pedophiles can use computer networks to solicit illicit sex with young children; individuals and organizations can use cybertechnology to distribute child pornography, traffic in drugs, and engage in illegal gambling activities.

Although each of these activities is clearly illegal, it is not clear that any of them necessarily result from insecure computers. Perhaps greater security mechanisms on computer networks could deter crimes and detect criminals in cyberspace, but cyberrelated crimes involving pedophilia, stalking, and pornography do not typically result from security flaws in computer system design, nor do these crimes occur because of computer systems that are undependable.

There are, then, important distinctions between issues of security and crime involving cybertechnology. We will discuss cybercrime in Chapter 7, and focus our concern in this chapter on actual and potential threats to security in cyberspace.

Just as computer security overlaps with computer crime, security concerns intersect with personal privacy. We discussed confidentiality and data integrity in our examination of privacy in Chapter 5. Now we ask, how are issues pertaining to security in cyberspace different from those involving privacy?

6.1.2 Security and Privacy: Similarities and Differences

The concepts of privacy and security are not always easy to separate when discussing civil liberties and basic human rights. In the United States, arguments for a right to privacy that appeal to the Fourth Amendment have often been made on the basis of *securing* the person (and the person's papers, etc.) from the physical intrusion of searches and seizures. Paul Thompson (2001) argues that many of our claims involving an alleged right to privacy are rooted in the concept of security and can be better understood as arguments having to do with a "right to being secure."

Although cyberrelated issues involving privacy and security often overlap, some important distinctions are worth drawing. Privacy concerns often arise because on-line users fear losing control over personal information that can be accessed by organizations (especially businesses and government agencies), many of whom claim to have some *legitimate* need for that information in order to make important decisions. Security concerns, on the other hand, typically arise because on-line users worry that personal data or proprietary information, or both, could be retrieved, and possibly altered, by unauthorized individuals and organizations. Privacy and security concerns can be thought of as two sides of a single coin: People need personal privacy, and they wish to control who has information about them as well as how that information is accessed by others. Making sure that personal information stored in computer databases is secure is important in helping them achieve and maintain their privacy. In this sense, then, the objectives of privacy would seem compatible with, and even complementary to, security. In another sense, however, there is a certain tension between privacy and security. From the perspective of security, the protection of system resources and proprietary data are generally considered more critical, while from the vantage point of privacy, the protection of personal information and personal autonomy will receive a higher priority.

Privacy concerns tend to focus on protecting personal data from unauthorized access, abuse, and alteration, reflecting values that preserve individual autonomy and individual respect for persons. And while anonymity tools (discussed in Section 6.6.4) help to ensure the privacy of individuals navigating in cyberspace, those tools can also cause serious concerns for security since anonymous behavior makes it difficult to identify security violators. So in some cases, there is a natural tension between security and privacy; and at other times, the objectives and goals of privacy and security—for example, with respect to confidentiality and data integrity—are the same (Tavani 2000).

6.1.3 How Do Security Issues in Cyberspace Raise Ethical Concerns?

Our main focus in this chapter is to determine what ethically is at stake with respect to computer security. In previous chapters we saw that ethical concerns arise because of issues having to do with fairness, respect, autonomy, and so forth. So how do ethical concerns arise in the context of cybersecurity? To be autonomous, individuals need to have some control over how information about them is gathered and used. In Chapter 5, we saw how important this kind of control is for privacy. Computer security helps users control their own personal information; it also ensures that information stored in electronic databases is kept confidential.

However, there is also another side to questions surrounding ethics and security. Some individuals in cyberspace have, unfortunately, threatened and even violated security. Some have caused only minor nuisances and others have disrupted major networks, resulting in severe financial loss and significant physical damage. Anonymity tools enable users to navigate the Web without having to reveal their true identities. While this might help to protect an individual's privacy, it also poses a risk for computer security, so some argue individual freedom and autonomy sometimes have to yield to public safety and security. An ethical analysis of these issues will seek to find a balance that is both appropriate and fair between the autonomy expected by individual users and the security needed to protect both the community of users in cyberspace and the overall infrastructure on which we all critically depend. A primary objective of this chapter is to isolate and examine controversial issues that challenge and threaten this balance.

▶ 6.2 TWO DISTINCT ASPECTS OF COMPUTER SECURITY

In information and communications technology, the term "security" is used in two ways (Spinello and Tavani 2001). In one sense, "computer security" refers to a computer system's vulnerability to attacks from "malicious programs," such as viruses and worms, on its hardware and software resources, including operating system software and applications programs. We refer to this aspect of computer security as *system security*. Here, the concern is that individual computer systems connected to the Internet, as well as the Internet itself as a system of computer networks, could be sabotaged because of inadequate security. Saboteurs can, through the distribution and execution of rogue programs, severely disrupt activities on the Internet and potentially render the Internet itself inoperable.

A second sense of "computer security" is concerned not with the vulnerability of a computer system's software and hardware resources but with vulnerability to unauthorized access to data. The data can be either (a) resident in one or more disk drives or databases in a computer system, or (b) transmitted between two or more computer systems. We will refer to this aspect of computer security as *data security*. Figure 6-1 shows the relationship between the two senses of computer security.

6.2.1 System Security: Protecting Networked Computers against Rogue Computer Programs and Computer Rogues

As noted above, *system security* is concerned with cyberattacks that either threaten to disrupt activities on a computer system or network or damage and destroy system resources.

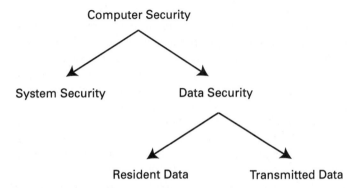

Figure 6-1 Two Kinds of Computer Security

Among the resources that contribute to this threat are computer viruses, worms, and other malicious programs that threaten secure and stable computer systems.

▶ **CASE ILLUSTRATION:** The Code Red Worm

In August 2001, departments and agencies of the United States Government, members of e-commerce communities, and ordinary Internet users all prepared once again for another attack by a potentially dangerous computer worm. This time, the malicious program was referred to as the *Code Red Worm*. Taking advantage of a hole in the Microsoft NT 4.0 operating system, the worm was designed to infect servers running that particular version of software. Fortunately, security experts were able to anticipate the implications of this particular computer worm. The Code Red Worm was to infect systems during the first eighteen days of a month and then activate on the nineteenth day, when infected computers would flood a target site with bogus data. The worm would then sit dormant in the newly infected computers until the first day of the next month when the reactivated worm would spread further, infecting more systems.

System security, as described above, is concerned with various kinds of viruses, worms, and related malicious computer programs that can cause disruption, sabotage, and vandalism of computer systems. What are the differences between computer viruses and worms? Richard Rosenberg (1997) defines a computer *virus* as a "program that can insert executable copies of itself into programs." He distinguishes a virus from a *worm*, which he defines as a program or program segment that "searches computer systems for idle resources and then disables them by erasing various locations in memory." Richard Power (2000) differentiates between a virus and a worm in the following way: A virus is a "program that can 'infect' other programs by modifying them to include a possibly evolved copy of itself." A worm, on the other hand, is an "independent program that replicates from machine to machine across network connections often clogging networks and information systems as it spreads."

Some security analysts differentiate further between the two types of disruptive programs by pointing out that a worm, such as Code Red, is less virulent than a virus, such as the "Love Bug" (described in Chapter 7). Worms are generally considered less virulent for two reasons: (i) Worms do less harm to computers than viruses, and (ii) Worms can be "killed" just by turning off and rebooting an infected machine. On the other hand, worms can spread more quickly than viruses, because worms, unlike viruses, do not need any action to trigger them. A computer virus is often activated when an unsuspecting user opens an e-mail attachment; viruses cannot run on their own but are inserted into other programs. Worms, on the other hand, can move from machine to machine across networks and can have parts of themselves running on different machines.

Certain notorious worms and viruses have become household names. You have probably heard of the Michelangelo, Melissa, and ILOVEYOU viruses. If the distinction between viruses and worms were not confusing enough, some analysts suggest that we further differentiate disruptive programs to include Trojan horses, logic bombs, and bacteria. A *Trojan horse* often appears to be a benign program, but it can do significant system damage behind the scenes. *Logic bombs*, on the other hand, check for certain conditions or states in a computer system and then execute when one of those conditions arise. And *bacteria* (or "rabbits") multiply quickly and are designed to fill a computer system's memory.

So malicious software, or what some call "programmed threats" (see Spafford et al., 1989), can take many forms. But when it comes to understanding and responding to these disruptive computer programs, not all security experts care about the nuances and subtleties of such distinctions. Following Anne Branscomb (1990), we can refer to all flavors of malicious programs or programmed threats, including the various forms of worms and viruses, simply as *rogue computer programs*. And we can refer to those who program them as *computer rogues*.

6.2.2 Data Security: Protecting the Integrity of Information

As noted above, we can differentiate between the security attacks directed at computer systems themselves and the security threats posed to the data that either resides in or is transmitted through computer systems. In the latter case, the concern is primarily with the "integrity" of data rather than with the vulnerability of a computer system's resources. Perhaps the key elements involving the integrity of data and information are best captured by Richard Spinello (2000) when he notes that information integrity requires that the

> proprietary or sensitive information under one's custodial care is kept confidential and secure, that information being transmitted is not altered in form or content and cannot be read by unauthorized parties, and that all information being disseminated or otherwise made accessible through Web sites and on-line data repositories is as accessible and reliable as possible.

Three points in this definition are worth highlighting. First, the information to be protected can be either proprietary or sensitive: it can be "owned" by corporations or by individuals, and it can generally be considered personal or intimate.

Second, the information must be secured not only from tampering and alteration by unauthorized parties, but also from mere access by unauthorized parties. It is critical for information integrity that data resident either in the hard drive of a personal computer or in a proprietary database (such as a corporate database) is secure from unauthorized access. For example, a university needs to ensure that hackers cannot alter, or even read, student transcripts. Government offices, especially military departments, must ensure that sensitive data cannot be accessed. And businesses must also ensure that data resident in their databases or on their password-protected Web sites, whether that data identifies customer records or sensitive information about the business itself, cannot be accessed by unauthorized users.

Third, authorized parties must readily be able to access the information from the repositories in which it is stored. Not only must the information residing in a computer database or in a password-protected Web site be available at peak times or times of highest request, it must be accessible to authorized users on demand.

▶ 6.3 COMPUTER SECURITY AND COMPUTER HACKERS

Although we earlier described those who launch malicious computer programs as "computer rogues," they are more commonly referred to as computer *hackers*. We will examine the profile of a "typical" computer hacker in our discussion of cybercrime in Chapter 7, where we will discuss hacking as it relates to crime and criminal behavior, and we will draw some useful distinctions between hacking and "cracking." In this chapter, we examine hacking as it relates to computer security. In particular, we consider whether such activities are ever ethically justified.

Imagine that some instances of hacking, whether by intention or accident, resulted in saving the lives of one or more persons. Further imagine an instance in which hacking made a segment of cyberspace more secure or at least less vulnerable to serious disruptions. Could such instances of hacking ever be considered ethical? Or is hacking inherently wrong and thus always immoral, regardless of whether it might bring about some desirable outcomes? We examine these and similar questions in the next two sections.

6.3.1 Hacking and the "Hacker Ethic"

Hackers are sometimes described as behaving in accordance with a "code of ethics." Some forms of hacker behavior, however, would hardly appear ethical, at least in a conventional sense of "ethics." In documenting early computer hackers, who were often associated with "the MIT culture," some authors have used the expressions "hacker ethic" and "hacker code of ethics." Steven Levy (1984) suggests that a "strong and distinctive code of ethics," in which freedom and elegance are primary values, could be found in the hacker community. Levy describes the hacker code as "a philosophy, an ethic, and a dream," based on the following principles:

i. Access to computers should be unlimited and total.

ii. All information should be free.

iii. Mistrust Authority—Promote Decentralization.

iv. Hackers should be judged by their hacking (not by bogus criteria such as degrees, age, race, or position).

v. You can create art and beauty on a computer.

vi. Computers can change your life for the better.

Perhaps what Levy really describes is not so much a code of ethics but rather a code for the way that hackers approach their craft, that is, in terms of a certain ethic, as in "work ethic." Pekka Himanen (2001) has described the hacker ethic as a "new work ethic," which he contrasts with the classic "Protestant work ethic" (coined originally by Max Weber in his classic work *The Protestant Ethic and the Spirit of Capitalism*). In addition to an ethic, hackers also seem to have a distinct "ethos," that is, they have a distinct way of looking at the world, especially the world of computers.

Many hackers believe that computer systems are inherently flawed and thus need to be improved. As a result, some hackers believe that they need total access to all computer systems in order to take them apart, see how they work, and make the needed improvements. Not surprisingly, then, hackers want to remove any barriers to free access to computers. More recently, hackers have seemed to embrace, either explicitly or implicitly, the following three principles:

1. Information should be free.

2. Hackers provide society with a useful and important service.

3. Activities in cyberspace are virtual in nature and thus do not harm real people in the real (physical) world.

We briefly consider each principle.

6.3.1.1 Information Should Be Free

Should information be totally free? If so, on what grounds can this claim be justified? The expression "Information wants to be free" has become a mantra for many hackers who see proprietary software and systems as obstacles to realizing the freedom of the Internet, where users would otherwise have total access to information. The debate over whether information should be free, or even to what extent information should be freely accessible to Internet users, is a complicated one. As we shall see in Chapter 8, this debate is rooted in complex property laws and policies that have been disputed in the courts, resulting in Supreme Court decisions. So we will postpone our fuller discussion of this particular point raised by hackers until our analysis of intellectual property in cyberspace. However, a few brief comments need to be made at this point.

Some critics regard the view that information should be free as idealistic or romantic. According to Eugene Spafford (1992), it is also a very naive view. He points out that if information were free, privacy would not be possible because individuals could not control how information about them was collected and used. Also, it would not be possible to ensure integrity and accuracy of that information, since information that was freely available could always be modified and changed by anyone who happened to access it. So from the points of view of privacy and confidentiality, a world in which all information was literally and completely free would not be desirable. Perhaps what hackers really intend to assert is that sharing and distributing nonpersonal proprietary information over the Internet should not be restricted. This is, however, a very different claim than asserting that (all) information should be free. So the first hacker principle is certainly questionable.

6.3.1.2 Hackers Provide Society with an Important Service

Does the second hacker principle fare any better? Many are suspicious of claims that hackers perform a useful service for society by searching for and exposing security holes in cyberspace. According to this rationale, hackers are doing us a favor, because pointing out these security holes will force those responsible for the holes to fix them.

Eugene Spafford (1992) has produced a series of counterexamples to this version of the hacker argument, and he uses an analogy to counter the hacker's position that exposing security vulnerabilities is doing the computer user community a favor. Spafford asks, Would we permit someone to start a fire in a crowded shopping mall in order to expose the fact that the mall's sprinkler system was not adequate? Similarly we could also ask, Would you be willing to thank a burglar, who in the process of burglarizing your house, was able to show that your home security system was inadequate? If not, then why, Spafford would ask, should we thank hackers for showing us that our computers are insecure?

6.3.1.3 Hacking Causes Only Virtual Harm, Not Real Harm

According to third hacker principle, break-ins and vandalism in cyberspace cause no real harm because they occur only in the *virtual* world. This argument commits a logical fallacy in that it confuses the relationship between the notions of "harm" and "space" by reasoning that

> the virtual world is not the real (physical) world, so any harms that occur in the virtual world are not real harms.

Consider how this reasoning is flawed. If someone sends you an e-mail message in which they unfairly accuse you of being a malicious person, they have communicated with you in cyberspace, which is a form of "virtual," as opposed to physical, space. But does it follow that the content of the e-mail is any less real than if it had been printed in a hardcopy letter that had been sent to you in the physical mail? Would any harm you experience because of the e-mail's content be any less real than the harm you would experience from identical information in a letter written on physical paper? James Moor (2001) has described a variation of this type of reasoning as the "virtuality fallacy," which we discussed in Section 3.2.

6.3.2 Can Computer Break-ins Ever Be Justified on Ethical Grounds?

We have given counterexamples for each of the three principles that we identified as the "hacker code of ethics." Yet we still might question whether a computer break-in could ever be ethically justified. Eugene Spafford (1992) believes that in certain extreme cases, breaking into a computer could be the "right thing to do." He also argues, however, that computer break-ins always cause harm; and from this point, he infers that hacker break-ins are never ethically justifiable.

How can Spafford defend his seemingly contradictory principle: Sometimes it could be right to do something that is ethically unjustifiable? Spafford asks us to consider a scenario in which vital medical data that resided in a computer was needed in an emergency to save someone's life. Further imagine that the authorized users of the computer system cannot be located. In this case, Spafford believes that breaking into that computer system would be the right thing to do, but that such an act is still unethical. His rationale is that a greater wrong would be committed if the break-in (i.e., the unethical act) were not carried out.

Independent of whether some cases of hacking might be justified on ethical grounds is the question as to whether certain forms of hacking ought to be legally permissible. Should all forms of hacking behavior be declared illegal? And are all hackers necessarily criminals? Should we distinguish between hacking and "cracking" as some authors do? For example, Power (2000) describes a cracker as one who breaks into systems to steal or destroy, as opposed to a hacker who breaks in simply to explore. (However, as Power and others have noted, breaking in to explore is still a form of breaking and entering.) We address these and similar questions in Chapter 7, where we examine legal issues involving hacking in our discussion of computer crime.

Thus far we have differentiated two types of computer security—system security and data security—and we have considered whether some forms of hacking might be defended from an ethical perspective. We have not yet considered the implications that hacker attacks have for our financial infrastructure, which increasingly depends on available networked computers. Nor have we yet considered the threats that hacking poses to our national security. In the next two sections we examine both security-related concerns.

▶ 6.4 CYBERTERRORISM

On February 7, 2002, the United States House of Representatives passed a bill (HR 3394) by a margin of 400 to 12 to expand research on protecting computer networks from terrorist attacks. The author of the House bill, Representative Sherwood Boehlert (R, New Hartford, NY), argued that we must allocate funding for university research into yet another variation of terrorist threat (in addition to hijackings and bombings), which he describes as "cyberterrorism."

Dorothy Denning (2000) defines *cyberterrorism* as the "convergence of cyberspace and terrorism." As such, it covers politically motivated hacking operations intended to cause grave harm, that is, resulting in either loss of life or severe economic loss, or both. In some cases, it is difficult to separate acts of hacking and cybervandalism from cyberterrorism. It is sometimes even difficult to determine whether a major computer network disruption is due to a system failure (in either the hardware or software of a networked computer system) or is the result of the work of hackers or cyberterrorists.

▶ **CASE ILLUSTRATION:** A Computer Network Failure or an Instance of Cyberterrorism?

On January 15, 1990, AT&T long distance telephone service experienced a power outage that lasted for several hours and resulted in the loss of millions of dollars in revenue for businesses. The official explanation given for the outage was that a software glitch in the programming code in the AT&T computer system caused the network to crash. Some have been suspicious of this explanation, believing instead that the crash was the result of the work of hackers. Others have gone so far as to suggest that this particular incident was the first cyberterrorist attack on the United States infrastructure. The disruption of the AT&T computer system—regardless of how it was caused, or who or what caused it—showed for the first time just how vulnerable certain elements of the infrastructure and economy were to software failures involving networked computers.

Immediately following the AT&T incident, the FBI increased surveillance on hackers and terrorist organizations suspected of being able to damage, disrupt, or possibly bring down altogether elements of the United States infrastructure. Notorious computer hackers, such as Kevin Mitnick (code named Condor), and individuals in hacker groups, such as Cyberpunks, the Legion of Doom (LOD), and the Masters of Deception (MOD), were closely watched.

To what extent are attacks on our infrastructure and on our military defense systems random attacks perpetrated by individual hackers and hacker groups, possibly as pranks, and to what extent are these the attacks of highly coordinated efforts of organized terrorist groups? It is not always easy to determine, based on the motives that separate these individuals and groups.

6.4.1 Cyberterrorism vs. Hacktivism

In February 2000, "denial-of-service" attacks that were perpetrated against e-commerce Web sites prevented tens of thousands of people from accessing them. Although these attacks might not have been acts of terrorism in its truest form, and although they might not have been politically motivated, they resulted in severe economic loss for major corporations. Should these cyberattacks be classified as cyberterrorism? Or are they better understood as malicious hacking by individuals with no particular political agenda or ideology?

Mark Manion and Abby Goodrum (2000) have questioned whether some cyberattacks might not be better understood as acts of *hacktivism*. Considering the growing outrage on the part of some hackers and political activists over an increasingly "commodified Internet," Manion and Goodrum question whether these kinds of cyberattacks suggest a new form of civil disobedience that integrates the talent of traditional computer hackers with the interests and social consciousness of political activists. They also point out that while hackers have been and continue to be portrayed as vandals, terrorists, and saboteurs, hardly anyone has considered the possibility that at least some of these individuals might be "electronic political activists" or what they call hacktivists. Can a meaningful distinction be drawn between acts of hacktivism and cyberterrorism?

Dorothy Denning (1999b) attempts to draw some critical distinctions among three related notions: *activism*, *hacktivism*, and *cyberterrorism*. She suggests that activism can be viewed as normal, nondisruptive use of the Internet to support a cause; for example, an activist could use the Internet to discuss issues, form coalitions, and plan and coordinate activities. Activists could engage in browsing the Web, sending e-mail, posting material to a Web site, constructing a Web site dedicated to their political cause or causes, and so forth.

Hacktivism, the convergence of activism and computer hacking, uses hacking techniques against a target Internet site with intent to disrupt normal operations but without intending to cause serious damage. These disruptions could be caused by "e-mail" bombs and "low grade" viruses that cause only minimal disruption but would not result in severe economic damage or loss of life.

Cyberterrorism, as we saw earlier, consists of activities intended to cause great harm, such as loss of life or severe economic damage, or both. For example, a cyberterrorist might attempt to bring down the United States stock market or take control of a transportation unit in order to cause trains to crash. Denning believes that conceptual distinctions can be used to differentiate activism, hacktivism, and cyberterrorism. She admits, however, that as we progress from activism to cyberterrorism the boundaries become fuzzy. For example, should an e-mail bomb sent by a hacker who is also a political activist be classified as a form of hacktivism or as an act of cyberterrorism? Many in law enforcement would no doubt argue that rather than trying to understand the ideological beliefs, goals, and objectives of those who engage in malicious forms of hacking, much more effort should be devoted to finding ways to deter and catch these individuals.

6.4.2 Cybertechnology and Terrorist Organizations

A major security concern, especially since September 11, 2001, has been how and when terrorist organizations, such as Al Qaeda, might use cybertechnology to carry out their objectives. We now know that the terrorists who carried out the highly coordinated attacks on the Twin Towers of the World Trade Center communicated by e-mail in the days preceding the attack. We also have discovered that many members of Al Qaeda, despite the fact that some operated out of caves in Afghanistan, had fairly sophisticated computer devices. Yet it does not seem that these terrorists have taken full advantage of currently available forms of cybertechnology in executing their campaigns.

Why not? One possible explanation is that they have not yet gained the needed expertise with cybertechnology. This, of course, may change as the next generation of terrorists, who will likely be more skilled in the use of computers and cybertechnology, replace current leadership. Two terrorists gave up their lives in targeting the Navy ship USS *Cole* in 2000. Similar activities might be done remotely, in the future via cybertechnology, in which case no terrorists would be required to give up their lives in carrying out their missions. A scenario is also possible in which terrorists gain control of an airplane's onboard computer systems and even block the ability of a pilot to override those controls.

▶ 6.5 INFORMATION WARFARE

In the preceding section, we saw that it is not always easy to differentiate acts of cyberterrorism from those of hacktivism, activism, and cybervandalism. It can also be difficult to distinguish between acts of cyberterrorism and acts of *information warfare* (IW). Dorothy Denning (1999a) defines IW as "operations that target or exploit information media in order to win some objective over an adversary." But certain aspects of cyberterrorism also conform to Denning's definition of IW, so what distinguishes information warfare from cyberterrorism? For one thing, information warfare is a broader concept than cyberterrorism, and for another, it need not involve loss of life or severe economic loss, even though such results can occur.

James Moor (1998) has pointed out that in the computer era the concept of warfare has become "informationally enriched." He notes that while information has always played a vital role in warfare, now its importance is overwhelming, because the battlefield is becoming increasingly computerized. In the past, warfare was conducted by physical means: Human beings engaged in combat, using weapons such as guns, tanks, and aircraft. During the Gulf War in the early 1990s, we saw for the first time the importance of information technology in contemporary warfare strategies. Arguably, the war was won quickly by the multinational coalition because it had advantages in cybertechnology. Destroying the Iraqi communications technologies at the outset put the Iraqi army at a severe disadvantage. Also the use of "smart bombs" helped the American military pinpoint targets with accuracy not possible before the advent of computers and computer-related technologies. Moor points out that in the future, warfare may have more to do with information and cybertechnology than with human beings going into combat.

Some have pointed out that IW, unlike conventional or physical warfare, often tends to be more disruptive than destructive. The "weapons" of IW, consisting of logic bombs, viruses, and worms deployable from cyberspace, typically strike at a nation's infrastructure. Although these are not the traditional weapons of warfare, the disruption can be more damaging than physical damage from conventional weapons.

We have discussed various security threats, from hacking to hacktivism, and from cyberterrorism to information warfare, as summarized in Table 6-1. We have also seen that it is not always easy to differentiate clearly among them. What is important, of course, is that we continue to develop measures for deterring, detecting, preventing, and responding to future attacks on computer systems. In the next section, we examine some come currently available security countermeasures.

▶ 6.6 SECURITY COUNTERMEASURES

Richard Power (2000) defines a *countermeasure* as an action, device, procedure, technique ,or other measure that reduces the vulnerability of a threat to a computer system. Although we have come to rely increasingly on countermeasures, some security analysts believe that we would not need them as much if better security features were built into computer

TABLE 6-1   Hacktivism, Cyberterrorism, and Information Warfare

Hacktivism	The convergence of political activism and computer hacking techniques to engage in a new form of civil disobedience.
Cyberterrorism	The convergence of cybertechnology and terrorism for carrying out acts of terror in (or via) cyberspace.
Information Warfare	Using information to jam the enemy's communication systems, and using technology to take out an enemy's computer and information systems.

systems in the first place. Eugene Spafford (2002), for example, argues that successful security cannot be thought of as an "add-on" to computer systems; instead, it should be embedded in the systems themselves. Although we can agree with Spafford, it would perhaps be prudent to use existing tools and technologies to combat security threats until better security is built into computer systems.

Arguably, the best tactical approach to security threats, at present, is through available security countermeasures. These countermeasures come in a variety of forms. In this section, we briefly examine four common types: firewall technology, antivirus software, encryption devices, and anonymity tools.

6.6.1 Firewall Technology

Many businesses, government agencies, and on-line service providers have come to depend on security environments, such as firewalls, to help protect the data in the computer systems. Richard Power (2000) defines a *firewall* as a system or combination of systems that enforces a boundary between two or more networks. Firewalls not only help to secure systems from unauthorized access to information in databases, but also help prevent unwanted and unauthorized communication into or out of a privately owned network.

Rolf Oppliger (1997) describes a firewall as a "blockade" between an internal privately owned network (such as an intranet) that is believed to be secure and an external network, such as the Internet, which is not assumed to be secure. The metaphor of a blockade is perhaps useful, but others have suggested that a firewall can be compared more accurately to a "moat around a castle." Steven Lodin and Christoph Schuba (1998), for example, point out that a firewall protects against those outside the castle.

Firewall technology consists of a set of mechanisms that are embedded in hardware, software, or both. This technology includes filters and gateways that are designed to secure communication traffic entering or leaving a specific network domain. As such, firewalls attempt to ensure the authenticity of data communications that pass through the domain's boundaries. They are also designed to ensure that stored data on the computers within the network domain does not get accessed and possibly altered by unauthorized users. But firewalls are only effective at protecting the traffic that enters or leaves a particular domain and thus offer very little protection from security threats (such as sabotages) perpetrated inside the domain. Thus firewalls are, at best, only one part of a comprehensive network protection scheme.

6.6.2 Antivirus Software

Another commonly used security countermeasure is *antivirus software*, which is designed to "inoculate" computer systems against viruses, worms, and other forms of malicious, or rogue, programs. Antivirus software, which is now considered by many to be a standard security countermeasure, has been installed on most networked computer systems, including desktop computers. This software is typically used in conjunction with firewall technology to protect individual computer systems as well as network domains in universities, governmental organizations, and commercial institutions.

Lee Garber and Richard Raucci (1997) note that work on computer virus theory began more than fifty years ago with computer science pioneer and mathematician John von Neumann, who was among the first to describe the phenomenon "self-replicating systems."

(von Neumann is credited with designing the architecture for the first stored computer program in electronic computers.) Over the years, an antivirus industry emerged, and it has grown significantly since the advent of the Internet and the Web. Many contemporary antivirus programs are very sophisticated; some are able not only to detect and eliminate viruses but also to delete them as well. Certain antivirus programs can repair "infected files" and can remove "infected sectors" from system memory and disk drives.

Much of the current antivirus software is "scan-based" in that it is designed to scan a computer system for infected files. These programs can scan either at the time of system startup or after certain events (such as when a file is downloaded) or both. Antivirus software has had to keep pace as virus writers have become more sophisticated, but unfortunately, antivirus software can become quickly outdated and obsolete. Sophisticated hackers, such as members of the group that designed the Back Orifice program (described in Chapter 7) have figured out ways to disable older versions of antivirus software on systems that have not been upgraded. In some cases, hackers leave messages on their victims' computer systems, informing them that their antivirus software is outdated and useless. So users and system administrators must continue to remain vigilant and must make sure that they are running the very latest versions of antivirus programs.

In addition to having their computer systems secured against attacks by rogue programs and hacker break-ins, users expect that the data they transmit between computer systems will not be compromised. Whereas firewalls and antivirus software protect against incoming rogue programs and hacker break-ins, they do not ensure that electronic data sent beyond the "walls" of the protected system are secure from interference and possible tampering. To ensure the integrity of the electronic data they transmit, some users and many organizations have turned to data-encryption tools.

6.6.3 Encryption Tools

We already noted that some data security issues arise because of the threat to information that is transmitted over the Internet. In our discussion of privacy in Chapter 5, we saw that certain privacy-enhancing tools (PETs) could be used to protect the content of a user's communications in cyberspace. For example, Pretty Good Privacy (PGP), which was one of the earliest and perhaps best known PETs, was designed to ensure the confidentiality and integrity of data transmitted via e-mail. PGP employs a technique known as *data encryption*, which can also be viewed as a type of security countermeasure. Currently, much information that is transmitted in the cyberrealm, especially information communicated via e-mail, occurs through messages that are encrypted.

The use of data encryption, or cryptography, techniques in communicating sensitive information is hardly new; in fact, it is believed to date back at least as far as the Roman era, when Julius Caesar encrypted messages he sent to his generals. Essentially, encryption is converting the information in a message, composed in ordinary text (or "plain text"), into "ciphertext." The party receiving the encrypted message then uses a "key" to decrypt the ciphertext back into plain text. So long as both parties have the appropriate key, they can decode a message back into its original form (i.e., plain text). One challenge in ensuring the integrity of encrypted communications has been to make sure that the key, which must remain private, can be successfully communicated. Thus, an encrypted communication will be only as secure and private as its key.

6.6.3.1 Private-key and Public-key Encryption Schemes

The cryptographic technique described in the preceding paragraph is referred to as private-key encryption, a system in which both parties use the same encryption algorithm and the same private key. A more recent technology, called public cryptography, uses two keys: one public and the other private. If *A* wishes to communicate with *B*, *A* uses *B*'s public key to encode the message. That message can then only be decoded with *B*'s private key, which is secret. Similarly when *B* responds to *A*, *B* uses *A*'s public key to encrypt the message. That message can be decrypted only by using *A*'s private key. Although information about an individual's public key is accessible to others, that individual's ability to communicate encrypted information is not compromised. Public-key encryption is of particular interest to governmental agencies responsible for protecting national security and military intelligence, preventing terrorism, and enforcing laws.

Perhaps no group has been more interested in the security features made possible by strong forms of encryption than those involved in e-commerce. Because many on-line entrepreneurs believe that strong encryption is essential for realizing the full potential of e-commerce, they have looked to encryption-based applications to resolve some of their security-related worries. One solution involves a verification technique that ensures authentication between on-line consumers and merchants through strong-encryption tools.

While certain members of the e-commerce community might favor a solution to security problems through the implementation of strong encryption programs, those representing government and law enforcement agencies would not find a proposal of this type acceptable. At present, many lawmakers are concerned that criminals and terrorists can use strong-encrypted communications to carry out illegal and subversive activities. And law enforcement agencies have been frustrated in their attempts to monitor and intercept messages sent by terrorists and criminals who can use strong-encryption programs in their electronic communications.

6.6.3.2 Encryption Techniques Used in E-commerce Transactions

In the preceding section we noted that the e-commerce sector was particularly interested in the security features made possible by strong-encryption techniques. Many in that sector are concerned that the perception of insecure communications features will deter consumers from engaging in e-commerce transactions, so the e-commerce community has looked for solutions based on tools and applications using strong-encryption technology.

One application that has been used to ensure authentication between on-line consumers and merchants is a form of encryption involving *digital signatures*. VeriSign, for example, uses a public-key encryption technology to produce a "digital certificate," used to authenticate on-line transactions between consumers and merchants. Digital signatures not only ensure that the information sent from one destination to another is secure, they also verify that the party alleged to have sent the information in question is, in fact, the party who sent it. They are also designed to ensure that the party who received the information is indeed the party for whom the message was intended.

More will be said about encryption in Chapter 7, where we examine certain practices involving the use of cryptography by governmental and law enforcement agencies to combat crime. We next consider some ways in which anonymity tools can be used as a type of security countermeasure.

6.6.4 Anonymity Tools

Not only do users want to secure the integrity and confidentiality of their electronic communications, but many also wish to protect their identity while engaging in on-line activities. The recent introduction of anonymity tools, such as the Anonymizer, and pseudonymity agents, such as Lucent's Personalized Web Assistant, enable users to roam the Web either anonymously or pseudonymously.

What is anonymity, and how does it raise ethical concerns involving security in cyberspace? In its simplest sense, being anonymous means not being recognized or known as an individual with a certain name, identity, and so forth. Kathleen Wallace (1999) describes a person as being anonymous when that person has no traits that can be coordinated in way that would make that person uniquely identifiable. So an individual is anonymous in cyberspace when that person is able to navigate the Internet in a way that his or her personal identity is not revealed. Even though a user's movements in cyberspace can be tracked by data-monitoring tools such as cookies (see Chapter 5), an anonymous user cannot be identified beyond certain technical information such as the user's IP (Internet protocol) address, and ISP.

Many users have found the opportunity to interact anonymously or pseudonymously a desirable feature of the Internet, but some security analysts and many law enforcement officials fear that criminals and terrorists will abuse Internet anonymity and thereby exploit that medium for their own sinister ends. It is fairly easy to see how anonymity in cyberspace has raised moral concerns. Deborah Johnson (1997) believes that Internet anonymity makes it possible for people on-line to behave in ways that are not possible in off-line contexts. Although people can behave anonymously in the off-line world, Johnson argues that it requires much more effort. Because Internet anonymity has made possible certain kinds of undesirable, and arguably immoral, behavior, some have questioned whether anonymity in cyberspace should continue to be protected. The answer to this question depends on our answer to the related questions: What kind of value is anonymity? Is it a core value? Do we have an expected right to anonymity? Should we, by default, presume "in favor of" anonymity?

We noted in Chapter 5 that anonymity is often closely associated with privacy, which is generally believed to be a positive human value. Does a defense of personal privacy necessarily entail that we must embrace anonymity as well? Not all privacy advocates and civil libertarians who currently defend anonymous behavior on the Internet believe that anonymity itself is a core human value or a basic right. For example, some argue that while we have a right to privacy, we have no right to anonymity. Others, however, believe that without some degree of anonymity in cyberspace, users are vulnerable to having all of their movements tracked.

Anonymity on the Internet, despite its many positive features, has made it possible for individuals to behave in undesirable or even harmful ways. It has also made the process of identifying and catching criminals more difficult. So we return to the question: Should Internet anonymity always be protected? This is a very difficult and important question. As Helen Nissenbaum (1999) so aptly puts the matter, "…after all is said and done, we would not want to discover that the thing we have fought so hard to protect was not worth protecting after all." A number of arguments for and against policies involving Internet anonymity have been put forth. Unfortunately, we are unable to examine those arguments in detail.

▶ 6.7 IS A CODE OF NETWORK ETHICS NEEDED TO ADDRESS SECURITY CONCERNS IN CYBERSPACE?

Many worry that currently available countermeasures are not sufficient to safeguard our contemporary infrastructure, which increasingly depends on secure and reliable networked computer systems. Some have suggested that computer corporations should be required by law to produce more secure computer systems than those that are currently being sold to consumers and to organizations. Robert Steele (2000) has argued that computer systems are not secure because the software on which they run is not reliable and that the software is not reliable because it is not properly tested and regulated. He notes that regulating agencies require the testing of comparable products, yet we seem willing to accept the fact that software products and systems are neither exhaustively tested nor regulated, and thus not fully secure. Steele asks whether people would purchase automobiles if wheels on cars routinely fell off while motorists were driving in their cars.

Steele also asks whether you would be willing to purchase an automobile that could not be locked (secured) and thus protected against theft. He points out that there are no adequate "locks" for computers, and he blames Microsoft and other large computer corporations for not ensuring and guaranteeing that the computer software products are more secure. Steele also believes that corporations that produce computer software should assume full responsibility, legal and moral, for any insecure software products they sell. Because of this egregious lack of security, Steele concludes that we need a "code of network ethics" with a "due diligence" clause, which would spell out specific requirements for businesses engaged in the production of software. Recall our discussion of codes of ethics, professional responsibility, and reliability issues in Chapter 4. Do we need yet another ethical code? Would such a code be effective?

Steele raises a number of important points, but we will examine just two of his claims: First, we can agree with Steele's assumptions that consumers desire reliable products and that they expect dependable computer systems that are reasonably secure. But we can also question whether the analogy that Steele draws between computer systems and automobiles is useful or whether it breaks down in crucial respects. It is not yet possible to test computer systems for reliability in the same way that we can test automobile systems; we saw in our discussion of computer malfunctions such as in the case of the Therac 25 in Chapter 4 that it is virtually impossible to test for every variation and permutation of software code. The same is not true for testing the component parts of automobiles. Therefore, we ought to establish different thresholds of reliability testing and expectations for automobiles and computers. That said, there is still no reason why we cannot, with Steele, demand better security for computer systems.

Second, we can respond to Steele's claim that a code of network ethics is necessary. Few would dispute that such a code might be helpful, but it is not clear how a formal code of network ethics of the type that Steele suggests would necessarily ensure that security in computer systems could be foolproof. Perhaps, then, it would be prudent for us to continue to look for alternative measures to combat security issues involving cybertechnology.

▶ 6.8 IS TOTAL SECURITY IN CYBERSPACE A REASONABLE EXPECTATION?

Can total security in cyberspace be achieved? If so, would it be a desirable goal? Different answers to both questions have been given by different computer security experts. Many of us would no doubt prefer a secure cyberspace; however, some security analysts believe that we might not be willing to accept the consequences of such a level of security. More secure systems might require features that would make computer systems less friendly (and thus more difficult to operate). And while e-businesses might desire more secure systems, they might not want them if they discourage prospective on-line customers because of stricter security guidelines or requirements.

Stronger security requirements, strictly mandated and regulated by law, could mean more bureaucratic red tape for computer manufacturers, resulting in delays in getting their products to market. So stricter security requirements could have a negative financial impact on both computer manufacturers and e-commerce.

6.8.1 Tradeoffs in Computer Security

In any decisions to produce computer systems with enhanced security features, there are clearly tradeoffs that can be measured in cost, convenience, and flexibility. Having more secure computer systems might result in products that are more expensive to purchase, for both individual consumers and businesses. Would consumers be willing to spend more money for more security? And would commercial organizations be willing to incur costs that might be prohibitive because of the sheer numbers of computer systems with enhanced security that they would need to purchase at higher prices? Nonmonetary costs could be measured in terms of restrictions to user autonomy—more secure systems could eliminate anonymity and reduce privacy. And we've discussed how more secure systems might result in computers that are less user-friendly—and thus less convenient and less flexible.

But there are certain levels of insecurity that most of us seem willing to accept. For example, most of us drive automobiles, despite the fact that they are vulnerable to collisions and breakdowns that result in the deaths of thousands of motorists and pedestrians each year. Of course, we could invest billions of dollars into programs designed to make cars safer, but how much are we willing (or able) to spend for safer cars? Would consumers spend $90,000 on average for a car that was slightly, or even significantly, safer than current standard automobiles? Could they afford to do so?

We might, as a society, decide that it would be safer to drive and ride in armored vehicles. We could design automobiles to be more like military-style tanks in order to reduce the number of deaths and injuries that result from the use of automobiles. But even if we could figure out how to produce such vehicles economically, we would still have to be sure they offered convenience and flexibility. As a society, we have decided that we will accept a certain level of risk associated with automobile fatalities and injuries rather than either driving tanks (for automobiles) or not driving motor vehicles altogether. Can we, and should we, accept similar levels of risk associated with computer security? In the final section of this chapter, we examine computer security issues from the vantage point of risk analysis.

6.8.2 Viewing Security as a Process, Not a Product

We still have not decided whether foolproof security is possible for computer systems, even if we are willing to pay the price of increased cost, less convenience, and less flexibility. Joseph Kizza (1998) suggests that complete security can be guaranteed when four mechanisms are in place: deterrence, prevention, detection, and response, but Kizza does not specify how their conjunction guarantees security. Others have suggested that total security is not possible.

Bruce Schneier (2000) claims that anyone who promises a totally secure, or hacker-proof, system is selling snake oil, because there is no magic wand to make a system secure. Schneier points out that many security experts mistakenly assume that security solutions are simply a question of finding the right technology or the foolproof mathematical combination for an encryption device. He also believes that traditional approaches to security have been ineffective because they have relied to heavily on technology itself; this is especially apparent in the case of conventional security countermeasures.

For Schneier, the thesis that *security is a process, not a product* has become a mantra. Schneier also believes that an important element in that process is one involving risk assessment. He argues that seeking perfect security would make a system useless, because "anything worth doing requires some risk."

▶ 6.9 COMPUTER SECURITY AND RISK ANALYSIS

Bruce Schneier argues that security, at bottom, is an ongoing process (not a product) and that this process is essentially about risk analysis and risk management. (Recall that we briefly considered the concept of risk analysis in Section 4.6, where we examined a model for assessing risk in the development of safety-critical software systems.) Risk analysis is one of several methodologies used to reach an informed decision about the most cost-effective way to limit the risks (i.e., protect) to your assets. Consider that banks and credit card companies can tolerate a considerable amount of credit risk and fraud because they know how to anticipate losses and price their services accordingly. But what exactly is the level of risk that can be acceptable in computer systems? And how can we assess that kind of risk?

Consider how risk analysis could be applied in the following thought experiment: Imagine that you recently purchased a 1990 Toyota, and suppose that you live in an urban area where there is a high degree of automobile theft. Even though a 1990 Toyota has a low Blue-Book value (say, for example, $800), it might be good for parts that could be sold once the stolen vehicle has been "stripped." So you decide that you need to take the appropriate measures to make your car secure against theft and vandalism. You find out that purchasing a security system for your car would cost approximately $1100. Is your asset (the 1990 Toyota) worth the price required to secure it? According to most risk-assessment models, including Schneier's, it would be advisable to find some alternative means to secure your car.

Schneier believes that risk can be understood and assessed in terms of the net result of the impacts of five elements: assets, threats, vulnerabilities, impact, and safeguards. Although we will not analyze Schneier's model of risk analysis in detail, you can, on your own, consider how these five elements apply in the thought experiment above.

We will try to determine whether Schneier's model can help us to frame an adequate security policy that also addresses ethical challenges; for example, we can ask whether we can apply a cost-benefits analysis to computer security issues that impact the safety and lives of individuals. Financial considerations alone might be adequate for determining the "bottom line" when individual corporations who invest in e-commerce ventures decide how to increase their computer security. But should all decisions involving computer security be market driven—that is, determined by how much consumers are willing to spend and how much businesses are willing to invest? (Recall Don Gotterbarn's claim in Chapter 4 that an expanded sense of both "ethical risks" and "system stakeholder" should be taken into account in models of risk assessment for software development.) Should the results of a procedure based on conventional risk analysis be used to determine security policies involving our national infrastructure, with implications for the safety and well being of millions of people? And if the private sector is not willing to pay for enhanced security, does the federal government have an obligation to do so?

The ethical issues surrounding computer security are not trivial; they have implications for public safety that can result in the deaths of significant numbers of persons. So it is not clear that all computer security issues can be understood simply in terms of the risk analysis model advocated by Schneier. On the other hand, it is also not clear where the moral responsibility for ensuring greater computer security lies.

▶ 6.10 CHAPTER SUMMARY

In this chapter we examined the ethical implications of a wide range of computer security issues. We argued that it is useful to draw distinctions between such concepts as system security and data security, hacking and hacktivism, and information warfare and cyberterrorism. We also considered arguments for the view that foolproof security for computer systems may be neither possible nor desirable. Finally, we described some ethical challenges involved in trying to understand computer security issues solely in terms of models for risk analysis.

We considered whether some forms of hacking might, in certain extreme circumstances, be ethically justified. In Chapter 7 we will focus on legal and criminal aspects of hacking and hacking-related behavior in cyberspace.

▶ REVIEW QUESTIONS

1. What do we mean by "computer security"?
2. How are computer security issues similar to and different from computer privacy issues?
3. How do security issues in cyberspace raise ethical concerns?
4. Identify some of the key differences between "system security" and "data security."
5. What do we mean by "rogue computer programs" and "computer rogues"?
6. Who are computer hackers? How do hacking activities threaten security on the Internet?
7. Are there any cases where hacking might be justified from an ethical point of view?
8. What exactly is meant by "hacktivism"?
9. Can "hacktivist" activities be justified on the grounds of civil disobedience toward unjust laws?
10. What is cyberterrorism?
11. Can cyberterrorist activities be distinguished from hacktivist activities?
12. What is meant by "information warfare"?
13. How can information warfare be distinguished from cyberterrorism?
14. Identify and describe four types of countermeasures that can be used to combat computer security.
15. What are some controversies surrounding data encryption in cyberspace?
16. Describe some controversies associated with Internet anonymity as it relates to computer security.
17. Is complete security in cyberspace possible?

18. Is total security a reasonable goal? Why or why not?

19. What is meant by the expression "Security is a process, not a product"?

20. How might our understanding of computer security be enhanced by the principles of risk management and risk assessment?

▶ DISCUSSION QUESTIONS

1. Consider some of the tradeoffs regarding security and convenience that we examined in this chapter. Is it possible to strike an appropriate or reasonable balance? For example, suppose that in the United States, 20,000 lives could be saved each year if the speed limit were reduced from fifty-five to thirty miles per hour. Is reducing the speed limit that drastically plausible? What implications does your answer have for tradeoffs involving computer security and considerations of convenience?

2. Recall Eugene Spafford's argument as to why computer break-ins can be justified under extraordinary circumstances. On the one hand, his argument seems to make perfectly good sense, but it is difficult to understand what Spafford means when he suggests that "doing the right thing" (i.e., breaking into a computer system in the case of a medical emergency) would also be ethically unjustifiable. Perhaps what he intends to say is that performing an undesirable act, which causes some harm and which could never be justified in ordinary circumstances, can in certain cases be the (ethically) right thing to do. For example, assume that you have a moral obligation to save a person's life when it is in your power to do so. Further assume that saving the person's life would result in some, but not significant, harm to others: Imagine that you had to break into a neighbor's car in order to drive a friend, who would otherwise die, to the hospital. You would be morally obligated to save the person's life, and, arguably, what you did, even though it might have violated the law and even though it may have caused some harm to your neighbor, was not only the right thing to do but was also ethically justifiable.

   If we apply the analogy used in the preceding paragraph to the Spafford's case involving a computer break-in, then it would seem that breaking into the computer database containing the medical information is ethically justifiable as well; that is, it is in the hacker's power to save someone's life without causing significant harm to others, so we should break into the computer system to get the vital medical information that we need. Spafford may be correct in asserting that computer break-ins are never harmless, but even if they result in some harm, would it follow on that criterion alone that every computer break-in is necessarily unethical? Explain.

3. In our discussion of Internet anonymity, we saw how some forms of anonymous behavior in cyberspace can have profound ethical implications. Imagine that there is a very close political election involving two candidates who are running for a seat in a state legislature. The weekend before citizens will cast their votes, one candidate decides to defame his opponent by using an anonymous re-mailer service (which strips away the original address of the sender of the e-mail) to send a message of questionable truth to an electronic distribution list of his opponent's supporters. The information included in this email is so defamatory that it may threaten the outcome of the election by influencing many undecided voters, as well as the libeled candidate's regular supporters, to vote against her. Does the "injured" candidate in this instance have the right to demand that the identity of the person using the anonymous re-mailer (whom she suspects for good reasons to be her opponent in this election) be revealed?

4. We have seen that strong arguments can be given as to why encryption tools are needed to safeguard communications in cyberspace, yet we have also seen that these tools can be used by terrorists and criminals to protect their communications in cyberspace. In the wake of September 11, can a case be made for not allowing ordinary users to employ strong encryption tools in

Internet communications? On the other hand, can we still claim to live in a free society if plans for government interception of e-mail communications, as provided for in the Homeland Security Act, are implemented?

► REFERENCES

Branscomb, Anne W. (1990). "Rogue Computer Programs and Computer Rogues: Tailoring the Punishment to Fit the Crime," *Rutgers Computer and Technology Law Journal*, Vol. 16, pp. 1–6.

Denning, Dorothy E. (1999a). *Information Warfare and Security*. New York: ACM Press and Reading, MA: Addison Wesley.

Denning, Dorothy E. (1999b). "Activism, Hacktivism, and Cyberterrorism: The Internet as a Tool For Influencing Foreign Policy." Paper presented to the World Affairs Council (Dec. 10). Available at: http://www.nautilus.org/info-policy/workshop/papers/denning.html.

Denning, Dorothy E. (2000). "Cyberterrorism." Testimony before the Special Oversight Panel on Terrorism, Committee on Armed Services, United States House of Representatives (May 23). Available at: http://www.cs.georgetown.edu/~denning/infosec/cyberterror.html.

Garfinkel, Simson, and Eugene Spafford (1996). *Practical UNIX and Internet Security*. 2d ed. Cambridge, MA: O'Reilly & Associates, Inc.

Garber, Lee, and Richard Raucci (1997). "Antivirus Technology Offers New Cures," *IEEE Computer*, Vol. 31, No. 2, pp. 12–14.

Himanen, Pekka (2001). *The Hacker Ethic: A Radical Approach to the Philosophy of Business*. New York: Random House.

Johnson, Deborah G. (1997). "Ethics On-line," *Communications of the ACM*, Vol. 40, No. 1, pp. 60–69.

Kizza, Joseph M. (1998). *Ethical and Social Issues in the Information Age*. New York: Springer-Verlag.

Levy, Steve (1984). *Hackers: Heroes of the Computer Revolution*. Garden City, NY: Doubleday.

Lodin, Steven W., and Christopher L. Schuba (1998). "Firewalls Fend Off Invasions from the Net," *IEEE Spectrum*, Vol. 35, No. 2, pp. 26–34.

Manion, Mark, and Abby Goodrum (2000). "Terrorism or Civil Disobedience: Toward a Hacktivist Ethic," *Computers and Society*, Vol. 30, No. 2, pp. 14–19.

Moor, James H. (1997). "Towards a Theory of Privacy for the Information Age," *Computers and Society*, Vol. 27, No. 3, pp. 349–359.

Moor, James H. (1998). "Reason, Relativity, and Responsibility in Computer Ethics," *Computers and Society*, Vol. 28, No. 1, pp. 14–21.

Nissenbaum, Helen (1999). "The Meaning of Anonymity in an Information Age," *The Information Society, Vol.* 15, No. 2, pp. 141–144.

Oppliger, Rolf (1997). "Internet Security: Firewalls and Beyond," *Communications of the ACM*, Vol. 40, No. 5, pp. 93–102.

Power, Richard (2000). *Tangled Web: Tales of Digital Crime from the Shadows of Cyberspace*. Indianapolis, IN: Que Corp.

Rosenberg, Richard S. (1997). *The Social Impact of Computers*. 2d ed. San Diego: Academic Press.

Schneier, Bruce (2000). *Secrets and Lies: Digital Security in a Networked World*. New York: John Wiley and Sons.

Spafford, Eugene H. (1992). "Are Computer Hacker Break-Ins Ethical?" *Journal of Systems Software*, Vol. 17, pp. 41–47.

Spafford, Eugene H. (2002). Interview in *PKI Forum*, conducted on January 26. Available at: http://pkiforum.com/books/interview_spafford_1a.html.

Spafford, Eugene H., Kathleen A. Heaphy, and David J. Ferbrache (1989). *Computer Viruses: Dealing With Electronic Vandalism and Programmed Threats*. Arlington, VA: ADAPSO Press.

Spinello, Richard A. (2000). "Information Integrity." In D. Langford, ed. *Internet Ethics*. London, UK: Macmillan Publishers, pp. 158–180.

Spinello, Richard A., and Herman T. Tavani. (2001). "Security and Cyberspace." In R. A. Spinello and H. T. Tavani, eds. *Readings in Cyberethics*. Sudbury, MA: Jones and Bartlett Publishers, pp. 443–450.

Steele, Robert (2000). Interview conducted in the PBS television series *Frontline* special entitled "Hackers."

Tavani, Herman T. (2000). "Privacy and Security." Chap. 4 in D. Langford, ed. *Internet Ethics*. London, UK: Macmillan and New York: St. Martin's Press.

Thompson, Paul B. (2001). "Privacy, Secrecy, and Security," *Ethics and Information Technology*, Vol. 3, No. 1, pp. 13–19.

Wallace, Kathleen A. (1999). "Anonymity," *Ethics and Information Technology*, Vol. 1, No. 1, pp. 22–35.

► FURTHER READINGS

Arquilla, John, and David F. Ronfeldt, eds. (1998). *In Athena's Camp: Preparing for Conflict in the Information Age*. Santa Monica, CA: Rand Corporation.

Baase, Sara (2003). "Encryption and Interception of Communications." Chapter 3 in *A Gift of Fire: Social, Legal, and Ethical Issues in Computing*. 2d ed. Upper Saddle River, NJ: Prentice Hall.

Camp, L. Jean (2000). *Trust and Risk in Internet Commerce*. Cambridge, MA: MIT Press.

Chaum, David (1984). "A New Paradigm for Individuals in the Information Age." In *Proceedings of from IEEE 5th Symposium on Security and Privacy*, Oakland, CA, pp. 99–103.

Denning, Dorothy E., and Peter J. Denning, eds. (1998) *Internet Besieged: Countering Cyberspace Scofflaws*. New York: ACM Press.

Diffie, Whitield, and Susan Landau (1998). *Privacy on the Line: The Politics of Wiretapping and Encryption*. Cambridge, MA: MIT Press.

Garfinkel, Simson (1999). *Database Nation: The Death of Privacy in the 21st Century*. Cambridge, MA: O'Reilly and Associates.

Ghosh, Anup K., and Jeffrey M. Voas (1999). "Innoculating Software for Survivability," *Communications of the ACM*, Vol. 42, No. 7, July, pp. 38–44.

Goodrum, Abby, and Mark Manion (2000). "The Ethics of Hacktivism," *Journal of Information Ethics*, Vol. 9, No., 2, pp. 51–59.

Jajodia, Sushil, Catherine D. McCollum, and Paul Ammann (1999). "Trusted Recovery," *Communications of the ACM*, Vol. 42, No. 7, July, pp. 71–75.

Ludlow, Peter, ed. (2001). *Crypto Anarchy, Cyberstates, and Pirate Utopia*. Cambridge, MA: MIT Press.

Marx, Gary (1999). "What's in a Name: Some Reflections on the Sociology of Anonymity," *The Information Society,* Vol. 15, No. 2, pp. 1–15.

Marx, Gary (2001). "Identity and Anonymity: Some Conceptual Distinctions and Issues for Research." In J. Caplani and J. Topley, eds. *Documenting Individual Identity*. Princeton, NJ: Princeton University Press.

Neuman, Peter. "Inside Risks." A column that appears regularly in *Communications of the ACM*.

Reiter, M. K. and A. D. Rubin (1999). "Anonymous Web Transactions With Crowds," *Communications of the ACM*, Vol. 42, No. 2, February, pp. 32–38.

Rotenberg, Marc (1995). "Computer Virus Legislation." In D. G. Johnson and H. Nissenbaum, eds. *Computing, Ethics & Social Values*, Englewood Cliffs, NJ: Prentice Hall, pp. 135–147.

Simons, Barbara, and Eugene H. Spafford (2003). "Risks of Total Surveillance," *Communications of the ACM*, Vol. 46, No. 3, p. 120.

Spinello, Richard A. (2003). "Securing the Electronic Frontier." Chapter 6 in *CyberEthics: Morality and Law in Cyberspace*. 2d ed. Sudbury, MA: Jones and Bartlett Publishers.

Thomas, Douglas (2002). *Hacker Culture*. Minneapolis: University of Minnesota Press.

Vlug, Albert, and Johan van der Lei (2001). "Double Encryption of Anonymized Electronic Interchange." In R. A. Spinello and H. T. Tavani, eds. *Readings in Cyberethics*. Sudbury, MA: Jones and Bartlett Publishers, pp. 493–500.

7

CYBERCRIME AND CYBERRELATED CRIMES

In Chapter 6, we examined computer security issues independent of their implications for crime, even though issues involving crime and security in cyberspace sometimes overlap. In Chapter 7, we focus specifically on criminal activities involving cybertechnology. Among the questions examined in this chapter are:

- What is cybercrime, and how can it be distinguished from cyberrelated crimes?
- Is there a typical cybercriminal?
- Is there a difference between computer hacking and cracking?
- Why are jurisdictional issues problematic for prosecuting cybercrimes?
- How do encryption technologies pose a special challenge for law enforcement agencies?
- How can biometric technologies assist law enforcement groups in identifying criminals?

We begin our examination with a brief look at some cybercrimes that have received world-wide media attention.

▶ 7.1 CYBERCRIMES AND CYBERCRIMINALS

Reports of criminal activities involving cybertechnology have appeared as cover stories in periodicals, as headlines in major newspapers, and as lead stories on television news programs in the United States and around the globe. Consider three incidents, each of which illustrates a different type of criminal activity involving the use of cybertechnology. In May 2000, the

ILOVEYOU computer virus, also called the Love Bug, infected computer systems in the United States, Europe, and Asia, disrupting e-commerce activities as well as the operations of many governmental agencies. In February 2000, a series of cyberattacks on major commercial Web sites owned and operated by Amazon, eBay, CNN, Yahoo!, and others, resulted in "denial of service" to users who wished to access them for legitimate purposes. And in December 1999, the owners and operators of the Napster Web site were sued by the Recording Industry Association of America for wrongfully and willingly distributing proprietary information (in the form of MP3 files that contained copyrighted music) on the Internet. Although the flurry of criminal activities involving cybertechnology was the subject of much media attention, the use of computers to carry out criminal activities is not exactly new.

7.1.1 Background Events: A Brief Sketch

In the 1970s and 1980s, stories surfaced about disgruntled employees who altered files in computer databases or who sabotaged computer systems to seek revenge against employers. Other highly publicized news stories described teenage hackers breaking into computer systems, either as a prank or as a malicious attempt to subvert data or disrupt its flow. There were also reports, frequently sensationalized and occasionally glamorized by some members of the press, involving hackers who used computers to transfer money from wealthy individuals and corporations to poorer individuals and organizations.

In Chapter 6 we saw that hackers have engaged in a wide range of illicit, or at least questionable, activities. As a society, our attitude toward hacking has changed: In the past, young computer hackers were sometimes portrayed as countercultural heroes who single-handedly took on the establishment, like David taking down Goliath (e.g., big government or big business), or Robin Hood robbing the rich to give to the poor. Today, however, there is a growing concern among those both in the private sector and in the public sector that hacking activities of any type should not be tolerated. The media, which itself has been a victim of cyberattacks (e.g., denial-of-service attacks on the New York Times and the CNN Web sites mentioned above), as well as ordinary computer users have shifted their attitude considerably. Perhaps this change in sentiment is due to our society's increased dependence on networked computers and the Internet.

Of course, hacking-related crimes are only one of the many kinds of crimes made possible by cybertechnology. Most computer crimes involve either fraud or abuse, or both. Richard Power (2000) distinguishes computer fraud from computer abuse in the following way. He identifies computer fraud as computer-related crimes involving deliberate misrepresentation or alteration of data in order to get something of value; he defines *computer abuse,* on the other hand, as willful or negligent unauthorized activity that affects the availability, confidentiality, or integrity of computer resources. Criminal computer abuse includes fraud, embezzlement, theft, malicious damage, unauthorized use, denial of service, and misappropriation.

Analysts believe that many computer crimes go unreported because the victims fear the negative repercussions: reporting the crimes would be tantamount to admitting that their computer security practices are inadequate. Consider, for example, what might happen if a customer discovered that the bank where she deposits and saves money had been broken into by hackers—she might decide to transfer her funds to a bank that she perceives to be more secure. And if computer-related crimes committed by employees working inside a financial institution were reported and publicized, the institution could suffer a loss of customer confidence.

7.1.2 A Typical Cybercriminal

Can we construct a profile for a typical cybercriminal? Some people associate cybercriminals with hackers; computer crime expert Donn Parker (1998) believes that typical hackers tend to exhibit three common traits: precociousness, curiosity, and persistence. Many people think of the typical computer hacker as the very bright, technically sophisticated, young white male in the popular movie *War Games*. Is such a portrayal accurate? Parker suggests that it might be, provided that we carefully distinguish between hackers as nonprofessional, or amateur, criminals, and hackers as professional criminals. He points out that stereotypical computer hackers, unlike most professional criminals, are not generally motivated by greed, and they seem to enjoy "joyriding" (the thrill experienced in figuring out how to break into unauthorized systems), another characteristic that allegedly distinguishes them from professional criminals. But is this stereotyping of computer criminals as either professionals or nonprofessionals adequate?

Tom Forester and Perry Morrison (1994) have pointed out that many computer criminals have been company employees who were formerly loyal and trustworthy and who did not necessarily possess great computer expertise but were tempted by flaws in computer systems or by loopholes in the controls monitoring their daily activities. So in this case, opportunity seems to be the root cause of many computer crimes. If Forester and Morrison are correct, then typical computer criminals are either (amateur) teenage hackers, professional criminals, or (once) loyal employees unable to resist a criminal opportunity presented by cybertechnology.

Although many hackers are considered amateur criminals, some possess an expertise with computers comparable to that of the best technical experts in computer science. On the other hand, many hackers do not possess outstanding technical skills but are savvy enough to locate sophisticated hacking tools that can be downloaded from the Internet for free, and many of these hackers are sufficiently astute to take advantage of "holes" in computer systems and programs.

7.1.3 Some Notorious Cybercriminals

Many of the crimes we will describe in this section have involved either teenagers or college students and have become classic cases of malicious hacking and computer crime.

Kevin Mitnick: Public Cyberenemy No. 1?

Kevin Mitnick has been described as "Public Cyberenemy No. 1" (Power 2000). Mitnick's criminal activities span nearly twenty years. In 1982, eighteen-year-old Mitnick broke into the computer system of the North American Air Defense Command. Six years later, he broke into the computer network of Digital Equipment Corporation and monitored its e-mail. Douglas Thomas (2002), who describes Mitnick as an *überhacker* (or super hacker), tells how Mitnick stole Digital's entire VMS operating system while security experts at Digital "simply watched millions of lines of their code being downloaded, unable to do anything about it." Mitnick was arrested, prosecuted, and convicted for the first time in 1989.

Mitnick cleverly avoided detection and arrest in several later criminal incidents, but he was eventually caught and prosecuted each time. He has since been sentenced to serving jail terms on multiple occasions. Even when on parole from prison, however, Mitnick repeatedly engaged in cyberrelated criminal activities. His crimes exemplify the behavior of a hacker whose motives are far more sinister and malicious than earlier computer hackers who engaged in "pranks."

Robert Morris and the "Internet Worm"

One of the earliest Internet-related crimes was perpetrated by a Cornell University graduate student named Robert Morris. In 1988, Morris released a worm (now referred to as the "Internet worm" or the "Cornell Virus") that brought activity on the Internet virtually to a halt. The Morris case is a classic because it was the first cybercrime to have a profound effect in terms of the scope and scale of disruption it caused for Internet users.

Authorities easily traced the origin of the Cornell Virus to Morris, who was brought to trial. In his defense, Morris testified that he did not intend to cause any damage, arguing that his program (the virus) was just an experiment that got out of control. Prosecutors had a difficult time finding a specific legal violation with which to charge Morris; it was not clear how the 1986 Computer Fraud and Abuse Act could be applied. Many believe that the sentence finally handed to Morris—primarily, probation and community service—was far too lenient given the serious nature of his crime.

It is interesting to note that Robert Morris is the son of one of the government's leading experts on computer security; Morris's father was employed as a scientist at NSA (the National Security Agency).

Onel de Guzman and the ILOVEYOU Virus

Several disruptive worms and viruses, for example, Michelangelo and Melissa, followed in the wake of the "Cornell Virus" and caused severe disruption and damage to networked computers systems. On May 3, 2000, Onel de Guzman, a student in the Philippines, allegedly launched a computer virus that came to be known as the Love Bug, or the ILOVEYOU virus; it wreaked havoc for computer users worldwide.

In writing the software code for his virus, Guzman took advantage of a hole in Microsoft's Outlook program for e-mail. We will discuss the prosecution of the Guzman case in Section 7.5.1, which addresses the problem of legal jurisdiction in cyberspace.

Mafia Boy and the Cyberattacks on E-commerce Sites

In early February 2000, a fifteen-year-old Canadian resident whose Internet alias was "Mafia Boy" issued a series of "denial of service attacks" on e-commerce sites owned and operated by American corporations. Because of the thousands of bogus requests they received, the Web sites of Yahoo!, CNN, eBay, and others were not fully functional for more than twenty-four hours. This disruption resulted in the loss of billions of dollars for the affected sites. Because Mafia Boy was underage, his true identity was not revealed.

Dimitri and Microsoft Corporation

A Russian teenager, code-named Dimitri, took advantage of a bug in a Microsoft program to break into computers at the Microsoft Corporation. Microsoft had informed its users, via the Internet, that it was necessary to install a software "patch" to a known bug in one of

Microsoft's operating systems in order to keep their computer systems secure. The patch was available for free and could easily be downloaded from Microsoft's Web page. Ironically, however, Microsoft had failed to apply the patch to its own system. Dmitri noticed Microsoft's oversight and decided to take advantage of it in his successful attempt to gain access to computers at Microsoft's headquarters; his success has raised concerns about Microsoft's own internal security practices.

Curador and Identity Theft

Rafael Grey, a teenager living in England who used the hacker code name "Curador," stole thousands of credit card numbers. He was eventually caught, many believe, because he boasted on-line about the theft. Although some might view Grey's activities as "cybermischief" (he did not use the stolen credit card numbers), his activities still involved unauthorized on-line activities.

Unlike Grey's cybermischief foray on the Internet, some identity-theft cases have resulted in serious damage. For example, a hacker was able to steal Mari Frank's credit card number from a database via the Internet, assume her (electronic) identity, and then make $50,000 in purchases in Frank's name. In November 2002, the federal government broke up a ring of identity-theft criminals who had used Internet technology to gain access to the credit information of thousands of individuals. Consumers have since been warned that they might be vulnerable to identity theft via electronic transactions.

Notorious Hacker Cults

Malicious hackers have not always acted alone in carrying out their criminal acts; some banded together to form groups such as Chaos and the Legion of Doom. More recently a group that calls itself the Cult of the Dead Cow created the Back Orifice Program to take advantage of a bug in Microsoft software and gain access to and control of computer systems running Microsoft operating system software. Using the Back Orifice program, hackers can not only break into computer systems but once they have penetrated a system they can also take control of a user's keyboard and mouse.

7.1.4 Hacking vs. Cracking: Is There a Legal Distinction?

We have already noted that computer criminals are often called hackers. Consequently "hacker" has taken on a pejorative connotation. Pekka Himanen (2001) notes that hacker originally meant anyone who "programmed enthusiastically" and who believed that "information sharing is a powerful positive good." The hacker Jargon File (maintained on the Web by Eric Raymond at www.tuxedo.org/esr/jargon) defines a hacker as an expert or enthusiast of any kind. Note that, according to this definition, a person can be an astronomy hacker: A hacker need not be a computer enthusiast. In fact, a hacker, in the generic sense of the term, might have no interest in computers at all.

As we saw in our examination of hacking activities vis-à-vis computer security in Chapter 6, many hackers believe that they have an ethical duty to share their expertise by writing free software and facilitating access to computer resources. This was the view of the "hacker ethic," as described by Steve Levy (1984), which emerged in the 1960s at institutions such as MIT. Himanen points out that this earlier understanding of a hacker began to change in the 1980s when "the media started applying the term [hacker] to criminals. In order to avoid the confusion with virus writers and intruders into information systems, hackers began calling these destructive computer users *crackers*." According to the hacker Jargon File, a cracker is one "who breaks security on a system." Crackers often engage in theft and vandalism once they have gained access to computer systems.

Some authors also use the expressions *white hat* and *black hat* to distinguish between the two types of hacking behavior. The phrase "white hat hackers" is used to refer to those "innocent," or nonmalicious, forms of hacking, while "black hat hackers" refers roughly to what we described above as "cracking."

Unfortunately, distinctions between hacking and cracking, and between white hat hackers and black hat hackers are generally not recognized and observed in the world beyond the computer community. So the media often refer to crackers, or black hat hackers, simply as hackers. This, in turn, has perpetuated the negative image of hackers and hacking in society at large.

In this chapter, many of our uses of "hacker" reflect the broader societal (i.e., negative) meaning of the term. Because of the way "hacker" has been used in the media, it is difficult, if not impossible to refer to classic cases of computer crime without invoking it. So it is important to keep in mind that many activities and crimes described in this chapter as hacking would be better understood as instances of cracking.

In Chapter 6, we considered whether at least some hacking cases, under extraordinary conditions, might be ethically justifiable. In this chapter, our concern is with hacking-related issues from a legal perspective. For example, we ask, Should all forms of computer hacking be declared illegal? Should every hacker be prosecuted as a criminal? Can some forms of hacking be defended on constitutional grounds in the United States? Certain First Amendment rights advocates see some forms of hacking as an expression of individual freedoms. Advocates for "hacker's rights," such as Mitch Kapor (1991), sometimes note that traditional forms of hacking played an important role in computer developments and breakthroughs, and they point out that many of today's "computer heroes" and successful entrepreneurs could also be accused of having been hackers in the past.

7.1.5 Hackers and the Law

Even though hackers may enjoy some support for their activities from civil liberties organizations, many in the government and business sectors view hacking as an invasive activity, and some see it as a form of trespass. They argue that trespassing in cyberspace is a criminal offense, regardless of whether hackers claim to be engaging merely in fun or pranks or whether they also go on to steal, abuse, or disrupt. Current legislation against hacking clearly takes the side of business, government, and law enforcement agencies. Many on both sides of the debate, however, support legislation that would distinguish between the degree of punishment handed to "nonmalicious" vs. "malicious" hackers. Earlier computer crime legislation did not always allow for such distinctions.

To see that some laws for prosecuting computer break-ins have not been adequate, we need only look at comparable laws that apply to analogous crimes in physical space. Courts and juries understand very well distinctions in crimes involving breaking and entering into property in physical space; for example, a person who only picks the lock of a door handle or one who turns an unlocked door handle but does not enter someone's house, would not likely receive the same punishment as someone who also turns the door handle and then enters the house. Similarly, a person who illegally enters someone's house only to snoop, and not to steal or vandalize, would probably not receive the same punishment as someone who illegally enters a person's house and then goes on to steal items or vandalize property, or both. Yet in crimes committed in cyberspace, these distinctions have not always been made by judges and juries in determining sentences.

We describe some national and international laws and proposals in Section 7.5.2. Before considering those laws, it is useful to define what we mean by "cybercrime."

▶ 7.2 DEFINING CYBERCRIME

We have seen that crimes involving cybertechnology, especially those involving teenage hackers, have received considerable attention in the popular press. The criteria used for determining which kinds of crimes should be labeled "computer crimes" have been neither clear nor consistent. Some news reporters and journalists suggest that any crime involving the presence of a computer is a computer crime; others, however, have argued that there is nothing special about crimes that involve computers. Don Gotterbarn (1991) has criticized much of the media hype surrounding computer-related crimes as a new species of "yellow journalism." As we saw in Chapter 1, Gotterbarn argues that a crime in which an individual uses a surgeon's scalpel to commit a murder would not be considered an issue in medical ethics, even though a medical instrument was used in the criminal act; so, by analogy, Gotterbarn concludes that crimes involving computers are not necessarily issues in computer ethics.

If Gotterbarn is correct, we can reasonably ask whether a separate category, cybercrime, is necessary or even useful. Consider the crimes that have involved technologies other than computers. Do we have separate categories for them? People steal televisions, but we don't have a category, television crime. People also steal automobiles, and some people have used automobiles to assist criminals in "getaway" operations, but we don't have a category, automobile crime. So why do we need a separate category, cybercrime, for criminal acts involving cybertechnology? Yet lawmakers have determined it necessary, or at least useful, to enact specific laws for crimes involving computers and cybertechnology. Have the criteria used by lawmakers to frame various categories of computer crime been coherent? We next take up the question of criteria for distinguishing between computer crimes and noncomputer crimes.

7.2.1 Determining the Criteria

Do any of these three scenarios, each of which illustrates criminal activity involving a computer lab, convincingly demonstrate the need for a distinct category of computer crime?

> **SCENARIO 1:** Lee steals a computer device (e.g., a printer) from a computer lab.

> **SCENARIO 2:** Lee breaks into a computer lab and then snoops around.

> **SCENARIO 3:** Lee enters a computer lab that he is authorized to use and then places an explosive device, set to detonate a short time later, on a computer system in the lab.

Clearly each of the acts in these three scenarios is criminal. But should any of these criminal acts necessarily be viewed as a computer crime or cybercrime? One could point out that it would not have been possible to commit any of them if computer technology had never existed, and this might initially influence some to believe that the three criminal acts are somehow unique to computer technology. Even though each act involves the presence of computer technology, however, they each can easily be understood and prosecuted as a specific example of ordinary crime involving theft, breaking and entering, and vandalism, respectively. So we might infer that there are no legitimate grounds for having a separate category of computer crime. Can we justify such an inference?

7.2.2 A Preliminary Definition of Cybercrime

A computer crime could, as Forester and Morrison (1994) suggest, be defined as "a criminal act in which a computer is used as the *principal tool*" [Italics added]. According to this definition, the theft of a computer hardware device (or, for that matter, the theft of an automobile or a television which also happened to contain a computer component), would not qualify as a computer crime. If we apply the definition to Scenario 2, involving breaking and entering into the computer lab, and 3, vandalizing a computer system in the lab, Forester and Morrison's definition eliminates these criminal acts as well, so their definition of computer crime seems plausible. But is it adequate? Consider the following scenario:

> **SCENARIO 4:** Lee uses a computer to file a fraudulent income tax return.

In the process of entering data into his electronic income tax forms, Lee decides to cheat the government by providing false information. Since income tax fraud is a crime and Lee uses a computer in committing this crime, is this criminal act a computer crime?

Lee uses a computer as the principal tool to commit fraud, so according to Forester and Morrison's definition, it would seem that Lee has committed a computer crime. But has he? Lee could commit the same crime by manually filling out a hardcopy version of the income tax forms using a pencil or pen. Lee's using a computer is coincident with, but by no means essential to, this particular criminal act, so Forester and Morrison's definition of computer crime, which fails to rule out Lee's criminal act of income-tax fraud as a computer crime, is not adequate.

7.2.3 Toward a Coherent and Comprehensive Definition of Cybercrime

Roy Girasa (2002) offers a more comprehensive definition of cybercrime than Forester and Morrison's. He defines cybercrime as "a generic term covering the multiplicity of crimes found in penal codes or in legislation having the use of a computer as a central component." Is this definition any more helpful than Forester and Morrison's? What does it mean for a crime to have a computer as its "central component?" Was a computer a "central component" in our example of Lee's cheating on his income tax return? It is difficult to distinguish which crimes have and which do not have a computer as their central component, so Girasa's definition of computer crime is not much of an improvement over the one advanced by Forester and Morrison.

Recall our discussion in Chapter 1 of James Moor's insight that computer technology is "logically malleable" and thus creates "new possibilities for human action." We saw that these new possibilities, in turn, sometimes generate both policy vacuums and conceptual muddles. By extension, these new possibilities for human action include new possibilities for crime. Many of these possibilities have resulted in criminal actions that have forced us to stretch and tweak concepts and laws dealing with crime, requiring conceptual clarification as well as new or revised policies and laws. Applying Moor's insight, we can ask whether any new forms of crime have been made possible by cybertechnology. If we answer "yes," then some crimes are unique to computers and cybertechnology.

By thinking about cybercrimes in terms of their unique or special features—i.e., conditions that separate them from ordinary crimes—we could distinguish authentic or "genuine" cybercrimes from other crimes that involve cybertechnology. We can propose a definition of a (genuine) *cybercrime* as a crime in which the criminal act can be carried out only through the use of cybertechnology and can take place only in the cyberrealm.

As in the case of Forester and Morrison's definition, this definition of cybercrime would rule out the three scenarios in the computer lab. But unlike Forester and Morrison's definition, it would also rule out crimes in which the use of a computer is either trivial or insignificant; for example, cases in which individuals used computers and computing devices to commit traditional crimes such as filing a fraudulent income tax return or physically assaulting one or more persons. If we accept our working definition of cybercrime, then we can isolate specific cybercrimes and place them into appropriate categories.

▶ 7.3 THREE CATEGORIES OF GENUINE CYBERCRIME: PIRACY, TRESPASS, AND VANDALISM IN CYBERSPACE

Using our proposed definition of cybercrime in the preceding section, we can categorize genuine cybercrimes as follows:

1. *Cyberpiracy*: using cybertechnology in unauthorized ways to
   a. reproduce copies of proprietary software and proprietary information or
   b. distribute proprietary information (in digital form) across a computer network.
2. *Cybertrespass*: using cybertechnology to gain unauthorized access to
   a. an individual's or an organization's computer system or
   b. a password-protected Web site.
3. *Cybervandalism*: using cybertechnology to unleash one or more programs that
   a. disrupt the transmission of electronic information across one or more computer networks, including the Internet, or
   b. destroy data resident in a computer or damage a computer system's resources, or both.

Recall the three incidents described in Section 7.1: unleashing the ILOVEYOU computer virus; launching the denial-of-service attacks on commercial Web sites; and distributing proprietary MP3 files on the Internet. Using our model of cybercrime, each incident falls into at least one of the three categories. Crimes involving the distribution of MP3 files that contain proprietary material are cyberpiracy (Category 1); the ILOVEYOU or "love bug" virus is cybervandalism (Category 3); and the denial-of-service attacks on the e-commerce Web sites are cybertrespass (Category 2), because they involved the unauthorized use of (i.e., the breaking into) third-party computer systems and sending spurious requests to their Web sites rather than the kind of "genuine" request sent by users who wish to access those sites for legitimate purposes (such as e-commerce transactions). Since denial-of-service attacks also cause serious disruption of services for the targeted Web sites, they can also be classified as cybervandalism (Category 3); some cybercrimes will span more than one category (Tavani 2000).

If our model is correct, then many crimes that use cybertechnology are not genuine cybercrimes. Pedophilia, stalking, and pornography can each be carried out with or without computers; there is nothing about them that is unique to cybertechnology, so we could describe them as *cyberrelated* crimes.

In Chapter 6, we saw that it was difficult to draw a coherent distinction between cyberterrorism and hacktivism. We now see that both can be understood as instances of cybervandalism, regardless whether they were perpetrated by "electronic political activists" or by cyberterrorists. If, however, hackers, hacktivists, and cyberterrorists also break into computer systems in order to disrupt or vandalize computer systems and networks, then they have committed cybertrespass as well. According to our scheme, there is no need to consider motive, political cause, ideology, etc., when determining how the criminal acts best fit into one of our three categories.

▶ 7.4 CYBERRELATED CRIMES

Cyberrelated crimes can be divided into two subcategories: *cyberexacerbated* crimes and *cyberassisted* crimes, so we can classify crimes involving cybertechnology as

- cyberspecific crimes (genuine cybercrimes),
- cyberrelated crimes, which include

    cyberexacerbated crimes, and

    cyberassisted crimes.

This enables us to distinguish between a crime in which someone merely uses a personal computer (e.g., to file a fraudulent income-tax return) from crimes such as Internet pedophilia and cyberstalking, which require a computer. The role that cybertechnology plays in the first case seems at best trivial and possibly altogether irrelevant, but in the latter two, cybertechnology does much more than merely *assist* someone in carrying out a crime—cybertechnology *exacerbates* it.

Certain kinds of crimes aided by cybertechnology can increase significantly because of that technology. For example, in the case of cyberexacerbated crimes, the scale on which crimes of a certain type can be carried out is significantly affected. Consider the potential increase in the number of stalking and pedophile-related crimes that can now occur because of cybertechnology vs. the likely increase in the number of income tax crimes, which are also assisted by computer technology (Grodzinsky and Tavani 2001, 2002).

Figure 7-1 illustrates some ways in which crimes involving the use of cybertechnology can be catalogued according to this threefold scheme.

Next we focus our discussion on cyberrelated organized crimes (involving racketeering) and cyberrelated espionage.

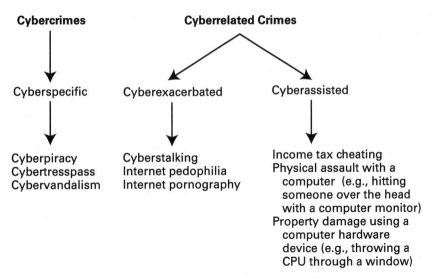

Figure 7-1 Cybercrimes and Cyberrelated Crimes

7.4.1 Organized Crime and the Internet

Career criminals, including those involved in organized crime, are using cyberspace to conduct gambling, drug trafficking, and racketeering scams, some involving Internet adoptions and Internet auctions. Yet these "old-style" crimes receive far less attention in the popular media than those perpetrated by teenage hackers. Because amateur hackers tend to grab the headlines, our attention is diverted from crimes committed in cyberspace by professionals. Richard Power (2000) believes that youthful hacker stereotypes provide a convenient foil for both professional criminals and foreign intelligence agents. Unlike hackers, professionals do not seek technological adventure; rather they hope to gain a technological advantage. And since professional criminals have superior skills, they are less likely than (amateur) hackers to get caught in carrying out their criminal acts.

In addition to placing wiretaps on phones, law enforcement agencies are using several electronic methods to track the activities of criminals who use cybertechnology. *Keystroke monitoring* is a specialized form of audit-trail software that carefully records every key struck by a user and every character of the response that the system returns to the user (Power 2000). This software can trace the text included in electronic messages back to the original sequence of keys and characters entered at a user's computer keyboard, so it is especially useful in tracking the activities of criminals who use encryption tools to encode their messages. *Echelon* is the federal government's once super-secret system for monitoring voice and data communication worldwide. They detect and track criminal activities with Carnivore, a "packet sniffing" program that monitors the data traveling between networked computers; a packet sniffer or "sniffer" is a program that captures data across a computer network. These programs have also been used by hackers to capture user IDs and passwords.

Police and federal agents employ entrapment techniques to catch members of organized crime involved in drug dealing, gambling, pornography, and so forth. Walter Sinnott-Armstrong (1999) describes a controversial case of entrapment involving cybertechnology that was intended to lure and catch pedophiles who used the Internet to meet young boys:

▶ **CASE ILLUSTRATION:** Entrapment on the Internet

Under an alias, detective James McLaughlin of Keene, New Hampshire, posed as a young boy in boy-love chat rooms, searching for adults using the Internet to seek sex with underage boys and gathering evidence from conversations recorded in the chat rooms. Philip Rankin, a British marine-insurance expert living in Norway, communicated with McLaughlin under the assumption that the police officer was a young boy. The unsuspecting pedophile then agreed to travel to Keene to meet his on-line contact in person at a McDonald's restaurant. Upon his arrival at the restaurant, Rankin was arrested by McLaughlin on the charge of child molestation. Some, including Sinnott-Armstrong (1999), have questioned whether such practices for catching child molesters in cyberspace are ethically justifiable even if they are legal.

Supporters of entrapment operations on the Internet argue that it can save many innocent lives and can significantly lessen the harm to individuals. For example, one could speculate about the Amy Boyer stalking case (described in Chapter 1) if an entrapment scheme, similar to the one used in the pedophile case, had been in place to catch cyberstalkers like Liam Youens—If police officers had been able to entrap Youens in cyberspace, Boyer might be alive today. Of course, a critical question from the point of view of many civil libertarians is whether the ends achieved by entrapment operations justify the means. Are such means morally acceptable? At the root of this question are some of the same issues involving civil liberties that we examined in our discussion of computerized record-matching in Chapter 5, where we saw that the end achieved, catching welfare cheats and deadbeat parents, was desirable, but the means used to accomplish this end were questionable.

The USA *Patriot Act*, which was passed overwhelmingly by the US Congress in October 2001, and the Homeland Security Act, passed in November 2002, gave increased powers to law enforcement agencies to track down suspected terrorists and criminals. Under these acts, authorities have been able to increase their monitoring of e-mail communications and cell phone conversations. While many have applauded these provisions, others fear that the government's increased powers to "snoop" will have overall negative consequences for a nation that values both freedom and the presumption of innocence.

We should note that many, possibly even most, crimes involving cybertechnology have involved neither terrorists nor members of organized crime syndicates. Should the government be permitted to use the same aggressive tactics that it claims are needed to counter terrorism and organized crime in catching lesser criminals who commit crimes that do not impact our security and safety as a nation? Should measures designed to detect and trap terrorists also be used to catch those who engage in "white collar" cyberrelated crimes such as corporate espionage?

7.4.2 Corporate Espionage

Considerable fortunes have been made and lost by computer corporations, especially the "dot.com" companies that spearheaded the venture into e-commerce. Not surprisingly, this provided great opportunities for corporate spies to steal trade secrets, both nationally and internationally, and the number of espionage-related crimes involving high-tech companies has risen accordingly.

Corporate spies in the high-tech capital, the Silicon Valley of California, have intercepted cell phone conversations between corporate executives and acquired highly sensitive and confidential information, including company secrets. Richard Power (2000) describes a case in which an ingenious spy, posing as a consultant, visited a corporation at a time when he knew the senior manager was on vacation. The consultant cleverly managed to get the inside information he needed by claiming to be a close associate of the vacationing manager and by convincing employees of the corporation that the manager had given him permission to consult during the manager's absence; he was able to get the source code for a software product the corporation was developing and then deliver that product to market before its developers could do so. Tales describing recent cases of economic espionage abound, but there is no need to examine any of these incidents in detail to understand the severe harm caused by corporate spies.

Corporate espionage has been made easier because of cybertechnology, which has provided spies with data-gathering opportunities that were not possible in the pre-Internet era. In posting information about their products and their missions on company Web sites that are freely accessible to the public, corporations sometimes inadvertently supply corporate spies with valuable "inside information." Of course, crimes of this type need not involve the use of cybertechnology; nor need they be directed at computer corporations, but there is concern about the increasing use of cybertechnology in economic espionage crimes in general.

On October 2, 1996, Congress passed the Economic Espionage Act of 1996, making it a federal crime to profit from the misappropriation of someone else's trade secret. Although the Economic Espionage Act is not exclusively a computer crime law, it specifically includes language about "downloads," "uploads," "e-mails," etc. Some economic analysts worry that economic espionage, especially in the high-tech industry, threatens the American position in a global market. Ironically, cybertechnology in general, and the Internet in particular, have made it much easier for spies to carry out their espionage operations against the very corporations that develop that technology.

▶ 7.5 NATIONAL AND INTERNATIONAL EFFORTS TO COMBAT CYBERCRIME

The Economic Espionage Act of 1996 is enforceable only in the United States. Laws are typically limited in jurisdiction to nations where they are enacted. Other laws involving cybercrime and also intended to have international reach have been enacted, but issues involving legal jurisdiction have impeded their prosecution.

7.5.1 The Problem of Jurisdiction in Cyberspace

Traditionally, crimes are prosecuted in the legal jurisdictions in which they were committed. In certain cases, suspected criminals have been extradited from one legal jurisdiction to another (and sometimes from one country to another) to stand trial for an accused crime. Roy Girasa (2002) points out that jurisdiction is based on the concept of boundaries, and laws are based on "territorial sovereignty." Cyberspace, of course, has no physical boundaries, so does the concept of jurisdiction make any sense in cyberspace?

States, as well as nations, are often perplexed when they try to determine how to enforce local laws when crimes are perpetrated within their jurisdictional boundaries by criminals residing outside those boundaries. In the United States, for example, different states have different laws regarding gambling. How can those laws be prosecuted in the case of on-line gambling, which can span multiple states? Consider the following scenario.

▶ **SCENARIO:** A "Virtual Casino"

Imagine that someone who resides in Nevada has set up a Web site, Virtual Casino, dedicated to on-line gambling. Because gambling is legal in the state of Nevada, let us assume that on-line gambling is also legal there, provided that the owners and operators of an on-line gambling site comply with the state's overall gambling regulations and laws. But what happens if residents of different states where gambling is illegal wish to engage in gambling activities on this Web site?

Suppose, for example, that gambling is illegal in the state of Texas and a person living in Texas who has Internet access visits the Virtual Casino Web site physically located on a computer in Nevada. Technically, the gambler in Texas who engages in gambling activities on the Web site in Nevada has broken the law in Texas, but where exactly has the violation of the law taken place—in Texas, where the "illegal" gambling activities are carried out from an individual's home, or in Nevada where the Virtual Casino resides? And where should the "crime" be prosecuted?

Can the state of Texas prosecute such individuals? Can the state of Texas demand the extradition of the Nevada resident who owns and operates the on-line gambling site on grounds that the Web site owner has assisted (or has made possible) the "crime" that was committed by the resident of Texas? These are thorny legal issues that still need to be worked out and fine-tuned in the United States. (In this particular scenario no interstate transmission of illegal material, in the strict legal sense of that definition, has occurred. Interstate statutes have been established to combat crimes of this type.)

Our scenario is, of course, hypothetical. But there have been some actual jurisdictional quagmires. An Internet bulletin board system (BBS) located on a server in California contained pornographic material that was legal in that state, but the BBS's content was illegal in Tennessee, where it was viewed by a resident of that state. In our discussion of pornography laws in Chapter 9, we examine this case more closely, and we will also see why it is important to reach consensus about how cyberspace should be viewed in order to both regulate it and determine whether specific laws have been broken. We will consider whether cyberspace should be regarded as a "place" or public space, like a bookstore, or whether it is a broadcast medium, like television and radio.

Not only have there been problems in prosecuting Internet crimes that span state borders, but criminal enforcement has been hampered as well by a lack of international legal agreements and treaties. Consider once again the case of the ILOVEYOU virus that wreaked havoc worldwide in May 2000 and which was allegedly launched by Onel de Guzman from the Philippines.

Where, exactly, did the crime take place? In the Philippines? In the United States? In Europe? Or in all of the above? Even though it originated in the Philippines, its effect was global. And if in the Philippines there is no explicit crime against launching computer viruses, did an actual crime even occur? Furthermore, if no crime was committed by Guzman in the Philippines, should he be extradited to nations that do have cyberrelated crime laws, and should he be required to stand trial in those nations?

On the one hand, it might be argued that Guzman should stand trial in any country that was affected by the virus he launched; after all, individuals and institutions in those countries were harmed by Guzman's act. However, we might also wish to consider the flip side of that argument: Would we want all cases of crimes or controversial Internet practices that have a global reach prosecuted by multiple nations? Consider the following scenario.

▶ **SCENARIO:** International Corporate Lawsuits

Suppose that Microsoft Corporation has developed and released a new software product that has been distributed globally. Further suppose that this product has a serious defect that causes computer systems using it to crash under certain conditions. These system crashes, in turn, result in both severe disruption and damage to system resources. What recourse do those who purchase this product have in their complaint against Microsoft?

In America, there are strict liability laws; but there are also disclaimers and caveats issued by manufacturers to protect themselves against litigation. Suppose that several countries where Microsoft has sold its new product also have strict liability laws. Should Microsoft Corporation be held legally liable and then be forced to stand trial in each of these countries? By the logic used in the Guzman case, perhaps the answer is yes. (Of course, one might argue that the principle of legal liability used in civil law suits for defective products is not strictly analogous to the principle used in crimes involving malicious intent. Nonetheless, the reasoning seems analogous in relevant ways.) If Microsoft were forced to stand trial in each country, and if it were found guilty in their courts, the litigation costs could force Microsoft into bankruptcy. So we need to think through the ramifications that broadening jurisdictional practices could have for corporations, or any organizations, even if they are not overtly engaged in criminal activities in cyberspace.

7.5.2 Legislative Efforts to Combat Cybercrime

After Congress passed the USA Patriot Act, authorizing the government to conduct unannounced "sneak and peek" attacks on individuals and organizations that it suspected of criminal activities, news stories reported that the FBI intended to plant a "Trojan horse" program, code-named Magic Lantern, on the computers of citizens it suspected of crimes. With this program, the government could use keystroke monitoring technology (described in Section 7.4.1) to obtain encryption keys for the suspects' computers. According to published reports, this technique was used in a case that resulted in the arrest of Nicodemo Scarfo, an alleged member of an organized crime syndicate.

The government's tactics in the Scarfo case, as well as in similar cases, required complicity with security software vendors; antivirus software vendors, such as McAfee, agreed not to detect trespasses by government snoops. Some worried that by pledging not to allow antivirus software to detect the FBI's illicit code, these vendors violated basic laws and civil liberties. Others point out that this practice deceived ordinary users who were not told the truth as to which kinds of illicit programs were and which were not being detected by the antivirus software they purchased.

Another worry was that the antivirus software programs used by government agencies to track down criminals would require "back doors" in the software, that is, holes in a security system deliberately left in place by designers and maintainers. ("Back door" is sometimes used interchangeably with "trap door," a hidden software or hardware mechanism used to circumvent security.) The prospect of a back door with a potential blind spot was worrisome

TABLE 7-1   United States Criminal Laws Involving Computers and Cybertechnology

18 U.S.C. Sec. 1029.	Fraud and Related Activity in Connection with Access Device
18 U.S.C. Sec. 1030.	Fraud and Related Activity in Connection with Computers
18 U.S.C. Sec. 1362.	Communication Lines, Stations, or Systems
18 U.S.C. Sec. 2511.	Interception and Disclosure of Wire, Oral, or Electronic Communication Prohibited
18 U.S.C. Sec. 270.	Unlawful Access to Stored Communication
18 U.S.C. Sec. 2701.	Disclosure of Contents
18 U.S.C. Sec. 2703.	Requirements for Governmental Access

because it meant that hackers and corporate spies might also be able to exploit the holes in computer systems, which were made possible by the government's snooping program. Some have also worried that the government itself could use this new snooping software in ways that are unconstitutional.

In response to crimes committed in cyberspace, several laws have been enacted (and revised), but many analysts continue to argue that they have failed to keep pace with ever-changing technology. The National Information Infrastructure Protection Act of 1996, for example, was enacted as part of Public Law 104-294; it amended the Computer Fraud and Abuse Act (originally passed in 1986). Table 7-1 includes a list of federal laws that address computer-related crimes. For more information about these laws, see the United States government's cybercrime Web site (http://www.cybercrime.gov).

The Council of Europe (COE) has considered ways to implement an international legal code that would apply to members of the European Union. Because cybercrimes can involve multiple law enforcement agencies and multiple ISPs in diverse countries under diverse rules of law, the G8 countries met in May 2000 to discuss an international treaty involving cybercrime. The G8 is an informal group of eight countries: Canada, France, Germany, Italy, Japan, Russia, the United Kingdom and the United States of America; the European Union also participates as a permanent nonhosting member. In conjunction with the G8 conference, the Council of Europe (COE) released its first draft of the COE Convention on Cybercrime on April 27, 2000. It addresses four types of criminal activity in cyberspace:

- Offenses against the confidentiality, availability, and integrity of data and computer systems
- Computer-related offenses (such as fraud)
- Content-related offenses (such as child pornography)
- Copyright-related offenses

Crimes involving economic espionage are not considered in the COE draft. For more information on the COE proposal, see http://conventions.coe.in/treaty/en/projects/ cybercrime.htm.

▶ 7.6 TECHNOLOGIES AND TOOLS FOR COMBATING CYBERCRIME

In Chapter 5 we saw that in response to privacy threats involving cybertechnology, some users have turned to technology itself to protect their privacy. Analogously, many now believe that the best way to combat crimes involving cybertechnology is through the use of the latest available tools and technologies. We saw in Section 7.4.1 of this chapter that the federal government has used programs such as Echelon and Carnivore, both of which are controversial from the perspective of civil liberties groups. In this section, we examine two controversial technologies that are currently used by law enforcement agencies: encryption and biometrics.

7.6.1 Encryption Technologies

In our discussion of security countermeasures in Chapter 6, we saw that one virtue of encryption tools is that they help to ensure the integrity of electronic data communicated by individuals between two or more computer systems. That same technology, however, has made it possible for criminals and terrorists to send and receive electronic communications.

Electronic communications devices that employ strong encryption features threaten the ability of law enforcement agencies to conduct wiretap operations. As a result, many crime and security experts believe that encryption technologies can provide a communication shield for individuals involved in terrorism and organized crime.

7.6.1.1 The Clipper Chip and Its Critics

In February 1994, the Clinton Administration proposed that an encryption system, which came to be known as the *Clipper Chip*, be installed in all electronic communications devices. Such a device would provide an antidote for law enforcement agents in their attempts to crack encrypted messages sent by individuals and organizations suspected of violating the law. The proposal also called for the keys to this encryption system to be held in escrow by the federal government. (See the description of public-key encryption in Chapter 6.) So if one government agency determined that it needed to intercept information transmitted via a certain electronic device, it would first get the necessary court order and then request the keys from another federal agency that was holding those keys.

Critics of Clipper, which included groups and individuals as diverse as the American Civil Liberties Union and Rush Limbaugh, argued that the federal government should not be allowed to proceed with this controversial encryption system. The arguments fell into four categories: security/reliability, trust in government, economic impact, and implications for civil liberties.

First, those who designed the chip argued that it was virtually foolproof, but some critics questioned whether Clipper was really as secure as it was alleged to be. Because no one outside of the government had access to Clipper, tests regarding the security and reliability of this technology could not be independently confirmed.

Some critics questioned whether we can/should actually trust the federal government with Clipper at its disposal. What were the chances, for example, that the government would abuse it? Could they appeal to national security as a rationale for using Clipper in questionable political practices? Government officials and supporters of Clipper responded to this objection by noting that this particular encryption technology would help to better ensure legitimate, private communications among ordinary citizens while deterring criminals. Steven Levy (1995) notes, however, that with Clipper, or with any government-controlled encryption system like it, we could be sure that our communications would be completely private—except, of course, from the government itself!

Other critics raised concerns about the economic implications of the Clipper Chip; for example, nations that trade with the United States made it clear that they would not continue to purchase electronic communications devices from the United States if those devices contained Clipper. This also raised concerns that tradeoffs might have to be made between national security and the interests of powerful individuals in the commercial sector.

7.6.1.2 Encryption Technologies and Civil-liberties Concerns

Members of both the political left and the political right raised the concern that encryption technologies such as Clipper threaten civil liberties. Would the government's use of strong encryption technology violate the Fourth Amendment of the Constitution, which protects against unwarranted search and seizure? Defenders of Clipper, both inside and outside the federal government, argued that it did not pose a threat to individual civil liberties. They argued that individual rights were no more threatened or compromised by Clipper than they were under existing laws, since government agencies were already permitted to eavesdrop on the communications of both private citizens and organizations, provided that they have a legal warrant to do so. In this case, Clipper would be only one more tool that could be used in court-approved surveillance activities. The main argument put forth by Clipper's proponents was that a strong encryption technology was essential for keeping tabs on organized crime members, international drug dealers, terrorists, and so forth.

Because of the sustained efforts on the part of the anti-Clipper coalition, the Clinton administration withdrew its support for the chip. Although the controversy has subsided, many believe that the federal government will try again in the future to introduce an encryption standard similar to Clipper.

7.6.2 Biometric Technologies

Biometrics can be defined as the biological identification of a person, which includes eyes, voice, hand prints, finger prints, retina patterns, and handwritten signatures (Power 2002); biometrics technologies are considered by many computer security experts as one of the most reliable forms of authentication. Irma van der Ploeg (2001) points out that through biometric technologies, one's iris can be read in the same way that one's voice can be printed. She also notes that one's fingerprints can be read by a computer that, in turn, has become touch sensitive and endowed with hearing and seeing capacities. The digital representation of this biometric data is usually transformed via some algorithm to produce a template, which is stored in a central computer database.

In February 2002 a biometric identification scheme was first tested at London's Heathrow Airport; the iris-scanning device captures a digital image of one's iris, which is then stored in a database and can then be matched against images of the irises of other individuals entering and leaving public places such as airports. If the testing of the new scanning device proves successful, security officials at Heathrow Airport will consider adopting this technique for authenticating an individual's identity, in combination with (or possibly even in place of) passports.

Possibly you have heard the expression, "Eyes are the window to the soul." In an age of biometrics, however, one's eyes may become the window to one's identity in a much more tangible sense than the classic metaphor ever intended. We will see that while biometric devices are a highly accurate means for validating an individual's identity, they are also controversial.

7.6.2.1 Using Face-Recognition Technologies at Super Bowl XXXV

It is difficult to determine whether the iris-scanner technology we described will, in fact, replace passports or whether it will become the preferred new device for authentication that some have predicted. Recall our case illustration in Chapter 5 that described how at Super Bowl XXXV in January 2001, a biometric identification tool that uses face-recognition technology was used by law enforcement agencies to scan the faces of people entering the football stadium. The scanned images were then instantly matched against the facial templates of suspected criminals and terrorists, which were contained in a central computer database.

This use of technology drew scathing criticism from civil liberties groups and privacy advocates. In the post–September 11 world, however, practices that employ technologies such as face-recognition devices have received overwhelming support from the American public; a poll conducted in October 2001 indicated that more than 86% of Americans approved of using biometric technologies in public places, including sports stadiums and airports.

7.6.2.2 The Eurodac Project

Proposals to use biometric identifiers in Europe have also generated controversy. The Eurodac project, a European Union proposal to use biometrics in controlling illegal immigration and border crossing in European countries by asylum seekers, was first considered by the European Council on November 24, 1997. A study to analyze the policy was then conducted, and a proposal made to implement it in 2002 (van der Ploeg 1999). Like the Clipper Chip in the United States, the Eurodac proposal has been a subject of debate in Europe.

Does the use of biometric technologies violate human rights? Would American citizens be supportive of their use had it not been for the tragic events of September 11, 2001? One might be tempted to assume that the arguments surrounding computerized record matching (examined in Chapter 5) would apply equally to biometric techniques, but in Chapter 5, we saw at least one significant difference in the two practices. In nonbiometric computerized record matching, databases contain records of individuals all of whom are presumed to be innocent; for example, records of government workers matched against records of welfare recipients to generate a hit. In matching practices involving biometric technology, on the other hand, images of people who are presumed innocent have been recorded and matched against a database of known or suspected criminals and terrorists.

Those critical of the use of face-recognition technologies in particular, and biometrics in general, point to at least three problems: error, abuse, and privacy (Brey 2001). Errors occur in matches resulting from biometrics technology, and the rate of error increases when the criteria for what qualifies as an acceptable match is expanded. Second, the uses for which biometric technologies are originally authorized can expand significantly and can lead to possible abuses, such as those described by the critics of the Clipper Chip (in the preceding section). And finally, some privacy advocates argue that the net security gained in the use of biometrics is not commensurate with the loss of privacy and civil liberty for individuals. The responses given by defenders of the Clipper Chip in Section 7.6.1.2 are similar to those that can be advanced in the case of biometrics.

▶ 7.7 CHAPTER SUMMARY

In this chapter, we examined crimes involving cybertechnology. We considered arguments as to whether a profile for a typical computer criminal could be constructed and whether a reasonable distinction could be drawn between hacking and cracking. We drew a distinction between "genuine" cybercrimes and cyberrelated crimes and considered some examples of each type. We also identified and briefly discussed some national and international laws that have been enacted to facilitate the prosecution of cybercrimes, especially where legal jurisdiction is unclear. We have also seen that, in many instances, laws and policies have not managed to keep pace with the technology.

▶ REVIEW QUESTIONS

1. Is there a typical cybercriminal?
2. Can a meaningful distinction be drawn between hacking and "cracking"?
3. Can certain forms of hacking be protected by the Constitution?
4. Why has the media attention given to hackers made it difficult for law enforcement authorities to track down professional criminals who use cybertechnology?
5. Identify some laws that have been drafted to combat crime in cyberspace.
6. What problems do issues of jurisdiction pose for understanding and prosecuting crimes committed in cyberspace?
7. What exactly is cybercrime? Can a coherent definition of cybercrime be framed?
8. How can we distinguish between genuine cybercrimes and "cyberrelated" crimes?
9. How might we distinguish between "cyberexacerbated" and "cyberassisted" crimes?
10. Which ethical questions does the use of encryption technology raise with respect to computer crime and computer criminals?
11. Describe some of the national and international efforts currently used to combat cybercrime.
12. What are some problems in enforcing national and international crime laws and treaties?
13. Describe some of the controversies associated with strong encryption technologies, such as the Clipper Chip, in combating crime.
14. How can biometric technologies be used to fight cybercrime and cyberrelated crimes?

▶ DISCUSSION QUESTIONS

1. Recall the case of Internet entrapment involving a pedophile that we discussed in Section 7.4.1. Which arguments can be made in favor of entrapment or "sting operations" on the Internet? From a utilitarian perspective, entrapment might seem like a good thing because it may achieve desirable consequences. But can it be defended on constitutional grounds in the United States? Justify your position by appealing to one or more of the ethical theories described in Chapter 2.
2. Assess arguments for and against the use of biometric technologies for security, especially in airports and large stadiums. Should biometric technologies such as face-recognition programs and iris scanners be used in public places to catch criminals? In the post–September 11 world, there is much more support for these technologies than there was when biometrics were used at Super Bowl XXXV in January 2001. Granted that such technologies can help the government to catch criminals and suspected terrorists, what kinds of issues do they raise from a civil liberties perspective? Compare the arguments for and against the use of biometric technologies in tracking down criminals to arguments we examined for and against computerized record matching in our discussion of privacy in Chapter 5. Do you support the use of biometrics in large, public gathering places in the United States? Defend your answer.

3. What do you believe were the core issues in the debate over the controversial Clipper Chip? Should the United States government be permitted to hold encryption "keys" in escrow? And can the government be trusted with these keys? In which ways, if any, have the events of September 11 affected your thinking about the federal government's role in the controversy over strong encryption? Explain.

4. Are the distinctions that we drew between cyberspecific and cyberrelated crimes useful? Why would cyberstalking be classified as a cyberrelated crime, according to this distinction? Among cyberrelated crimes, is it useful to distinguish further between cyberexacerbated and cyberassisted crimes? Why would cyberstalking be categorized as a "cyberexacerbated" rather than a cyberassisted crime? Why not simply call every crime in which cybertechnology is either used or present a cybercrime? Would doing so pose any problems for drafting coherent cybercrime legislation?

▶ REFERENCES

Brey, Philip (2001). "Ethical Aspects of Facial Recognition Systems in Public Places." In R. Chadwick, L. Introna, and A. Marturano, eds. *Proceedings of the Fourth Conference on Computer Ethics: Philosophical Enquiry (CEPE 2001)*, Lancaster University, UK, pp. 14–25.

Forester, Tom, and Perry Morrison (1994). *Computer Ethics: Cautionary Tales and Ethical Dilemmas in Computing*. 2d ed. Cambridge, MA: MIT Press.

Girasa, Roy J. (2002) *Cyberlaw: National and International Perspectives*. Upper-Saddle River, NJ: Prentice Hall.

Gotterbarn, Don (1991). "Computer Ethics: Responsibility Regained," *National Forum: The Phi Kappa Phi Journal*. Vol. LXXI, No. 3.

Grodzinsky, Frances S., and Herman T. Tavani. (2001). "Is Cyberstalking a Special Type of Computer Crime?" In T. W. Bynum et al., eds. *Proceedings of the Fifth International Conference on the Social and Ethical Impacts of Information and Communications Technologies: Ethicomp 2001*. Vol. 2. Gdansk, Poland: Mikom Publishers, pp. 73–85.

Grodzinsky, Frances S. (2002). "Some Ethical Reflections on Cyberstalking," *Computers and Society*, Vol. 42, No. 1, pp. 22–32.

Hacker Jargon File. Available at www.tuxedo.org/esr/jargon. Maintained by Eric Raymond.

Himanen, Pekka (2001). *The Hacker Ethic: A Radical Approach to the Philosophy of Business*. New York: Random House.

Kapor, Mitch (1991). "Civil Liberties in Cyberspace," *Scientific American*, Vol. 265, No. 3, pp. 23–32.

Levy, Steve (1984). *Hackers: Heroes of the Computer Revolution*. Garden City, NY: Doubleday.

Levy, Steve (1995). "The Battle Over the Clipper Chip." In D. G. Johnson and H. Nissenbaum, eds. *Computing, Ethics and Social Values*, Englewood Cliffs, NJ: Prentice Hall, pp. 651–663.

Moor, James H. (1985). "What Is Computer Ethics?" *Metaphilosophy*, Vol. 16, No. 4, pp. 266–275.

Parker, Donn B. (1998). *Fighting Computer Crime: A Framework for Protecting Information*. New York: John Wiley and Sons.

Power, Richard (2000). *Tangled Web: Tales of Digital Crime from the Shadows of Cyberspace*. Indianapolis, IN: Que Corp.

Sinnott-Armstrong, Walter (1999). "Entrapment in the Net?" *Ethics and Information Technology*, Vol. 1, No. 2, pp. 95–104.

Tavani, Herman T. (2000). "Defining the Boundaries of Computer Crime: Piracy, Break-ins, and Sabotage in Cyberspace," *Computers and Society*, Vol. 30, No. 3, pp. 3–9

van der Ploeg, Irma (1999). "The Illegal Body: 'Eurodac' and the Politics of Biometric Identification," *Ethics and Information Technology*, Vol. 1, No. 4, pp. 295–302.

van der Ploeg, Irma (2001). "Written on the Body: Biometrics and Identity." In R. A. Spinello and H. T. Tavani, eds. *Readings in CyberEthics*. Sudbury, MA: Jones and Bartlett Publishers, pp. 501–514.

▶ FURTHER READINGS

Baase, Sara (2003). "Computer Crime." Chapter 7 in *A Gift of Fire: Social, Legal, and Ethical Issues in Computing*. 2d ed. Upper Saddle River, NJ: Prentice Hall.

Denning, Dorothy E., and Peter J. Denning, eds. (1998) *Internet Besieged: Countering Cyberspace Scofflaws*. New York: ACM Press.

Grosso, Andrew (2000). "The Promise and the Problems of the No Electronic Theft Act," *Communications of the ACM*, Vol. 43, No. 2, February, pp. 23–26.

Hafner, Katie, and John Markoff (1995). *Cyberpunk: Outlaws and Hackers on the Electronic Frontier*. New York: Touchstone Books.

Johnson, Deborah G., and Helen Nissenbaum (1995). "Crime, Abuse, and Hackers." In D. G. Johnson and H. Nissenbaum, eds. *Computing, Ethics and Social Values*, Englewood Cliffs, NJ: Prentice Hall, pp. 57–60.

Spafford, Eugene H. (1992). "Are Computer Hacker Break-ins Ethical?" *Journal of Systems Software*, Vol. 17, pp. 41–47.

Stallman, Richard (1995). "Why Software Should Be Free." In D. G. Johnson and H. Nissenbaum, eds. *Computing, Ethics and Social Values*, Englewood Cliffs, NJ: Prentice Hall, pp. 190–200.

Thomas, Douglas (2002). *Hacker Culture*. Minneapolis: University of Minnesota Press.

Wall, David S. (1997). "Policing the Virtual Community: The Internet, Cybercrimes, and the Policing of Cyberspace." In P. Francis, P. Davies, and V. Jupp, eds. *Policing Futures*. London: Macmillan, pp. 208–236.

Wall, David S. (1998). "Catching Cybercriminals: Policing the Internet," *International Review of Law, Computers and Technology*, Vol. 12, No. 2, pp. 201–218.

8

INTELLECTUAL PROPERTY DISPUTES IN CYBERSPACE

What exactly is intellectual property? And how should it be protected in cyberspace? These are two of the questions examined in Chapter 8. Other questions include:

- Should computer software be protected by copyright law as well as by patent law?
- What are the differences between copyright protection and patent protection?
- How can copyright principles involving "fair use" be applied to digital information?
- Should MP3 files that contain proprietary information be distributed freely on the Internet?
- Is the "public domain of ideas" beginning to disappear because of copyright laws?
- Do current intellectual property laws sufficiently balance the interests of the public good against those of individuals and corporations who own copyrights and hold patents?

▶ 8.1 BACKGROUND: THE INTELLECTUAL PROPERTY DEBATE INVOLVING CYBERTECHNOLOGY

The debate over intellectual property rights in cyberspace has become one of the defining ethical issues of the Internet era. Deciding who should have ownership rights to, and thus control over, digitized information will ultimately determine who can and cannot access that form of information. In many ways, the controversy over property rights in cyberspace can be viewed as a battle between two groups whose interests are diametrically opposed: One camp advocates greater *control* of proprietary information and the other champions unrestricted *access* to electronic information that is now available globally because of cybertechnology.

Recall that the disputes surrounding privacy issues we examined in Chapter 5 turned on arguments generated by the same rival camps. There, we saw that privacy advocates and most consumers argued for legislation that would provide individuals with greater control over the personal information about them that is collected and stored in computer databases. The business sector, on the other hand, argued for the right to access that information. Many "information brokers" in the business sector, as well as journalists and private investigators, have appealed to such principles as the public's right to know and the free flow of information in defending their right to collect, access, and exchange personal information about individuals. But in disputes involving intellectual property in cyberspace, the two camps reverse their positions: Entrepreneurs and business interests argue for strong legal measures that will enable them to control proprietary information in cyberspace, while ordinary users argue for greater access to that information.

The subjects of these disputes range from claims pertaining to ownership of software programs to arguments about who has the right to distribute (or even make available for use) proprietary software and other forms of proprietary information on the Internet. The disputes consider whether computer software programs should be patentable or copyrightable, or both, and whether the "look and feel" of a user interface deserves the protection of intellectual property laws. Additionally, they ask whether Web sites, which are privately operated but also reside in "public space" on the Internet, should qualify for legal protection as property. Perhaps no property issue has been more contentious in the past few years than the question as to whether computer users should be able to transfer and download MP3 files that include proprietary information.

▶ 8.2 WHAT IS INTELLECTUAL PROPERTY, AND WHY SHOULD IT BE PROTECTED?

An adequate analysis of *intellectual property* issues requires that we first have an understanding of the concept of property in general. Like privacy, property is a complex notion that is neither easily defined nor clearly understood. Yet, as legal scholars and philosophers have pointed out, property laws and norms play a fundamental role in shaping a society and in preserving its legal order; that is, laws and norms involving property rights establish relationships between individuals, different sorts of objects, and the state. When discussing issues involving property, we tend to think of tangible items. Originally, "property" referred to land; however, it now also includes objects that an individual can own, such as an automobile, articles of clothing, or a stamp collection.

In a more sophisticated scheme, property is not considered in terms of things, but rather as a *relationship between individuals in reference to things*. Hence, there are three elements to consider:

1. an individual, X
2. an object, Y
3. $X's$ relation to other individuals (A, B, C, etc.) in reference to Y

In this sense, X (as the owner of property Y) can control Y relative to persons A, B, C, and so forth. So if Harry owns a Toshiba laptop computer, then he can control who has access to his computer and how it is used; for example, Harry has the right to exclude Sally from using the laptop computer, or, as its owner he can grant her unlimited access to it. Ownership claims involving "intellectual objects" are similar in certain respects but less straightforward in others to claims involving the ownership of tangible objects.

8.2.1 Intellectual Objects

Some philosophers use the expression *intellectual objects* when referring to forms of intellectual property. Unlike physical property, intellectual property consists of objects that are not tangible. These nontangible, or intellectual, objects represent creative works and inventions, which are the manifestations or expressions of ideas. Unlike tangible objects, which are exclusionary in nature, intellectual objects (e.g., software programs) are *nonexclusionary* (Spinello and tavani 2001a): Consider once again Harry's laptop computer, which is a physical object. If Harry owns it, then Sally cannot own it, and vice versa. Harry's laptop is an exclusionary object. Next consider a word-processing program that resides in Harry's computer. If Sally makes a copy of that program, then both Sally and Harry own copies of it. The word-processing program is nonexclusionary.

Note that scarcity (which often causes competition and rivalry when applied to physical objects), need not exist in the case of intellectual objects, which can be easily reproduced. Note also that there are practical limitations to the number of physical objects one can own and that there are natural as well as political limitations to the amount of land that can be owned, but that countless digital copies of a Microsoft Word program can be produced and each at a relatively low cost.

Another feature that distinguishes intellectual objects from physical objects has to do with exactly what it is that one can lay legal claim to. One cannot own an idea in the same sense that one can own a physical object; ideas themselves are not the kinds of things for which governments are willing to grant ownership rights to individuals. Rather, legal protection is given only to the tangible *expression* of an idea that is creative or original. For a literary or artistic idea to be protected it must be expressed (or "fixed") in some tangible medium such as a physical book or a sheet of paper containing a musical score. If the idea is functional in nature, such as an invention, it must be expressed as a machine or a process. Whereas authors are granted copyright protections for expressions of their literary ideas, inventors are given an incentive, in the form of a patent protection, for their functional ideas. Both copyright law and patent law, along with other legal schemes for protecting intellectual property, are discussed in detail in Sections 8.4 and 8.5.

8.2.2 Why Protect Intellectual Objects?

What is our basis for saying that intellectual property, or for that matter any kind of property, ought to be protected? One answer lies in our current laws. Of course, we could then further ask on what philosophical grounds are our laws themselves based? In Section 8.6 of this chapter, we will see that in Anglo-American law the philosophical justification for granting property rights is grounded in two different theories about property. One theory is based on the rationale that a property right is a type of "natural right" that should be granted to individuals for the products that result from the labor expended in producing an artistic work or a practical invention. The other theory is based on the notion that property rights themselves are not natural rights but rather social constructs designed to encourage creators and inventors to better serve society in general by bringing forth their artistic works and practical inventions into the marketplace. To encourage authors and inventors, utilitarians believe that it is necessary to grant them property rights in the form of limited monopolies that result in financial advantages.

In many continental European countries, neither individual labor nor social utility are used as a justification for granting intellectual property rights and corresponding protections. Instead, literary works and inventions represent the expression and personality of their creators, who should, it is argued, have the right to determine how their works are displayed and distributed. This view is sometimes referred to as the personality theory of intellectual property. In Section 8.6, where we consider, in greater depth, examples of each kind of property theory, we will see that some philosophers reject the notion that intellectual property rights should be extended to computer software; we will also consider an alternative framework for understanding intellectual property that incorporates various aspects of traditional property theories.

Philosophers and legal theorists point out that the introduction of computer software has created questions regarding intellectual property laws for which there are no easy answers. Innovations in computer hardware, on the other hand, have clearly qualified for patent protection, and in this sense, computer hardware inventions are no different than other kinds of inventions involving physical objects. But the question of how software, a kind of intellectual object, should be protected has been fiercely debated in the courts.

▶ 8.3 SOFTWARE AS INTELLECTUAL PROPERTY

Should computer programs be protected by patents? Or should copyright law protect them? Or is computer software a special kind of intellectual object that deserves both, or perhaps neither, kind of protection? Computer software, which consists of lines of programming code (or codified thought), is not exactly expressed, or "fixed," in a tangible medium as literary works are. To complicate matters, a program's source code consists of symbols, whereas its object code is made up of "executable images" that run on the computer's hardware after they have been converted from the original source code. Because of conceptual muddles and confusions surrounding the nature of programming code, computer programs were not, initially, eligible for either copyright or patent protection. Eventually, however, they were granted legal protection. Although software programs seem like inventions that could be patented, they also resemble algorithms, which, like mathematical ideas or "mental steps," are not typically eligible for patent protection.

As late as the 1970s and early 1980s software was often given away without concern for copyright. I worked in the software industry in the early 1980s, and I recall incidents where software developers freely exchanged with each other copies of programs on which they were working: A software developer might lend a fellow developer a copy of a database program in return for a copy of a word-processing program. Some have argued that these kinds of exchanges actually improved the software products that eventually went to market. The important point, however, is that lawyers were not involved. By the late 1980s, the cavalier attitude that surrounded the exchange of software programs had changed considerably, and by the 1990s, software companies carefully guarded their proprietary software, sometimes to the point of encouraging law enforcement officials to raid private homes where they suspected that unauthorized software was being used.

Many nations have enacted specific laws and statutes to protect the rights and interests of "owners" of intellectual property, including computer software programs and applications. We next examine four different types of schemes for protecting intellectual property rights: copyright law, patents, trademarks, and trade secrets.

▶ 8.4 COPYRIGHT LAW

Legal scholars trace the development of Anglo-American copyright law to a response to the widespread publishing of pamphlets made possible by the printing press. On the one hand, the British monarchy wanted to control the spread of "subversive" and "heretical" works that were being printed. On the other hand, authors had a vested interest in protecting their works from unauthorized reproduction. The English Statute of Anne, enacted in 1710, was the first law to give protection to authors for works attributed to them. The American colonies followed English law regarding copyright; the Framers later included these ideas in Article 1, Section 8, of the United States Constitution:

> The congress shall have the power...to promote the Progress of Science and the useful Arts, by securing for limited Times to authors and inventors the exclusive Rights to their respective Writings and Discoveries.

8.4.1 The Evolution of Copyright Law in the United States

The first copyright law in the United States was enacted in 1790 and applied primarily to books, maps, and charts. As newer forms of media were developed, it was extended to include photography, movies, and audio recordings. In 1909 the copyright law was amended to include any "form that could be seen and read visually" by humans; this modification was motivated by a new technology, namely the player piano, which could copy a song onto a perforated roll. Since the musical copy could not be read from the piano roll visually (by humans), the copy was not considered a violation of the song's copyright. The "machine readable" vs. "human readable" distinction has implications for decisions as to whether software programs qualify for copyright protection: Although a program's source code can be read by humans, its executable code, which runs on a computer, cannot. Beginning in the 1960s, arguments were made that computer programs, or at least parts of computer programs, should be eligible for copyright protection.

The Copyright Act of 1976 modified copyright law, but computer programs still did not clearly satisfy the requirements necessary for making them eligible for copyright protection. It was amended again in 1980 to address the status of software programs, and the concept of a literary work was extended to include programs, computers, and databases that "exhibit authorship." The amendment defined a computer program as a "set of statements or instructions to be used directly in a computer in order to bring about certain results." To obtain a copyright for a computer program, however, its author had to show that the program contained an original expression (or arrangement) of ideas and not simply the ideas themselves.

The Copyright Act of 1976 has been amended several times to keep pace with the changing world of digital technology; for example, it was amended in 1984 with the Semiconductor Chip Protection Act. In the early 1990s, some argued that the user interface (features such as icons and pull-down menus), that is, the "look and feel" of software, as well as the software code itself, should be copyrightable. Programs that have a similar user interface are sometimes referred to as "workalike" programs, and while the source code for these programs may differ significantly, their user interfaces look similar. In 1987, Lotus Development Corporation filed a lawsuit against Paperback Software International, LTD, whose user interface included menus and buttons that resembled the Lotus 1-2-3 product. In 1990, a federal court judge in Boston decided in favor of Lotus (in *Lotus v. Paperback*). Lotus initially won a copyright infringement suit against Borland International Inc. However, the decision in the Borland case was overturned in 1995. In a similar case, Apple lost its suits against Microsoft and Hewlett-Packard for using features that Apple believed were similar to its icon-based graphical user interface. In ruling against Apple and Lotus, the courts determined that icons and menus in a computer interface were analogous to buttons on a VCR or to controls on a car.

In 1998, two more important amendments were made to the 1976 Copyright Act: the Sonny Bono Copyright Term Extension Act (SBCTEA), and the Digital Millennium Copyright Act (DMCA). The SBCTEA extended the length of copyright protection from the life of the author plus fifty years to the life of the author plus seventy years. Protection for "works of hire" produced before 1978 were extended from seventy-five years to ninety-five years. (When an author receives payment from a corporation or organization to produce a creative or artistic work, it can be considered a "work of hire.") Critics of the SBCTEA noted that the law was passed just in time to keep Mickey Mouse from entering the public domain, and they also pointed out that the Disney Corporation lobbied very hard for the passage of this act.

The DMCA has also been severely criticized—not because it extends the amount of time that a copyrighted work is protected, but because of the manner in which copyrights are extended. Many worry that the DMCA potentially restricts the development and use of digital technology. It contains a highly controversial anti-circumvention clause, which forbids the development of any software or hardware technology that *circumvents* (or devises a technological workaround) to copyrighted digital media. We will see why this clause is so controversial in our discussion of the "fair-use" principle of copyright in Section 8.4.3.

8.4.2   What Does Copyright Law Protect?

A copyright is a legal protection given to a "person," or author. The author can be an entity (an organization or a corporation, such as Microsoft) or the author can be an individual. A copyright protection is given for an expression of an idea such as a book, poem, musical composition, photograph, dance movement, motion picture, audiovisual work, or computer software. For a work to be protected under copyright law, it must be

- original,
- nonfunctional, and
- fixed in a tangible medium.

First, a literary or artistic work must be *original* in the sense that it "owes its origins to the author." The work must also be *nonfunctional* or nonutilitarian in nature. Functions and processes, including inventions, are protected by patents; and, typically, are not eligible for copyright protection. Finally, in order to qualify for a copyright, the work must be *fixed* or expressed concretely in a tangible medium such as a book, poem, or musical score. Note that ideas, concepts, facts, processes, and methods are not protected by copyright law.

Section 106 of the 1976 Copyright Act (Title 17 of the United States Code) defines the set of exclusive rights granted to copyright owners under the law. Copyright holders have the exclusive right to

- make copies of the work,
- produce derivative works (e.g., translations into other languages, movies based on the book, etc.),
- distribute copies,
- perform works in public (e.g., musicals, plays, etc.), and
- display works in public (e.g., art works).

In certain cases, exceptions have been made to the exclusive rights given to a copyright holder. For example, in the case of software programs, the purchaser is permitted to make one archival copy of the program.

8.4.3 The Fair-Use and First-Sale Doctrines: Challenges Posed by Recent Amendments to Copyright Law

To balance the exclusive controls given to copyright holders against the broader interests of society, two doctrines have been developed: *fair use* and *first sale*. Fair use means that every author or publisher may make limited use of another person's copyrighted work for purposes such as criticism, comment, news, reporting, teaching, scholarship, and research, restricting the (total) control that the copyright holder would otherwise enjoy. And the fair-use principle is important to the computer industry in particular and to engineering in general, because it supports the practice of "reverse engineering," allowing someone to buy a product for the purpose of taking it apart to see how it works.

Another balancing scheme in copyright law is the first-sale doctrine, which applies once the original work has been sold for the first time, at which point the original owner loses rights over the work of art. For example, once you purchase a copy of a book, audio-tape, painting, etc., you are free to give away, resell, or even destroy your copy. It is not clear, however, that one can give away software that is licensed for use but not, strictly speaking, owned by a user.

Both the fair-use and first-sale doctrines have been threatened by recent copyright legislation. The DMCA, it has been argued, has serious implications for the fair-use doctrine because its anticircumvention clause would make it illegal to reverse engineer a competitor's product to see how it works. Innovators and competitors have depended on the use of reverse engineering, which has been protected by the Copyright Act's fair-use doctrine.

We next consider two cases that illustrate some implications for copyright legislation. The first case demonstrates one way in which the SBCTEA threatens the communication of information once in the public domain but now protected by copyright law. The second case illustrates how the DMCA threatens our ability to use electronic books the same way that we have been able to use physical books.

▶ **CASE ILLUSTRATION:** Eric Eldred's Web Site

Eric Eldred of Derry, New Hampshire, operates a personal, nonprofit Web site on which he includes electronic versions of classic books that are in the public domain. While helping his daughters locate

some older and out-of-print books for a high school literature project, Eldred found that it was difficult to find electronic versions of books such as *The Scarlet Letter*, so he decided to set up a Web site
(www.eldritchpress.org) dedicated to on-line versions of older books. He has included on his site, for
example, the complete works of Nathaniel Hawthorne. Legally, Eldred was permitted to post electronic versions of these books on his site because their copyright protection had expired. But with the
passage of SBCTEA in 1998, some of the books that were previously in the public domain (and also
included on Eldred's site) have since come back under copyright protection. Rather than remove
books from his site, Eldred decided to challenge the legality of the amended Copyright Act, which he
argued is incompatible with the fair-use provision and in violation of Article 1, Section 8, Clause 8, of
the Constitution (see the opening of Section 8.4). His court challenge (*Eldred v. Attorney General
John Ashcroft*), while turned down by a lower circuit court, was appealed, and some believed that the
initial decision had a good chance of being overturned. In January 2003, however, the Supreme Court
upheld the lower court's decision in a 7-2 ruling.

▶ **CASE ILLUSTRATION:** Dimitri Sklyarov's Decryption Program

In the summer of 2001, Dimitri Sklyarov traveled from Moscow to Las Vegas to speak at the Def Con
Computer Security Conference. While in Las Vegas, Sklyarov was arrested and handcuffed by United
States federal agents—not because of what he had to say at the conference, but because of what he
was carrying in his briefcase. Working for a Moscow-based company called ElcomSoft while completing his Ph.D., Sklyarov had written a program that could decrypt the code for the book-reading
software developed by Adobe, an American company. Adobe's Acrobat eBook Reader software
enables computer users to read digital books, available on-line for a fee. Adobe feared that because of
Sklyarov's software program, software pirates would now be able to read e-books for free. And the
United States government was eager to test the Digital Millennium Copyright Act (DMCA), especially its anticircumvention clause, which was passed in 1998 but was not enforceable until 2000.

Sklyarov's arrest sparked considerable controversy and protest, especially among software engineers. In fact, a "Free Sklyarov" movement arose from the protest. Some of the protesters thought Adobe
had a legitimate concern, but were troubled that the principle of "fair use" was being technologically
undermined by Adobe and legally undermined by the DMCA. Even some conservatives, who tend to be
proponents of intellectual property protection, believe that the DMCA may have gone too far.

Critics pointed out that in the case of a physical (paper and glue) book, one could do whatever one
wishes after purchasing it. For example, one could lend the book or parts of the book to a friend. Also,
one could make a photocopy of the physical book. And, finally one could resell that book, in compliance with the first-sale doctrine of copyright protection. The same is not true, however, of e-books,
because information contained in those books cannot be subsequently exchanged without permission
of the copyright holder. To the dismay of the United States Government, and to the delight of
Sklyarov's supporters, Adobe dropped its charges; however, many believe that the principles involved
in the Sklyarov incident will be challenged again in future court cases.

8.4.4 Software Piracy as Copyright Infringement

With the proliferation of personal computers in the 1980s, many users discovered how easy
it was to duplicate software, but as we saw in Chapter 1, there was some legitimate confusion during that period as to whether it was legal to make a copy of someone else's software
program. A policy vacuum existed with respect to copying proprietary software for personal
use; the vacuum arose, in large part, because of certain confusions or "conceptual muddles"
in our understanding of software. Earlier in this chapter, we noted that in the 1970s and

early 1980s, software developers sometimes shared and exchanged programs with one another, and that by the late 1980s, many software companies had become extremely zealous when it came to protecting their proprietary software.

Software manufacturers, who claim to have lost millions of dollars of potential revenue because of software piracy, seem justified in their concerns regarding the pirating of proprietary software by individuals and organizations, both nationally and globally. However, critics have argued that claims made by American software manufacturers about their loss of revenue due to the use of pirated software in developing countries are either greatly exaggerated or altogether bogus. They point out that many people and organizations in those countries could not afford to pay the prices set by American software companies for their products, so the companies have not lost any (real) revenues, because their (expensive, by American standards) software would not sell on the open market in most developing countries. And worse yet, if it were not for the pirated copies, individuals and organizations in those nations would have no access to software at all.

Software companies also worry about revenues lost in developed nations, including the United States, due to the illegal copying of software. Some people believe that a distinction should be drawn between an individual's unauthorized copying of a friend's software program for personal use and the pirating of software in a systematic way for profit by corporations and criminals. The economic impact of systematic software piracy by organizations and individuals, is far more significant than the impact of individuals copying their friends' programs. From a moral point of view, however, if unauthorized copying of proprietary software is wrong, then it is just as wrong for individuals as it is for organizations interested in profiting from it.

But is the unauthorized copying of software always morally wrong? Helen Nissenbaum (1995) has made an interesting case for why, in certain cases, making a copy of a neighbor's software program can be morally justified, even if it is illegal. She defends her position on both utilitarian and deontological grounds, appealing to the case of a graduate student who cannot afford to purchase a word-processing program to complete her dissertation. Some critics of Nissenbaum argue that breaking the law itself is morally wrong; and others point out that all immoral (and many illegal) acts cause harm to someone. Nissenbaum, however, suggests that more harm results when the student, who cannot afford the word-processing program, is denied the use of that program.

Others might argue that despite the fact that pirating software is illegal, no harm has come to anyone by the act of copying of the software program: for instance, Microsoft is so well-off that it will not suffer if it loses the revenue from one sale of its Word program. You can probably see the danger that might result if everyone used this line of reasoning. Recall our discussion of the slippery slope and virtuality fallacies in Chapter 3.

Many argue that the unauthorized copying of software is never morally permissible. Some point out that making an unauthorized copy of a program is a form of theft, and since theft always results in harm to someone, software piracy can never be morally justified—it is morally unjustifiable, independent of whether the particular instance of piracy has a negative financial impact for the company that has ownership rights to the program.

Corporations such as Microsoft have been far more concerned with piracy as a form of organized crime, both domestically and internationally, than they have been about individuals making occasional unauthorized copies of their proprietary software. From a financial point view, it would seem to make perfectly good sense for Microsoft to allow some illicit copying of its software by individuals rather than spend money to pursue their arrest and prosecution. However, many corporations have been quite willing to pursue those who engage in piracy for commercial gain. And corporations have been especially concerned about the ways that their proprietary information can be pirated over a computer network. As we saw in Chapter 7, cyberpiracy applies to more than the mere unauthorized copying of software; it also covers the unauthorized distribution (or facilitation of the distribution) of digital information on a computer network. The software industry confronted this phenomenon for the first time in 1994.

▶ **CASE ILLUSTRATION:** Distributing Proprietary Software in Cyberspace

In the spring of 1994, Robert LaMacchia, then a student at MIT, operated an Internet Bulletin Board System (BBS) called Cynosure and invited its users to upload and download (for free) copyrighted software to and from an anonymous server that resided in Finland. LaMacchia was arrested on charges that he had pirated software, but since LaMacchia himself did not make unauthorized copies of the proprietary software, and since he did not receive a fee for his services, law enforcement authorities had a difficult time bringing piracy charges against him. In fact, they had a difficult time finding any clear criminal grounds for prosecuting LaMacchia—there were no explicit provisions in the 1986 Computer Fraud and Abuse Act (see Chapter 7) under which he could be prosecuted. Eventually, federal authorities decided to bring charges against him (*United States v. LaMacchia*) by appealing to the Wire Fraud Act, a federal statute. Charges against LaMacchia, were eventually dropped, however, and the indictment was officially struck down by District Judge Richard Stearns, who ruled that, for constitutional reasons, any criminal copyright charge must be brought under copyright laws and not under general federal criminal laws.

Software companies followed the case closely, and, not surprisingly, they were disappointed with the outcome. They had hoped to make an example of LaMacchia, and they believed that his conviction would have set a precedent. Following the LaMacchia incident, the 1986 Computer Fraud and Abuse Act was amended to broaden the scope of criminal behavior that could be prosecuted under it, and the No Electronic Theft (NET) Act was passed in 1997, criminalizing the dissemination of copyrighted information by electronic means.

While many agree with the spirit of this act, some believe that it goes too far. Prior to the NET Act, a person had to "infringe a copyright willfully and for purposes of commercial or financial gain" in order to be punished under the criminal provisions of the Copyright Act. The NET Act, however, has made criminal the "reproduction or distribution, including by electronic means . . . one or more copies or vinyl disks (such as LPs) of one or more copyrighted works, which have a total retail value of more than $1,000."

Andrew Grosso (2000) believes that the meaning of "copyright infringement" has been expanded under this Act. He points out that a copyright infringement can occur either in "fixation" (in print or paper) or in virtual space, that is, by means of a mere electronic distribution, regardless of whether the copyrighted work is ever printed on paper or downloaded on to a disk, etc. According to the NET Act, merely viewing a copyrighted work posted on the Internet can be interpreted as a criminal violation of copyright. One possible interpretation is that "fixation" occurs in on-line viewing, because a temporary copy is "fixed" in the memory (i.e., in RAM) of the host computer, no matter how briefly the information is stored there.

In some ways, the LaMacchia incident foreshadowed many issues in the highly publicized Napster debate. Like LaMacchia's Cynosure BBS, Napster also provided a distribution center for proprietary electronic information, although Napster was not distributing software. We should note, however, that piracy laws apply to the illegal copying and distribution over a computer network of any kind of proprietary information in digital form.

▶ **CASE ILLUSTRATION:** The Napster Debate

In December 1999, the Recording Industry Association of America sued the owners and operators of the Napster Web site for distributing copyrighted music on the Internet. Moving Picture Exports Group had, in 1987, developed the format for the electronic media that Napster distributed, a standard digital-format file for storage of audio recordings originally known as MPEG-3, but later abbreviated to MP3. By a process called "ripping," the software permits the user of a computer to copy an audio compact disc onto a computer's hard drive by compressing the audio information on the CD into the MP3 format. Once that is accomplished, any person may use the format to transmit audio files electronically from one computer to another.

The recording industry accused Napster of illegally distributing copyrighted information through its centralized server. Napster responded that its activities were perfectly legal under the fair-use doctrine. Thus far, the courts have ruled against Napster, but many believe that the Napster controversy is just the beginning of an ongoing battle with the recording industry over the use of the latest available technologies to exchange proprietary music on-line.

Internet music providers such as Gnutella, Morpheus, and KaZaA also support the distribution of MP3 files containing copyrighted music over the Internet. They have avoided the plight of Napster thus far because, unlike Napster, which used a centralized distribution point consisting of a centralized server, index, and registry of names, Gnutella, Morpheus, and KaZaA use a decentralized system. Why should the centralization/decentralization distinction be considered a relevant legal distinction in the current controversy? Does this distinction make a moral difference? Once again, as in the early days of software development, we have a conceptual muddle involving a new technology and the exchange of proprietary information.

8.4.5 The DeCSS Case: A Further Challenge to the Fair-use Doctrine

In the summer of 2000, Paramount Pictures, Universal Studies, and MGM Studios brought a lawsuit against the owners and operators of three commercial Web sites, each of which included software that users could download for free and that would enable them to view DVDs (Digital Versatile Discs) on machines that were not authorized to use that technology. Jan Johansen and two of his teenage friends in Norway developed the controversial program, called DeCSS, in 1999; it enables users to decrypt the CSS (Content Scrambling System) code that lies at the base of DVD technology. CSS is an access-control system for encrypting DVDs, which would otherwise be vulnerable to copying; and CSS technology was designed to prevent the kind of easy reproduction features associated with VHS tapes using videocassette recorders.

▶ **CASE ILLUSTRATION:** Decrypting Code for DVD Technology

In *Universal City Studios, Inc. v. Reimerdes*, the court found the defendants liable under the anti-circumvention clause of the DMCA. Judge Kaplan rejected the defendants' claim that their actions constituted fair use and therefore could not be illegal. They pointed out that the DeCSS software had been developed by Johansen in order to play DVDs on a computer running the Linux operating system; unlike computers running MS Windows or Macintosh operating system software, Linux was not equipped to support CSS software. The defendants argued that writing DeCSS code was both consistent with and necessary to realize fair use. The plaintiffs, however, appealed to a controversial anti-circumvention clause in the DMCA, which explicitly states that it is illegal to "circumvent" or construct a workaround through a process that decodes or decrypts a technology. The defendants countered by arguing that the DMCA's anticircumvention clause is unconstitutional in that it deprives individuals of fair use.

Should it be illegal to include DeCSS software on a Web site merely because that software could be used in activities that would violate the law? If so, should the sale of scissors, knives, and razors also be banned from the Internet? Critics of the DMCA point out that many items currently available for purchase on the Internet should also be banned for sale if we employ the rationale that such an item could be used illegally. A central argument made by the defense in the Reimerdes case involved a precedent from *Sony Corp of America v. Universal City Studios, Inc.* (1984), where it had to be resolved whether it was legal to forbid the use of technology because it *could* result in copyright infringement. Universal sued to bar the sale of such technology, claiming that Sony, who manufactured the Betamax home video recorder (the rival technology of the current VHS recording devices), was liable for copyright infringement either directly or indirectly because the new technology could be used to make illegal copies of movies. Sony argued, however, that people who used VCR machines could record movies already being televised at a certain time and then view those movies at their own convenience.

By a very narrow decision—one decided by a 5–4—vote the Supreme Court ruled in favor of Sony. (It is very difficult to imagine the consequences for both the entertainment industry and consumers if the decision had gone the other way.) The Court ruled that simply because VCR technology could be used to do something illegal is not sufficient grounds for banning that technology. In essence, it concluded that as long as the technology was capable of substantial noninfringing issues, it could not be barred from sale and distribution. So, in effect, the Court also determined that VCRs did not violate copyright law merely because they were capable of substantial copyright infringement. Courts have since been reluctant to ban or limit the use of technological advances due to the highly controversial but precedent-setting decision of the Supreme Court in the Sony case. Yet in the Reimerdes case, the judge sided with Universal City Studios. The case is currently under appeal.

8.4.6 Jurisdictional Issues Involving Intellectual Property Laws and Contracts

The specific copyright laws and cases described in this chapter apply mostly to the United States even though their implications are global. In recent years, international treaties pertaining to intellectual property and copyright have also been signed; for example, the TRIPS (Trade Relationship Aspects of Intellectual Property Standards) agreement implemented requirements from the Berne Convention for the Protection of Literary and Artistic Works. This agreement is recognized by signatories to the World Intellectual Property Organization (WIPO). International intellectual property laws have been very difficult to enforce at the international level, in large part because of jurisdictional issues. In countries such as the United States, laws applicable to the sale of goods, as well as to contracts involved in those sales, often vary from state to state. Attempts have been made to improve the uniformity of legislation across states, resulting in three pieces of legislation: The Uniform Commerce Code (UCC), aimed at clarifying the rights and obligations of parties to the "sale of goods and contracts" and to the "lease of goods"; the Uniform Computer and Information Transactions Act (UCITA); and the Uniform Electronic Transactions Act (UETA).

Whereas UETA applies to electronic contracts in general, UCITA is designed to govern computer information transactions and all contracts for the development, sale, licensing, maintenance, and support of computer software. It would also extend to all shrink-wrap licenses and "click-wrap" agreements. In the case of shrink-wrap licenses, the act of opening the sealed package indicates your full consent to the terms and conditions of use for the product. Click-wrap agreements give the user an on-screen choice to agree or not agree with the product requirements, and a program might not open until a user consents by clicking on the words "I agree" (Girasa 2002). Should such agreements be valid and enforceable against users? Under UCITA, they would be. Thus far, UCITA has been enacted into law in the states of Virginia and Maryland.

Even though UCITA is not law in most states, its effects can be felt in all states because contracts involving electronic goods and services can span multiple states and thus potentially involve Virginia and Maryland law in the process. Although there is general agreement that a uniform law across states pertaining to electronic contracts would be desirable, many worry about the effects that universal passage of UCITA would have for American consumers.

UCITA has been criticized by the Software Engineering Ethics Research Institute and the American Library Association, as well as by many consumer advocacy groups. Many critics believe that it overreaches because it would (a) give software vendors the right to repossess software by disabling it remotely, and (b) prevent the transfer of licenses from one party to another without vendor permission. Some also worry that UCITA would undermine existing consumer protection laws and threaten current copyright exceptions for fair use and first sale.

On the other hand, companies such as Microsoft and AOL have lobbied hard for UCITA. They have tried to persuade lawmakers that it would be good for e-commerce and that it would create more jobs in the computer industry. Critics, however, believe that these companies simply want increased control over the products they license—controls that UCITA's opponents argue would further ensure that these products could not be passed along from one party to another without vendor approval. Other critics ironically note that at the same time software vendors argue for the need for greater control over the licensing of their products, they lobby for the right to be exempt from responsibility and liability for those products.

Efforts have also been made to address jurisdictional issues having to do with contracts at the international level; for example, the United Nations Convention on Contracts for the Sale of Goods has unified the laws of the nations that ratified the Convention. And efforts are currently underway by the European Union to unify the contract laws of the member nations so that greater consistency will apply to contracts involving computer information and electronics. As we have suggested, enforcing international laws involving property and contracts can be very difficult. Recall our analysis of international aspects of cybercrime in Chapter 7, where we examined issues involving jurisdiction in cyberspace. We consider the question of jurisdiction again in Chapter 9, where we examine jurisdictional issues involved in prosecuting a case of Internet pornography.

TABLE 8-1   Abbreviations and Acronyms Pertaining to Copyright

CSS	Content Scrambling System
DeCSS	De-Content Scrambling System
DMCA	Digital Millennium Copyright Act (Public Law 304, 1998)
DVD	Digital Versatile Disc
MP3	Standard file digital format (developed in 1987 by the Moving Picture Exports Group)
NET Act	No Electronic Theft Act
SBCTEA	Sonny Bono Copyright Term Extension Act
TRIPS	Trade Relationship Aspects of Intellectual Property Standards
UCC	Uniform Commerce Code (for electronic contracts)
UCITA	Uniform Computer and Information Transactions Act
UETA	Uniform Electronic Transactions Act
WIPO	World Intellectual Property Organization

In our discussions involving copyright protection and electronic contracts, we have used several acronyms and abbreviations to describe and refer to national and international policies, treaties, and statutes. Table 8-1 contains a list of those acronyms.

▷ 8.5 PATENTS, TRADEMARKS, AND TRADE SECRETS

In addition to copyright law, other kinds of legal protection schemes have been devised to safeguard intellectual property. Depending on the nature of the property, protective measures such as patents, trademarks, and trade secrets can apply. We examine examples of each form of protection with respect to how each can be applied to cybertechnology.

8.5.1   Patent Protections

A patent is a form of legal protection given to individuals who create an invention or process. Patent protection is covered in Title 35 of the United States Code, and, as in the case of copyright law, the basis for patent protection can be found in Article 1, Section 8 of the Constitution. Unlike copyright protection, patents offer a twenty-year exclusive monopoly over an expression or implementation of a protected work. The first explicit American patent law, the Patent Act of 1793, was passed when Thomas Jefferson was the administrator of the patent system. The present United States patent statute is based on the Patent Act of 1952, as amended in 1995.

Patent protection can be applied to inventions and discoveries that include utilitarian or functional devices such as machines, articles of manufacture, or "compositions of matter." The Patent Act requires that inventions satisfy three conditions:

- usefulness
- novelty
- nonobviousness

First, an invention must have a certain *usefulness,* or utility, in order to be awarded a patent; inventing a machine that does nothing useful would not merit its inventor a patent. Also, the invention must be *novel,* or new, in order to qualify for a patent. One cannot simply modify an existing invention and expect to be granted a patent for it; the modification would have to be significant enough to make a qualified difference. Finally, the invention or process must be *nonobvious*. For example, it is possible that no one has yet recorded directions for how to travel from Buffalo, New York to Cleveland, Ohio, through Pittsburgh, Pennsylvania, but describing the route would not satisfy the condition of nonobviousness.

There are three different kinds of patents: design patents and utility patents (both of particular interest with respect to computers and computer software) and plant patents. Whereas design patents protect any new, original, and ornamental design for an article of manufacture, utility patents protect any new, useful, and nonobvious process, machine, or article of manufacture. Patent protection excludes others from making, using, or selling the invention. The owner of a patent has a complete monopoly over the use of the machine or process for twenty years.

Although computer hardware inventions clearly satisfied the requirements of patent law, this was not initially the case with computer software. John Snapper (1995) points out that in the 1960s, most of the discussion involving the protection of software focused on patents, but in a series of decisions beginning with *Gotshalk v. Benson* (1972), the United States Patent Office and the courts established a strong opposition to patenting software. Benson applied for a patent for an algorithm that translated the representation of numbers from base 10 to base 2; such an algorithm is an important feature of all programs. If granted a patent for his algorithm, however, Benson would have controlled almost every computer in use for a number of years. He was denied the patent on the basis of a policy that bars the granting of patents for mere mathematical formulas or abstract processes that can be performed by a series of "mental steps" with the aid of pencil and paper.

▶ **CASE ILLUSTRATION:** A Pivotal Court Decision Involving Software Patents

In *Diamond v. Deihr*, the Supreme Court decided 5–4 that a patent could be awarded for a computer program under certain conditions; in this instance, the program assisted in converting rubber into tires. On the one hand, Deihr had developed a new process that physically transformed raw rubber into rubber tires, and on the other hand, Deihr had only a new computer program, since every other part of the machinery used in the conversion process consisted of traditional technology. Initially, Deihr's request for a patent was denied by Diamond, the director of the Patent Office. Deihr appealed, and his case was taken to the Supreme Court. Although the Court ruled in favor of Deihr, the justices, in their decision, continued to affirm the view that computer algorithms themselves are not patentable. They pointed out that the patent awarded to Deihr was not for the computer program but for the rubber tire transformation process as a whole.

Since the Deihr case, patents have been granted to computer programs and software applications. Some fear that now patent protection has gone too far—the United States Patent and Trademark Office (PTO) currently issues about 20,000 new software patents every year. Gregory Aharonian (1999) points out that between 1990 and 1999 the number of patents increased from 1,300 to 22,5000; and between 1993 and 1999, the number of patents issued increased tenfold. He also points out that between 1979 and 1999, more than 700,000 patents were issued for electronics inventions, including software products.

Recently, the generous granting of patent protections has raised concerns about which features of the user interfaces on e-commerce sites should be eligible for patent protection. For example, should an e-commerce site that is the first to display a "shopping cart" icon in its user interface be able to patent that icon? We briefly consider a recent e-commerce dispute involving two well-known "e-tailers."

▶ **CASE ILLUSTRATION:** Amazon.com v. BarnesandNoble.com

Amazon.com, a major on-line retailer of books and related products, developed a process for purchasing items on-line that involved a single mouse click (a one-click express check-out system). Barnes and Noble later developed a similar procedure, called "express lane," where its users could click on a single button to accomplish the same form of one-click check-out. Amazon argued that Barnes and Noble had simply copied the procedure that Amazon had previously patented. Barnes and Noble objected, claiming that it was not infringing on a feature patented by Amazon. Barnes and Noble argued that the feature in question did not meet the patent criterion of nonobviousness, since express lanes and one-stop shopping practices are commonplace. However, the Court concluded that Amazon's patent was valid and granted an injunction against Barnes and Noble. Many have been skeptical about a decision that would enable an on-line company to have exclusive rights to a process that did not seem to meet the nonobvious requirement for a patent.

8.5.2   Trademarks

A trademark is a word, name, phrase, or symbol that identifies a product or service. In 1946 the Lanham Act, also referred to as the Trademark Act, was passed to provide protection for registered trademarks. It helps ensure that the quality associated with a certain logo or symbol used by a business actually represents the quality that consumers expect. So for example, when a consumer sees a Mercedes-Benz emblem, he or she can expect that the product will live up to the standards of the Mercedes-Benz Company. Consider three common trademarks: the apple that symbolizes Apple and Macintosh computers; the golden arches that have come to symbolize McDonald's restaurants; and the expression "Coke," which symbolizes Coca-Cola. To qualify for a trademark, the "mark," or name, is supposed to be distinctive. As Debora Halbert (1999) notes, however, a (not very distinctive) trademark for "uh-huh" was granted to Pepsi-Cola. Because of decisions such as this, she and others have argued that trademark protections are being expanded in ways that are inappropriate and potentially damaging to the market place. Consider the following example, which may support Halbert's point that entrepreneurs are trying to expand the scope of trademarks.

▶ **CASE ILLUSTRATION:** AOL v. AT&T

America On-Line (AOL), a major ISP, applied for trademarks for its expressions "You've Got Mail," "Buddy List," and "IM" (Instant Messenger). If AOL owns such trademarks, other providers who use them would be infringing on AOL's registered trademarks. AT&T challenged AOL as to the legality of such trademarks, and the court decided that the expressions were not unique to AOL.

You can acquire a trademark in most cases in which you are the first to use a word or expression publicly or when you explicitly register the trademark with the United States Patent Office. An owner's trademark is violated when someone else infringes on it in connection with the sale of goods and services. A trademark owner can also bring forth a legal claim in the event that his or her trademark is "diluted" or "blurred." We examine the issue of trademark dilution in our discussion of Internet domain names, (HTML) metatags, and Web hyperlinks in Chapter 9.

8.5.3 Trade Secrets

A *trade secret* consists of information used in the operation of a business or other enterprise that is sufficiently valuable and secret to afford an actual or potential economic advantage over others. Trade secrets can be used to protect

- formulas (such as the one used by Coca-Cola),
- blueprints for future projects,
- chemical compounds,
- processes of manufacturing.

Trade secrets are generally recognized as "secrets" on which a company has expended money and energy and that are shown only to a select few within an organization. Owners of a trade secret have exclusive rights to make use of it, but they have this right only as long as the secret is maintained.

Many states in America have adopted the Uniform Trade Secrets Act (UTSA). According to this act, a trade secret is "information, including a formula, pattern, compilation, program, device, technique, or process that (i) derives independent economic value from not being generally known to . . . other persons who can obtain economic value, actual or potential, from its disclosure or use, and (ii) is the subject of efforts that are reasonable under the circumstances to maintain its secrecy."

One problem with protecting trade secrets is that trade secret law is difficult to enforce at the international level. Not only have corporate spies in the United States tried to steal secrets from their corporate rivals, but there is evidence to suggest that international industrial espionage has become a growing industry. Recently, the world community has acknowledged the need for member states to protect against the disclosure of trade secrets. The TRIPS agreement, which was part of the WIPO agreements, provides a platform for protecting trade secrets at the international level; specifically, Article 39 of the TRIPS agreement protects trade secrets by stating explicitly that disclosure of trade secrets "comes within the meaning of unfair competition in the global community."

Of course, trade secrets are not peculiar to the computer industry or to the high-tech industry. However, because of the considerable amount of research and development conducted in those industries in recent years, they have experienced a higher incidence of trade-secret violations than other industrial markets.

► 8.6 PHILOSOPHICAL FOUNDATIONS FOR INTELLECTUAL PROPERTY

Although some philosophers and political theorists have opposed the notion of private property rights, we will presume that property ownership is justifiable. We should note that some believe that property ownership rights make sense in the physical realm but are skeptical that property rights can be extended to intellectual objects in cyberspace. We will examine arguments for this position in Section 8.6.4.

In Section 8.2.2, we alluded to three philosophical theories—labor, utilitarian, and personality—that have been used to justify property rights. We next examine each of those theories in greater detail and then consider an alternative framework for analyzing intellectual-property-rights claims and information-ownership disputes in cyberspace.

8.6.1 The Labor Theory of Property

The labor theory of property, based on the notion of "just deserts" for one's (physical) labor, traces its origins to seventeenth-century philosopher John Locke. In the fifth chapter of his *Second Treatise on Civil Government* (1690), Locke argues that when a person "mixes" his or her labor with the environment, that person is entitled to the fruit of his or her labor. So if a person tills and plants crops—an act which, Locke notes, requires considerable toil— on land that is not already owned by another, that person has a right to claim ownership of the crops. Similarly, if a person goes into the woods, cuts down a tree, and saws it into several pieces, then the person is entitled to the pieces of wood that result from his or her labor. Locke also includes an important qualification, the "enough as good" proviso, according to which a person has neither the right to cut down all of the trees in the forest nor the right to take the last tree. Even with this sufficiency qualification, however, some argue that Locke's theory falls short of an adequate account of property rights.

Locke claims that an individual's right to own property is a natural right, as opposed to an artificial (or man-made) right, but he gives no argument to explain his position. Furthermore, Locke's theory of property also presupposes that persons making property claims "own their own bodies." If the right to own property is indeed a natural right, then it should apply to all persons, but consider the example of slavery, a relevant issue in Locke's time. Slaves do not legally own their bodies and it would follow, on Locke's reasoning, that they have no claim to the fruits of their labor—they do not have property rights. So property rights, according to Locke's labor theory, do not apply equally to all people; if they did, Native Americans who mixed their labor with the soil should have been granted property rights to their land in North and South America. It is not clear how Locke can claim that property ownership is a natural right, and yet at the same time allow that such a right could possibly be denied to some individuals who happen to be slaves or Native Americans.

Some critics also argue that even if Locke's theory made sense for physical property, it could not be easily extended to the intellectual realm. Noting that Locke associates labor with arduous physical labor, some critics argue that the production of intellectual objects does not require the same kind of onerous toil (or "sweat") that goes into producing tangible goods. But we can see how an author might claim a natural right to the ownership of intellectual objects generated by his or her labor, because writing a book, a poem, or a software program does require a fair amount of toil. Other critics of Locke point out that intellectual objects are nonexclusionary in nature. From this, they go on to infer that there is no need to grant property rights for those objects in a way that would be strictly analogous to rights involving physical property. Consider a scenario in which an appeal for copyright protection is made on the basis of the labor theory of property.

▶ **SCENARIO:** ABC Corporation v. XYZ, Inc.

ABC Corporation, a software company with eighty employees, has spent the last year developing a database program that it is about to release. Thirty software developers have been employed full time on this project, and each software developer worked an average of sixty hours per week. The company expects that it will take more than one year to recoup the investment of labor and time put into this project. ABC applies for a copyright for its product.

XYZ, Inc., which also produces database software, files a suit against ABC Corporation for allegedly infringing on its copyright: XYZ claims that ABC has copied a feature used in the interface in one of XYZ's software products. ABC objects by arguing the feature is, in fact, not original and thus XYZ, Inc., should not be eligible for copyright protection. More importantly, ABC further argues that it has invested considerable labor and "sweat" in its database program, so it should be rewarded for its hard work.

Does ABC's claim make sense in light of the labor theory of property? Is the labor expended on a particular project, in itself, sufficient to make the case for copyright protection? According to Locke's theory, ABC has a reasonable case, but XYZ sees the matter very differently. Do you agree with ABC's position or with the case made by XYZ?

8.6.2 The Utilitarian Theory of Property

Critics of the labor theory argue that a rationale for granting property rights should not be confused with an individual's labor or with a natural right; rather, property rights are better understood as artificial rights or conventions devised by the state to achieve certain practical ends. According to utilitarian theory, granting property rights will maximize the good for the greatest number of people in a given society. (Recall our Chapter 2 discussion of utilitarianism and Jeremy Bentham and John Stuart Mill's arguments for it.) In many respects, utilitarian theory underpins the rationale used by the framers of the Constitution for granting intellectual property rights. The Founders reasoned that if incentives (i.e., a system of copyrights an patents) were given for individuals to bring out their creative products (literary works and inventions), American society in general would benefit.

An advantage of the utilitarian theory is that it does not need to appeal to an abstract principle such as a "natural right to property" in order to justify the granting of property rights to creators and inventors of intellectual objects. However, utilitarians have their critics as well. In Chapter 2, we saw some shortcomings of utilitarian theory with respect to protecting the interests of individuals who fall outside the scope of "the greatest number" in a given society. For this reason, many find utilitarianism in general, as well as the utilitarian argument for granting property rights, inadequate. The next scenario is concerned with the utilitarian argument for property rights.

▶ **SCENARIO:** Sam's Multiple CD Loader/Reader

Sam is a very talented and creative person, but he is not terribly industrious when it comes to following through with his ideas. He has an idea for loading multiple CDs onto a desktop computer and then retrieving and playing them individually through a series of mouse clicks. Many of Sam's friends are interested in his idea, and some have strongly encouraged him to develop his CD loading device so that they can use it on their home computers. But Sam remains unconvinced and unmotivated. Then Sam's friend, Pat, tells him that an acquaintance of hers patented an analogous invention and parleyed it into a profit of several thousand dollars. Pat tries to persuade Sam that not only would his invention benefit his friends but also that he would stand to gain financially if he patents the product and sells it. After considering Pat's advice, Sam decides to work on his multiple CD-retrieval invention and apply for a patent for it.

Was a utilitarian incentive (i.e., financial benefits) necessary to get Sam to follow through on his invention? Would he have brought his invention into the marketplace if there were not a financial enticement?

8.6.3 The Personality Theory of Property

Critics of the labor and utilitarian theories believe that a theory that links the granting of property rights to either (a) an individual's onerous labor or (b) the notion of social utility, misses an important point about the nature of the creative work involved in the production of intellectual objects. Both the labor and utilitarian theories appeal to criteria external to the individual as the rationale for granting a property right. Note that in each case, the criterion is a reward that is directly monetary in the case of utilitarian theory, and indirectly monetary in the case of labor theory. Both theories assume a financial or economic basis for property rights; neither considers the possibility that an internal criterion could provide a ground for granting property rights to individuals.. In failing to do so, both theories underestimate the investment of the *personality* of the creator in his or her artistic or intellectual work. According to the personality theory of property, the intellectual object is an extension of the creator's or author's personality. And it is because of this relationship between the object and the author's personality (i.e., the person's being, or soul) that advocates of the personality theory believe that artistic works deserve legal protection.

The personality theory traces its origins to the writings of G. W. F. Hegel, a nineteenth-century philosopher, and it has served as a foundational element in intellectual property laws enacted by nations in continental Europe. In France, the personality account of property is sometimes referred to as the "moral rights" theory of property. The personality theory provides an interesting interpretation of *why* an author should have control over the ways in which his or her work can be displayed and distributed. To ensure this control, personality theorists argue that authors should be given protection for their artistic work even if they have no legal claim to any monetary reward associated with it. Consider an actual case in which the personality theory of property can be applied.

▶ **CASE ILLUSTRATION:** A Television Commercial for Nike

In the late 1980s the Nike Corporation aired a television commercial for it sneakers that featured the song "Revolution," composed by John Lennon in the late 1960s (when he was a member of The Beatles). Lennon was assassinated in 1980, so when the Nike ad aired on commercial television, he could neither approve nor disapprove of how his song was being used. Many of Lennon's fans, however, were outraged that a song penned by Lennon to address the serious political and social concerns of the turbulent 1960s could be used so frivolously in a TV commercial. Critics argued that Lennon would not have approved of his song being used in this manner.

Legally, however, even if he had been alive, Lennon may not have had recourse when the TV commercial aired, because the entire Lennon-McCartney corpus of songs was purchased by Michael Jackson in the 1980s; Michael Jackson owned the copyright to "Revolution." By appealing to a "moral rights" theory of property, such as the personality theory, however, the case could be made that Lennon—or in this instance, his widow—should have some say in how his song was represented in a commercial forum.

Next consider a hypothetical scenario involving the personality theory of property.

▶ **SCENARIO:** Angela's B++ Programming Tool

Imagine that Angela, a graduate student who has been struggling to make ends meet, has developed a new programming tool, called B++. This software application, which is based on a "reduced instruction set" design, can be used in conjunction with the standard C++ programming language to execute certain tasks more quickly than the C++ instruction set. Angela has recently published an article that describes, in detail, the reduced set of instructions, how they work, and why she was motivated to develop B++. She was delighted to have her article published in the prestigious journal *CyberTechnology*. As part of the conditions for publication, however, Angela had to agree to sign over the copyright for her article to *CyberPress* (the publisher of *CyberTechnology*), but she will receive royalties for future reprints of her article.

Next imagine that a textbook publisher, *CyberTextbooks, Inc.*, wishes to include a portion of Angela's article in a textbook. As the copyright holder for Angela's article, *CyberPress* is legally authorized to allow *CyberTextbooks* to reprint all or selected portions of her article. Suppose, however, that Angela protests that mere excerpts from her article neither truly convey the important features of her programming tool nor explain how it works. She further argues that the article is an extension of her persona and that only in total does the article reveal her creative talents as a future programmer. *CyberPress* responds by pointing out that she will receive a royalty payment for the inclusion of the abridged version of her article in the textbook, but Angela maintains her objections.

Should Angela, the original author of the article and the creator of the new programming tool, have the right to prevent her article from being republished in an abridged form? Is her claim, that an abridged from of her work should not be reprinted in the forthcoming book published by *CyberTextbooks,* a reasonable one? Can her argument, based on the notion of intellectual property as an expression of one's personality, be defended on moral grounds?

Table 8-2 summarizes the three philosophical theories of property.

8.6.4 An Alternative Framework for Analyzing Intellectual-Property-Right Claims

We have examined three traditional theories that are sometimes used to justify intellectual-property-right claims from a philosophical perspective. In Section 8.6.1 we noted that some have argued for the claim that no formal legal protection should be given to intellectual property even if we do grant such protection to physical property. One of the best known, and perhaps most controversial, arguments for that position, as applied to software, has been made by Richard Stallman (1995). Stallman's position on intellectual property rights for software may seem inconsistent, because he copyrighted his Emacs software editor. However, Stallman claimed that he did so to prevent others from copyrighting and then making a profit from his software application. Stallman's claim might be viewed as a variation of the personality theory of property, in that he seems to view the Emacs editor as an

TABLE 8-2 Three Philosophical Theories of Property

Labor Theory	Argues that a property right is a natural right and that property rights can be justified by the labor, or toil, that one invests in cultivating land or in creating a work of art.
Utilitarian Theory	Argues that property rights are not natural rights but rather artificial rights created by the state. Property rights are granted to individuals and to corporations because they result in greater overall social utility.
Personality Theory	Argues that a property right is a moral right and that property rights are justified not because of labor or social utility but because creative works express the personalities of the authors who create them.

extension of his personality. Nonetheless, Stallman has been a staunch advocate for the view that software should be free, and many of his disciples subscribe to the mantra *Information wants to be free.*

Stallman's argument for why information should be free is fairly complex, so some important aspects of his broader argument cannot be considered here in depth. Stallman believes that programmers would continue to write software programs even if they received no financial rewards in the form of copyright protections. Utilitarians, of course, would disagree with Stallman on this point, and so too would labor theorists as well as many laypeople who have never reflected seriously on the notion of intellectual property rights.

One point that Stallman makes is particularly useful in helping us think about issues involving intellectual property from a radically different perspective: *Information* is something that humans desire to share with one another. This particular insight also undergirds Stallman's broader claim that information should be free. We do not need to defend this claim, however, to appreciate Stallman's insight. In order to be shared, of course, information must be communicated, so elaborate intellectual property structures and mechanisms that prohibit, or even discourage, the communication of information would seem to undermine its very purpose—as something to be shared.

Although proportionately few may agree with Stallman's claim that information should be completely free, some have found Stallman's insight about the nature and purpose of information (i.e., as something that humans naturally want to share and communicate) to be compelling. Some have also noted that this insight dovetails with a central tenet of *natural law* theory. Although there is no systematic natural law theory of property, recent attempts have been made by David Carey (1997) and Michael McFarland (2001) to draw from principles in virtue ethics (see Chapter 2) and natural law theory in discussions about intellectual property. Neither Carey nor McFarland are willing to accept Stallman's claim that software should be totally free and thus legally unprotected, but both authors believe that Stallman is correct in his insight that the essential purpose of information is to be shared. From that premise, Carey and McFarland each construct arguments for a system of intellectual property along the lines of a natural law theory.

8.6.4.1 Applying Natural Law Theory to the Intellectual Property Debate

First articulated in a systematic way by St. Thomas Aquinas (1225–1274), natural law theory has its roots in Aristotle's *Nicomachean Ethics*. In Chapter 2, we saw that key elements of Aristotle's theory serve as the cornerstone for virtue ethics, or character ethics. How can these basic doctrines be extended to form a framework for discussing intellectual property issues? First, it is important to note that Aristotle believed that every object had a nature, end, or purpose, which he called its *good*. Following his method of inquiry, we begin any philosophical investigation by asking what the good, or purpose, of an object *is*. To investigate information as an intellectual object, we should aim at understanding its ultimate purpose.

Although information can certainly be understood as a form of self-expression (as the personality theory rightly suggests), and as a product that performs some useful functions (as utilitarians correctly suggest), it also has an even more fundamental purpose than personal expression and utility. Information, McFarland and Carey argue, is ultimately about communication; hence the nature and purpose of intellectual property in the form of information is communication, and thus an adequate account of the purpose of information (as something to be communicated) must take that into consideration.

McFarland points out that if we begin our analysis of intellectual property issues simply by analyzing the notion of property itself, then the central point of debate tends to be ownership and control; and this is indeed how property issues are typically conceived and debated. McFarland also believes, however, that if we are willing to step outside that conventional framework, we can get a more complete view of the issues surrounding the intellectual property debate. In doing this, we gain the insight that an adequate theory of information must take into account its *social nature*, an important feature that we tend to overlook when we think of intellectual objects only in terms of rights and property.

How is a natural law approach to intellectual property issues, which takes into account the overall good of society, different from a utilitarian theory? We noted earlier that a utilitarian system's primary concern is with maximizing the good for the majority, but utilitarianism does not always take individual rights into consideration in producing the greatest good for the greatest number. McFarland points out that a utilitarian analysis based solely on cost-benefits criteria might determine that it is desirable to publish a person's private diary because many people would enjoy reading it. Although the benefit to the overall majority would outweigh any embarrassment to the individual writer of the diary, such a practice is not morally correct, because it violates the basic right of humans to be respected.

8.6.4.2 Acknowledging Information's Social Role

Traditional concepts of property often overlook the ethically significant relationships that some kinds of property have with the rest of society. The three traditional theories of property focus on either an individual's (or a corporation's) labor, social utility (cost-benefits), or the author's personality. But none considers the purpose of information as something whose essential nature is to be shared and communicated. Hence, McFarland, Carey, and others believe that a natural law analysis of property, which examines the nature of information in terms of a broader social context, can provide us with an attractive alternative to the traditional property theories.

Critics could point out that while the alternative framework proposed by McFarland and others sounds fine in concept, its important details are yet to be worked out. And they could question aspects of natural law theory in general, especially the essential presupposition that objects have an inherent purpose, or end. In spite of these criticisms, this alternative framework for approaching intellectual property has exposed a major flaw in traditional property theories.

Some theorists believe that our current intellectual property laws also tend to overlook both the social role of the creator and the social role of the work itself. McFarland points out that because our conventional concept of property is individualistic, it focuses only on the creator/developer of the work (i.e., on his or her labor, personality, or financial gain). James Boyle (2001) makes a similar point when he notes that we have romanticized the notion of "author," attributing to individuals a sense of originality that is not always warranted. We often forget that authors do borrow from one another and in so doing make a greater overall contribution to society.

Debora Halbert (1999) believes that the concept of the individual author as someone who is in control of his or her creative work is deceptive. She points out that such a view of "author" has served to "conceal the larger political and economic implications" of the intellectual property system, where major owners such as Microsoft can own as well as control both information systems and information itself. This control tends to deter, rather than facilitate, the sharing of information. Thus recent trends in United States intellectual property law runs counter to the view that the purpose of information is something to be shared.

▶ 8.7 INFORMATION WANTS TO BE SHARED VS. INFORMATION WANTS TO BE FREE

Perhaps a new principle will emerge from the insight of McFarland, Carey, and others: *Information wants to be shared* (Tavani 2002). I believe that it has a chance to be taken far more seriously than "Information wants to be free." In fact, others, including some who do not necessarily advocate a natural law approach to intellectual property echo many of the concerns that McFarland and Carey raise with respect to the sharing of information. Richard De George (2001), for example, has pointed out a great advantage of information: One can usually share it with others while retaining it oneself; that is, we can share in its benefits without depriving others of it. De George believes that the cyberage, which makes possible the sharing of information in ways that were not previously possible, has provided us with greater opportunity to move from the level of individual to the level of community. Yet, paradoxically, by focusing on information as a commodity, the software industry has highlighted its commercial value, and as a result, policies and schemes have been constructed to control information for commercial purposes rather than to share it freely.

To see the force of De George's claim, consider that copyright laws, originally intended to cover print media, were designed to encourage the distribution of information. We have seen that these laws have since been extended to cover digital media, inhibiting the distribution of electronic information. The distribution of digitized information is now being discouraged, despite the fact that cybertechnology has made information exchange easy and inexpensive. To illustrate this point, consider the interlibrary loan, a practice that has helped expand the notion of a learning community. Physical books are exchanged between libraries so that students can borrow, for a limited time, books not physically available at their local library. When I was a graduate student, I would sometimes take advantage of my university's interlibrary loan policy: If the books that I so easily borrowed then were available only in digitized form now, it might no longer be possible to borrow them because the DMCA discourages the sharing of electronic books by granting copyright holders of digital media the ability to prohibit their exchange.

There is a certain irony here. The ability to share, not to hoard, information contributed to the development of the World Wide Web. Consider what might have happened if the inventors of the Web had been more entrepreneurial-minded and less concerned with sharing information. Tim Berners-Lee, who invented HTTP, never bothered to apply for a patent for his invention or for a copyright for his code. As a physicist working at CERN (a laboratory in Switzerland), he desired to develop a common protocol for Internet communication so that scientists could share information more easily with each other. Note that Berners-Lee's goal in developing the Web was to provide a forum where information could be *shared*. A person whose interest was more entrepreneurial could have sought intellectual property protection for his or her contribution, thereby reducing the amount of information that could be shared. Also consider that Doug Englebart, who invented the mouse, received no patent or copyright for his contribution, but virtually every major computer manufacturer, as well as every computer user who has used a graphical interface, has benefited by his seminal contribution to what we have come to know as a "windows interface."

Consider also how the sharing of information has benefited many of those entrepreneurs who now seek to control the flow of information in cyberspace. It has been argued that Microsoft benefited significantly from the work done by Apple Corporation on its graphical user interface (the system of icons that users can point to and click on to accomplish a task). And it is well known that when Steve Jobs was at Apple, he visited Xerox Park, where he discovered that a graphical interface had already been invented by researchers there. So it is reasonably accurate to say that current user interfaces have benefited from the sharing of information along the way. Would it be fair to credit any one company or person with exclusive rights to a graphical user interface? Would doing so not also eliminate, or certainly impede, the possibility of incremental development and innovation? And more importantly, would it not also prevent us from sharing that important information?

How can a proposal espousing the principle "Information wants to be shared" be taken seriously in a world where recent laws and policies seem to have conspired against the sharing of information? Perhaps the recent "open source" software movement is one response to that challenge. In the open source model, software is distributed for free, and its source code is openly published and also allowed to be modified by users. (Contrast this with the source code for proprietary software programs, which typically cannot be viewed and modified.) Eric Raymond (2001) has argued that open source software can actually be superior to proprietary software produced by large corporations such as Microsoft. He believes that the decentralized open source model promotes a climate in which software bugs can be more easily identified and fixed by the many individuals who will want to use the software. Although open software is free to users, companies who provide services for it will be able to make money by supporting it. So the open source movement promotes the principle that "information wants to be shared" even though it does not necessarily endorse the stronger view that "information wants to be (absolutely) free."

It is interesting to note that in 1994 John Perry Barlow confidently predicted the end of intellectual property laws in cyberspace, arguing that such laws no longer made sense in the information age. Although he correctly noted that existing property laws were grossly inadequate in an age of digital media, his prediction that intellectual-property laws in cyberspace would disappear has, so far at least, turned out to be mistaken. Instead, one could make a plausible case, given the recent trends affecting property protection examined in this chapter, that the opposite has happened. Debora Halbert (1999) has remarked that the boundaries of intellectual property have become so expanded as to become oppressive. As a result, many critics fear that that digital information is now becoming less available and that we as a society are worse off because of it. Some also fear that if the public domain of ideas continues to shrink, our intellectual commons may eventually disappear.

▶ 8.8 PRESERVING THE INTELLECTUAL COMMONS

What do we mean by "intellectual commons?" Perhaps we can better understand the concept by drawing an analogy with a physical commons, a common area that has been set aside and is open to an entire community. You may have heard the "tragedy of the commons" as described by Garret Hardin (1968), a tale about the disappearance of the public space, or commons, that farmers living in a certain community had once enjoyed. A public plot of land is shared by ten farmers but owned by none of them; by sharing the land in a reasonable and mutually agreed manner, the commons benefits all of the farmers. They agree collectively that each is allowed to have no more than ten cows graze on the commons on a given day. Suppose, however, one day a farmer decides to cheat a little by having eleven or twelve of his cattle graze on the commons, reasoning that having one or two additional cows graze will not deplete the land's resources and will also enable him to profit slightly. If a second farmer uses the same rationale, you can see that before long the entire commons would be depleted.

It is very easy to underestimate the importance of the commons, or the public domain. We often take for granted the public parks, public beaches, and public gathering places that have been set aside for general use. Imagine the quality of our lives without them, and consider that without proper foresight, planning, and management our parks could easily have been turned over to entrepreneurs for private development. Imagine, for example, if early city planners in New York City had not had the wisdom to set aside the area of Manhattan called Central Park; yet there was nothing inevitable about this. An entrepreneurial-minded city council might have sold the land to developers and businesses on the grounds that doing so would bring revenue to the city. In the short term, the city might have realized significant financial gain, but they would have been very shortsighted, and it would likely have been economically disadvantageous in the long term as well. Although Central Park is a tourist attraction that draws many people to New York City, it is not valued simply as a tourist attraction—it is a gathering place for city residents as well as visitors, a place to hear a concert on a summer evening, have a picnic in the fall, or ice skate in the winter. Imagine if Central Park were to disappear from the New York City landscape.

8.8.1 The Public Domain of Ideas

Now imagine what it would be like if the public domain of ideas, that is, the "intellectual commons," that we have all enjoyed and benefited from, disappeared. In a book subtitled *The Fate of the Commons in a Connected World*, Larry Lessig (2002) raises some serious concerns about the future of ideas in a medium that is overly regulated and controlled by economic interests. Recall Section 8.4.3, where we discussed Eric Eldred's Web site, which included classic books from the public domain available in electronic form. We saw that Eldred had to remove the books from his Web site because of the retroactive provisions of the Sonny Bono Copyright Extension Term Act, which extended copyright protection by twenty years.

Of course, Congress could continue to pass laws extending the term limits of copyright law to the point where precious little, if anything, remains in the public domain. We have already seen how the Digital Millennium Copyright Act, with its controversial anticircumvention clause, contributes to the erosion, and possible elimination, of the intellectual commons in the future. We may wish to consider the short-term vs. long-term gains and losses that can result from current trends in information policy. In the near term, corporations and some individuals will profit handsomely from privatization of information policy. In the long term, however, our society may be worse off intellectually, spiritually, and even economically if the short-term goals of privatization are not balanced against the interests of the greater public.

Imagine if all information that we have traditionally shared freely were to disappear from the public domain and enter the world of copyright protection. Suppose, for example, that beginning tomorrow every recipe will be copyrighted and thus not be able to be disseminated without the permission of the new rights holder, that is, the legal owner of that recipe.

We would not even be permitted to use, let alone improve on, a particular recipe without first getting permission from the copyright holder. In the past, chefs could use recipes freely and improve upon them. Would it be fair if those chefs who had previously benefited from the sharing of recipes were all of a sudden awarded exclusive rights to them? And would it be fair if they were awarded the exclusive rights simply because they just happened to be experimenting with food at a time when the legal system favored the privatizing of information for commercial interests? Does it matter that society would be deprived of communicating freely the kind of information it has always had the luxury to share? What would this mean for the public domain of ideas and for ordinary discourse and information exchange?

8.8.2 The Environmental Movement: An Analogy for Cyberspace

In response to concerns about the disappearance of the public domain of intellectual objects, James Boyle (2001) has recently argued for a political movement similar to the environmental movement that emerged in the 1970s: just as a political movement was necessary to save the environment from inevitable destruction, so is an analogous movement needed to save the intellectual commons. To illustrate his claim, Boyle notes that the environment almost disappeared under the simplistic claim of (highly individualistic) property rights, and in a similar way the public domain of information is disappearing under an intellectual property system built around the interests of the current stakeholders. As the environmental movement invented the concept of the environment so that farmers, consumers, hunters, and bird watchers could all "discover themselves as environmentalists," perhaps we also need to invent (or reinvent) the concept of the public domain to call into being the coalition that might protect it. Boyle also suggests that we might still reclaim the public domain of ideas if we act responsibly.

We have defended the view that the ultimate purpose of information (as an intellectual object) is something to be shared and communicated and we have made the case that the intellectual commons should be preserved. Of course, the rights and interests of both software manufacturers and individual creators of literary and artistic works also deserve serious consideration in any debate about intellectual property rights in cyberspace. And we do not need to advocate for the controversial view that "information should be free" to move the debate forward. Indeed, companies and individuals need fair compensation for both their costs and the risks they undertake in developing their creative products and bringing them to market. The key phrase here, of course, is "fair compensation;" a fair intellectual property system is one that would enable us to achieve a proper balance. In reaching that state of equilibrium, however, we must not lose sight of the fact that information is more than merely a commodity that has commercial value.

If we presume in favor of the principle that information wants to be shared (but not necessarily for free), then I believe that it is possible to frame a reasonable policy for the information age that will both (a) allow the flow of information and (b) reward fairly the creators of intellectual objects, including software manufacturers, in the cyberage.

▶ 8.9 CHAPTER SUMMARY

In this chapter we have examined disputes involving intellectual property right claims in cyberspace. In particular, we considered how current intellectual property laws, especially those involving copyright and patents can be applied to cybertechnology. We saw that various philosophical theories of property underpin much of the rationale for our current schemes of legal protection, and we also saw that an alternative framework for approaching property disputes suggests that we need to take into account that fact that the essential purpose of information is to be shared. Ironically, many copyright laws, such as the DMCA, restrict the distribution, and thus the sharing, of information in the Information Age. Perhaps our greatest challenge, then, is to persuade policy makers to develop a scheme that will enable the software industry to enjoy certain legal protections for the creation of its products without jeopardizing the sharing of information among ordinary users. If we fail to do that, we as a society will be unable to share in the promises that cybertechnology makes possible with respect to both the communication and the sharing of information.

We mentioned trademark infringement only in passing in this chapter, but we will examine this notion in more detail in our discussions of Internet domain names, (HTML) metatags, and Web hyperlinks in Chapter 9, where we consider Internet regulation. We will also examine the claim that information policy affecting copyright law in cyberspace is becoming increasingly privatized. And we will see why this trend furthers what we have described in this chapter as the disappearance of the intellectual commons.

▶ REVIEW QUESTIONS

1. What is intellectual property?
2. How is intellectual property different from tangible property?
3. What is meant by an "intellectual object?"
4. Do intellectual objects deserve legal or normative protection?
5. Describe the difficulties that arose in determining whether computer software should be eligible for the kinds of legal protection (i.e., copyrights and patents) that are typically granted to authors of creative works.
6. Describe some differences between the legal schemes for protecting intellectual property: copyrights, patents, trademarks, and trade secrets.
7. What is the Digital Millennium Copyright Act, and what are its implications for the future of copyright protection in cyberspace?
8. What are the doctrines of fair use and first sale?
9. How is the principle of fair use, as illustrated in the Eldred and Sklyarov cases, threatened by recent changes to copyright law?
10. What property rights issues surround the Napster case?
11. How were the controversies involving the Napster dispute anticipated by the 1994 case involving MIT student Robert LaMacchia?
12. What are the arguments for and against protecting software with patents?
13. Describe the three philosophical property theories that we considered.
14. How can each of the three philosophical theories of property be extended to intellectual property claims? Which theory seems most plausible in the Internet era?
15. What do we mean by the expression "Information wants to be shared?"
16. How is the expression "Information wants to be shared" different from the position "Information wants to be free?"

▶ DISCUSSION QUESTIONS

1. Recall Michael McFarland's argument for an alternative way of looking at the intellectual property dispute. How can we use a natural law framework to analyze the debate involving intellectual property rights for proprietary information? How can the claim that "information should be free" be incorporated into that framework?

2. What do we mean by "intellectual commons?" How is this commons disappearing in the cyberage? Does James Boyle's suggestion that a political movement, similar to the environmental movement in the 1970s, is needed to save the commons merit further consideration? Explain.

3. Has protection for proprietary software gone too far, as some critics suggest? If so, what are the implications for innovation and competition in the computer industry? How can we achieve an appropriate balance between those who hold legal rights to proprietary information and ordinary users who wish to access, share, and communicate that information?

4. In Chapter 5 we saw that privacy advocates argue for greater control of personal information by individuals, while many in the commercial sector argue for access to that information. In Chapter 8, we saw that those positions have become reversed—entrepreneurs argue for control of the flow of information on the Internet, while ordinary users argue for access to that information. Is there an irony, perhaps even an inconsistency, here? Can this inconsistency be resolved in a logically coherent manner? How? Explain.

▶ REFERENCES

Aharonian, Gregory (1999). "Does the Patent Office Respect the Software Community?" *IEEE Software*, Vol. 16, No. 4, pp. 87–89.

Barlow, John Perry (1994). "The Economy of Ideas: A Framework for Copyrights and Patents (Everything You Know About Intellectual Property is Wrong)," *Wired*, Vol. 2, No. 3, March, pp. 47–50.

Boyle, James (2001). "A Politics of Intellectual Property: Environmentalism for the Net." In R. A. Spinello and H. T. Tavani, eds (2001). *Readings in CyberEthics*. Sudbury, MA: Jones and Bartlett Publishers, pp. 231–251.

Carey, David H. (1997). "The Virtues of Software Ownership." In A. D. Moore, ed. *Intellectual Property: Moral, Legal, and International Dilemmas*. Lanham, MD: Rowan and Littlefield, pp. 299–305.

De George, Richard T. (2001). "Ethics and Law in the Information Age." Paper presented at the 2000–2001 Rivier College Humanities Series Lectures, Nashua, NH, April 5.

Grosso, Andrew (2000). "The Promise and the Problems of the No Electronic Theft Act," *Communications of the ACM*, Vol. 43, No. 2, February, pp. 23–26.

Halbert, Debora J. (1999). *Intellectual Property in the Information Age: The Politics of Expanding Ownership Rights*. Westport, CT: Quorum Books.

Hardin, Garret (1968). "The Tragedy of the Commons" *Science*, Vol. 162, pp. 1243-1248.

Lessig, Larry (2002). *The Future of Ideas: The Fate of the Commons in a Connected World*. New York: Random House.

McFarland, Michael C. (2001). "Intellectual Property, Information, and the Common Good." In R. A. Spinello and H. T. Tavani, eds. (2001). *Readings in CyberEthics*. Sudbury, MA: Jones and Bartlett Publishers, pp. 252–263.

Nissenbaum, Helen (1995). "Should I Copy My Neighbor's Software?" In D. G. Johnson and H. Nissenbaum, eds. *Computing, Ethics, and Social Values*, Englewood Cliffs, NJ: Prentice Hall, pp. 200–213.

Raymond, Eric (2001). "The Cathedral and the Bazaar." In R. A. Spinello and H. T. Tavani, eds. (2001). *Readings in CyberEthics*. Sudbury, MA: Jones and Bartlett Publishers, pp. 309–338.

Snapper, John W. (1995). "Intellectual Property Protections for Computer Software." In D. G. Johnson and H. Nissenbaum, eds. (1995). *Computing, Ethics, and Social Values*, Englewood Cliffs, NJ: Prentice Hall, pp. 181–189.

Spinello, Richard A., and Herman T. Tavani (2001a). "Intellectual Property in Cyberspace." In *Readings in CyberEthics*. Sudbury, MA: Jones and Bartlett Publishers, pp. 210–214.

Spinello, Richard A., and Herman T. Tavani (2001b). "Notes on the DeCSS Trial." In *Readings in CyberEthics*. Sudbury, MA: Jones and Bartlett Publishers, pp. 226–230.

Stallman, Richard (1995). "Why Software Should Be Free." In D. Johnson and H. Nissenbaum, eds. *Computing, Ethics, and Social Values*, Englewood Cliffs, NJ: Prentice Hall, pp. 199–200.

Tavani, Herman T. (2002). "'Information Wants to Be Shared: An Alternative Framework for Analyzing Intellectual Property Disputes in an Information Age, *Catholic Library World*, Vol. 73, No. 2, pp. 94–104.

▶ FURTHER READINGS

Baase, Sara (2003). "Protecting Software and Other Intellectual Property." Chapter 5 in *A Gift of Fire: Social, Legal, and Ethical Issues in Computing*. 2d ed. Upper Saddle River, NJ: Prentice Hall.

Burk, Dan L. (1994). "Transborder Intellectual Property Issues on the Electronic Frontier," *Stanford Law & Policy Issues*, Vol. 6, No. 1, pp. 9–16.

Burk, Dan L. (2002). "Anti-Circumvention Misuse, or, How I Stopped Worrying and Love the DMCA." In . J. R. Herkert, ed. *Proceedings of the 2002 International Symposium on Technology and Society ISTAS '02)*. Piscataway, NJ: IEEE Press, pp. 244–251

Boyle, James (1996). *Shamans, Software, and Spleens: Law and Construction of the Information Society*. Cambridge, MA: Harvard University Press.

Davis, J. C. (1998). "Protecting Intellectual Property in Cyberspace," *IEEE Technology and Society*, Vol. 17, No. 2, pp. 12–25.

Digital Millennium Copyright Act. Public Law 105-304, passed by the United States Congress on October 28, 1998. Excerpts from this Act are included in R. A. Spinello and H. T. Tavani, eds. (2001). *Readings in CyberEthics*. Sudbury, MA: Jones and Bartlett Publishers, pp. 215–225.

Girasa, Roy J. (2002). *Cyberlaw: National and International Perspectives*. Upper Saddle River, NJ: Prentice Hall.

Johnson, Deborah G. (2001). "Property Rights in Computer Software." Chap. 6 in *Computer Ethics*. 3d. ed. Upper Saddle River, NJ: Prentice Hall.

Kuflik, Arthur (1995). "Moral Foundations of Intellectual Property Rights." In D. G. Johnson and H. Nissenbaum, eds. (1995). *Computing, Ethics, and Social Values*, Englewood Cliffs, NJ: Prentice Hall, pp. 169–180.

Lessig, Larry (1999). *Code and Other Laws of Cyberspace*. New York: Basic Books.

Lipinski, Thomas A., and Johannes J. Britz (2000). "Rethinking the Ownership of Information in the 21st Century: Ethical Implications," *Ethics and Information Technology*, Vol. 2, No. 1, pp. 49–71.

Litman, Jessica (1990). "The Public Domain," *Emory Law Journal*, Vol. 39, pp. 965-1023.

Litman, Jessica (2001). *Digital Copyright*. New York: Prometheus Books.

Moore, Adam D., ed. (1997). *Intellectual Property: Moral, Legal, and International Dilemmas*. Lanham, MD: Rowman and Littlefield.

Moorse, Adam D. (2001). *Intellectual Property and Information Control*. New Brunswick, NJ: Transaction Publishers.

Nozick, Robert (1974). *Anarchy, State, and Utopia*. New York: Basic Books.

Samuelson, Pamela (1989). "Why the Look and Feel of Software user Interfaces Should Not Be Protected By Copyright Law," *Communications of the ACM*, Vol. 32, No. 5, pp. 563–572.

Samuelson, Pamela (1999). "Intellectual Property and the Digital Economy: Why the Anticircumvention Regulations Need to Be Revised," *Berkeley Technology Law Journal*, Vol. 14, pp. 519–566.

Snapper, John W. (1999). "On the Web Plagiarism Matters More Than Copyright Piracy," *Ethics and Information Technology*, Vol. 1, No. 2, pp. 127–136.

Spinello, Richard A. (2003). "Intellectual Property in Cyberspace." Chapter 4 in *Cyberethics: Morality and Law in Cyberspace*. 2d ed. Sudbury, MA: Jones and Bartlett Publishers.

Warwick, Shelly (2001). "Is Copyright Ethical? An Examination of the Theories, Laws, and Practices Regarding the Private Ownership of Intellectual Work in the United States." In R. A. Spinello and H. T. Tavani, eds. *Readings in CyberEthics*. Sudbury, MA: Jones and Bartlett Publishers, pp. 263–279.

9

REGULATING COMMERCE AND SPEECH IN CYBERSPACE

Should cyberspace be regulated? Can it be regulated? If the answer to both questions is yes, which aspects of the Internet should be regulated? Who should be responsible for carrying out the regulatory functions—the government? Private organizations? Or perhaps Internet users themselves? In this chapter, we examine issues that have led to a call for strong regulatory proposals in cyberspace by considering the following:

- How should Internet domain names be assigned and registered?
- Should trademarks registered in physical space apply in cyberspace as well?
- Should Web users presume a right to include hyperlinks to proprietary Web sites?
- Should the distribution of electronic spam on the Internet be permitted?
- Should on-line pornography, especially pornographic images involving minors, be censored?
- Should hate speech, as well as speech that can cause physical harm to others, be tolerated on the Internet?
- Can software filters provide a satisfactory alternative to censorship and government regulation of speech on the Internet?
- Who should be held responsible for on-line defamation?
- Should Internet Service Providers be held legally liable, morally responsible, or both, for the content of speech communicated in their on-line forums?

Many conservative organizations have argued for censorship of certain kinds of speech in cyberspace. Some liberal groups, on the other hand, who oppose any restrictions on free speech in cyberspace, argue that e-commerce, not speech, needs to be regulated. We consider "speech" to include issues involving pornography, hate speech, and defamation. And somewhat more loosely we consider e-commerce regulation issues to include concerns involving electronic spam, Internet domain names, and hyperlinking on the Web.

We will also see why we should be concerned about Internet regulation that can be implemented with technology itself, by means of "regulation by code." In the absence of clear and explicit Internet laws, regulation by code is becoming the default regulatory scheme in cyberspace. We begin with background issues.

▶ 9.1 BACKGROUND ISSUES AND PRELIMINARY DISTINCTIONS

What do we mean by "Internet regulation"? John Weckert (2000) believes that we need to ask two separate questions: (A) *Can* the Internet be regulated? And (B) *should* it be regulated? Asking question A implies that it is not clear whether the Internet can be effectively regulated, but we will operate on the assumption that it can, in fact, be regulated. We also acknowledge, however, that regulation schemes can be difficult to implement and enforce, and we concede that regulation can have undesirable side effects in terms of both cost and efficiency. We will focus on question (B), that is, the normative question as to whether the Internet, or cyberspace, *ought* to be regulated. To answer this question, it is useful to consider two additional questions:

1. What do we mean by *cyberspace*?
2. What do we mean by *regulation*, particularly as it applies to cyberspace?

9.1.1 The Ontology of Cyberspace: Is the Internet a Medium or a Place?

In Chapter 1, we loosely defined the Internet as the network of interconnected computers, and we suggested that the terms "Internet" and "cyberspace" were roughly equivalent. In this chapter, we use the two terms interchangeably. But we have not yet described the ontology of cyberspace, that is, we have not said what exactly cyberspace *is*. Is it a place, that is, a virtual space that consists of all the data and information that resides in the connected servers and databases that make up the Internet? Or is cyberspace a medium of some sort?

Mike Goodwin (1995) believes that the Internet is a new kind of medium, significantly different from earlier media, such as the telephone or television. Describing the telephone as a "one-to-one medium," and television as a "one-to-many medium," Goodman suggests that the Internet is a "many-to-many medium." He notes that one does not need to be wealthy to have access to it, and one does not need to win the approval of an editor or a publisher to speak his or her mind there. But is the Internet a medium, or can it be better understood as a public space?

Jean Camp and Y. T. Chien (2000) note four types of media: *publisher*, *broadcast*, *distributor*, and *common carrier*. An example of a publisher is a newspaper or a magazine; and broadcast media include television and radio. Telephone companies and cable companies are instances of common carriers, conduits for the distribution of information. Camp and Chien argue that none of the media models are appropriate for understanding the Internet. Instead, they believe that a spatial model—one in which cyberspace is viewed as a "public space with certain digital characteristics"—is more plausible.

But can we model the Internet accurately as a public space, as Camp and Chien suggest? Or is it better understood as a new kind of *medium*, as Goodwin and others have argued? We are making more than a mere semantic distinction, because, as Camp and Chien believe, the model we use can influence our decisions about public policies on the Internet. If the Internet is viewed as a public space, for example, then there are good legal and moral reasons for ensuring that everyone has access to it. The ontology of cyberspace will ultimately determine whether and how we should (or perhaps should not) regulate it.

Consider the rules used to regulate the distribution of videotapes of "adult" movies in physical space. Bookstores and video rental stores are permitted to carry and sell such videos, and because a store is a physical place, certain sections can be partitioned so that adults can visit them but individuals under a certain age cannot, preventing them from viewing or purchasing adult movies. The rules are drastically different, however, for broadcast media such as television, where the Federal Communications Commission (FCC) regulates which kinds of movies can be broadcast over the airwaves. Videotapes of movies that can be rented and sold only to adults in stores can also be deemed inappropriate (by the FCC) for general television viewers. So before we can successfully resolve questions about Internet regulation, we need to keep in mind that the model we use to understand cyberspace will also strongly influence which regulatory schemes are appropriate.

Figure 9-1 illustrates our two models of cyberspace.

9.1.2 Two Categories of Internet Regulation

To regulate means to monitor or control a product, process, or set of behaviors according to certain requirements, standards, or protocols. Sometimes regulatory discussions about cyberspace have centered on the *content*, for example, whether on-line pornography and hate speech should be censored on the Internet. And sometimes the regulatory discussions have focused on which kinds of processes, that is, rules and policies, should be implemented and enforced in commercial transactions in cyberspace. Physical space is regulated in both ways.

Some regulatory agencies monitor the content, and others the process, of items in physical space. The Federal Drug Administration (FDA) monitors food products on the shelves of supermarkets to ensure that they meet health and nutrition standards; FDA regulations ensure that the contents of each food item both matches and is accurately described by its

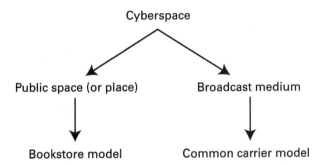

Figure 9-1 The Ontology of Cyberspace

label. Unlike the FDA, state public health boards do not regulate contents; their regulations apply to conditions for compliance with community health standards. For example, public health officials inspect restaurants and grocery stores to ensure that they meet sanitation standards in their preparation and sale of food. So an agency can regulate for content or process, or both.

In the commerce sector, federal and state agencies, such as the Federal Trade Commission (FTC) and the Securities and Exchange Commission (SEC), enforce laws and policies that apply to commercial activities and transactions; for example, they regulate against monopolies and other unfair business practices, like those alleged in the Microsoft antitrust case. Regulatory principles in the commerce sector also determine whether to permit mergers, such as the one between America Online (AOL) and Time Warner. Some believe that in cyberspace, an additional set of criteria is needed to regulate the e-commerce, or so-called dot.com sector.

Figure 9-2 illustrates the ways in which cyberspace can be regulated.

It is not difficult to point out positive effects that regulatory practices in physical space have for health and safety. Consider, for example, the role that state liquor boards play in regulating the distribution and sale of liquor: they determine who is and is not eligible for a license to distribute liquor in their state, and if a board determines that a licensed distributor has violated its licensing agreement with the state, its license can be revoked. And boards that regulate liquor can help to keep liquor out of the hands of minors and help to discourage an underground, or black market, for the sale of bootleg liquor, which is not tested and certified as meeting standards of quality and authenticity. State liquor boards also help determine fair pricing to prevent unscrupulous merchants from price gouging. So there are many good reasons for regulating the distribution and sale of liquor. But how can we extend this analogy to the Internet?

First, we can ask how we can possibly regulate cyberspace, which is inherently decentralized. Cyberspace is not compartmentalized neatly into state jurisdictions that can set up their own control boards. Does this mean that effective regulation of any type is impossible in cyberspace? Not according to Larry Lessig (1999), who believes that although cyberspace might seem "less regulable" than physical space, Internet regulation can be carried out quite effectively. Lessig argues that in cyberspace, understanding architecture, or what he calls *code*, is the key to understanding how regulation works.

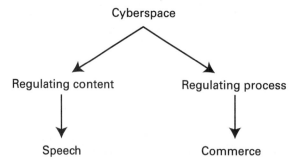

Figure 9-2 Two Categories of Cyberspace Regulation

▶ 9.2 FOUR MODES OF REGULATION: THE LESSIG MODEL

Lessig describes four distinct but interdependent constraints, which he calls "modalities," for regulating behavior: *laws*, social *norms*, *market* pressures, and *architecture*. Before we apply each modality to cyberspace, consider how each can be applied in regulating behaviors in the physical world.

Cigarette smoking can be regulated through the passage and enforcement of explicit laws that make it illegal to smoke in public buildings. And we have specific laws that prohibit cigarette manufacturers from advertising on television or in magazines targeted at teenage audiences. Independent of explicit laws, however, social norms can also discourage cigarette smoking in public; for example, it is socially acceptable for homeowners to place "Thank you for not smoking in our house" signs on their front doors. And restaurant owners can, under social pressure from patrons, partition smoking and nonsmoking sections of their establishments even when there is no explicit law requiring them to do so.

Market pressures can also affect smoking behavior: Cigarettes can be priced so that only the wealthiest people can afford to buy them. Finally, merchants can impose an architecture of control on cigarettes by using physical constraints. All cigarettes sold in grocery stores could be located behind locked doors, causing interruptions in check-out transactions. A cashier might have to temporarily suspend the transaction, locate the store's manager, and get the proper authorization and the key to open the locked doors to remove the cigarettes. Contrast this architecture with one in which cigarettes are available in vending machines easily accessible to everyone, including minors.

To apply Lessig's fourfold distinction to cyberspace, we replace architecture, which is in physical or geographic space, with *code*. Code, for Lessig, consists of programs, devices, and protocols—that is, the sum total of the software and hardware—that constitute cyberspace. Like physical architecture in geographic space, code sets the terms upon which one can enter or exit cyberspace. Also like architecture, code is not optional. Lessig notes that we do not choose to obey the structures that architecture establishes. Just as we are subject to architectures of physical space, so we are subject to code in cyberspace; a physical door can block you from entering a physical building, and a password requirement can prevent you entering a Web site. And code can be used to limit access to Web sites by requiring that users accept cookies (see Chapter 5) if they wish to visit those sites. Lessig believes that code can either facilitate or deter access to, or transfer of, information in cyberspace.

In Chapter 1, we saw that James Moor (1985) described computer technology as "logically malleable" because, unlike most other technologies that are dedicated to performing specific tasks, computers can be instructed through software to perform an indefinite number of diverse functions. Lessig (2001) also recognizes that computer technology is not fixed, noting that different computer architectures create very different kinds of environments. He compares the Internet of 1995, which he calls NET 95 and which he believes has a "libertarian architecture," to the Internet of 1999. To illustrate differences between these tow architectures, Lessig offers a comparison of the computer network systems at the University of Chicago and Harvard University. The University of Chicago's network was like NET 95, because anyone could connect his or her machine to jacks on the campus. As such, the code at Chicago favored freedom, or free speech. At Harvard, on the other hand, one must first register his or her machine before getting on the Harvard's network. Once registered, all interactions with the network are potentially monitored and identified by Harvard's network administrators. Lessig points out that at the University of Chicago, facilitating access was the ideal; at Harvard, controlling access is the ideal. The University of Chicago's network had the architecture of NET 95, whereas the architecture of Harvard's system is a contemporary "intranet architecture."

Note that the underlying network protocols (i.e., TCP/IP) are the same for both Harvard and the University of Chicago. But layered on top of Harvard's TCP/IP protocol is an additional set of protocols, or *code*, which Lessig says "facilitates control." Why should we care about the differences between the two kinds of architectures? Lessig notes that in the NET 95 environment, one could roam the Internet freely and anonymously. Today, one cannot. Lessig concludes from this that we are moving from an architecture of freedom to an architecture of control. He also concludes that in cyberspace, code is a more effective regulator than law. In fact, Lessig claims that in cyberspace, *code is the law*.

▶ 9.3 REGULATION BY CODE AND THE PRIVATIZATION OF INFORMATION POLICY

To understand the force of Lessig's claim that code is regulating cyberspace, consider how information policy has become "privatized." Niva Elkin-Koren (2000) argues that this privatization process is being accomplished, in large part, through the technological controls embedded in software code. To illustrate her case, she points to recent copyright laws. We saw in Chapter 8 that the Digital Millennium Copyright Act (DMCA) prohibits the development and use of technologies designed to circumvent copyright management systems, and recent technology has made possible the enforcement of information policies and laws in cyberspace to a degree that never existed in the physical realm. Rather than directly regulating the behavior of users (i.e., prohibiting unauthorized copying of a copyrighted work), the DMCA regulates technologies that enable access to and use of informational products. As Elkin-Koren puts it, regulation focuses on the *technologies* that affect users' behavior rather than on the behaviors themselves. She notes that regulation by code can prevent behaviors deemed undesirable by the software industry. This, in turn, enables the industry to act in its own behalf by developing codes that support *its* values and interests.

9.3.1 Developing Technology That Precludes the Possibility of Certain Kinds of Immoral and Illegal Behavior

What is wrong with designing technology that makes software piracy, or for that matter any kind of illegal behavior, virtually impossible? Imagine that an automobile manufacturer has designed a system that makes it impossible to steal automobiles. For example, a predefined sequence of software instructions could be required to start an automobile's engine, so that even if a potential car thief could break into an automobile, he could not start the car's engine. (Don't ask how this is done; merely imagine that it could be done!) Who would object to such a foolproof device? Consider what would happen if someone needed to gain access to the automobile for legitimate purposes but did not know the sequence of instructions. Suppose, for example, a heart attack left the automobile owner speechless (and thus unable to reveal the required sequence of instructions needed to start the car), and a friend needed to drive her to the hospital.

There is also a deeper, less obvious concern regarding the use of technology to prevent one's engaging in illegal behavior. In the past, people were free to choose to break laws, such as those against software piracy, knowing full well what the ramifications would be.

Individuals were held responsible for their choices and in that sense could exercise autonomy. However, if breaking a certain law becomes impossible because of technology, can humans still exercise individual autonomy by choosing whether or not to break that law? (Similarly, if humans could be programmed so that they were not capable of choosing to commit crimes, then crime would be eliminated; but could those persons still be considered fully human?)

9.3.2 Closing Down the Possibility of Public Debate on Copyright Issues

There is also a practical side to the concern raised about the loss of individual autonomy in the preceding paragraph, a concern that goes beyond philosophical speculation. Consider, for example, public policy debates regarding copyright law. In the past, when individuals duplicated proprietary information by using the latest available technologies, we were often forced to question the viability of existing copyright laws in light of those new technologies vis-à-vis principles such as fair use and first sale. We could then engage in meaningful public policy debates about whether traditional copyright laws should apply or whether some laws needed to be amended. Most importantly, we could challenge the viability and constitutionality of such laws through the judicial process.

Because code is being developed and used with the express purpose of precluding the possibility of copyright infringement, this traditional mechanism for debating public policy may now be closed to us. If computer manufacturers can decide what the copyright rules should be, and if they are permitted to embed certain code in their products that enforces those rules, then there is no longer a need for, or even the possibility of, public policy debate about copyright issues. So Elkin-Koren fears that a framework *balancing* the interests of individuals and the public, which in the past had been supported by spirited policy debates and judicial review, is not possible in a world in which such policies are predetermined by code. And as Richard Spinello (2000) notes, restrictions embedded into computer code end up having "the force of law without the checks and balances provided by the legal system."

9.3.3 Privatizing Information Policy: Implications for the Internet

Jessica Litman (1999) suggests that information policies involving cyberspace are becoming increasingly privatized. She notes, for example, that in 1998 the Internet was transformed into what she describes as a giant American shopping mall. In that year the 105th Congress passed three copyright-related acts that strongly favored commercial interests: the DMCA, SBCTEA, and the NET Act (each discussed in Chapter 8). In the same year, the federal government transferred the process of registering domain names from the National Science Foundation—an independent government regulatory body—to ICANN (Internet Corporation for Assigned Names and Numbers), a private group favorable to commercial interests.

Litman also notes that the Recording Industry of America sought to ban the manufacture of portable MP3 players on grounds that such devices *could* be used to play pirated music, even though the MP3 file format is perfectly legal and even though many MP3 files do not contain copyrighted music. The recording industry has tried to pressure computer manufacturers to embed code in their computer systems, making it impossible to use personal computers to download MP3 files and to burn CDs.

Others have worried about potential conflicts of interest in the e-commerce sector. Lines are now beginning to blur between common carriers (such as telephone companies) and commercial content providers, which in the past were closely regulated and monitored by the FCC. Consider that the recent merger involving AOL and Time Warner brings a carrier and a content provider together under one major corporation. Some analysts worry that such mergers create conflicts of interest in cyberspace; the content provided by Time Warner could receive preferential consideration in offerings provided to AOL subscribers.

▶ 9.4 INTERNET DOMAIN NAMES, (HTML) METATAGS, AND HYPERLINKING ON THE WEB

We have seen how intellectual property laws involving copyright threaten to privatize cyberspace. Some also worry that decisions involving trademark law also have significant implications for privatization. In our analysis of trademark protections in Chapter 8, we briefly alluded to the fact that trademark-related questions have surfaced in the policy for registering Internet domain names, along with related concerns about hyperlinking, especially "deep linking" into proprietary Web sites, and the use of metatags.

9.4.1 Internet Domain Names and the Registration Process

A *domain name*, an alphanumeric string used to identify a unique address on the World Wide Web, is included in the address of a URL (universal resource locator) such as http://www.mysite.net. Immediately following the Hypertext Transfer Protocol (http://) and the Web (www.) portions of the URL is the domain name (in this case, "mysite.com"). Examples of complete or "fully qualified" domain names are yahoo.com, harvard.edu, and 123xyz.org. The ".com," ".edu," and ".org" sections of the full domain name are also referred to as *generic top-level domain names* (gTLDs). The gTLD designations have been used to identify sites that are commercial (.com), organizational (.org), educational (.edu), governmental (.gov), and network-related (.net).

Prior to 1998, the registration of domain names in the United States was administered by the National Science Foundation (NSF), a federally funded organization that had set up a network division (NSFNET) to oversee certain aspects of Internet governance. In 1992, Congress had approved commerce on the Internet and charged NSFNET with the task of working with a private organization, Network Solutions, to develop a scheme for determining the future assignment of domain names.

Domain names were registered on a first-come, first-served basis. There was no clear or systematic policy for deciding which domain names one was eligible or ineligible to register, and this practice resulted in confusion for Web users, especially those who assumed that there would be a correlation between a Web site's domain name and its content. If someone wishing to visit the White House's Web site entered the address "www.whitehouse.com," that user would be taken to a pornographic site—the actual White House site is www.whitehouse.gov. Users unfamiliar with gTLDs might not realize that a ".com" extension in a URL typically represents a commercial Web site. Also, search engines could be less helpful to users who are unfamiliar with domain name extensions, since a general search under the keyword "White House" would return the addresses of both the ".com" and the ".gov" sites. Because of the relative ease with which one can be inadvertently directed to pornographic sites, some members of Congress proposed that all pornographic sites have a special gTLD (such as ".porn," for example) to warn unsuspecting Internet users about that site's content. On the one hand, confusion about Internet domain names might seem like a minor nuisance, but being unexpectedly directed to a pornographic Web site such as www.whitehouse.com can be both annoying and embarrassing.

Anyone could, in principle, register domain names that contain "Disney," or "Playboy," and a serious issue arose when certain individuals registered domain names containing such key phrases and symbols that were previously registered as legal trademarks in physical space. In one case, the first applicant for the candyland.com domain name was not Hasbro, who manufacturers and markets the Candy Land game; it was instead the operator of a pornographic Web site. Many trademark owners became outraged that their trademarks were being co-opted in cyberspace, and some filed trademark infringement suits against those whose domain names included symbols identical to their registered trademarks.

9.4.2 Cybersquatting

Not only was it unclear whether trademarks registered in physical space necessarily applied to cyberspace, but there were also no explicit laws in place to prevent an individual or an organization from registering a domain name that potentially conflicted with a registered trademark in physical space. And because there were no explicit laws or policies governing domain name registration, there was also nothing to prevent individuals and companies from registering as many domain names as they could afford. A few did, and some of them became wealthy when they later sold the rights to their registered domain names to corporations who wanted to have domain names that were either identical to or closely resembled the trademarks they had registered in physical space.

But not all individuals and corporations were willing to pay an exorbitant price for domain names that, by virtue of their registered trademarks, they believed they already had the legal right to own. A dispute arose over the legal status of Internet domain names vis-à-vis the claims of trademark owners. Those who had first registered these domain names were referred to as cybersquatters. Trademark owners had a legitimate concern about the abuse of the "marks" that identified them to millions of people. To protect owners of legitimate trademarks from the abuse of their marks, trademark law includes a provision for nullifying a registered trademark if it can be shown that the mark was registered in bad faith. And the cybersquatters who tried to corner the market on domain names for the sole purpose of becoming wealthy at the expense of legitimate trademark owners clearly acted in bad faith. Trademark owners, insisting that cybersquatters were unfairly using a trademark that already had been registered, petitioned Congress for legislation, and in 1999, the Anticybersquatting Consumer Protection Act was passed.

The dispute involving the abuse of domain names extends beyond trademarks per se. Someone acting in bad faith could also register the name of an actor or other famous person as part of an Internet domain name. There was no law prohibiting a fan of actor Robert Redford, for example, from registering the domain name RobertRedford.com. Someone did, in fact, register the domain name BillGates.com and as a result, some e-mail that was intended for Bill Gates never reached him.

9.4.3 The Emergence of ICANN

The policy for assigning domain names tightened considerably in 1998, when the federal government directed the Department of Commerce to supervise the administration of the Domain Name System. The Internet Corporation for Assigned Names and Numbers (ICANN) has since become responsible for assigning and registering domain names. ICANN has been criticized as being neither broadly representative of Internet users, nor accountable to its constituents. Critics also believe that the policy ICANN used to resolve trademark disputes was heavily biased towards those who owned trademarks previously registered in physical space; however, defenders of the new ICANN policy, especially trademark owners themselves, see the matter quite differently. Trademark owners point out that in many cases their registered trademarks had been "diluted" because of unclear policies in the earlier system for assigning domain names.

Jessica Litman (1999) believes that ICANN could have devised alternative or compromise strategies to resolve trademark disputes in cyberspace, but, she believes, such strategies were never seriously explored. For example, the number of generic top-level domains (gTLDs) could have been expanded to include extensions such as ".biz," ".firm," ".arts," and ".music." Even with this compromise, however, it is likely that many trademark owners would still have complained that their marks were being diluted in cyberspace because of so many similar-sounding domain names. In the following case illustration, consider whether the Amazon.com trademark would be diluted if some variation of it were allowed to be registered by a "bricks-and-mortar" bookstore that had previously used the Amazon name.

▶ **CASE ILLUSTRATION:** Amazon Bookstore Cooperative v. Amazon.com

Amazon.com is one of the best-known e-commerce sites. Initially an on-line bookstore, Amazon.com has expanded its e-commerce operations to include the sale of additional products on-line, and it has developed an international reputation as a robust e-commerce site, so Amazon.com would have a good case for registering "Amazon" both as a trademark and a domain name. Prior to the inception of the Amazon.com e-commerce site, however, a bookstore named the Amazon Bookstore Cooperative had been operating in Minneapolis, Minnesota and was familiar to many people who lived in the Minneapolis area. In April 1999, the Amazon Bookstore Cooperative sued Amazon.com for trademark infringement.

It is quite possible that Amazon.com was unaware of the existence of the Minneapolis store. In fact, a systematic search of existing trademarks that included the symbol "Amazon" would not have revealed any information about the bricks-and-mortar bookstore in Minnesota, since the bricks-and-mortar Amazon bookstore had never formally registered the Amazon trademark (We should note, however, that in the United States there is also "common law" trademark, which would apply to the physical bookstore so long as the store simply used the Amazon mark.) Defenders of Amazon.com questioned why the Amazon bookstore waited so long to file its suit. In trademark disputes, "delay in filing a suit" can be a relevant factor in determining the suit's legal outcome.

One way to resolve this dispute would have been to let the Amazon trademark hold for the bookstore in Minneapolis, which would have precluded Amazon.com from conducting business in that region. Since cyberspace boundaries are porous, however, it would not be possible to enforce a trademark law in which Amazon.com would not be allowed to engage in commerce in the Minneapolis area. Another way to resolve this domain-name dispute would have been to expand the gTLDs to allow both Amazon.com, and Amazon.books. As we noted above, however, ICANN never seriously considered this strategy. A company as powerful as Amazon.com might not have accepted it in any case, arguing that its Amazon mark would be diluted and that the Minneapolis-based Amazon would benefit significantly from the exposure to the Amazon name that the on-line company had established. They might further argue that Amazon.com could lose business if prospective Amazon.com customers were inadvertently sent to the Web site for the bricks-and-mortar store.

9.4.4 Issues Surrounding the Use of (HTML) Metatags

The use of metatags has also raised questions of possible trademark infringement. A *metatag* is embedded in HTML code, which is transparent, or "invisible" to most Web users. To see which metatags have been included in a Web site, one can simply "view" the HTML source code used to construct the site, and most Web browsers enable users to do this. Metatags can be either *keyword metatags* or *description metatags*. Keyword metatags, such as <baseball> and <Barry Bonds> enable Web-page designers to identify terms that can be used by search engines. Descriptive metatags, on the other hand, enable the designer of a Web page to describe the page contents. For example, the description of a Web site for Barry Bonds might read: "Barry Bonds . . . plays for the San Francisco Giants . . . broke major league baseball's home run record in 2001 . . ." The description typically appears as one or more sentence fragments, directly beneath the Web page's listing in an Internet search result.

Search engines examine keyword metatags to help determine how best to organize the listings of Web sites they return to queries, according to meaningful labels or categories that a user might request. For example, if I were constructing a Web site on cyberethics that I wanted students to visit, I might include the following keyword metatags in my HTML source code: <cyberethics>, <cyberethics courses>, <computer ethics instruction>, and <issues in Internet ethics>. In doing this, my objective is to make the contents of my Web site known to search engines so that they can direct Internet users who request cyberethics-related information to my Web site.

Metatags hardly seem controversial; however, a number of cases illustrate some questionable, and at times seemingly deceptive, uses of metatags. Consider the following scenario illustrating a sinister way that metatags might be used.

▶ **SCENARIO:** A Misuse of Metatags

Keith, a student at Technical University, recently completed a cyberethics course taught by Professor Bright. But Keith did not do well in the class, and he wishes to express his opinion about Professor Bright to anyone who will listen. Suppose Keith decides to construct a Web site called Cyberethics Review, where he intends to comment on the course and its instructor. Note that his Web site, despite its title, has nothing at all to do with cyberethics per se. In the HTML code for his site, Keith includes the keyword metatag <cyberethics> as well as the following descriptive metatag: "Professor Bright is a jerk . . . unfair to students . . . terrible instructor . . ." Now if someone enters the keyword "cyberethics" in a search engine's entry box, that person may receive information about the Cyberethics Review site in the list of entries returned by the search. Directly under that site's name and corresponding URL, the user will also find the (summary) descriptive sentence fragments containing the disparaging remarks about Professor Bright.

Keith could also accomplish his goal, by using only a series of keyword metatags. Suppose he decides to call his Web site "Professor Bright." Of course, no search engine responding to a query about cyberethics would ordinarily return in its list (of relevant sites) information about Keith's Professor Bright site. Keith, however, is very shrewd when it comes to writing the code for his Web site. He decides to embed keyword metatags such as <Professor Bright>, <cyberethics>, and <computer ethics instructors> in the HTML source code. Suppose also that he decides not to use any descriptive metatags that might give away the true nature of the site he has constructed. Now a search engine will likely determine that Keith's site does pertain to cyberethics and will return its URL (as part of a list) to a user who has conducted a search query for the keyword "cyberethics." Unsuspecting users who may be interested in visiting a site that they assume was constructed by Professor Bright for the purposes of discussing cyberethics issues, will be surprised when they click on the URL for Keith's site: Users will receive no information pertaining cyberethics but instead a Web page dedicated to derogatory, and possibly defamatory, remarks about Professor Bright. (We will discuss online defamation in Section 9.7.)

The scenario involving Keith and Professor Bright is, of course, hypothetical; however, there have been actual cases involving the deceptive use of metatags that have been contested in court. One such incident is the *Bihari v. Gross*, 2000.

▶ **CASE ILLUSTRATION:** Bihari v. Gross

Bihari, a company in New York City, provides interior design services. Gross, a former associate of Bihari, registered the "bihari.com" and "bahiriinteriors.com" domain names and included derogatory remarks about Bihari on his Web sites. Bihari sued Gross, and as a condition of the settlement Gross agreed to relinquish both Bihari domain names. Gross then registered the domain names "design-scam.com" and "manhattaninteriordesign.com," and embedded the keyword metatag "Bihari Interiors" in the HTML code for his Web sites. He included the same derogatory remarks about Bihari in the new site, which search engines could reference via the metatag identifying Bihari Interiors. At issue in this case was the question as to whether Gross's actions violated either the Anticybersquatting Consumer Protection Act or the Trademark (Lanham) Act. This time the court ruled in favor of Gross, requiring that Bihari demonstrate the likelihood of irreparable harm caused before it would grant the Bihari Company the preliminary injunction it sought against Gross.

9.4.5 Hyperlinking and Deep Linking

Users can navigate the World Wide Web from one site to another via direct connections called *hyperlinks*: Clicking on a hyperlink takes the user directly to the target Web site. Without hyperlinks, users have to either use search engines to locate and access related Web sites before being able to link to them or enter by hand (i.e., key in) the complete URL of a site in order to access it. Without hyperlinks, it is much slower to navigate the Internet.

Before electronic commerce, the practice of including direct links to related Web pages had become the default mode of operation on the Web; Internet users gave little thought as to whether they needed permission to include a hyperlink to a target Web site (or to any particular section of that targeted site). They did not consider, from a legal perspective, whether they had an explicit right to link directly to another person's Web site, or to any portion of it, without first acquiring the express consent of its owner.

Consider the case of a professor who has, as part of her Web site, a page devoted to bibliographic material on a certain topic. Should Internet users be able to link directly to the bibliographic portion of her site? Or should, if she prefers, they be required to first access her (top-level) home page and then click down to the bibliography page? The professor may not care whether visitors to her site access the top level of her site before going to the bibliography section, but the operators of some commercial Web sites have objected to visitors linking "deep" into their sites, thus bypassing the top-level pages. They point out that on-line advertisers, who typically place ad banners on the top-level pages of Web sites, want their ads to be seen by all visitors to the sites they are sponsoring. Also, "counter mechanisms" (which track both the number of users who visit a site over a certain period and information about the time of day most visitors connect to that site) usually appear on a Web site's top-level page, and this kind of information can be a key factor in determining whether advertisers will sponsor a particular site. Commercial Web-site owners, especially those who depend on advertisers, have a legitimate concern about how users access their sites.

Proprietors of noncommercial Web sites might also want to be able to exercise control over how visitors enter their sites, just as a homeowner may prefer that guests enter his house by way of the front door instead of the side or back door. We next consider two cases of deep hyperlinking: one in a commercial context, and the other in a personal Web site.

▶ **CASE ILLUSTRATION:** Ticketmaster v. Microsoft Corporation

As a service to its employees, Microsoft included a link from its Web site directly to a page on the Seattle-based Ticketmaster Web site that both listed cultural events in the Seattle area and enabled users to purchase tickets for them. Ticketmaster objected to Microsoft's use of this direct link to their subpage, arguing that it should have a right to determine how information on its site is viewed. Ticketmaster also worried about revenue that might be lost from its advertisers, if the site's visitors systematically bypassed its top-level page, which contained various advertising banners. Ticketmaster sued Microsoft, and Microsoft eventually settled out of court. So we have no court ruling on the legality of deep linking, but many legal observers believe that Microsoft had a strong case and would have prevailed.

From the standpoint of commercial interests, Ticketmaster's position seems reasonable: Ticketmaster stood to lose valuable revenue from advertisers, which could eventually have resulted in Ticketmaster's demise as a player in the e-commerce market. But what about our earlier example of a college professor who may wish visitors to her site to enter via her top-level home page before accessing her bibliography? Is her position also reasonable? Compare this example with the scenario we presented in Chapter 8, where the author of a journal article wanted her article reprinted only in its entirety, even though the copyright holder authorized an abridgment to be included in a textbook. Is the professor's position similar to the author's?

Richard Spinello (2000) describes a scenario where Maria, an artist, has set up an on-line exhibit of her paintings on her Web site. One of Maria's paintings is highly controversial and has aroused the interest both within and outside the art community, so many people would like to link directly to the image on Maria's Web site. But Maria reasons that the artist determines the sequential arrangement of paintings in a physical art gallery, so analogously, she should be able to determine how visitors to her on-line gallery are required to view the paintings there. The controversial painting in question, she further argues, is best understood within the context of other paintings that both precede and follow it in the on-line exhibit.

Is Maria's position reasonable? If a Web site is viewed as a form of intellectual property (see Chapter 8), then she may have a strong case. Consider that Maria, as a property owner, could determine how people enter her site in the same way that a home owner in physical space can require that visitors enter the house only through the front door. If a Web site is considered private property, however, another controversial issue arises: an unwelcome visitor to a Web site could be accused of trespassing. The notion of trespass in cyberspace is far from clear; however, some believe that the practice of sending unsolicited e-mail, that is, electronic spam, qualifies as a form of trespass in cyberspace.

▶ 9.5 SPAM

What is electronic *spam*, and why is it problematic from a social and moral perspective? There is no universally agreed-upon definition of spam, but we will distinguish it from other forms of e-mail because it is *unsolicited*, *promotional*, and *sent in bulk* to multiple users. Because spam is unsolicited, it is also nonconsensual. However, not all nonconsensual e-mail is spam.

If you have an e-mail account, you have probably received unsolicited e-mail messages requesting information from you or informing you about an upcoming event; they may have been sent to you because you are a member of an e-mail distribution list or a listserv. You may have considered some of these messages annoying, but they are not considered spam, because they are not overtly commercial, or promotional. Even though such messages might have been distributed in bulk (i.e., to an e-mail list or listserv), they were most likely directed to people in the group who are known by the sender; there is some personal or professional connection between the sender and receiver of the e-mail message.

One disturbing feature of spam is that it is inherently impersonal as well as commercial. Bulk commercial e-mail is not intended for you personally; it is sent to you only because you are a member of an on-line discussion group or e-mail distribution list whose address has become know to spammers. If you have an e-mail account with Hotmail or AOL, spammers might target you simply because of your e-mail address.

Spam is very similar to the "junk mail" that we receive via the postal delivery system, so why shouldn't the same rules that apply to physical junk mail also apply to electronic spam? Although there are certain similarities between the two forms of junk mail, there are also relevant differences: practical and financial constraints determine how much junk mail merchants can send in physical space, but in cyberspace opportunities to distribute bulk mail are virtually limitless. In physical space, junk mailers bear the brunt of the expense for sending their mail, even though junk mail is subsidized through bulk rates that the United States Postal Service grants to distributors who send mail in that form. Richard Spinello (1999) notes that in cyberspace spam shifts costs from the advertiser to several other parties, including Internet Service Providers (ISPs) and the recipients of their service. The cost-shifting even affects users of the Internet who are only indirectly inconvenienced by spam. Because others must bear the cost for its delivery, spam is not cost free, as Spinello correctly notes.

Spam consumes valuable computer resources. When it is sent through ISPs, it wastes their network bandwidth. Spam also puts an increased strain on system resources, such as disk storage space. For these reasons and others, critics have argued that spam is an abuse of the e-mail system.

9.5.1 Is Spam Unethical?

Spinello believes that spam is morally objectionable for two reasons; one utilitarian and the other deontological. Spam not only has harmful consequences, but it also violates the individual autonomy of Internet users. We have already considered some of the harmful consequences of spam—its financial impacts, such as cost shifting and the consumption of valuable network resources. Spam also consumes and strains valuable computing resources, and thus contributes to what some now see as the degradation of the fragile ecology of the Internet. (Recall our discussion of the tragedy of the commons in Chapter 8.) But what about the claim that spam violates individual autonomy?

Spinello argues that even if Internet resources were infinite and there were no negative utilitarian consequences, spam would still be morally objectionable because it does not respect individual users as persons. He believes that deontological arguments, such as those introduced by Immanuel Kant (see Chapter 2), can be used to show why this so. Recall that Kant argues that a practice has moral worth only if it can be universalizable. And, in Kant's system, a practice is universalizable only if it can coherently apply to all persons without exception. So we need to ask: Could we universalize a coherent practice in which each e-mail user would allow spam to be sent and received by every other user? Could such a practice, if instituted, be logically coherent? If such a practice were universalized, then the current distributors of spam would have to allow that they too could be spammed. If everyone freely engaged in spamming, however, would the practice of using e-mail to communicate in a reasonable and effective way still make sense? Could the Internet, as we currently understand it, still exist?

On Kantian grounds, if spammers did not accept the principle that everyone should be able to send and receive spam, then they would be inconsistent. If spammers believed that only they should be permitted to send spam, then they would be making an exception for themselves. And if they granted themselves this exception, while relying on the good will of ordinary users not to engage in the practice of spamming others, then spammers would be treating ordinary users as a means to their ends.

Of course, those who engage in spam would no doubt point out that not everyone would send spam. While this may be factually true, it ignores what would happen *if* everyone did! Assuming the truth of the deontological principle that we are all equal players from a moral perspective, then either each of us has a right to send spam, or none of us has a right to do so. Because spammers are making an exception for themselves, they violate the principles of fair play and respect for persons, which are required by a Kantian system of morality. So Spinello makes a strong case that spam is morally objectionable on deontological as well as utilitarian grounds.

9.5.2 What Can Be Done about Spam?

It is one thing to say that spam is morally objectionable, but it is another to ask what can be done about it from a legal and a public policy perspective. Legal scholars have argued that we need explicit laws and regulations to combat spam. Others have suggested that users themselves, in conjunction with network managers, regulate spam by using software filter programs. Network managers can control the influx of spam into their systems with antispam tools, and antispam programs, such as MailEssentials, can block messages by matching the domain name included in the source of the originating e-mail message with domain names on the list of known spammers. Antispam programs also can scan messages for key words or phrases that indicate the likelihood of spam.

David Post (2001) describes a way to block spam using Realtime Blackhole List (RBL) software, which is managed by a nonprofit organization known as the Mail Abuse Prevention System (MAPS). Essentially, RBL is a list of Internet Protocol (IP) addresses that have been determined to be spammers. The names and addresses of spammers get included on the RBL, once a complaint has been filed against them and verified by MAPS, a private organization operated by Paul Vixie. Individuals and organizations that are black-listed will have their e-mail messages bounced by ISPs and other providers that subscribe to the RBL list. Some believe that MAPS-RBL is an effective way to handle spam, but others have questioned it from a public policy perspective.

Are these approaches to spam, such as MAPS-RBL, adequate? Or do we need specific laws to deal with this problem? Post suggests that a decentralized policy, such as MAPS, is reasonable, given both the decentralized nature of the Internet and what he calls the "judicial conundrum" of cyberspace. Larry Lessig (1999) and others, however, note that while the possibility of self-regulation is enhanced by filtering, there is also a great danger (or risk of "myopic perspective") in policies, such as the one involving MAPS-RBL, that depend on excessive filtering. Lessig believes that the RBL solution is simply one more example of "regulation by code" by private parties. He asks if private organizations should have the prerogative to determine whether millions of e-mail messages reach their targets. Lessig believes that the central problem in this case is that "vigilantes and network service providers are deciding fundamental questions about how the Internet will work," and each is deciding from its own perspective.

Lessig sees at least two problems with the use of filtering as a remedy: (i) Policy is being made by an "invisible hand," and (ii) those making the policy are not accountable to anyone. Lessig objects that this is not how policy should be made. Rather, policy should be open and debated in a public forum, and it should not be left to the whims of those in the private sector to determine outcomes through the use of software code. Others, such as Post, believe that we should not be too quick in dismissing the notion that at least some Internet regulatory problems can best be solved by less formal means—that is, through a decentralized system that Post admits is both messy and semi-chaotic.

Because there is no clear-cut policy for dealing with spam, legal analysts are not sure how complaints about it are best adjudicated. We have already mentioned that spam consumes valuable network and computer resources and that some argue it is a form of trespass. Cases either involving or bordering on spam have appealed to both notions. In *Hotmail Corporation v. Van$ Money Pie Inc.* 1998, the court ruled in favor of Hotmail, and spam was found to be trespassing. Two court cases (*CompuServe, Incorporated v. Cyber Promotions, Inc.* 1997) and (*Cyber Promotions, Inc. v. America Online, Inc.*, 1996) have involved ISPs who sought to block senders of spam, and in both cases, the ISPs were successful. Another case, which technically is not a spam lawsuit, considers several issues at the heart of the spam controversy.

▶ **CASE ILLUSTRATION:** eBay v. Bidder's Edge

EBay is one of the best known among the many Web sites that handle electronic auctions on the Web. Bidder's Edge was an "aggregate" auction site; it compiled goods listed on various auction sites and then directed prospective auction customers to them. To do this, Bidder's Edge sent out "web crawlers," which are "metasearch engines," to search the Web for e-auction sites and collect data from them. Bidder's Edge then compiled the data into an aggregate list.

EBay had entered into a tentative, but nonlegally binding, agreement with Bidder's Edge that allowed Bidder's Edge to gather data from eBay's Web site for its list. Then, however, eBay changed its mind and informed Bidder's Edge that its search engines were no longer permitted to gather data from the eBay site. Nevertheless, Bidder's Edge continued to search and extract data from eBay's site, arguing that the information it was compiling was not proprietary. EBay then filed a lawsuit against Bidder's Edge.

EBay's position would be compelling if it could show that the information on its site was indeed proprietary, but eBay's lawyers did not make that argument. The information in eBay's database contained personal information about eBay's customers. That information technically belonged to the individual customers themselves and not to eBay. EBay could have claimed that its particular scheme for arranging the personal data made its database proprietary so that the information in it was copyrightable, but eBay did not take that tack either. Instead, eBay's lawyers appealed to a law in physical space that involved the "consumption" of a business' resources by a competitor: EBay argued that Bidder's Edge was consuming valuable computing resources, such as bandwidth, by instructing its search engines to crawl through eBay's database.

On the one hand, eBay's Web site is not password-protected, so it is open to the public, even though it is a privately owned e-commerce site; eBay cannot prevent any individual who wishes to visit its site from doing so. However, eBay argued that Bidder's Edge's intense use of search engines on eBay's site was consuming eBay's computer system resources in ways that individual users who visit its site do not.

The judge in this case sided with eBay and ordered an injunction against Bidder's Edge, effectively forcing it to shut down its operations. Bidder's Edge objected by arguing that because its search engines crawled through eBay's site during nonpeak hours—usually after midnight and before 6:00 A.M., when customer-presence on eBay was extremely low and possibly nonexistent—it did not significantly consume eBay's computer resources. However, the judge reasoned that if several companies had acted in a manner similar to Bidder's Edge, eBay's resources could have been drained to the point that it might not be able to conduct its e-commerce effectively. The ruling in this case has been considered controversial and because it was based in large part on the notion of "consumption of resources," it may have implications for future lawsuits involving spam.

▶ 9.6 FREE SPEECH VS. CENSORSHIP AND CONTENT CONTROL IN CYBERSPACE

We have examined a set of regulatory issues that either involved, or had implications for, electronic commerce. In this section we turn our attention to regulatory issues involving the *content* of cyberspace. Such issues center on the question as to whether all forms of on-line speech should be tolerated. Some issues concerning the regulation of on-line speech and on-line commerce overlap. For example, questions concerning electronic spam, considered in the preceding section, straddle the divide. Some purveyors of spam have defended their practice on the grounds of free speech. Should certain forms of speech on the Internet be censored? Or do they deserve to be protected under the constitutional guarantee of free speech?

According to the First Amendment of the United States Constitution, "Congress shall make no law . . . abridging the freedom of speech, or of the press." This passage, consisting of a scant fourteen words, has often been quoted by libertarians who strongly believe that the government should not intrude in matters involving our constitutionally guaranteed right to free speech. We should note, however, that free speech is not an absolute right. As in the case of other rights contained in the Bill of Rights, which comprise the first ten amendments to the Constitution, the right to free speech is *conditional*, in the sense that it is only a right if all things are equal. While your right to free speech protects your freedom to express controversial ideas concerning politics, religion, and the like, it does not grant you the right to shout "Fire!" in a crowded shopping mall or in a movie theater.

Also, during times of war, one's ability to speak freely is sometimes constrained. For example, in the fall of 2001 some labeled the news commentators, reporters, and talk show hosts who criticized the Bush White House "unpatriotic." Ordinarily such criticisms are considered normal and in accordance with the principle of free speech accorded to the press. But at other times, social norms and market forces rather than law itself can regulate free speech. Television viewers who were offended by remarks they perceived as either anti-Bush or antigovernment pressured advertisers not to sponsor programs that expressed viewpoints that could be considered unpatriotic. This, in turn, caused television networks either to cancel some programs or not to broadcast them in certain areas of the country. (Note that this is an example of Lessig's claim that, in certain cases, social norms and market forces can be more effective regulators than laws themselves.) Nonetheless, free speech is a broad right, cited time and again by publishers of unpopular tabloids and also appealed to by many who distribute pornography. Many believe, however, that some forms of speech on the Internet, including pornography, should be censored.

What exactly is censorship? Jacques Catudal (1999) believes that an important distinction can be drawn between two types of censorship that he describes as "censorship by suppression" and "censorship by deterrence." Both forms presuppose that some "authorized person or group of persons" has judged some text or "type of text" objectionable on moral, political, or other grounds.

Censorship by suppression prohibits the objectionable text or material from being published, displayed, or circulated. Banning certain books from being published or prohibiting certain kinds of movies from being made are both examples of censorship by suppression. In this scheme, pornography and other objectionable forms of speech would not be allowed on the Internet.

Censorship by deterrence, on the other hand, is less drastic. It neither suppresses nor blocks out objectionable material, nor does it forbid such material from being published. Rather, it depends on threats of arrest, prosecution, conviction, and punishment of both those who make an objectionable text available and those who acquire it. Heavy fines and possible imprisonment can deter the publication and acquisition of objectionable content. Again, using Larry Lessig's regulatory model, social norms, such as social disenfranchisement, personal disgrace, and public censure, can also work to deter individuals from engaging in the publication, display, and transmission of objectionable speech.

9.6.1 Pornography in Cyberspace

Before examining the issue of pornography on the Internet, it is instructive to understand what legally qualifies as pornography. It is often debated in terms of notions such as obscenity and indecent speech. In *Miller v. California*, 1973, the court established a three-part guideline for determining whether material is obscene under the law and thus not protected by the First Amendment. According to this criteria, something is obscene if it

1. depicts sexual (or excretory) acts whose depiction is specifically prohibited by law,
2. depicts these acts in a patently offensive manner, appealing to prurient interest as judged by a reasonable person using community standards,
3. has no serious literary, artistic, social, political, or scientific value.

These criteria have proved problematic in attempts to enforce pornography laws. For example, the second criterion includes three controversial notions: "prurient interest," "reasonable person," and "community standards." *Prurient* is usually defined as having to do with lust and lewd behavior, concepts that, in turn, have been challenged as being vague and arbitrary. Also, many ask who, exactly, counts as a "reasonable person." Until the advent of cybertechnology, we might have assumed a fairly straightforward notion of "community standard" because traditionally a community has been defined in terms of geographical space. But what, exactly, is a community in cyberspace? And when more than one community is involved in a dispute involving pornography, whose community standards should apply?

9.6.1.1 Interpreting "Community Standards" in Cyberspace

Interpretations of "community" and "community standards" were among the issues debated in a court case involving pornography and the Amateur Auction (Electronic) Bulletin Board System. This particular Bulletin Board System (BBS), which made sexually explicit images available to its members, was operated by a couple who lived in California. Because it was an electronic forum, its contents were available not only to residents of California but to users who had Internet access in other states and countries. A resident of Memphis, Tennessee, became a member of the BBS and then downloaded sexually explicit pictures onto his computer in Tennessee. Although including sexually explicit images on a BBS may not have been illegal in California, viewing such images was illegal under Tennessee state law, and criminal charges were brought against the California operators of the BBS, who were prosecuted in Tennessee.

The California couple was found guilty under Tennessee law of distributing obscenity as defined under the local community standards that applied in Memphis. Not surprisingly, this case raised issues of what was meant by "community standards" on the Internet. Can a community in cyberspace be defined simply in terms of geography? Or in the age of the Internet, should "community" be defined by other criteria? For example, can a cybercommunity be better understood as an electronic gathering place where individuals who share common interests come together? (We discuss on-line communsiteis in Chapter 11.)

The Amateur Action case also raised another important issue: Were the pornographic files *distributed* over the Internet by the operators of the BBS in California, as alleged? Or, instead, did the resident in Tennessee who actually downloaded them via the interstate telephone lines that transmit information between the two states *retrieve* those controversial files from the Internet? Questions involving distribution and community standards in cyberspace contribute to the difficulty of interpreting and enforcing pornography laws on-line.

9.6.1.2 Internet Pornography Laws and Protecting Children On-line

Many people first became aware of the amount of pornographic material available on the Internet through a news story, entitled "CyberPorn," which appeared in *TIME* magazine in the summer of 1995. Drawing wide media coverage, *TIME* reported that there were 900,000 sexually explicit pornographic materials (pictures, film clips, etc.) available on the Internet. Many people, including most lawmakers, were outraged when they learned about the amount of pornographic material that was so easily accessible to Internet users, including minors. Later, however, the *Time* magazine story, based on an Internet study that had been conducted by a researcher at Carnegie Mellon University, was shown to be seriously flawed.

Although the Carnegie Mellon study accurately reported the number of pornographic images and pornographic Web sites that were available, it failed to put this information into proper perspective—it made no mention of the fact that the percentage of pornographic sites relative to other sites on the Web was very low. However, the report caught the eye of many influential politicians who set out to draft legislation in response to what they saw as the growth of the "pornography industry" on the Internet. The result was the passage of the Communications Decency Act (CDA) in early 1996.

The CDA caused controversy from the outset, especially the section referred to as the Exon Amendment, which dealt exclusively with on-line pornography. The ACLU and other organizations soon challenged the constitutionality of CDA. In the summer of 1996, a court in Philadelphia struck down CDA on grounds that it was too broad and that it violated the United States Constitution; in the summer of 1997 the Supreme Court upheld the lower court's ruling. A portion of the CDA, known as the Child Pornography Protection Act (CPPA) of 1996, was determined to be constitutional. According to the CPPA, it was a crime to "knowingly send, receive, distribute, reproduce, sell, or possess more than three child pornographic images." So even though CDA itself was overturned, critics took some refuge in the fact that the provision for child pornography remained intact.

In June 1998, Congress passed the Child On-line Pornography Act (COPA). Many of COPA's proponents believed that this act would pass constitutional muster, but as in the case of CDA, COPA was ill-fated. In February 1999, the Supreme Court ruled that COPA was unconstitutional. The only remaining federal law that was specifically directed at on-line pornography and that had managed to withstand constitutional scrutiny was the CPPA of 1996, a section of the original CDA. Although it appeared that CPPA would remain intact, many critics argued that provisions of this act also conflicted with the Constitution. On April 16, 2002, the Supreme Court, in a ruling of 6-3, struck down CPPA as unconstitutional.

Table 9-1 identifies the three on-line child pornography laws that have been enacted at the federal level, including when the laws were passed and when they were eventually struck down.

Jacques Catudal (1999) has argued that the CPPA broadens the definition of child pornography to include entire categories of images that many would not judge to be "child pornographic." He notes, for example, that visual depictions of sexually explicit conduct that do not involve *actual* minors would be included as child pornography under CPPA. Catudal also believes that the CPPA's definition of child pornography includes categories of images that some would judge not pornographic at all. Child pornography, according to CPPA, is "any depiction, including a photograph, film, video, picture, or computer or computer-generated image or picture, whether made or produced by electronic, mechanical, or other means, of sexually explicit conduct." The definition goes on to list four categories of such depictions:

A. the production of such visual depiction involves the use of a minor engaging in sexually explicit conduct;

B. such visual depiction is, or appears to be, of a minor engaging in sexually explicit conduct; or

C. such visual depiction has been created, adapted, or modified to appear that an identifiable minor is engaging in sexually explicit conduct; or

D. such visual depiction is advertised, promoted, presented, described, or distributed in such a manner that conveys the impression that the material is or contains a visual depiction of a minor engaging in sexually explicit conduct.

Whereas category (A) images represent depictions of what has been traditionally regarded as child pornography, Catudal argues that the same is not true of category (B) images by considering the case of a nineteen-year-old girl who appears in a pornographic image in which she looks much younger. Catudal notes that sexual depictions of this sort are sometimes referred to as the "little girl" genre; they have been used in many artistic works. (The "little girl" type does not, by definition, actually involve little girls or minors of any age.) In the United States, the on-line sexually explicit depiction of a "young looking" nineteen-year-old would be considered child pornography under CPPA, but in some other countries, such as Norway, it would not. Catudal believes that CPPA fails to note that category (A) and category (B) depictions represent two different types of prurient images.

Note also that in categories (C) and (D), the pornographic image can consist of a depiction of someone who *appears* to be a minor engaging in sexual activity, or *conveys the impression* of a minor engaging in such an activity. So, a computer-generated image that does not refer to an actual human being would also qualify as a child-pornography image under CPPA. In its decision to strike down portions of the CPPA, the Supreme Court reasoned that a distinction needed to be made between a pornographic image of an actual child and that of a "virtual," or computer-generated, image of a minor.

9.6.2 Controversial Speech in Cyberspace

In addition to pornography, which is sometimes referred to in legal venues as a form of obscene speech, *hate speech* and forms of speech that can *cause physical harm* to individuals

TABLE 9-1   Internet-specific Child Pornography Laws

CDA (Communications Decency Act)	Passed in January 1996 and declared unconstitutional in July 1996. The Supreme Court upheld the lower court's decision in 1997.
CPPA (Child Pornography Protection Act)	Passed as part of the larger CDA, but not initially struck down in 1997 with the CDA. It was declared unconstitutional in April 2002.
COPA (Child On-line Pornography Act)	Passed in June 1998 and declared unconstitutional by the Supreme Court in February 1999.

and communities have both caused controversy in cyberspace. Hate speech on the Internet often targets racial and ethnic groups. For example, white supremacist organizations such as the Klu Klux Klan (KKK) can include offensive remarks about African-Americans and Jews on their Web pages. Because of the Internet, international hate groups, such as "skin heads" in America, Europe, and Russia, can spread their messages of hate in ways that were not previously possible.

9.6.2.1 Hate Speech

Whereas the United States has focused its attention on controversial Internet speech issues that involve on-line pornography, European countries such as France and Germany have been more concerned about on-line hate speech. In 1997, Germany enacted the Information and Communications Act, which was directed at censoring neo-Nazi propaganda. The German statute, however, applies only to persons who reside in Germany, although it was initially intended to regulate the speech transmitted by ISPs outside of Germany as well. Roy Girasa (2002) believes that if the German government had tried to enforce this act, countries such as the United States would have refused to extradite individuals to Germany. He also points out that ISPs in the United States have broader constitutional rights that allow them to relay neo-Nazi propaganda. Whereas United States law protects ISPs from liability for the transmission of their content, German law holds ISPs accountable. For example, a United States citizen wishing to espouse pro-Nazi views, so long as that citizen does not instigate any violent activities, would have the constitutional right to do so, but according to German law, such a person would be criminally liable within Germany.

Another form of hate speech has involved radical elements of conservative organizations; for example, right-wing militia groups, whose ideology is often anti-federal-government, can broadcast information on the Internet about how to harm or even kill agents of the government. Recall the anti-government rhetoric that emanated from the militia movements in the United States in the early 1990s, which some believe led to the Oklahoma City bombing.

Also consider the case of anti-abortion groups in the United States who have set up Web sites dedicated to distributing hate-related information about doctors who perform abortions. Some of these sites have included information about where these doctors live, what times they travel to and from abortion clinics, where they go in their free time, etc. As in the case of the anti-government rhetoric used by militia groups in the United States, this type of (hate) speech can also result in physical harm to others: Some information made available on anti-abortion Web sites has been linked to the murder of doctors who perform abortions.

9.6.2.2 Speech That Can Cause Harm to Others

Some forms of hate speech on the Internet are such that they *might* also result in physical harm being caused to individuals. Other forms of this speech, however, are by the very nature of their content, biased towards violence and physical harm to others. Consider two examples of how of speech communicated on the Internet can result in serious physical harm: one involving information on how to construct bombs, and another that provides information on how to abduct children for the purpose of molesting them. Should this information be censored in cyberspace? This kind of information was available before the Internet era and it may even have been (and still may be) available in public libraries. If it is available elsewhere, should it be censored on the Internet?

Critics point out that Internet access now makes it much easier to acquire all kinds of information, including information about how to make and do things that cause physical harm. They also note that it is possible to access and read this information in the privacy and comfort of one's home. Even more disturbing is that it is now far easier for international and domestic terrorists to obtain information about how to construct bombs. Some believe that these are good enough reasons for censoring this kind of speech on the Internet.

Recall our discussion in Section 9.1.1 about whether the Internet should be conceived as a broadcast medium, like television or radio, or as a place, like a bookstore. We saw that the rules that apply in each are significantly different. Viewing the Internet as a medium of some sort makes it far easier to control the dissemination (or broadcast) of certain kinds of information than viewing it as a public place, such as a bookstore or library.

Also recall our example in Chapter 1 of the cyberstalking case of Amy Boyer. Was the posting on Liam Youen's Web site describing his plans to murder Boyer an example of hate speech? Consider that it resulted in physical harm to Boyer—viz., her death. Should the ISPs that enable users to construct Web sites containing such speech be held legally liable? We take up the question of the legal liability/moral responsibility of ISPs in the final section of this chapter.

9.6.3 Software Filtering Programs as an Alternative to Censorship

We have already noted that software filters can be used to block undesirable material; for example, in our discussion of spam we considered how the MAPS-RBL filtering scheme could be used to prevent significant amounts of spam from reaching its targeted destinations. Many believe that filtering also provides a reasonable alternative to censoring speech on the Internet. Others, however, are less enthusiastic about software filters as a panacea for resolving the censorship–free-speech debate in cyberspace.

Essentially, software filters are programs that screen Internet content and block access to unacceptable Web sites. Some filters have been criticized because they screen too much. Consider that filtering out objectionable material through the use of the keyword "sex" could block out important literary and scientific works, precluding the ability to access works by Shakespeare as well as books on biology and health. Other filters are criticized because they screen too little; such schemes might not successfully block nonobvious pornographic Web sites, such as www.whitehouse.com. A number of software filtering programs, including Net Nanny, have been available to Internet users, but most of them are inadequate for one or more reasons.

9.6.3.1 PICS

In the mid-1990s, the Platform for Internet Content Selection (PICS) devised a labeling scheme for Internet users who wanted to self-rate (or, depending on one's point of view, "self-censor") Web sites. PICS divides the task of filtering into two activities: labeling, which involves rating the content of the Web site, and then filtering the content based on those labels. The PICS protocol provides a standard format and supports multiple labeling schemes or rating services. For example, Internet content providers who comply with PICS standards could embed a label within their Web site, or a third party could rate its content according to the PICS criteria if the Web site's owners and operators elect not to do so. Users also have the option of selecting a rating system approved by a specific organization, such as the Christian Coalition, so if families are not sure about which sites to filter for pornographic content, they can purchase a Web browser with a PICS-compatible filter and then choose a rating system sanctioned by a specific religious organization.

Proponents of PICS believe that their rating system will help solve the problem of pornography as well as other undesirable forms of speech in cyberspace without having to resort to formal legal mechanisms that would suppress altogether the distribution of controversial speech on the Web. These proponents also that believe filtering via content-based labels will control pornography on-line more effectively than censoring by suppression. And they believe that PICS provides individual Internet users and their families the autonomy they need to determine for themselves which kinds of content they will view on-line. In this sense, some believe that PICS perform a function analogous to that of the PETs (Privacy Enhancing Technologies) we considered in Chapter 5.

9.6.3.2 Objections to Filtering

Not everyone, however, has been impressed with the use of software filters for self-regulatory purposes. Larry Lessig (1999) believes that architectures like PICS are a form of regulation by code, which is why he is skeptical of filtering schemes in cyberspace. He argues that PICS is, in effect, a universal censorship system, which can censor any kind of material, not just pornography and hate speech. For example, software filters can be used to block unpopular political speech or dissenting points of view. Richard Rosenberg (2001), whose position is similar to Lessig's, points out that filters could also be used by conservative school boards to block out information about evolutionary theory. The ACLU has also recently taken a similar position on the use of filtering. Their 2001 report expressed the fear that using censoring mechanisms such as filters may "burn the global village to roast the pig."

Whereas defenders of PICS, such as Resnick and Miller (1996), assume that the PICS protocol is neutral or value free, Lessig argues that such protocols will always reflect the biases of those who are the content-labelers. For Lessig, the fundamental flaw of rating systems for software filters is that we, as citizens, will be turning over to those who rate content (e.g., private industry, public interest groups, etc.) the government's role as an arbiter of speech rights. Thus privately owned corporations and their computer programmers will ultimately make decisions about which Web sites children should and should not see.

Software filters can be used at two different levels: We have already considered some pros and cons of parents using "downstream filtering" to control what their children see in the home; however, "upstream filtering," done at the ISP level, or at the government level is more controversial. Some argue that upstream filtering is repressive because it fences out many legitimate voices in the act of filtering. These critics also believe that filtering upstream prevents the free flow of information, undermining the democratizing feature of the Internet. The following case illustrates one difficulty with upstream filtering.

▶ **CASE ILLUSTRATION:** Mainstream Loudon v. Board of Trustees

In 1998, a number of adult patrons of the Loudon County (Virginia) Public Library (who were also members of an association called Mainstream Loudon) sued the library's board of trustees for "impermissible block[ing] of access to Internet sites." The library pointed out that its use of filtering was designed to block child pornography and obscene material; the plaintiffs, however, complained that the filtering devices also blocked access to nonpornographic sites such as the Quaker Home Page, the American Association of University Women, and others.

The district court ruled in favor of the plaintiffs. It determined that the installation of filtering software on public-access computers in libraries violates the First Amendment. Unfortunately, the court gave no clear direction as to how to resolve this and similar problems, but one solution would have libraries provide no Internet access at all, an unsatisfactory alternative for obvious reasons. And because at that time children were protected under the Child Pornography Protection Act (CPPA) of 1996, some argued that it would be permissible for libraries to include filtering devices on computers intended for use by children in restricted sections of the library.

▶ 9.7 DEFAMATION IN CYBERSPACE AND THE ROLE OF ISPs

We have described instances of on-line speech that border on defamation. In our discussion of hate speech in Section 9.6.2.1, for example, we saw how certain racial and ethnic groups have been harassed on the Internet through the posting of offensive remarks. And in our discussion of metatags in Section 9.4.4, we saw how HTML code could be used deceptively to demean and insult individuals, organizations, or corporations. Recall our scenario in which a student included derogatory remarks about his professor on the student's Web site. Also recall our case illustration in which Gross, a former associate in Bihari's interior design company, used metatags to broadcast disparaging remarks about Bihari on the Internet.

Which kinds of speech actually constitute legal defamation? Who should be held legally liable and morally accountable for defamatory remarks that occur in cyberspace? We address both questions in the next section.

9.7.1 Defining Defamation

Richard Spinello (2000) defines *defamation* as "communication that harms the reputation of another and lowers that person's self esteem in the eyes of the community." Defamatory remarks can take two forms: *libel*, which refers to written or printed defamation, and *slander*, which refers to oral defamation. John Mawhood and Daniel Tysver (2000) point out that defamation can also occur through pictures, images, gestures, and other methods of signifying meaning. They note both that a picture of a person that has been scanned and changed by merging with another image can suggest something defamatory and that anyone passing on such an image can also be held liable by the person filing defamation charges. Our concern, however, is primarily with defamatory speech in the form of written words on the Internet.

We should also point out that libelous speech on the Internet can be distinguished from certain kinds of inflammatory speech. Inflammatory remarks made in on-line forums are sometimes referred to as "flames," and the person who is the victim of such a remark has been "flamed." A flame need not meet the legal standards of defamation; nonetheless, flames, as in the case of genuine defamatory remarks, are problematic. In response to exchanges of inflammatory remarks, on-line user groups have developed their own rules of behavior or "netiquette" (etiquette on the Internet) to deal with this problem. Some Internet chat rooms, for example, have instituted the rule that any individual who flames another member of the group will be banned from the chat room. Although informal schemes based on netiquette might work well in Internet chat rooms to regulate certain kinds of unwelcome speech, they tend to be ineffective in regulating speech on the Internet in general. Hence, many believe we need more explicit laws involving on-line defamation.

Legal analysts point out that there are different standards of liability for distributing defamatory information depending on the role that an individual or organization plays in the process. Under the standard of publisher liability, "one who repeats or otherwise publishes defamatory material is subject to liability as if he had originally published it." Thus publishers such as newspapers and magazines are held liable and accountable for the defamation that appears on their pages, since they exercise editorial control over those publications.

Can the rules that apply to defamation in physical space be extended to cyberspace? Is there an instructive analogy that can link our understanding of defamation in the two realms? If an individual is defamed in print, he or she can hold the publisher of the periodical (newspaper, magazine, etc.) legally liable. Would it follow that if an individual is defamed in an on-line forum, he or she should be able to hold the on-line service provider, or ISP, legally liable? To consider this question, we briefly examine the evolution of rulings in three court cases: *Cubby, Inc. v. CompuServe Inc,* 1991; *Stratton Oakmont, Inc. v. Prodigy Services Company,* 1995; and *Zeran v. America Online Inc.,* 1997.

9.7.2 The Role of ISPs in Defamation Suits

In the case of *Cubby, Inc. v. CompuServe Inc,* the court ruled that CompuServe was not liable for disseminating an electronic newsletter with libelous content. The court determined that CompuServe had acted as a distributor, and not as a publisher, since the service provider did not exercise editorial control over the contents of its bulletin boards or other on-line publications. However, a different interpretation of the role of ISPs was rendered in the 1995 case of *Stratton Oakmont, Inc. v. Prodigy Services Company.* There, a court found that Prodigy was legally liable since it had advertised that it had "editorial control" over the computer bulletin board system it hosted. The court noted that Prodigy had positioned itself as a proprietary, family-oriented, electronic network that screened out objectionable content, thereby making the network more suitable for children. In the eyes of the court, Prodigy's claim to have editorial control over its electronic forums made it seem much like a newspaper, in which case the standard of strict legal liability used for original publishers would apply. In light of the Prodigy case, many ISPs have since argued that they should be understood not as "original publishers," but rather as "common carriers," similar to telephone companies. Their argument rested, in part, on the notion that ISPs provide the "conduits for communication but not the content." This view of ISPs was used in the *Zeran v. America Online Inc.* case in 1997, where AOL was found not to be legally liable for content disseminated in its electronic forums.

The Zeran case was the first to test the new provisions for ISPs included in Section 230(c) of the Communications Decency Act, which we examined in our discussion of on-line pornography in Section 9.6.1.2. Although, as we noted, portions of the CDA were struck down as unconstitutional, Section 230 remains intact; the 1996 law protects ISPs from lawsuits similar to the one filed against Prodigy. According to the relevant section of the CDA, "[n]o provider or user of an interactive computer service shall be treated as the publisher or speaker of any information provided by another information content provider." Some refer to this policy as the "Good Samaritan immunity for ISPs."

Although ISPs cannot currently be held legally liable for content that is communicated in their electronic forums, they have been encouraged to monitor and filter that content, to the extent that they can. But this has presented a thorny legal problem: The more an ISP edits content, the more it becomes like a publisher (such as a newspaper). And the more it becomes like a publisher, with editorial control, the more it becomes legally liable. So there may be an unintended disincentive for ISPs to monitor and filter content, and this, in turn, raises a moral dilemma for ISPs (Grodzinsky and Tavani, 2002).

9.7.3 Distinguishing Between Legal Liability and Moral Accountability for ISPs

In Chapter 4 we discussed distinctions between legal liability and moral responsibility. We also drew distinctions between these two notions and the concept of accountability. (You may want to review Section 4.5 and Table 4-2 at this point.) We now consider whether ISPs should be held morally accountable for objectionable behavior that occurs in their forums. We have seen that attempts have been made to hold ISPs legally liable for content on their electronic forums, and we have also seen that the courts have flip-flopped in their decisions involving three cases. Recently Richard Spinello (2001) and Anton Vedder (2001) have each tried to show, by very different kinds of arguments, why ISPs should be held *accountable* to some extent. We briefly examine both arguments.

9.7.3.1 The Spinello View
Arguing that ISPs should be held morally accountable in defamation cases, Spinello first distinguishes between "moral responsibility" and "moral accountability." In making this distinction, he uses a scheme introduced by Helen Nissenbaum (1994). According to Nissenbaum's view, accountability, unlike responsibility, does not require *causality,* or a causal connection. Spinello points out that because ISPs do not cause defamation, they cannot be held responsible in the strict or narrow arrow sense of the term. He argues that they could, nonetheless, be held accountable in the sense that they "provide an occasion or forum" for defamation. Spinello is careful to point out that simply because an ISP presents an occasion for defamation, this does not necessarily imply that the ISP is accountable. Rather, for an ISP to be accountable, two conditions are required:

    A. the ISP must have had the *capability* to do something about the defamation, and

    B. the ISP failed to take action once it was informed that a victim had been defamed.

Spinello believes that this standard of accountability takes into consideration what ISPs can reasonably do—that is, what they are *capable* of doing—to prevent defamation or at least to limit its damage. So the fact that an ISP might not have caused the defamation does not rule out the possibility that the ISP can be held accountable in some sense for defamatory remarks.

Spinello concedes that technical and economic factors make it virtually impossible for ISPs to take preventative, or what he calls "pre-screening," measures that would detect or filter out defamatory messages. Thus we cannot hold ISPs responsible in a causal sense for defamation. Assuming that Spinello's overall argument is correct, however, we might hold them accountable if they failed to take certain actions once they are informed that a victim has been defamed. For Spinello, these steps would include

    1. prompt removal of the defamatory remarks,

    2. the issuance of a retraction on behalf of the victim,

    3. the initiation of a good faith effort to track down the originator so that the defamation does not reoccur.

Does this threefold requirement provide us with a standard of accountability that is, as Spinello suggests, a "reasonable middle ground?" That is, does it lie between the extremes of strict legal liability (as in the Prodigy case) and immunity from all responsibility (as in the Zeran case)? Or is this an unreasonable expectation for ISPs? Spinello notes that in the current system, a victim of defamation has no legal recourse because of the absolute immunity given to ISPs. On the other hand, the strict legal liability that was applied in the Prodigy case seems unduly harsh. So Spinello believes that his alternative scheme provides the appropriate middle ground, because it grants some protection to victims of defamation without burdening the ISP. So even if the law does not require ISPs to take any action, Spinello believes that "post-screening" in a diligent fashion for content along the lines of the threefold criteria described above is the morally right thing to do. He concedes, however, that ISPs do not have the capability to pre-screen content for defamation.

9.7.3.2 The Vedder Argument

Anton Vedder (2001) has advanced a very different kind of argument for why we should consider holding ISPs morally responsible for harm caused to individuals. Vedder suggests that we begin by drawing a distinction between *prospective* and *retrospective* responsibility. Whereas retrospective responsibility tends to be "backward looking," prospective responsibility is "forward looking." Vedder believes that in the past, arguments used to ascribe legal liability to ISPs have tended to be prospective, because the primary objective of liability laws has been to deter future on-line abuses rather than punish past offenses.

Vedder also notes that even though ISPs are not legally liable for their content under current United States law, the mere threat of legal liability can be used to deter ISPs from becoming lax about "policing" their electronic forums to some reasonable extent. So the utilitarian principle of deterring harm to individuals in the future underlies the reasoning of arguments for applying strict legal liability to ISPs. And this legal argument, in turn, is based on a notion of moral responsibility that is essentially *prospective* in nature. Vedder also points out that we are hesitant to attribute a retrospective sense of responsibility to ISPs because this sense of moral responsibility is usually applied to individuals (as opposed to organizations, or what Vedder calls "collectivities"), and it also often implies guilt. Vedder correctly notes that guilt is typically attributed to individuals and not to organizations or collecivities, but he suggests that in some cases it also makes sense to attribute guilt to a collectivity such as an ISP.

Attributing moral accountability to ISPs makes sense, on Vedder's view, because of the connection between retrospective and prospective responsibility. He argues that it makes no sense to hold an agent (i.e., either an individual or a collectivity) responsible for an act in a prospective sense if that agent could not be held responsible for the act in a retrospective sense as well. So he concludes that if we assume that collectivities such as ISPs can be held responsible in a prospective sense—a rationale that has been used for utilitarian arguments in attributing legal liability for ISPs—then we can also ascribe retrospective responsibility to them. So, like Spinello, Vedder believes that, to some extent, ISPs can be held morally accountable for speech that is communicated in their electronic forums.

9.7.4 Implications for the Amy Boyer Case

Next consider how Vedder's and Spinello's arguments might be applied to the cyberstalking case involving Amy Boyer, which we introduced in Chapter 1. Should Tripod and Geocities, the two ISPs that enabled Liam Youens to set up his Web sites about Boyer, be held morally accountable for the harm to her and to her family? And should those two ISPs be held morally accountable, even if they were not responsible (in the narrow sense) for causing harm to Boyer and even if they can be exonerated from charges of strict legal liability? If the arguments by Vedder and Spinello succeed, and if it can be shown that the ISPs were capable of limiting the harm to persons that result from their various on-line forums, then it is reasonable to hold them accountable.

Of course, one might ask what the purpose would be in attributing moral responsibility to ISPs if no legal action could be taken against them. There are two replies that can be given, both of which might also cause us to be more careful in our thinking about moral issues involving cyberspace. First, analyzing moral issues in this light could help us to distinguish further between moral and legal aspects of controversial cyberspace issues. Second, such an analysis can also help us consider ways that moral responsibility can be applied at the collective, as well as at the individual, level.

▶ 9.8 CHAPTER SUMMARY

In this chapter we have considered some challenges to regulating cyberspace. Specifically, we have considered Internet-regulation issues from two different perspectives: the regulation of commercial activities on the Internet and the regulation of content in cyberspace. We have seen that decisions to view cyberspace as a medium rather than as a public place or space, or vice versa, are significant, because they will determine which kinds of rules apply to regulating speech on the Internet. We have also seen that the enactment of formal or explicit laws is only one way to regulate cyberspace. As Larry Lessig and others have noted, much regulation of the Internet is being accomplished through "regulation by code."

In some ways, the legal issues examined in this chapter have overlapped with, and expanded on the issues involving intellectual property rights that we examined in Chapter 8. For example, issues involving domain names, metatags, hyperlinking, and spam each impact property-related concerns in cyberspace. Other issues, such as child pornography, hate speech, speech that can cause physical harm, and defamation, raise concerns in the ongoing dispute between censorship and free speech. Finally, we considered the role of ISPs with respect to legal liability, and possible moral responsibility, for defamatory speech and physical harm that can result from communication in their on-line forums.

▶ REVIEW QUESTIONS

1. What do we mean by "Internet regulation"?
2. Describe the two different senses of "regulation," as applied to the regulatory issues involving cyberspace that we examined.
3. What are the four modalities that Larry Lessig believes can be used to regulate behavior?
4. Give an example of how each of Lessig's modalities can be applied to regulating behavior on the Internet.
5. What does Lessig mean by the following claim: "In cyberspace, *code is the law*"?
6. What does Niva Elkin-Koren mean when she asserts that information policy is becoming increasingly privatized?
7. What does Elkin-Koren mean by "regulation by code," and why does she believe that it is problematic?

8. In which ways does Jessica Litman's analysis of trends in cyberspace having to do with e-commerce support Elkin-Koren's position regarding the privatization of information policy?

9. Describe the controversies surrounding the registration of Internet domain names.

10. What are (HTML) metatags and how can they be controversial?

11. What is the difference between a keyword metatag and a descriptive metatag? Give an example of how each type of metatag can be used controversially.

12. What do we mean by hyperlinking on the Web?

13. Do Web operators and owners have a right to include on their Web sites links to other Web sites?

14. What is electronic spam?

15. Why is spam controversial from a moral point of view?

16. What do we mean by "hate speech?" Give some examples of hate speech in cyberspace.

17. Should we tolerate hate speech on the Internet?

18. What do we mean by speech that can cause physical harm to others, and how is this form of speech different from hate speech in general?

19. Why is speech that can cause physical harm especially problematic in the Internet era?

20. What is defamation, and how has on-line defamation become problematic from a legal perspective? What responsibility, if any, should ISPs have for defamation that occurs in their electronic forums?

▶ DISCUSSION QUESTIONS

1. Should the assignment of domain names be made by a governmental agency, or should it be controlled by the private sector? What was the purpose behind the Anticybersquatting Consumer Protection Act of 1999? Is that law fair from a moral point of view?

2. What is deep linking, and why is it so controversial? Recall our discussion of the Microsoft-TicketMaster dispute over deep linking. Which side would you take in this dispute? Defend your answer by appealing to one or more of the ethical theories we considered in Chapter 2.

3. Assess the arguments that Richard Spinello uses to show that spam is morally objectionable. Are his arguments convincing? Could those arguments also be applied to the underlying dispute in the eBay-Bidder's Edge case that we examined? Can that dispute be adequately understood in terms of issues that are central to the problem of spam?

4. Describe some of the issues underlying the free speech vs. censorship debate in cyberspace. What do we mean by "free speech?" Describe the differences between what Jacques Catudal calls "censorship by suppression" and what he calls "censorship by deterrence"? Is this distinction useful for understanding some of the complex issues surrounding censorship?

5. Describe some concerns involving pornography in cyberspace. Why was the Communications Decency Act (CDA), sections of which were designed to protect children from concerns about pornography on the Internet, so controversial? Why was it eventually stuck down? Why were both COPA and (portions of) CPPA both struck down as being unconstitutional? Should they have been declared unconstitutional? Defend your answer.

6. What are some of the important distinctions between legal liability, moral responsibility, and accountability as applied to ISPs? Do Anton Vedder's and Richard Spinello's arguments succeed in showing why ISPs should be held morally accountable? Apply their arguments to the Amy Boyer case of cyberstalking introduced in Chapter 1. Should Tripod and Geocities be held accountable?

▶ REFERENCES

American Civil Liberties Union (2001). "Fahrenheit 451.2: Is Cyberspace Burning? (How Rating and Blocking Proposals May Torch Free Speech on the Internet)." In R. A. Spinello and H. T. Tavani, eds. *Readings in CyberEthics*. Sudbury, MA: Jones and Bartlett Publishers, pp. 149–162.

Camp, L. Jean, and Y. T. Chien (2000). "The Internet as Public Space: Concepts, Issues, and Implications in Public Policy," *Computers and Society*, Vol. 30, No. 3, pp. 13–19.

Catudal, Jacques (1999). "Censorship, the Internet, and the Child Pornography Law of 1996: A Critique," *Ethics and Information Technology*, Vol. 1, No. 2, pp. 105–116.

Elkin-Koren, Niva (2000). "The Privatization of Information Policy," *Ethics and Information Technology*, Vol. 2, No. 4, pp. 201–209.

Girasa, Roy J. (2002). *Cyberlaw: National and International Perspectives*. Upper Saddle River, NJ: Prentice Hall.

Goodwin, Mike (1995). "alt.sex.academic.freedom," *Wired*.

Grodzinsky, Frances S., and Herman T. Tavani (2002). "Cyberstalking, Moral Responsibility and Legal Liability Issues for Internet Service Providers" In *Proceedings of the 2002 International Symposium on Technology and Society*. Los Alamitos, CA: IEEE Computer Society Press, pp. 331–339.

Lessig, Larry (1999). *Code and Other Laws of Cyberspace*. New York: Basic Books.

Lessig, Larry (2001). "The Laws of Cyberspace." In R. A. Spinello and H. T. Tavani, eds. *Readings in CyberEthics*. Sudbury, MA: Jones and Bartlett Publishers, pp. 124–134.

Litman, Jessica (1999). "Electronic Commerce and Free Speech," *Ethics and Information Technology*, Vol. 1, No. 3, pp. 213—225.

Mawhood, John and Daniel Tysver (2000). "Law and the Internet." In D. Langford, ed. *Internet Ethics*. London: Macmillan, pp. 96–126.

Nissenbaum, Helen (1994). "Computing and Accountability," *Communications of the ACM*, Vol. 37, No. 1, pp. 73–80.

Post, David (2001). "Of Black Holes and Decentralized Law-Making in Cyberspace." In R. A. Spinello and H. T. Tavani, eds. *Readings in CyberEthics*. Sudbury, MA: Jones and Bartlett, pp. 135–148.

Resnick, Paul, and James Miller (1996). "PICS: Internet Access Controls without Censorship," *Communications of the ACM*, Vol. 40, No. 11, pp. 87–93.

Rosenberg, Richard S. (2001). "Controlling Access to the Internet: The Role of Filtering," *Ethics and Information Technology*, Vol. 3, No. 1, pp. 35–54.

Spinello, Richard A. (1997). *Case Studies in Information and Computer Ethics*. Upper Saddle River, NJ: Prentice Hall, Inc.

Spinello, Richard A. (1999). "Ethical Reflections on the Problem of Spam," *Ethics and Information Technology*, Vol. 1, No. 3, pp. 185–191.

Spinello, Richard A. (2000). "An Ethical Evaluation of Web-Site Linking," *Computers and Society*, Vol. 30, No. 4, pp. 25–32.

Spinello, Richard A. (2001). "Internet Service Providers and Defamation: New Standards of Liability." In R. A. Spinello and H. T. Tavani, eds. *Readings in CyberEthics*. Sudbury, MA: Jones and Bartlett Publishers, pp. 198–209.

Vedder, Anton H. (2001). "Accountability of Internet Access and Service Providers—Strict Liability Entering Ethics," *Ethics and Information Technology*, Vol. 3, No. 1, pp. 67–74.

Weckert, John (2000). "What Is So Bad about Internet Content Regulation?" *Ethics and Information Technology*, Vol. 2, No. 2, pp. 95–104.

▶ FURTHER READINGS

Baase, Sara (2003). "Freedom of Speech in Cyberspace." Chapter 5 in *A Gift of Fire: Social, Legal, and Ethical Issues in Computing*. 2d ed. Upper Saddle River, NJ: Prentice Hall.

Burk, Dan L. (2002). "Anti-circumvention Misuse, or Why I Learned to Stop Worrying and Love the DMCA." In *Proceedings of the 2002 International Symposium on Technology and Society*. Los Alamitos, CA: IEEE Computer Society Press, pp. 244–252.

Camp, L. Jean, and K. Lewis (2001). "Code as Speech: A Discussion of *Bernstein v. USDOJ*, *Karn v. USDOS*, and *Junger v. Daley* in Light of the U.S. Supreme Court's Recent Shift to Federalism," *Ethics and Information Technology*, Vol. 3, No. 1, pp. 21–33.

Goodwin, Mike (1998). *CyberRights*. New York: Random House.

Johnson, Deborah G. (2001). "Accountability and Computer and Information Technology." Chapter 7 in *Computer Ethics*. 3d ed. Upper Saddle Rivier, NJ: Prentice Hall.

Kapor, Mitchell (1991). "Civil Liberties in Cyberspace," *Scientific American*, September, pp. 159–164.

Koepsell, David P. (2000). "An Emerging Ontology of Jurisdiction in Cyberspace," *Ethics and Information Technology*, Vol. 2, No. 2, pp. 99–104.

Lessig, Larry (2002). *The Future of Ideas: The Fate of the Commons in a Connected World*. New York: Random House.

Lipinski, Thomas A., Elizabeth A. Buchanan, and Johannes J. Britz. (2002). "Sticks and Stones and Words That Harm: Liability vs. Responsibility, Section 230 and Defamatory Speech in Cyberspace," *Ethics and Information Technology*, Vol. 4, No. 2, pp. 143–158.

Litman, Jessica (2001). *Digital Copyright*. Amherst, NY: Prometheus Books.

Pool, Ithiel de Sola (1983). *Technologies of Freedom*. Cambridge, MA: Harvard University Press.

Rosenberg, Richard S. (2001). "Filtering the Internet in the USA: Free Speech Denied." In R. A. Spinello and H. T. Tavani, eds. *Readings in CyberEthics*. Sudbury, MA: Jones and Bartlett, pp. 163–169.

Shapiro, Andrew (1999). *The Control Revolution*. New York: Century Foundations Books.

Spinello, Richard A. (2001). "Code and Moral Values in Cyberspace," *Ethics and Information Technology*, Vol. 3, No. 2, pp. 137–150.

Spinello, Richard A. (2003). "Regulating and Governing the Internet." Chapter 2 in *Cyberethics: Morality and Law in Cyberspace*. 2d ed. Sudbury, MA: Jones and Bartlett Publishers.

Spinello, Richard A., and Herman T. Tavani (2001) "Regulating the Net: Free Speech and Content Controls," in R. A. Spinello and H. T. Tavani, eds. *Readings in CyberEthics*. Sudbury, MA: Jones and Bartlett Publishers, pp. 105–110.

Sunstein, Cass R. (1993). *Democracy and the Problems of Free Speech*. New York: Free Press.

Sunstein, Cass R. (2002). *Republic.com*. Princeton, NJ: Princeton University Press.

Tribe, Lawrence (1997). "The Constitution in Cyberspace." In M. D. Ermann, M. B. Williams, and M. S. Schauf, eds. *Computers, Ethics, and Society*. 2nd ed. New York: Oxford University Press, pp. 208–219.

CHAPTER

▼

10

SOCIAL ISSUES I: EQUITY AND ACCESS, EMPLOYMENT AND WORK

In Chapters 10 and 11 we examine social issues generated by the use of cybertechnology; we pay particular attention in Chapter 10 to how these issues impact

- *socio-demographic groups* (involving social class, race, and gender),
- *social and political institutions* (such as education and government),
- *social sectors* (such as the workplace).

The ethical and legal problems we examined in Chapters 5 through 9 typically centered on specific issues such as privacy, security, crime, or intellectual property. In this chapter and the next, however, we consider issues that cut across broader social categories, such as access and equity, employment and work, and identity and community. A common characteristic unifies these otherwise disparate issues: They are often approached from the perspective of *descriptive ethics*.

In Chapter 1 we drew the distinction between descriptive and normative approaches to the study of moral issues, noting that while social scientists conduct research that is essentially designed to report (or describe) sociological aspects of cybertechnology those aspects often have normative implications as well. In this chapter we examine some issues primarily from the vantage point of descriptive ethics. In other cases, we also examine normative aspects of those issues.

Specific questions examined in Chapter 10 include the following:

- What do we mean by "digital divide"?
- Are "universal service" policies needed to ensure Internet access for low-income and disabled populations?

- Has cybertechnology helped reduce racism, or does it enhance it?
- What implications does cybertechnology have for gender issues?
- Has cybertechnology transformed the nature of work?
- How has the use of cybertechnology affected the quality of work life?
- What kinds of social and ethical issues have been raised by computerized monitoring and surveillance in the workplace?

▶ 10.1 THE DIGITAL DIVIDE: WHAT IS IT?

According to Benjamin Compaine (2001), the phrase *digital divide* is essentially a new label for an earlier concept: "information haves and have-nots." Compaine defines the digital divide as the "perceived gap" between those who have and those who do not have both access to "information tools" *and* the ability to use those tools; we will understand it as the perceived or real gap between those who have and those who do not have either access to cybertechnology or the knowledge and ability to use that technology, or both.

First, we should note that an analysis of *the* digital divide might suggest that there is one overall divide—that is, a single divide as opposed to many "divides," or divisions. Actually, there are multiple divisions involving access to cybertechnology, which, for our purposes, can be organized into two categories: a divide *between* nations and a divide *within* nations. The division between information-rich and information-poor nations is sometimes referred to as the "global digital divide"; the technological divides within nations, on the other hand, exist between rich and poor persons, racial majority and minority groups, men and women, disabled and nondisabled persons, and so forth. We we examine disability issues involving universal access in Section 10.2, respectively; and examine access-and-equity issues involving race and gender in Sections 10.3 and 10.4. We begin with a look at the global digital divide.

10.1.1 The Global Digital Divide

Consider some statistics: As of 2000 it was estimated that 429 million people, approximately 6% of the world's population, were on-line. Of those 429 million people, 68% live in North America and Europe. According to the *Human Development Report* (2000), an estimated two billion people in the world do not even have electricity—for example, in Nepal where there are approximately 35,000 Internet users among a population of 21 million, only 15% of the houses have electricity.

Users in many developing countries who are fortunate to have Internet access often are required to deal with technical problems that include poor connectivity and low bandwidth. Libby Levison, William Thies, and Saman Amarasinghe (2002) point out that not only is Internet access prohibitively expensive in the African nation of Malawi, where telephone service (and corresponding Internet access) is metered at minutes used, but even those who can afford access must cope with many practical difficulties and limitations. For example, telephone connections are so slow and telecom failures are so frequent that using the Internet for conventional purposes—such as interactive searches, which most Internet users residing in North America and western Europe take for granted as part of a Web interface— is generally impractical. These problems are neither isolated nor peculiar to countries in sub-Saharan Africa. Rather, they are typical of the problems that users in many developing nations encounter.

Developing countries struggle with low literacy rates; many people in developing nations cannot read and write in their native language, let alone in English, but much of the material on the Internet is in English. This has influenced advocates for improved Internet service for global users to lobby for the development of Web applications that include more graphics and images that can serve as universal symbols.

Efforts to address problems involving the cybertechnology divide between industrialized and developing countries began in the early 1990s, when the idea of a Global Information Infrastructure, or GII, emerged. Al Gore described the initial plan for a GII in an address to the International Telecommunication Union in Brazil on March 21, 1994. A principle objective of Gore's plan was to develop a global infrastructure that would support *universal access* to cybertechnology. Critics argue that very little has resulted from this and other earlier proposals that address global concerns about unequal access to cybertechnology, but recently there have been signs that concerns about a global digital divide are being taken seriously. In the summer of 2000, for example, the Okinawa Charter on Global Information was announced at an annual Group of Eight (G8) summit in Japan. At that summit, the G8 leaders formed the Digital Opportunities Task Force (DOT Force), perhaps the first step in a serious effort to narrow the global digital divide, sometimes referred to as the "international information and knowledge divide."

10.1.2 The Digital Divide in the United States

In response to concerns about a growing digital divide in the United States, the Clinton administration announced its plans for a National Information Infrastructure (NII) in 1993 to ensure that all Americans have access to cybertechnology. To accomplish this goal, the National Telecommunications and Information Administration (NTIA) was charged with investigating the status of computer and Internet access among Americans. In 1995 the NTIA issued its first report, entitled *Falling Through the Net*, which confirmed the commonly held belief that Internet access was related to socio-demographic factors and noted that a disproportionate number of information "have-nots" lived in rural areas and inner cities. The NTIA's 1999 report, *Falling through the Net: Defining the Digital Divide*, noted that while more Americans were accessing the Internet, significant discrepancies in access were still related to socio-demographic factors involving race, education, income, and marital status. According to the NTIA's 2000 report, entitled *Toward Digital Inclusion*, digital inclusion is increasing in the United States across all socio-demographic sectors. Some interpret this to imply that the divide between cybertechnology haves and have-nots in the United States is narrowing; others, however, dispute this interpretation.

10.1.2.1 Universal Service vs. Universal Access

A key issue in the debate about the digital divide in the United States is whether some kind of *universal service* policy is needed to ensure that all Americans have an appropriate level of access to computer and Internet technologies. Before the Internet era, universal service in America applied to telephony (or telephone technology): When telephones became available in the early part of the twentieth century, there was concern that people living in less-populated rural areas would not be able to afford this new technology. Because having a telephone was determined to be essential for one's well-being, the Communications Act of 1934 provided for the subsidy of telephone service rates to ensure that all Americans could afford telephone service. (Today, telephone users still pay a universal connectivity fee or surcharge on their monthly telephone bills to support universal telephone service.) Now the question is whether Internet access is, or soon will be, essential for one's well-being.

Recent proposals have recommended special "E-rates," that is, federal technology discounts, to subsidize the cost of Internet access for public schools and libraries. Whereas universal service policies involving telephony are aimed at providing residential telephone service, E-rates are targeted for "community points of access" to provide universal Internet *access* for Americans, but critics point out that they do not ensure universal *service*. Why is a policy that ensures universal service, as opposed to universal access, to cybertechnology necessary? Gary Chapman and Marc Rotenberg (1995), representing Computer Professionals for Social Responsibility (CPSR), have argued that not only must everyone have access to the Internet but also pricing should be structured so that full Internet service is affordable to everyone. In their view, merely providing community points of access to the Internet is not sufficient for universal Internet service, just as placing telephones in public locations would not meet the requirements for universal telephone service.

While advocacy groups such as CPSR have lobbied Congress for a universal Internet service policy, opponents to such legislation, including many lawmakers as well as conservative political interest groups, have used three different arguments: First, a universal Internet service policy could create an entitlement that might grow out of control, setting a precedent for entitlements for other government-subsidized services. (This argument was used by John Ashcroft when he was a United States Senator.) Second, the revenue needed to implement a universal Internet service policy would have to be generated by tax subsidies unfair both to taxpayers in moderate-income brackets, who would shoulder the greatest burden, and to the telephone and utility companies, who would also be taxed. A third objection views issues concerning Internet access for poorer citizens as, at bottom, issues involving their personal priorities and values. Critics who appeal to this view point out that nearly everyone in the United States who wishes to can find a way to purchase a television and pay for cable service. They conclude that those who wish to can find a way to purchase a computer and pay for Internet service; no universal service policy for cybertechnology is needed. Supporters of universal service, however, argue that their opponents either overly simplify or greatly underestimate the problems that face those who are unable to afford Internet access in their homes.

10.1.2.2 The Public Education System and the Analog Divide
The digital divide cannot be explained solely in terms of disparities in levels of income. Torin Monahan (2001) and others have argued that the educational system perpetuates divisions involving cybertechnology. Consider statistics that provide a strong link between educational level and access to cybertechnology: It is estimated that 65% of households headed by college graduates have Internet access, compared to only 11.7% of households headed by people with less than a high-school education (Digital Divide Network, 2002).

Monahan questions whether discussing disparities in access to cybertechnology in terms of a *digital* divide accurately captures the essential issues at stake. He suggests instead that we describe the problem as an *analog* divide, referring to divisions or inequalities that already existed prior to digital technology and that continue to exist independently of that technology. Monahan argues that the fundamental problems that generate and perpetuate existing divisions among groups in the United States cannot be understood simply in terms of access to cybertechnology, because these divisions are not ultimately about access to material resources. Others, like A. Rhae Adams (2001), have presented similar arguments—that the problems creating the digital divide cannot be understood simply in terms of material resources, numbers, and other modes of quantitative measurement. Adams believes that focusing merely on numbers can actually mask other ongoing social inequalities relevant to understanding how the divide arises and is sustained.

These arguments for reconceptualizing the digital divide as an analog divide might initially seem appealing. However, they tend to underestimate the significant role that technology itself plays in understanding (and potentially resolving) problems associated with unequal access to cybertechnology (Tavani, 2003). There are good reasons, therefore, for retaining a technological metaphor when analyzing these problems.

10. 1.3   Why Is the Digital Divide an Ethical Issue?

We have examined sociological aspects of the digital divide and have seen how statistical data confirms unequal access to cybertechnology due to both socio-economic differences between groups within the United States as well as divisions between developing and developed nations. Granted that there are significant divisions between those who have and do not have access to cybertechnology, we can still ask whether these divisions also raise ethical issues.

What does it mean to say that the digital divide is an *ethical* issue? Is every kind of divide regarding unequal access to goods necessarily an ethical problem? Opponents of universal service policies might note the divide between those who have and do not have Mercedes Benz automobiles, arguing that there is a "Mercedes Benz divide" and many of us fall on the "wrong side" of it but that this is not an ethical issue. We could respond by noting the divisions between those who do and those who do not have access to vital resources such as food and health care, divisions that many ethicists believe raise questions of *distributive justice*. But what about unequal access to cybertechnology? Is it closer to the "Mercede Benz divide," or is it closer to divisions involving access to food and health care?

10.1.3.1 Vital Resources and Distributive Justice

If we can show that having access to cybertechnology provides a means to resources that are vital for one's well-being, then we can make a fairly strong case that questions involving equal access to cybertechnology deserve moral consideration. Additionally, if we can show that not having access to cybertechnology either denies or unfairly limits access to basic goods—what James Moor (1998) calls "core goods," or "core values," such as knowledge, ability, freedom, and so forth—then we can make a fairly strong case that unequal access to cybertechnology is a moral issue involving distributive justice. Jeremy Moss (2002 believes that persons who do not have access to cybertechnology are deprived of resources that are vital for their well-being. He argues that without access to cybertechnology, people are unfairly disadvantaged because

1. their access to knowledge is significantly limited,

2. their ability to participate fully in the political process and to receive important information is greatly diminished, and

3. their economic prospects are severely hindered.

First, Moss claims that people who are deprived of access to cybertechnology are not able to benefit from the increasing range of information on the Internet and thus are falling further behind. Second, because of political barriers to participation in the decision-making process in developing countries, people in remote areas without access to the Internet may have no means at all of participating in national debates or of receiving information about important developmental matters and policies that can significantly affect them. Third, Moss believes that because so much economic growth is driven by the information and communication sector, people living in countries that are not part of this sector will be disadvantaged.

In response to Moss, one could argue that some people and some nations have always been disadvantaged in access to new technologies such as automobiles, household appliances, and so forth. But this misses a crucial point: As we have noted, disparities in access to certain technologies, such as Mercedes Benz automobiles, do not in themselves constitute an ethical issue. We should also note that divisions of this type are generally accepted in capitalist societies. However, if Moss's thesis about why cybertechnology is important is correct, then having access to cybertechnology is essential for one's well-being in ways that having access to other kinds of technologies—that is, "discretionary technologies" that provide convenience and entertainment—is not.

10.1.3.2 Our Moral Obligation to Bridge the Digital Divide

If Moss's argument holds, does it follow that we have a moral obligation to provide Internet access to those who are disadvantaged? Some argue that while we are morally obligated to do no harm, we have no explicit obligation to do good—in this case, to provide Internet access to disadvantaged groups. According to this view, we are behaving morally as long as we do nothing to prevent others from acquiring cybertechnology and Internet access. But is this minimalist view of morality adequate? Recall our discussion of contractualist ethical theory in Chapter 2, where we saw that a moral obligation to do good (to others) applies only in cases where individuals or nations have an express (legal) contract in which they are required to come to the aid of others. However, we also saw some compelling reasons to be skeptical about such a limited theory of moral obligation. In Chapter 9, for example, we saw that a more robust theory of morality requires members of the on-line community to come to the aid of those in harm's way, whenever it is in their power to do so. For one thing, this ethos contributes to making the Internet a much safer place, especially for those disadvantaged individuals and groups vulnerable to on-line harm. And we could construct an analogous argument to show why coming to the aid of other kinds of disadvantaged individuals and groups—that is, those without Internet access—would be the right thing to do.

One way in which we could frame the debate about universal Internet access is to think of it as a dispute involving "negative and positive rights," a distinction we also discussed in Chapter 2. Recall that *negative* rights were like liberties in the sense that we have a (legal) right not to be interfered with in exercising them. So if I have a (negative) right to own a computer, and I purchase Internet access, then you are not permitted to interfere with my purchase and use of these items and services. Can one's legal rights involving access to cybertechnology possibly be understood in terms of *positive* (as well as negative) rights? In Chapter 2, we saw that there are very few positive rights; for example, we noted that in America, the right to access to health care is considered a negative rather than a positive right because the government is not required to provide citizens with health care. One of the few positive rights American citizens enjoy is the right to receive a free public education through high school—a positive right in the sense that the United States government is legally required to provide each citizen with access to such an education.

Perhaps the rationale used in determining why one has a right to receive a free public education in the United States can help us to frame an argument for why one might also have a right to universal Internet access. We begin by asking why public education is a positive, and not merely a negative, right. We can answer that without adequate access to an education, a child would not have equal access to employment opportunities. If we could also show that having Internet access at home is essential for students to participate equally in the educational process, then it we could show that students have a positive right to Internet access. We can construct the following argument for why we should view the right to home Internet access for students in the public education system as a positive right:

> Because public education (for grades 1–12) is a positive right in the United States, the American government must provide citizens with an education.
>
> Providing an education means that the government is required (legally obligated) to supply students with the tools (free textbooks, etc.) necessary to gain an education.
>
> Internet access is (or soon will be) a necessary tool for completing homework assignments required in the public educational process.
>
> Students who cannot afford Internet access at home are unfairly advantaged and will not have the same opportunities in completing their public education as students who can afford to pay for home Internet access.

> Therefore, the United States government should be required to provide home Internet access for those students whose families cannot afford to pay for it.

Is this argument plausible? Even if we accept it, it would justify an on-line service policy that ensured home Internet access only to school-aged children in low-income families attending public schools. Though it would not in itself justify an Internet service policy for all Americans, it might be the first step in that direction.

We could apply the criterion of "equal opportunity" that we used in our argument in analogous contexts as well; for example, consider that poor people who cannot afford home Internet access might be unfairly disadvantaged in finding and competing for jobs that are only posted on-line. Chapman and Rotenberg (1995) envision a future in which employment interviews are conducted on-line; if someone did not have on-line access, he or she would clearly be disadvantaged in the job market.

So based on equal opportunity, we could make a plausible case for providing an Internet service policy to members of low-income groups in general. We noted in Section 10.1.2.1 that some lawmakers and political-interest groups in the United States have opposed policies that guarantee universal Internet service. But if we could reframe the debate as involving equal access to resources that are vital to one's well-being, as opposed to merely supplying technology and service to poorer Americans, then perhaps we could make a stronger moral argument for providing universal service. Proponents of universal Internet service policies generally acknowledge that having such policies would not, in itself, be sufficient to bridge the digital divide; however, they also believe that full Internet service is nonetheless a *necessary* condition for resolving certain problems that perpetuate the divide.

▷ 10.2 CYBERTECHNOLOGY AND THE DISABLED

In addition to developing nations and low-income groups within developed nations, the digital divide has affected disabled people. There has been much discussion about implementing strategies and policies to make the Internet more accessible to this group. Tim Berners-Lee, director of the World Wide Web Consortium (W3C) and the inventor of the HTTP protocol that underlies the Web, has stated: "The power of the Web is in its universality. Access by everyone regardless of disability is an essential aspect."

The W3C was formed, in large part, to promote standards that ensure universal Web access. It established a Web Accessibility Initiative (WAI), which has produced guidelines and protocols for developing software applications that improve access for disabled persons, ranging from software used in speech synthesizers and screen magnifiers to proposed software applications that will benefit people with visual, hearing, physical, cognitive, and neurological disabilities. WAI representatives have recently worked with industry groups and governmental organizations to establish guidelines for the design of "user agents," which are intended to lower barriers to Web accessibility for people with disabilities. These user agents include Web browsers and other types of software that retrieve and render Web content; the agents are designed to conform and communicate with other technologies, especially "assistive technologies" such as screen readers (which perform a function similar to Braille applications in off-line contexts).

Proponents of the WAI point out that measures taken for the disabled have had positive outcomes for other groups, especially poor people who often are forced to deal with literacy problems and inadequate equipment. Recall our earlier discussion of literacy problems in developing nations. It may well turn out that voice-recognition technology designed to assist disabled persons who are unable to use keyboards may ultimately also benefit nondisabled persons with low literacy skills.

Consider an example of an accessibility-related initiative in the nondigital world that was intended to accommodate disabled persons but that has also benefited the public in general. Ramps designed for wheelchair accessibility have not only benefited people in wheelchairs, but have also been very useful to nondisabled persons as well, such as parents pushing baby carriages. Also consider some of the advantages that sloped curbs on street corners have provided to many nondisabled persons—bicyclists and skaters have benefited from these features, which were initially intended to serve disabled persons (Woodbury, 2002). It has been argued, analogously, that ordinary users will likely benefit from computer design enhancements to user interfaces that are initially intended to assist disabled persons.

Because improving access to cybertechnology for the disabled has potential benefits for society as a whole, we can formulate a utilitarian argument to advance this cause. However, we should also be cautious about extending this argument too far. What would happen if, in the future, the broader population did not realize any benefits from improving access to cybertechnology for the disabled? Would that provide for a utilitarian argument against investing in initiatives that improved access for the disabled? After considering this, you can better understand some of the possible dangers of relying too heavily on utilitarian principles when advancing a moral argument for improved access for the disabled.

In Section 10.5.3, we will return to issues involving the disabled in our discussion of telework. Next, we examine the impact of the digital divide on race.

▶ 10.3 RACE AND CYBERTECHNOLOGY

We have seen that in the United States many lower-income individuals and families, especially those in the inner cities, still do not have access to the Internet; many of these individuals also belong to racial and ethnic minority groups. Consider statistics that correlate income (social class) and race with the digital divide in the United States: 51% of all homes have at least one computer, and 41.5% of all homes have Internet access. In terms of income, 86.3% of households earning more than $75,000 per year have Internet access, while of those households earning below $15,000 per year, only 12.7% have access. From the vantage point of race, 46.1% of white Americans and 56.8% of Asian-Americans and Pacific Islanders have access, contrasted with only 23.5% of African-Americans and 23.1% of Hispanics who do (Digital Divide Network). Table 10-1 summarizes these figures based on statistics available as of 2000.

We next focus our analysis on the impact of cybertechnology for African-Americans by examining three kinds of concerns: Internet usage patterns vis-à-vis demographic statistics, technology policies and their implications for African-Americans, and the Internet as a medium to spread racial prejudice.

10.3.1 Access Issues: Internet Usage Patterns and Demographic Statistics

Based on a study conducted by Tom Spooner and Lee Rainie (2000), an estimated 7.5 million adult African-American users were on-line in 2000. Susan Kretchmer and Rod Karveth (2001) point out that African-American users differ from their white counterparts, in both usage patterns and demographic characteristics. They also claim that usage patterns between the two groups differ in several respects: first, African-American Internet users are more likely to use the Internet for entertainment and for locating information about quality-of-life activities, such as job training, school, health care, and hobbies; second, they are less likely to participate in Web-based auctions; and third, they are also less likely to feel that the Internet connects them with family and friends, and they are less likely to use e-mail to develop and sustain friendships. Kretchmer and Karveth also cite relevant socio-demographic differences between African-Americans and whites: the average age for African-American users tends to be younger than for whites; African-Americans typically access the Internet less frequently than whites; and adult African-American Internet users are much more likely than their white counterparts to have modest incomes, no college degrees, and children under eighteen.

What factors contribute to these differences between African-Americans and whites in levels and patterns of Internet access? Although it is difficult to identify the root causes, Kretchmer and Karveth provide two different explanations: cultural attitudes of many African-Americans toward technology and assumptions that those who control technology

TABLE 10-1 Internet Usage by Racial/Ethnic Groups in the United States

Whites	Asian-Americans	African-Americans	Hispanics
46.1%	56.8%	23.5%	23.1%

have about African-Americans. Robert Johnson (1997) points out that many African-Americans tend to view technology as something that is designed by white people for white people. African-Americans are aware that the culture that created and currently dominates the Internet is white, and according to Kretchmer and Karveth, some African-Americans believe that whites perceive them as not being very interested in computer technology.

A different set of explanations emerges from the perspective of the attitudes of whites, and in particular of those (whites) who control technology. Kretchmer and Karveth suggest that Web-site developers see little value (economic or otherwise) in supplying and developing content that appeals to small groups on the Internet. Because African-American users constitute a relatively small percentage of the total user population, there is little incentive for non-African-American e-commerce entrepreneurs to develop content that would appeal primarily to African-Americans. All these factors account for differences between African-American and white Internet usage patterns.

10.3.2 Technology, Race, and Public Policy

Access and usage patterns are only one part of the overall problem concerning cybertechnology and race. Another important element involves public policy decisions: Historically, African-Americans have not had a representative voice in policy decisions involving technology that have affected them. Robert Johnson (1997) argues that African-Americans need to take a more active role in these decisions; he believes that if African-Americans take up this challenge, they can help to reshape the course of technological development to better suit the needs and interests specific to their community. To illustrate his argument, Johnson describes policy decisions made in the development of the United States highway system.

▶ **CASE ILLUSTRATION:** The Development of the United States Highway System and Its Impact on African-Americans

Robert Johnson points out that when the federal government was developing plans for an interstate highway system, virtually no thought was given to the impact of the new highways on existing urban neighborhoods. He also notes that since "automobility" accelerated the exodus of both the middle class and businesses to suburbia, proportionately fewer white Americans were affected by the urban highway systems. African-Americans who stayed behind in inner-city neighborhoods, however, were adversely impacted. Many homogeneous African-American neighborhoods were arbitrarily divided into segments that conveniently conformed to plans for the highway system, and African-Americans who lived in the communities affected had no say in how the highway system would be developed. Consider that because of the highway policies that were implemented, proportionately more African-Americans were subject to pollution generated by highway traffic; also consider that they were more vulnerable to injuries and deaths from automobile accidents.

African-Americans also have much at stake in policies that involve the "information highway." To have a meaningful and effective voice in policy decisions that affect them, Johnson argues that African-Americans need to become involved in the process during its early stages. Perhaps African-Americans also need to see themselves as stakeholders in decisions involving cybertechnology policies affecting the information highway, just as they were (unknowingly at the time) stakeholders in policies that decided how the motor-vehicle highway system would be constructed. Johnson believes that in order for African-

Americans to have an effective voice in those decisions, they must be willing to make technology an integral part of their socialization.

10.3.3 Rhetoric and Racism on the Internet

Has the Internet eliminated, or even helped to reduce, considerations of race in communication? Because Internet communication does not reveal users' physical attributes, we might assume that the answer is "Yes." However, we need to question that assumption. Kretchmer and Karveth (2001) note that the study of race in cyberspace often leads to paradoxical inferences: On the one hand, cyberspace provides an opportunity and forum to discover and confront racial issues, but on the other, it can perpetuate, or perhaps even enhance, aspects of racism. For example, the Internet has introduced new tools for harassing members of certain groups. Thus Internet technology can be, and has been, used to magnify the *rhetoric* and significance of hate groups.

Lynn Theismeyer (1999) has pointed out the rhetorical role that the Internet can play with respect to race. She examines the rhetoric of racism, not as it applies specifically to racial and minority groups in the United States, such as African-Americans and Hispanics, but rather as it has been used internationally in the rise of neo-Nazi propaganda. Theismeyer believes that there are two kinds of racist speech on the Internet:

a. "*Hate speech* itself, including text, music, on-line radio broadcasts, and images that exhort users to act against targeted groups."

b. "*Persuasive rhetoric* that does not directly enunciate but ultimately promotes or justifies violence."

Theismeyer asks us to consider two questions:

1. "Does information technology make the reemergence of prejudicial messages and attitudes swifter and more likely?"

2. "Does the Internet's wide range of distribution make for more followers and finally more persuasion?"

She concludes that it is impossible to know at this point whether cybertechnology has been the main cause of the rapid spread of racism in neo-Nazism groups, but she is convinced that cybertechnology has been its principal tool.

▶ 10.4 GENDER AND CYBERTECHNOLOGY

Other equity- and access-concerns associated with cybertechnology in general and with the digital divide in particular can be analyzed with respect to gender. Feminist authors and others who advocate for women's issues proffer arguments similar to those advanced by or on behalf of African-Americans, which we examined in the preceding section. Women, like certain racial and ethnic groups, have not been granted equal access to technology and have not been included in important decisions about technology policies. In this section, we examine gender-related cybertechnology issues in terms of (i) access to jobs in technology, (ii) gender bias in the design and development of software, and (iii) methodological frameworks.

10.4.1 Access Issues

Some see the root of the gender and technology problem, at least as it applies to access issues, in educational practices that contribute to the overall socialization processes. For example, many social scientists point out that at an early age girls learn that science (and, by association, technology) is for boys and that computers reinforce certain stereotypes regarding technology and gender. Many critics are willing to acknowledge that girls and young women have not literally been denied access to computers, computer labs, and computer camps, but they point out that socialization—for example, processes that encourage males and females to adopt particular gender-based roles—has perpetuated the gender imbalance with respect to computing.

Tracy Camp (1997) and others center their concern on what they call "pipeline" issues by analyzing statistics involving the number of women entering the computer science and engineering professions—the data suggest that proportionately few women elect to pursue degrees in either field. Michael Wesells (1990) has pointed out that in 1989, fewer than 5% of those awarded Ph.D. degrees in computer science were women. According to more recent statistics provided by Camp (1997), this percentage increased to 15.4% in 1993–1994, but Camp also notes that the percentage of women pursuing bachelor's and master's degrees in computer science declined slightly during those years. Davies and Camp (2000) projected a slight increase in the number of women graduating with computer science degrees between 1998 and 2000, but they project a drastic decline between 2001 and 2002.

In addition to providing information used in projecting the number of women who will have access to jobs in the computer profession, analyses of pipeline statistics also provide projections of the proportion of women who will have access to important decision-making roles in the computer industry. The decisions they make will affect the future direction of cybertechnology as well as its impact on women.

10.4.2 Gender Bias and Educational Software

Design and development decisions involving educational software can not only influence whether women will elect to pursue degrees and careers in computer science and engineering, they can also affect the education that young girls and women receive. The following case illustrates one way that the design of computer software can have such an effect.

▶ **CASE ILLUSTRATION:** Designing Educational Software

Chuck Huff and Joel Cooper (1987) developed a study in which they had teachers design software for three categories of users: girls, boys, and (gender unspecified) children. They discovered that the programs the teachers designed for boys looked like games (with time pressure, hand-to-eye coordination, and competition the most important features). Programs the teachers designed for girls, on the other hand, looked like tools for learning (with conversation and goal-based learning features). And surprisingly the programs the teachers designed for children looked just like the ones they designed for boys. So, the researchers concluded, when teachers designed programs for children, or students in general, they actually designed them for boys.

It is worth noting that 80% of the program "designers" in Huff and Cooper's experiment were female, and, ironically, some of these women had originally expressed the concern that educational software was male-biased. Huff and Cooper's research also points to a paradox: A software designer may be able to identify bias in a particular software application but may still not be able to design and develop software applications that avoid bias. At this point, you may find it useful to review our Chapter 1 discussion of bias and embedded values in technology.

Elizabeth Buchanan (2000) argues that gender bias can also be found in video-game software and that this bias raises two ethical concerns: (1) Video games tend either to misrepresent or exclude female characters, and (2) they tend to perpetuate traditional sexist stereotypes. With respect to (1), she argues that the representational politics of gender in video games needs greater evaluation, because many computer games, especially virtual sports games, include no female characters at all. (We examine issues involving representation in virtual games and some of the broader ethical questions they raise in greater detail in Chapter 11.) And with respect to (2), Buchanan argues that video games such as Barbie Fashion Designer, a top-selling game for girls, reinforce traditional cultural stereotypes along gender lines. Buchanan also points out that Apollo Computers markets a "glitter-pink accented" Barbie printer aimed at young girls—girls can get pink computers and printers, while boys can get camouflage. Buchanan worries that both marketing schemes for computers and printers and gender bias in video games serve to perpetuate gender stereotypes.

10.4.3 Methodological Frameworks for Understanding Gender Issues

A third perspective from which to view issues involving cybertechnology and gender is one that questions the standard methodological framework used to identify and understand specific moral problems. Alison Adam (2001) believes that problems involving gender and cybertechnology are analyzed either by focusing on the low numbers of women in the computing profession, as in the case of the pipeline issues examined by Tracy Camp (1997) that we considered above, or by focusing on potential differences in moral decision making by males and females, as suggested in the research of Jennifer Kreie and Timothy Cronin (1998). Adam acknowledges that the first approach is important because it reveals existing inequities in the field; however, she also believes that this approach tends to limit the study of gender to access-related concerns. She believes that research from the second approach, which focuses on establishing differences in moral decision making between men and women, tends to reinforce behavioral stereotypes in males and females. Adam believes that both approaches miss the opportunity to use feminist ethical theory to analyze and understand contemporary cyberethics in light of the gender implications for broader issues such as privacy and power.

Adam argues that conventional methodological frameworks used to research gender, that is, gathering data via techniques based on student surveys, has prevented us from seeing larger issues. So she proposes an alternative strategy in which data is gathered via empirical observation and interviews and then tested against ethical theory. She argues that current computer-ethics research involving gender is "under-theorized"; what little theory is being applied, Adam points out, is generally based on traditional schemes such as utilitarianism and deontology. She also believes that traditional ethical theories not only ignore gender, they also tend to emphasize the *result* of an ethical decision over the *process* used to reach the decision.

Adam suggests we need a "gender-informed" ethics to improve the process, based on a feminist ethics—in particular, on the "ethic of care" introduced in a seminal work on feminist ethics by Carol Gilligan (1982). According to this ethic, care and justice are part of a moral framework in which individuals are obligated to help one another when it is in their power to do so. An ethic based on care, therefore, is more robust than a mere "noninterference" notion of ethics (see Chapter 2). It contrasts with traditional ethical systems, which Adam believes tend to engender individualism and are often based on simply following formal rules.

Adam believes that a theoretical framework built on an ethic of care improves the understanding of gender issues. First, it shows why gender issues cannot be reduced to access issues and cannot be approached merely in terms of statistical studies based on quantitative analysis; second, and perhaps more importantly, it provides us with an insight for understanding many typical computer-ethics issues that cannot be gained through the application of conventional ethical theories. For example, Adam argues that an ethic of care especially helps us both to see some of the relations of power involved in the development and use of computers and to see that the concept of privacy can be different for men and women and can vary according to age, class, ethnicity, etc. More recently, Adam (2002) has argued that a gender-based ethics can also help us to understand issues involving cyberstalking and Internet pornography in a way that traditional ethical theories cannot.

So Adam's methodological framework can do much more than simply help us to identify specific moral issues *as* gender issues (i.e., issues affecting women per se). It also helps us to analyze many standard computer-ethics issues using a more robust theoretical framework than traditional ones that fail to show the impact of many technology-related issues on gender.

▶ 10.5 EMPLOYMENT AND WORK IN AN AGE OF CYBERTECHNOLOGY

Thus far, we have focused on access-and-equity issues as they pertain to specific sociodemographic groups. Some access-related issues involving cybertechnology, however, affect a much broader segment of society: those in the contemporary workforce. Though relatively new, cybertechnology already has had a profound effect on employment as well as on the nature of work itself. Computers and cybertechnology also significantly affect the quality of work-life. Before considering this, we examine issues involving the transformation of the contemporary workplace.

Whether or not they believe that cybertechnology has benefited workers, few would seriously challenge the claim that it has significantly changed the workplace. Some have gone so far as to suggest that cybertechnology has *transformed* the nature of work itself with respect to social and ethical issues involving

- job displacement and automation,
- robotics and expert systems,
- remote work and virtual organizations.

10.5.1 Job Displacement and Automation

One question that frequently arises in discussions about the transformation of employment by cybertechnology is whether, on balance, it has created or eliminated more jobs. There are arguments to support both sides of this debate. Studies concluding that cybertechnology in the workplace has reduced the number of jobs often point to the number of factory and assembly jobs that have been automated. But even though cybertechnology has caused certain industries to eliminate human jobs, it has enabled other industries, such as computer-support companies, to create jobs; social scientists often refer to this shift as *job displacement*.

Job displacement is associated with, and sometimes linked to, *automation*. Social issues associated with automation are by no means new, nor are they unique to cybertechnology. Social scientists note that the Industrial Revolution transformed jobs into smaller, discrete tasks that could be automated by machines, creating working conditions that adversely affected the lives of many workers. When new automated technology threatened to replace many workers, one group of disenchanted workers in England—later referred to as "Luddites"—smashed machines used to make textiles. ("Luddite" is derived from a nineteenth-century British worker, Ned Ludd, who reputedly led workers in destroying factory machinery.) Just as the Luddites resisted factory technology in the nineteenth century because they thought it threatened their jobs and thus their livelihood, some oppose developments involving cybertechnology for similar reasons. In the 1970s, for example, workers tried to stall developments in microprocessor-based technology, fearing that it would lead to a loss of jobs. Workers as well individuals in general who have a pessimistic view of the impact of cybertechnology in the workplace are known as "neo-Luddites."

Not all analysts view automation solely in terms of its negative consequences. Shoshana Zuboff (1988) has argued that while many jobs in the computer era have been and will continue to be automated, information technology also provides positive outcomes for the workplace; for example, it *informates* as well as automates. What does Zuboff mean by "informate"? And how is it in contrast with "automate"? Consider that a scanning device at a supermarket checkout not only serves to automate the process of checking out customers, it also informs managers about inventory, enabling them to control inventory in ways not previously possible. Zuboff also notes that because cybertechnology informates, it reveals information that makes it easier to understand the processes underlying the structure and organization of work. A better understanding of these processes will in turn enable us to restructure work, as well as the social organizations that support it, so that work can be more meaningful and more productive.

10.5.2 Robotics and Expert Systems

Recent developments in *robotics* raise social concerns for industrial automation. A robot is essentially the integration of computer and electromechanical parts that can be manifested in various forms; for example, a robot can be just a mobile robotic limb or armor or it can be as a full-fledged robotic system. Because robots are composed of sensory, tactile, and motor abilities that enable them to manipulate objects, they can be programmed to perform tasks such as assembling parts, spray painting, and welding, or they can be programmed to perform tasks considered hazardous to humans, such as removing nuclear waste and making repairs in outer space or underwater.

Robots were once fairly unsophisticated and had very limited sensory capacity. These first-generation robots were often dedicated to performing specific tasks, such as those required in automobile assembly lines and on factory floors. New-generation robots, however, are now able to perform a broader range of tasks and are capable of recognizing a variety of objects by using visual and tactile information. Even though robots offer increased productivity and lower labor costs, their use has also raised social concerns similar to those we discussed involving automation and job displacement.

Another cyberrelated technology that has impacted professional jobs is the *expert system* (ES), a problem-solving computer program or a computer system that is "expert" at performing one particular task. Because it is essentially a software program, an ES is different than a robot, which is a physical or mechanical system. Growing out of research and development in artificial intelligence (discussed in Chapter 11), ESs use "inference engines" to capture the decision-making strategies of "experts" (usually professionals); they execute instructions that correspond to a set of rules an expert would use in performing a professional task. A "knowledge engineer," asks human experts in a given field a series of questions and then extracts rules and designs a program based on the responses to those questions.

Initially expert systems were designed to perform jobs in chemical engineering and geology that both required the professional expertise of highly educated persons and were generally considered too hazardous for humans. Next, expert systems were used to perform tasks in certain nonhazardous professions, such as medicine, where an early expert system called MYCIN was developed in the 1970s to assist physicians in recommending appropriate antibiotics to treat bacterial infections. More recently, expert systems have been developed for use in professional fields such as law, education, and finance. The following hypothetical scenario illustrates one ethically controversial application of an ES.

▶ **SCENARIO:** Designing an Expert Administrator

Tom Forester and Perry Morrison (1994) ask whether an "expert administrator" should be programmed so that it is permitted to lie or even to deceive human beings in cases where it might (generally, but unofficially) seem "appropriate" for human administrators to do so. Is lying, or at least being deceptive with respect to certain information, essential to being an expert (or at least successful) human administrator? If so, should the "skill" of lying be designed into such a system? If you were a member of the design team for this ES application, what would you do?

The use of expert systems, like the use of robotics, has raised ethical and social issues having to do with automation and others having to do with "de-skilling" and "worker alienation." In Section 10.5.1, we discussed the impact that automation had on some workers during the Industrial Revolution. Social scientists have suggested that prior to that period, workers generally felt connected to their labor and exhibited a strong sense of pride and craftsmanship. The relationship between worker and work began to change, however, when work became automated. Social scientists have used the term *alienation* to describe the effect that de-skilling had for workers whose skills were transferred to machines. Richard Mason (1991) cites as an example the introduction of Jacquard's loom and its effect on weavers during the Industrial Revolution: Skills were "disembodied" from weavers and craftsmen and then "re-embodied" into machines such as the loom.

Today, ES technology poses a similar threat to professional workers by allowing knowledge, in the form of knowledge-related skills, to be extracted from experts and then implanted into computer software. Mason points out that now knowledge can be "disemminded" from professional workers, or experts in a given field, and "emminded" into machines in the form of computer programs. Mason also believes that there is an interesting connection between the Industrial Revolution and the current era in that a proliferation of publications on ethics appear in each time period, and he suggests that working conditions during the Industrial Revolution may have been responsible for the greatest outpouring of moral philosophy since Plato and Aristotle. Works on ethics by Immanuel Kant, Jeremy Bentham, John Stuart Mill, and many others appeared during that era. Mason suggests that, similarly, contemporary workplace controversies associated with ES and other aspects of cybertechnology have contributed to the recent flurry of publications on ethics.

10.5.3 Virtual Organizations and Remote Work

Communications technologies such as teleconferencing and videoconferencing, e-mail and voice mail, fax machines, and personal digital assistants (PDAs) such as palm pilots have all had a significant affect on the way we work. Cybertechnology also makes it possible for many employees to work from their homes, thus creating *virtual organizations*, including "virtual offices," "virtual teams," and "virtual corporations." Abbe Mowshowitz (1997) defines a virtual corporation as "a virtually organized company dynamically . . . linked to a variety of seemingly disparate phenomena, including . . . virtual teams and virtual offices." Mowshowitz points out that *virtual teams* allow managers to "assemble groups of employees to meet transient, unanticipated needs." *Virtual offices*, on the other hand, allow employees to operate in "dynamically changing work environments."

Virtual teams, offices, and corporations raise a number of social concerns; one has to do with the commitment that employees can expect from their employers. Richard Spinello (1997), for example, points out that virtual organizations may feel less obligated to provide their employees with benefits or other workplace amenities. Another concern involves the role that social relationships, which often develop in the workplace, play in virtual organizations. When work is performed in an office or at a physical site, workers are required to interact with each other and with managers, resulting in certain dynamics and interpersonal relationships now threatened by virtual organizations.

10.5.3.1 Telework and Telecommuting

Once considered a perk for a few fortunate workers who were often employed in high-tech companies, millions of employees now do remote work. Some further distinctions involving remote work have been drawn. *Telework*, defined by Richard Rosenberg (1997) as "organizational work performed outside the organizational confines," can be contrasted with *telecommuting*, which Rosenberg defines as the "use of computer and communications technologies to transport work to the worker as a substitute for physical transportation of the worker to the workplace."

Even though remote work is a relatively recent practice, it has already raised social and ethical questions, one of which asks whether all workers benefit from remote work. For example, are white-collar employees affected in the same way as those less-educated and less-skilled employees who also perform remote work? It is one thing to be a white-collar professional with an option to work at home at your discretion and convenience. It is something altogether different, however, to be a clerical, or "pink collar," worker required to work remotely out of your home. Of course, some professional men and women may choose to work at home because of child-care considerations or because they wish to avoid a long and tedious daily commute, but employers may require other employees, especially those in lower-skilled and clerical jobs, to work at home.

Some employees may ultimately be deprived of career advancement and promotions because they are required to work remotely. Employers cannot directly observe (and therefore cannot evaluate) either the interpersonal skills of these workers or other relevant aspects of their job performance as they can for those who work in the traditional office or in a physical workplace setting.

In addition to job advancement equity-and-access issues for those workers in lower-skilled and lower-paying jobs, remote work has begun to threaten professionals. Corporations and business in developed countries (such as the United States) have elected to farm out professional work, especially work requiring programming skills, to employees in developing countries because skilled programmers in those countries are willing to work for a fraction of the wages acceptable to American programmers. This practice would not be feasible without the turnaround time that cybertechnology makes possible.

10.5.3.2 Remote Work and Disabled Persons

Although problems involving remote work, such as isolation and lost career opportunities, affect all employees, disabled as well as nondisabled, we might consider how disabled workers are particularly affected. Ben Fairweather (1998), who has carefully examined specific issues that affect remote workers with disabilities, acknowledges that remote work has provided opportunities to some disabled workers who otherwise would be denied access to a job. But he also worries that for some disabled employees, especially those who are capable of working in both conventional and remote workplace settings, telework can have unfortunate consequences.

Fairweather is concerned that the practice of remote work might provide employers with a convenient scheme for keeping disabled workers out of the physical workplace, and he finds it troubling for three reasons: First, it affects worker autonomy because it denies those disabled workers who could work *either* remotely or in a conventional workplace setting the choice of determining where they will work. Second, the practice of remote work can be used to hide disabled workers, keeping them out of sight and away from the physical workplace. Third, remote work provides employers with a convenient excuse not to make the physical workplace compatible with current ADA (Americans with Disabilities Act) guidelines and requirements.

▶ 10.6 THE QUALITY OF WORK-LIFE

Thus far, we have focused on social and ethical issues surrounding the transformation of work, but many social scientists have also questioned how cybertechnology impacts the *quality* of work-life. Quality issues address both health and safety concerns and employee stress. We begin with health and safety issues in the computerized workplace.

10.6.1 Health and Safety Issues

Cybertechnology-related health and safety issues have been associated with the use of computer hardware. Prolonged use of a monitor, or a Video Display Terminal (VDT), can cause eyestrain, fatigue, blurring, and double vision; together these problems are called Video Operator's Distress Syndrome (VODS). Keyboards and hand-held pointing/tracking devices can cause arm, hand, and finger trauma leading to Carpal Tunnel Syndrome (CTS), as well as other musculo-skeletal conditions associated with Cumulative Trauma Disorder (CTD); together these problems are called Repetitive Strain Injury (RSI). Catherine Romano (1998) notes that RSI was a problem as early as the eighteenth-century, when Italian clerks reported ailments caused by "repeated use of the hand." So RSI issues are by no means unique to computers and cybertechnology, but nevertheless, they have been greatly exacerbated by the increased use of computers, both within and outside the workplace.

Because of RSI-related litigation, employers, especially those who require employees to use computers extensively, have begun to pay close attention to ergonomics. L. L. Bean, for instance, has installed ergonomically adjustable workstations, and each worker's ergonomic measurements—that is, appropriate height-level for keyboards and desktop work surfaces, proper eye-to-monitor distance, and measurements that ensure the employee's neck, back, and feet are properly aligned when the employee is seated at the computer—are recorded. At the beginning of each employee's shift the workstation is automatically adjusted according to the individual's prerecorded ergonomic measurements. Other companies have also adopted similar ergonomic practices and policies.

10.6.2 Employee Stress, Workplace Surveillance, and Computer Monitoring

Another quality-of-work issue involves employee stress. Many workers experience sterss because their activities are now monitored closely by an "invisible supervisor"—i.e., the computer, which can record information about work habits. Citing a 1999 American Management Survey, Lucas Introna (2001) points out that "45% percent of major United States firms record and review employee communications and activities on the job, including their phone calls, e-mail, and computer files. Additional forms of monitoring and surveillance, such as review of phone logs or videotaping for security purposes, bring the overall figure on electronic oversight to 67.3%."

Introna believes that surveillance technology, which has become less expensive, has also become less overt and more diffused He also points out that current technology has created the potential to build surveillance features into the "very fabric of organizational processes," and in fact technology is now being used to measure such things as the number of computer keystrokes a worker enters per minute, the number of minutes he or she spends on the telephone completing a transaction (such as selling a product or booking a reservation), and the number and length of breaks he or she takes. Not surprisingly, these kinds of surveillance and monitoring techniques oftn cause employee stress.

Perhaps somewhat ironically, "information workers," whose work is dependent on the use of cybertechnology to process information, are the ones most subjected to monitoring by computer technology. However, while most computer-monitoring techniques track the activities of clerical workers, they also track and evaluate the performance of professionals, such as programmers, loan officers, commodities brokers, and plant managers. And nurses are frequently monitored to make sure that they do not spend too much time with one patient.

Workers in offices and hospitals are not the only employees monitored by computers; Safeway Corporation has installed a monitoring device, called the "Tripmaster," in their trucks to track the speed at which a driver travels, the distance the driver travels on a given trip, and the number of stops the driver makes en route. Not surprisingly, the Tripmaster and similar monitoring devices have caused considerable controversy and the practice has been disputed in negotiations among truck drivers, unions, and management officials.

TABLE 10-2 **Arguments Used to Support and to Oppose Computer Monitoring**

Arguments in Favor of Monitoring	Arguments Against Monitoring
Helps to reduce employee theft	Increases employee stress
Helps to eliminate waste	Undermines employee trust
Helps employers to train new employees	Reduces individual autonomy
Provides employers with a motivational tool	Invades worker privacy
Improves competitiveness	Focuses on quantity rather than quality of work
Saves the company money	Creates an "electronic sweatshop"
Guards against industrial espionage	Provides employers with an "electronic whip"
Improves worker productivity and profits	Reduces employee morale and overall productivity

Forester and Morrison describe some arguments used in favor of, and in opposition to, computer monitoring. They note that some employers defend computer monitoring on the grounds that it is useful for training new employees who will work with the public. Others defend it by claiming it saves money, is essential for improving efficiency and worker productivity, aids managers in motivating employees, or helps businesses to reduce industrial espionage and employee theft.

Opponents of monitoring have a very different perspective: Some see computer monitoring as a Big-Brother tactic or as an "electronic whip" used unfairly by management, and they believe it creates a work environment tantamount to an "electronic sweatshop." Others claim that managers are motivated to use monitoring because they distrust their employees or that because monitoring invades individual privacy, it disregards human rights. Some critics also charge that while monitoring may accurately measure the quantity of work an employee produces, it fails to measure the overall quality of that work. Others argue that computer monitoring is ultimately counterproductive, because employee morale generally declines along with overall workplace productivity. Table 10-2 summarizes arguments on both sides of the debate.

▷ 10.7 EMPLOYEE AUTONOMY AND PRIVACY IN A COMPUTERIZED WORKPLACE

Workplace surveillance raises some serious ethical and social issues; we now consider two proposals that address them. The first recommends that a fairly straightforward code of ethics be adopted and used in workplace monitoring. The other is more complicated, but nevertheless warrants careful consideration.

10.7.1 Proposal I: A Code of Ethics for Employee Monitoring

Although they do not endorse computer monitoring, Gary Marx and Sanford Sherizen (1991) have proposed a code of ethics that they believe would provide standards for determining when monitoring practices satisfy minimal criteria for fairness to workers. Their code has six guidelines:

- Apply to monitoring the same protection that applies to pre-employment background checks; that is, permit only information directly related to the job to be collected.
- Require employers to provide employees with advanced notice of the introduction of monitoring as well as appropriate mechanisms for appeal.
- Require people to verify machine-produced information before using it to evaluate employees.
- Provide workers with access to the information on themselves.
- Provide mechanisms for monetary redress for employees whose rights are violated or who are victims of erroneous information generated by a monitoring system.
- Apply a "statute of limitations" on data from monitoring. The older the data, the less their potential relevance and the greater the difficulty employees have in challenging the information.

Note that (2) requires that employees must be told in advance before computerized monitoring is used. This gives the employee a measure of autonomy because, once informed that a company plans to institute monitoring, he or she can elect not to work for that company. And according to (4), an employee has the right to review information collected via monitoring and to determine whether that information is accurate; (3) allows them to challenge inaccurate information before it can be used against them. Another important feature of Marx and Sherizen's code is that (6) requires that a statute of limitations be set with respect to how long computer-gathered information about an employee could be used and kept on record in an employee's file.

On the one hand, a code that protects at least some employees' interests in the monitoring process is better than no code at all. Some critics argue, however, that much more than a code similar to the one proposed by Marx and Sherizen is needed, and Lucas Introna (2001) proposes a different strategy.

10.7.2 Proposal II: An Alternative Strategy

Introna believes that employees do not necessarily fear surveillance, or what he calls the "transparency of surveillance," rather, they fear the choices that employers will likely make with respect to the information they collect. Employees are concerned both that these choices will reflect only the interests of the employer and that the information will provide the employer with only part of the picture needed to make subsequent judgments about employees.

Introna also sees a problem with the way that the workplace privacy debate itself has evolved. He notes that workplace privacy cannot be understood simply in terms of "bad" employees wanting to hide their unscrupulous behavior behind a shield of privacy protection, although he acknowledges that this may be the case in some instances. Introna believes that the current attitudes and conditions affecting employee monitoring make it difficult for the individual workers to secure their interests, leaving them "power-less," but not necessarily powerless; he argues that employees are, for the most part, in a relationship of severe *power asymmetry*.

10.7.2.1 An "Asymmetry of Power"

Introna sees power in the workplace as asymmetrical, that is, in one direction: employer over employee, and this suggests a legitimate concern for justice in the workplace. As we noted, Introna believes that the debate about workplace privacy has been framed by the wrong criteria; it has attached itself to "public vs. private" distinctions, because the employee is performing in a public, not a private, context (see Chapter 5). Introna believes this places employees in an asymmetrical position with respect to power. He argues for an alternative strategy where the workplace privacy debate is framed in terms of "fairness and organizational justice" rather than "public vs. private," where privacy is linked to personal space.

But what exactly does it mean to evaluate workplace surveillance in terms "fairness and organizational justice"? Introna believes that the debate should be an argument for competing but equally legitimate claims for what he calls "privacy and transparency." He points out that if individuals (employees) are given an absolute right to privacy, they may act only in their own interest and thereby defraud the employer, but he also notes that if the employer is given a complete right to transparency, it may strip the employee of autonomy and self-determination by making inappropriate judgments that only serve the interest of the employer. Thus, he concludes that we need a framework that would "distribute" the right to privacy of the employee and the right to transparency of the employer. Introna believes that such a framework can be found in John Rawls's class work *A Theory of Justice*.

10.7.2.2 Extending the "Rawls Model" to the Debate over Employee Monitoring

Using a model of "justice as fairness" developed by John Rawls (1971), Introna suggests that the Rawlsian "veil of ignorance" can be used to resolve the debate over privacy and transparency in the workplace; Rawls's "veil" is similar to Bernard Gert's "blindfold of justice," described in Chapter 2. Behind the "veil," the participants would not know their place in the new system, so employers could end up as employees, and vice versa. Rawls's model is fairly complicated, so we cannot describe its details here, but we can summarize what is needed for Introna's argument: "Rational self-interested" parties would not likely wish to construct an unfair or unjust system if they thought it were very possible for them to end up in one of the disadvantaged groups in the new system.

Introna believes that anyone "behind the veil" would adopt a position that biases the right of the employee—the worse off—over the employer. He also suggests that all "rational self-interested persons" would reach the same conclusion if they were completely ignorant about their own status in the subsequent contexts where the new rules would be applied. Introna concludes that this new policy would ensure that workplace surveillance becomes, and stays, *fair*. He also notes that a "fair regime of workplace surveillance" would tend to avoid monitoring unless explicitly justified by the employer; it would also provide mechanisms for the employee to have maximum control over the use of data gathered by monitoring activities.

10.7.3 E-mail Privacy and Employer Policies

We have seen that computerized monitoring of employees raises a number of ethical issues, but the central issue involves the privacy rights and expectations of individuals, especially as they pertain to the workplace. Employee privacy issues include the use of e-mail in the workplace: Do employees, for example, have a right to send and receive private e-mail on an employer's computer system? Many companies, such as Merrill Lynch, have developed explicit policies regarding the use of e-mail as well as other employer-owned computer-system resources, while other institutions and companies have not. As a result, it is not always clear what kinds of personal privacy protections employees can expect.

Many of the concerns at the root of other workplace privacy issues that we will not be able to examine in this chapter overlap with concerns involving computerized monitoring. So, some of the issues of e-mail privacy for employees can be analyzed via proposals that we have considered for surveillance and monitoring practices. And recall that we examined other concerns involving privacy and cybertechnology (in general) as well as privacy issues involving surveillance in nonworkplace settings in Chapter 5.

▶ 10.8 CHAPTER SUMMARY

We have examined social issues from the vantage point of access and equity. We have considered the implications of the digital divide for demographic groups, involving social class, race, gender, and disabled persons. We have also considered access-and-equity issues affecting employment and work. Finally, we examined some of the challenges that workplace surveillance and employee monitoring pose for our social values and system of ethics, especially with respect to autonomy, privacy, and trust.

▶ REVIEW QUESTIONS

1. What is the "digital divide," and why is it significant?
2. How do we distinguish the "digital divide" from the "analog divide"?
3. What are the differences between universal access and universal service?
4. Describe arguments that have been advanced for and against universal service.
5. How does the public education system in inner-city schools perpetuate problems involving the digital divide?
6. What are some of the global issues involving the digital divide?
7. Describe three ways, according to Jeremy Moss, that people in developing countries are currently disadvantaged because of lack of access to digital technology.
8. Describe three perspectives from which we can analyze issues involving race and cybertechnology.
9. Identify three perspectives from which we can view issues involving gender and cybertechnology.
10. Why does Alison Adam believe that traditional schemes used to understand gender issues involving cybertechnology are not adequate?
11. What are some of the special equity-and-access issues affecting disabled persons who use cybertechnology?
12. How has work been "transformed" in the computer age?
13. How has cybertechnology affected both the quantity of work and the quality of work?
14. What are some of the social problems associated with automation and job displacement?
15. Who were the Luddites, and what is meant by the expression "neo-Luddite"?
16. What are some of the social issues associated with expert systems (ES) and robotics?

17. Describe some of the social issues affecting virtual organizations and remote work. What special implications does Ben Fairweather believe that remote work, or telework, has for disabled employees?

18. What is employee monitoring, and why is it controversial from an ethical perspective?

19. What are some of the standard arguments used for and against the use of computers to monitor employees?

20. Describe the code of ethics for employee monitoring as suggested by Gary Marx and Sanford Scherizen. Is it adequate?

▶ DISCUSSION QUESTIONS

1. What obligations does the United States have, as a democratic nation concerned with guaranteeing equal opportunities for all it citizens, to ensure that all its citizens have full access to the Internet? Does the United States also have obligations to developing countries to ensure that they have global access to the Internet? If so, what is the extent of those obligation? For example, should engineers working in the United States and other developed countries design applications to ensure that people living in remote areas with low connectivity and poor bandwidth have reasonable Internet access? If so, who should pay for the development of these software applications?

2. Do we, as a society, have a special obligation to disabled persons to ensure that they have full Internet access? Is the argument that by providing improved access and services for disabled persons, nondisabled users will benefit as well a reasonable one? Consider that it can be dangerous to reason along this line; for example, suppose that nondisabled persons did not benefit from software applications designed for the disabled. Would that be a reason for not investing in software for disabled people?

3. Recall the kind of racist/hate Web sites described by Lynn Theismeyer in Section 10.3.3. Should Web sites that promote racist speech be allowed to thrive on the Internet? Has the proliferation of these sites increased the incidence of racism on a global scale? Or is the Internet, as some have suggested, a force that can help to reduce racism?

4. Recall our discussion of expert systems (ES) in Section 10.5.2. There, we saw that the increased use of ES technology in professional fields has generated some ethical and social concerns, and we also considered some ethical dilemmas that were raised in designing an "expert administrator." Other ethical controversies surrounding ES have to do with critical decisions, including life and death decisions; for example, should "expert doctors" be allowed to make decisions that could directly result in the death of, or cause serious harm to, a patient? If so, *who* is ultimately responsible for the ES's decision? Is the hospital that owns the particular ES responsible? Should the knowledge engineer who designed the ES be held responsible? Or is the ES itself responsible? In answering these questions, you may want to consult relevant sections of Chapter 4, where we discussed responsibility for software accidents such as the case involving Therac-25.

5. Assess Lucas Introna's arguments for how employee issues involving privacy and autonomy might be resolved in the context of computerized monitoring and workplace surveillance. What does Introna mean by the expression "asymmetry of power?" In particular, consider the role that John Rawls's "veil of ignorance" plays in Introna's scheme. Is the Rawlsian "veil" a plausible mechanism for resolving disputes such as the one between what Introna calls "transparency and privacy?" Also, compare Rawls's "veil" to Bernard Gert's "blindfold of justice" (see Chapter 2). Would Gert's blindfold work equally well in Introna's case? Can Introna's argument involving employee monitoring also be extended to other workplace privacy issues such as those involving employee e-mail? Explain.

▶ REFERENCES

Adam, Alison (2001). "Gender and Computer Ethics." In R. A. Spinello and H. T. Tavani, eds. *Readings in CyberEthics*. Sudbury, MA: Jones and Bartlett Publishers, pp. 63–76.

Adam, Alison (2002). "Cyberstalking and Internet Pornography: Gender and the Gaze," *Ethics and Information Technology*, Vol. 4, No. 2, pp. 133–142.

Adams, A. Rhae (2001). "Beyond Numbers and Demographics: 'Experience Near' Explorations of the Digital Divide," *Computers and Society*, Vol. 31, No. 3, pp. 5–8.

Buchanan, Elizabeth A. (2000). "Strangers in the 'Myst' of Video Gaming: Ethics and Representation," *CPSR Journal*, Vol. 18, No. 1.

Camp, Tracy (1997). "The Incredible Shrinking Pipeline," *Communications of the ACM*, Vol. 40, No. 2, October, pp. 103–110.

Chapman, Gary, and Marc Rotenberg (1995). "The National Information Infrastructure: A Public Interest Opportunity." In D. G. Johnson and H. Nissenbaum, eds. *Computers, Ethics, and Social Values*. Englewood Cliffs, NJ: Prentice Hall, pp. 628–644.

Compaine, Benjamin (2001). *The Digital Divide: Facing a Crisis or Creating a Myth*. Cambridge, MA: MIT Press.

Davies, Vanessa, and Tracy Camp (2000). "Where Have Women Gone, and Will They Be Returning? Predictions about Female Involvement in Computing," *CPSR Journal*, Vol. 18, No. 1.

Digital Divide Network. Available at http://www.digitaldividenetwork.org. Accessed Dec. 21, 2002.

Fairweather, N. Ben (1998). "Moral Dilemmas and Issues of Telework for Disabled People." In M. J. van den Hoven, ed. *Proceedings for the Conference on Computer Ethics: Philosophical Enquiry (CEPE '97)*. Rotterdam, The Netherlands: Erasmus University Press, pp. 130–141.

Forester, Tom, and Perry Morrison (1994). *Computer Ethics: Cautionary Tales and Ethical Dilemmas in Computing*. 2d ed. Cambridge, MA: MIT Press.

Gilligan, Carol (1982). *In a Different Voice: Psychological Theory and Women's Development*. Cambridge, MA: Harvard University Press.

Huff, Chuck, and Joel Cooper (1987). "Sex Bias in Educational Software: The Effects of Designers' Stereotypes on the Software They Design," *Journal of Applied Social Psychology*, Vol. 17, pp. 519–532.

Human Development Report 2000. (2000). Published for the United Nations Development Program (UNDP). New York: Oxford University Press.

Introna, Lucas (2001). "Workplace Surveillance, Privacy, and Distributive Justice." In R. A. Spinello and H. T. Tavani, eds. *Readings in CyberEthics*. Sudbury, MA: Jones and Bartlett Publishers, pp. 418–429.

Johnson, Robert C. (1997). "Science, Technology, and Black Community Development." In A. H. Teich, ed. *Technology and the Future*. 7th ed. New York: St. Martin's press, pp. 270–283.

Kreie, Jennifer, and Timothy Paul Cronan (1998). "How Men and Women View Ethics," *Communications of the ACM*, Vol. 41, No. 9, pp. 70–76.

Kretchmer, Susan, and Rod Karveth (2001). "The Color of the Net: African-Americans, Race, and Cyberspace," *Computers and Society*, Vol. 31, No. 3, pp. 9–14.

Levison, Libby, William Thies, and Saman Amarasinghe (2002). "Providing Web-Search Capability for Low-Connectivity Communities." In J. R. Herkert, ed. *Proceedings of the 2002 International Symposium on Technology and Society (ISTAS 02)*. Los Alamitos, CA: IEEE Computer Society Press, pp. 87–92.

Marx, Gary, and Sanford Sherizen (1991). "Monitoring on the Job: How to Protect Privacy as well as Property." In T. Forester, ed. *Computers in the Human Context: Information Technology, Productivity, and People*. Cambridge, MA: MIT Press, pp. 397–406.

Mason, Richard O. (1991). "Four Ethical Issues of the Information Age." In R. Dejoie, G. Fowler, and D. Paradice, eds. *Ethical Issues in Information Systems*. Boston, MA: Boyd and Fraser, pp. 46–55.

Monahan, Torin (2001). "The Analog Divide: Technology Practices in Public Education," *Computers and Society*, Vol. 31, No. 3, pp. 22–31.

Moor, James H. (1998). "Reason, Relativity, and Responsibility in Computer Ethics," *Computers and Society*, Vol. 28, No. 1, pp. 14–21.

Moss, Jeremy (2002). "Power and the Digital Divide," *Ethics and Information Technology*, Vol. 4, No. 2, pp. 159–165.

Mowshowitz, Abbe (1997). "Virtual Organization," *Communications of the ACM*, Vol. 40, No. 9, pp. 30–37.

National Telecommunications and Information Administration (NTIA) (1995). *Falling Through the Net: A Survey of the Have-nots in Rural and Urban America*. Washington, DC: United States Department of Commerce. Available at http://www.ntia.doc.gov/ntiahome/fallingthru.html.

National Telecommunications and Information Administration (NTIA) (1999). *Falling Through the Net: Defining the Digital Divide*. Washington, DC: United States Department of Commerce. Available at http://www.ntia.doc.gov/ntiahome/fttn99.html.

National Telecommunications and Information Administration (NTIA) (2000). *Falling Through the Net: Toward Digital Inclusion*. Washington, DC: United States Department of Commerce. Available at http://www.ntia.doc.gov/ntiahome/fttn00/contents00.html.

Rawls, John (1971). *A Theory of Justice*. Cambridge, MA: Harvard University Press.

Romano, Catherine (1998). "Working Out the Kinks." In K. Schellenberg, ed. *Computers in Society*. 7th ed. New York: Dushkin/McGraw Hill, pp. 63–65.

Rosenberg, Richard S. (1997). *The Social Impact of Computers*. San Diego, CA: Academic Press.

Spinello, Richard A. (1997). *Case Studies in Information and Computer Ethics*. Upper Saddle River, NJ: Prentice Hall.

Spooner, Tom, and Lee Rainie (2000). *African-Americans and the Internet*. Washington, DC: Pew Internet & American Life Project.

Tavani, Herman T. (2003). "Ethical Reflections on the Digital Divide," *Journal of Information, Communication, and Ethics in Society*, Vol. 1, No. 2. pp. 98–108.

Theismeyer, Lynn (1999). "Racism on the Web: Its Rhetoric and its Marketing," *Ethics and Information Technology*, Vol. 1, No. 2, pp. 117–125.

Web Accessibility Initiative (WAI). World Wide Web Consortium (W3C). Available at http://www.w3.org/WAI/.

Wessells, Michael G. (1990). *Computer, Self, and Society*. Englewood Cliffs, NJ: Prentice Hall.

Woodbury, Marsha (2002). *Computer and Information Ethics*. Champaigne, IL: Stipes Publishing.

Zuboff, Shoshana (1988). *In the Age of the Smart Machine: The Future of Work and Power*. New York: Basic Books.

▶ FURTHER READINGS

Adam, Alison, and Jacqueline Ofori-Amanfo (2000). "Does Gender Matter in Computer Ethics?" *Ethics and Information Technology*, Vol. 2, No. 1, pp. 37–47.

Baase, Sara (2003). "Computers and Work." Chap. 8 in *A Gift of Fire: Social, Legal, and Ethical Issues in Computing*. 2d ed. Upper Saddle River, NJ: Prentice Hall.

Ball, Kristen (2001). "Structuring Workplace Surveillance: Ethics and Computer-based Performance Monitoring," *Ethics and Information Technology*, Vol. 3, No. 3, pp. 211–223.

Bolt, David B., and Ray Crawford (2001). *Digital Divide: Computers and Our Children's Future*. TV Books, LLC.

Bush, Corlann Gee (1997). "Women and the Assessment of Technology." In A. H. Teich, ed. *Technology and the Future*. 7th ed. New York: St. Martin's Press, pp. 157–159.

Camp, L. Jean, and Rose P. Tsang (2000). "Universal Service in a Ubiquitous Digital Network," *Ethics and Information Technology*, Vol. 2, No. 4, pp. 211–221.

Epstein, Richard G. (1997). "The Wheel," *Computers and Society*, Vol. 27, No. 2, pp. 8–17.

Gabel, Joan T. A., and Nancy Mansfield (2001). "On the Increasing Presence of Remote Employees: An Analysis of the Internet's Impact on Employment Law as it Relates to Teleworkers," *Journal of Law Technology and Policy*, Vol. 2001, No. 2, pp. 233–266.

Ito, Mizuko, et al. (2001). "Making a Place for Seniors on the Net: Senior Net, Identity, and the Cultural Divide," *Computers and Society*, Vol. 31, No. 3, pp. 15–21.

Johnson, Deborah G. (2001). "Ethics and the Internet II: Social Implications and Social Values." Chap. 8 in *Computer Ethics*. 3d. ed. Upper Saddle River, NJ: Prentice Hall.

Kirkman, Geoffrey (2002). *The Global Information Technology Report 2001–2002: Readiness for the Networked World*. New York: Oxford University Press.

Lyon, David (1994). *The Electronic Eye: The Rise of the Surveillance Society*. Minneapolis, MN: University of Minnesota Press.

Lyon, David (2001). *Surveillance Society: Monitoring Everyday Life*. London: Open University Press.

McFarland, Michael C. (1996). "Humanizing the Information Highway," *IEEE Technology and Society*, Vol. 14, No. 4, pp. 11–18.

Norris, Pippa (2001). *Digital Divide? Civic Engagement, Information Poverty, and the Internet Worldwide*. Cambridge, MA: Cambridge University Press.

Prior, Mary (2001). "Surveillance in the Workplace: Experience in a University Setting." In T. W. Bynum, et. al, eds. *Proceedings of the Fifth International Conference on the Social and Ethical Impacts of Information and Communications Technologies (ETHICOMP 2001)*. Vol. 2. Gdansk, Poland: Wydawnictwo Mikom Publishers, pp. 102–111.

Scott, Anne (2001). "Grounded Politics: Some Thoughts on Feminist Process in the Information Age," *Computers and Society*, Vol. 31, No. 4, pp. 5–14.

Sewell, Graham, and James R. Barker (2001). "Neither Good, Nor Bad, But Dangerous: Surveillance as an Ethical Paradox," *Ethics and Information Technology*, Vol. 3, No. 3, pp. 183–196.

Shapiro, Andrew (1999). *The Control Revolution*. New York: Century Foundations Books.

Warschauer, Mark (2003). *Technology and Social Inclusion: Rethinking the Digital Divide*. MIT Press.

Weill, Nancy (2000). "Computers Open Doors for the Disabled." In K. Schellenberg, ed. *Computers in Society 00/01*: Guilford, CT: McGraw Hill, pp. 68–69.

Wresch, William (1998). "Disconnected: Haves and Have-Nots in the Information Age." In K. Schellenberg, ed. *Computers in Society*. 7th ed. Guilford, CT: Dushkin/McGraw Hill, pp. 207–212.

11

SOCIAL ISSUES II: COMMUNITY AND IDENTITY IN CYBERSPACE

In Chapter 10, we examined some ethical implications of social issues generated by the use of cybertechnology. We looked at equity-and-access issues that impact sociodemographic groups in particular and employment and work in general. In this chapter, we continue our analysis of social issues, focusing on the impact of cybertechnology on community and personal identity by asking

- How have on-line communities affected our traditional understanding of "community"?
- Does the Internet facilitate democracy, or does it threaten it?
- Do behaviors made possible by virtual reality (VR) environments raise special ethical issues?
- What implications does cybertechnology have for personal-identity issues?
- How have developments in artificial intelligence (AI) affected our sense of self and our conception of what it means to be a human being?
- Given concerns about the potential dangers of nanotechnology, should research and development in nanocomputing continue?

▶ 11.1 ON-LINE COMMUNITIES

Do we need to redefine our traditional notion of community in the age of the Internet? Do on-line communities pose any special social and ethical challenges? We consider both questions in this section.

11.1.1 On-line Communities vs. Traditional Communities

Webster's New World Dictionary of the American Language defines *community* as "people living in the same district, city, etc., under the same laws." This definition stresses the geographical aspects of community by associating it with concepts such as "district" and "city" that have typically constrained community life. Although modern transportation, such as the automobile, has made it possible to extend the geographical boundaries of communities, for the most part traditional communities remain limited by geography.

Interactions made possible by the Internet have caused us to re-examine our concept of community: It is now possible for individuals physically separated by continents and oceans to come together and "sit around an electronic camp fire" to discuss topics that bind them together as a community. Not surprisingly then, more recent definitions of "community" focus on the common interests of groups rather than on geographical and physical criteria.

What do we mean by *on-line community*? Howard Rheingold (2001) suggests that on-line communities can be understood as "computer-mediated social groups"; he describes his experience in joining the WELL (Whole Earth 'Lectronic Link), an early electronic community, in 1985:

> The idea of a community accessible only via my computer screen sounded cold to me at first, but . . . [f]inding the WELL was like discovering a cozy little world that had been flourishing without me. . . . The WELL felt like an authentic community to me from the start, because it was grounded in my everyday physical world. WELLites who don't live within driving distance of the San Francisco Bay area are constrained in their ability to participate in the local networks of face-to-face acquaintances. . . . I've attended real-life WELL marriages, WELL births, and even a WELL funeral.

Rheingold points out that because of the social contracts and collaborative negotiations that happened when members met on-line, the WELL became a community in that setting. He notes, for example, that in the WELL, norms were "established, challenged, changed, re-established, rechallenged, in a kind of speeded-up social evolution." When the members decided to get together occasionally at physical locations in the greater San Francisco Bay area, the WELL became a "hybrid community," spanning both physical and virtual space.

Michelle White (2002) notes that in cyberspace, "community" is a popular way of describing "synchronous on-line settings," because it suggests that they offer "social exchange, emotional support, and learning environments." White also points out that describing on-line settings as communities acknowledges the "complex and important activities" that people engage in through those forums. In effect, it also legitimizes these settings by making them seem as if they are physical and real.

11.1.2 Forming On-line Communities

We have noted that common interests can bring people together to form an on-line community. But what are some of these common interests? We have traditionally identified ourselves in terms of national heritage, religious and political affiliations, and so forth; some authors suggest that many of our traditional notions of identity, including nationality, are becoming antiquated in the age of the Internet. Young people who have grown up using the Internet may define themselves in terms of their consumer interests rather than the country or state that they happen to inhabit in the off-line world. Geographic and national boundaries may mean far less to this group than to those who came of age before cybertechnology, when distance and geographical remoteness precluded the formation of "natural" communities with international members. Now, in the age of computer networks, some speak of "the passing of remoteness."

Many see on-line communities as positive. Consider that on the Internet, people can meet new friends and future romantic partners as well as form medical support groups by joining Internet chat rooms. They can also join listservers and discussion forums to disseminate material to like-minded colleagues, and they can communicate by e-mail with people they might not otherwise communicate with by physical mail or telephone.

On the other hand, interactions on-line have also had negative effects. They have, for example, (possibly) threatened traditional communities, minimized face-to-face communications, and made it much easier to deceive people about who actually is communicating with them.

11.1.3 Assessing Pros and Cons of On-line Communities

Have on-line communities had an overall positive effect on communication and interaction? Gordon Graham (1999) points out that the Internet could have a major impact on social life by allowing for a "reconfiguration of human communities," based on the individual choices they provide to users. So on-line communities empower people to choose a community rather than accept the default community or society in which they are already situated. Graham believes that on-line communities also promote individual freedom because members can more easily disregard personal attributes, such as gender and ethnicity, which are more obvious in traditional communities.

Because on-line communities provide choices, they contribute positively to human interaction; however, on-line communities also contribute to increased social and political fragmentation, which we examine when we discuss democracy and the Internet in Section 11.2. Furthermore, on-line communities also reveal a darker side of the Internet because users in on-line communities can, under the shield of anonymity, engage in behavior that would not be tolerated in most physical communities. For instance, individuals can use aliases and "screen names" when they interact in on-line forums. Consider Julian Dibbell's 1993 report of an incident that occurred in an electronic community called a MOO (Multiuser Object-Oriented environment).

► **CASE ILLUSTRATION:** A Rape in Cyberspace

LambdaMOO is an electronic forum in which "MOO members" can interact. In LambdaMOO, participants have screen names, or virtual identities, to represent the characters they portray; for example, characters whose screen names are Mr. Bungle, Zippy, Legba, Starsinger, and Joe Feedback have interacted in LambdaMOO. Bungle designed a program called "voodoo doll" that enabled him to control the actions of other characters in the MOO and used it to take control of Legba and Starsinger to "perform" sexually offensive actions. When Bungle's program was "frozen" by Zippy, the incident ceased.

As you might imagine, the incident had a profound effect not only on the "MOOers" in the Lambda community but also on members of other electronic communities who heard

TABLE 11-1   Features of On-line Communities

Positive Features	Negative Features
Empower individuals by giving them choices regarding community membership	Discourage face-to-face interaction between individuals
Enable people living in geographically remote locations to interact regularly as members of the same community	Facilitate anonymity, making it easier to perform morally objectionable acts that are not tolerated in physical communities
Tend to provide individuals with greater freedom	Tend to increase social and political fragmentation

about it. Almost immediately, questions arose about how to deal with Bungle: Should he be evicted from LambdaMOO? Should the real person behind Bungle be prohibited from joining other on-line communities and forums?

We examine the LambdaMOO case in more detail in Section 11.3, where we consider ethical aspects of virtual environments. We also discuss the effects that MOOs and MUDs (Multiuser Dimensions) have on personal identity in Section 11.4.

Table 11-1 summarizes positive and negative features of on-line communities.

▶ 11.2 DEMOCRACY AND THE INTERNET

In the preceding section we indirectly considered governance, that is, which kinds of rules should apply in on-line forums and how those rules should be enforced. Consider once again the case of Bungle's behavior in the LambdaMOO community, which caused us to ask what kinds of decision-making powers its members had in determining whether and how Bungle should be punished. Can we simply extend existing rules that apply in physical communities to virtual communities and forums? Or do we need at least some new rules? These questions broach the larger question as to what kind of political structure should be established in cyberspace. Many authors believe that cyberspace should be developed and governed in accordance with democratic principles and values.

What is the relationship between democracy and the Internet? Is the Internet an inherently democratic medium? Does it enhance democracy? Should it be used to spread democracy and democratic ideals? Deborah Johnson (2000) points out that claims involving the connection between the Internet and democracy tend to be made in three different ways: Some authors claim that the Internet is an inherently democratic technology; others claim that the Internet tends to facilitate or even enhance democracy; still others claim that because democratic values are at stake in the cyberspace policies we adopt, we should develop the Internet along democratic principles. I believe that a fourth claim—that is, the Internet should be used to promote democracy and democratic ideals—also needs to be examined. We limit our discussion of the relationship between the Internet and democracy to two questions:

A. Does the Internet facilitate democracy and democratic ideals?

B. Should the Internet be used as a tool to promote democracy?

Notice that whereas question (A) is descriptive, (B) is normative. We begin with (A).

11.2.1 Does the Internet Facilitate Democracy?

Some authors who claim that cyberspace favors democracy and democratic ideals point to the Internet as an open forum in which ideas can generally be communicated freely and easily. Recall Gordon Graham's claim, in Section 11.1.3, that the Internet has provided individuals with greater choice and freedom in joining communities. Values involving freedom, choice, openness, etc., certainly seem to favor democratic ideals; however, other authors have seen the relationship between cybertechnology and democracy differently. Richard Sclove (1995), for instance, believes that technologies—and by implication, Internet technology—tend to undermine, rather than facilitate, democracy and community life. Arguably, there is truth in both positions, and Cass Sunstein (2002) suggests that the Internet has both democracy-enhancing and democracy-threatening aspects.

Sunstein believes that the Internet enhances democracy by providing greater access to information at a lower cost, but at the same time Sunstein worries that deliberative democracy, the process of rationally debating issues in a public forum, may suffer irreparable harm because the Internet can filter information. People using software filters will not be inclined to gather new information that might broaden their views but will instead, Sunstein believes, use information available to them on the Internet to reinforce their existing prejudices.

We can reconstruct Sunstein's argument as follows:

1. Because individuals use filtering schemes that provide them with information that
   a. reinforces ideas that they already hold and
   b. screens out novel information and different points of view; and
2. because an increasing number of people get their information only from the Internet,
3. the Internet will likely
   c. insulate more and more people from exposure to new ideas as well as to ideas that may question or conflict with their own;
   d. lead to greater isolation and polarization among groups;
   e. encourage extremism and radicalism rather than fostering compromise and moderation; and
   f. reduce the need for the traditional give-and-take process in resolving differences in a public forum.
4. Therefore, behavior facilitated by the Internet tends to undermine deliberative democracy and corresponding democratic ideals.

Not everyone agrees with Sunstein's conclusion. Thomas Ulen (2001), for example, is not convinced that the "net effect" of the Internet on democracy is "anywhere close to negative." Ulen also believes that even if Sunstein's analysis is correct so far, Sunstein fails to consider that the Internet is changing very rapidly and that, in the long term, these changes could have a positive impact for deliberative democracy. If Sunstein is correct, however, there are good reasons to be skeptical that the Internet necessarily facilitates democracy and democratic values. On the other hand, we have seen that it promotes democratic ideals such as openness, freedom, access to information, and so forth, and it facilitates communication in ways not possible in the pre-Internet era.

11.2.2   Should the Internet Be Used to Promote Democracy and Democratic Ideals?

We have focused on whether the Internet facilitates and possibly strengthens democratic values and goals or whether it undermines them. We have seen that while that while certain aspects of Internet technology threaten democracy, at least in its deliberative sense, others enhance democratic ideals and goals. So we can question the claim that the Internet should be used as a tool to promote and spread democracy, and we can begin by noting that democracy, when compared to alternative forms of government, seems an attractive political structure and, arguably, one of the fairest. In fact, Gordon Graham (1999) points out that it is difficult to get people, especially in the Western world, to engage in a serious debate about the merits of democracy. Entertaining the question "Is democracy a good thing?" he remarks, "So powerful are the presuppositions of the present age that it is difficult to persuade people to take [this question] seriously and approach it in the spirit of critical inquiry." Graham correctly notes that democracy, and its corresponding democratic ideal, has won "almost universal and largely unquestioning acceptance." It is worth noting, however, that political theorists and philosophers have not always regarded democracy as the best—or even as an adequate—form of government. In the *Republic*, Plato was highly critical of democratic government and viewed it as a form of mob rule in which important decisions could be made by a citizenry that typically was not well-informed on matters involving the state. And in the nineteenth century, John Stuart Mill also questioned whether democracy was the ideal government. Let us assume, for the sake of argument, that democracy is superior to alternative political structures. We can still ask whether the Internet should be used to advance democratic ideals and goals.

Defending the view that all technological decisions should attend primarily to strengthening democracy, Richard Sclove (1995) presents the foundations of a strong argument for why the Internet should be used to promote democracy, claiming that democracy provides the "necessary circumstances for deciding freely and fairly" which considerations must be taken into account in decision making. But we have also considered how Internet technology poses a serious threat to deliberative democracy. Gordon Graham (1999) has suggested that the Internet might, perhaps unwittingly, strengthen the "worst aspects" of democracy, because Internet technology facilitates

  i.   political and social *fragmentation*
 ii.   *irrationality* (i.e., irrational prejudice in "direct democracies")
iii.   *powerlessness* (in "representative democracies")

We briefly examine each aspect.

11.2.2.1 Political and Social Fragmentation

How does the Internet facilitate social fragmentation, and why is that problematic? We have already seen how the Internet can isolate individuals, insulate groups, and increase group polarization. We also have seen how the Internet can filter information, entrenching existing ideas and reinforcing prejudice and hatred rather than encouraging exposure to new ideas. The Internet also fragments society by facilitating the formation of groups who depart from the mainstream perspectives of a cohesive society. An analogy involving television news programming in physical space might help us appreciate how easily social fragmentation can occur and why it can be problematic.

▶ **CASE ILLUSTRATION:** Viewing News Programs from Multiple Ideological Perspectives

Until the advent of cable programming, American television viewers relied primarily on the three major networks for the evening news reports. Even though the program formats varied slightly and even though different anchors delivered the news to viewers, all three presented "mainstream" news reporting that satisfied certain standards of accuracy and credibility before the networks would broadcast it. At times, the members of political groups may have been annoyed with, or possibly even offended by, the way that a particular story was presented, but the news reports were generally descriptive, or factual. Some news programs also included commentaries, usually toward the end of the program, in which the commentator expressed an opinion, but there was a clear line between "factual" reporting and personal opinion.

Now you can select a news program that fits best with and reinforces your ideology. For example, consider a news report of hostilities between Israelis and Palestinians. If supporters of Israel do not like the way the story is reported on an American news network, and if they have cable or satellite access to Israeli television, they can tune into an Israeli station for their news. Similarly, if Palestinian supporters dislike the American media's coverage, and if they have cable access to an Arab news network such as Al-Jazeera, they can choose to view the news story as an Arab station broadcasts it. On the one hand, these options provide supporters of both sides in this conflict with greater choices and seemingly greater freedom. On the other hand, these options increase fragmentation in American society, which already comprises so many diverse groups.

We can apply a similar analogy to news reports of domestic political issues in the United States. Conservatives and liberals can each interact in on-line forums and visit web sites that promote the political views of these groups. Of course we could object at this point, noting that prior to the Internet, people subscribed to newspapers and magazines that were labeled as either radically liberal or radically conservative and therefore filtered in their ideology. But it is more difficult to filter information in physical space because people in most physical communities encounter individuals with ideological perspectives different from their own even when they seek out only those who share their belief systems. In on-line communities, however, it is possible for individuals to be in contact with only those people who share their ideological beliefs.

▶ **SCENARIO:** "Personalized Electronic Newspapers"

Richard Epstein (2000) envisions a scenario, set in the year 2028, where our personal (electronic) agents prepare a personalized electronic newspaper for us each morning. The "newspaper" contains information about only those topics that we, individually, select, and the information is presented to us from an ideological perspective that we choose. In other words, our electronic agents have been carefully instructed to filter information to meet our specifications and tastes. Contrast this kind of personalized newspaper of the future, which Nicholas Negroponte (1995) refers to as *The Daily Me*, with conventional newspapers.

Epstein describes a (hypothetical) party in which the guests, all of whom subscribe to personalized newspapers, assemble around the dinner table and soon discover that they have no common vocabulary, no common shared memories, and no common conceptual framework in which to share their conversation. One guest reads only news about sporting events, while another reads only about the "virtual economy." And even if two or more guests happen to read news reports about the same general topic, the perspectives from which the information is disseminated to them via their electronic agents is so radically different that they still would be unlikely to find any common ground for conversation. Not surprisingly, there is complete silence at the dinner party.

Epstein invites us to consider how we could maintain a democracy in a world with no shared vocabulary of civic concepts and principles. The character in Epstein's story who describes the conversation at the dinner party laments:

> We have the frightening proliferation of extremists groups who have their own private vocabularies and ideologies. These groups have become extremely isolated. They do not receive the feedback that they need nor are they under appropriate scrutiny.

Epstein asks how the "public square," which has been fragmented into "tens of thousands of highly specialized communities that do not communicate with one another," can be recreated. We next consider some ways that political and social fragmentation contribute to what Graham (1999) calls the "problem of irrationality" in democracy.

11.2.2.2 Democracy and the Problem of Irrationality

In some respects, the problem of irrationality overlaps with and is reinforced by the problem of social fragmentation. We have seen that people can join extremist political groups, both in cyberspace and in physical space, and we have seen that these groups often filter information in ways not acceptable in "mainstream forums." On the one hand, to join these groups is to exercise one's democratic freedoms and choices. On the other hand, doing so can fragment democracy and undermine the possibility of larger group cohesiveness. Although a plurality of perspectives and values can be consistent with democratic ideals, nonreflective and prejudiced views endorsed by groups can also undermine conventional standards for separating rational perspectives from irrational ones.

Although the Internet might help spread political opinions, Graham believes that it will not necessarily promote greater "rational evaluation" of these political opinions by people who are exposed to them. Sunstein also suggests that the Internet, because of the kinds of insulation and polarization it facilitates, can encourage entrenched prejudices that are often irrational. Consider that thus far there has been a much stronger tendency for Internet users to spread the opinions they already have rather than to use the Internet for debate with other users over which views are most rational and beneficial. From this, Graham concludes that the Internet may increase the problem of irrationality by putting the "rational exercise of political judgment" on a par with "prejudiced and irrational political choices."

Graham also suggests that the Internet can increase the level of irrationality found in many "direct democracies." For example, he suggests that because the Internet increases irrationality and social fragmentation, it facilitates the worst aspects of a direct democracy. To understand force of Graham's insight, we need to distinguish between *direct* and indirect, or *representative*, democracies.

To appreciate the differences between the two forms of democracy, consider the government of the United States, which is a representative, not a direct, democracy; that is, American voters elect delegates who, in turn, cast electoral votes for the nation's president. In the 2000 presidential election some voters were astonished to find out that a presidential candidate could actually receive more direct votes from American voters than his opponent and still lose the election. Of course, this is possible only in a representative democracy. Because the election results were contested, Americans from both major political parties engaged in a fresh debate over the political advantages and disadvantages of a representative vs. a direct democracy.

Some who recognize the historical necessity of a establishing a representative democracy in the eighteenth century because of prevailing conditions involving education, transportation, etc., during that period now question whether a representative democracy still makes sense in the twenty-first century. Arguably, average American citizens are now better educated and better informed than they were two centuries ago. (Conversely, one might also make the case that many of our current congressional representatives lack the talents of virtue and intellect that our founders thought so important for leaders to govern effectively.) Perhaps most importantly, technology and modes of transportation have changed so drastically in the past two centuries that many of the original conditions that lent support for a representative democracy in the United States may no longer hold.

Advocates of representative democracy, however, argue that there are still advantages in a representational form of government. For one thing, representative democracy frees up the ordinary citizenry from many of the obligations of running a government; they are not required to understand the nuances of legislation and policies, since their elected representatives do that for them. Also consider that in the United States, a representative democracy can prevent states with large populations from having considerably more political influence on matters involving national policy and law than states with smaller populations.

Although some political analysts continue to defend the virtues of a representative democracy over a direct one, many ordinary citizens believe that their votes should count directly. We take no position on this debate here; rather we use it to illustrate tensions in the debate over how best to set up a democratic government in cyberspace One way to view cyberspace is to think of it as a newly formed nation in need of political structure. Should we simply carry over the existing structure with its current form of government? Or should we reassess that structure and consider applying a different type of democracy or even an entirely new political system? If you were going to form a new government for a brand new nation, which kind of democracy would you prefer to establish?

As we noted, many people assume that a direct democracy is superior to a representative one. Past presidential candidate Ross Perot envisioned an "electronic town hall" where voters could not only elect their candidates but also vote directly on bills that would otherwise be debated by congressional representatives. But we have also seen that direct democracy can lead to irrationality and prejudice rather than a forum in which issues are rationally debated.

11.2.2.3 The Problem of Powerlessness in Representative Democracies

If direct democracies have negative characteristics, then there are good reasons for not using the Internet to promote them, in which case perhaps the Internet should be used to promote representative democracy. But should it? Graham suggests that although the Internet could be used to promote representative democracy, doing so could concentrate more power in the hands of representatives instead of ordinary citizens. Consider that elected political leaders tend to have both greater resources and the ability to use the Internet more skillfully than most ordinary citizens, so that they can use the Internet to maintain their power. Thus, using the Internet to promote representative democracy can be problematic.

Graham believes that the Internet is more likely to increase social fragmentation than to enhance political and social consensus. If his assessment is accurate, then the Internet could easily be used to promote the worst aspects of both direct and indirect democracies conceivably leading, as he suggests, to "moral anarchy." So we need to think seriously about whether to use the Internet to spread democracy in either its direct or representative forms.

TABLE 11-2   Considerations for Using the Internet to Promote Democracy

Advantages	Disadvantages
Empowers individuals by giving them choices regarding on-line communities	Increases social fragmentation and discourages rational debate
Promotes individual freedom and decision making	Increases irrationality and prejudice (in direct democracies)
Gives individuals a voice in governance issues in cyberspace	Increases powerlessness for individuals (in representative democracies)

Table 11-2 summarizes advantages and disadvantages of using the Internet to promote democracy and democratic ideals.

▶ 11.3 VIRTUAL ENVIRONMENTS

We have examined issues involving on-line democracy and on-line communities; on-line communities are often referred to as *virtual communities*. They are *virtual* because they exist in cyberspace, usually equated with *virtual space*. But what is virtual space? In contrast to physical space, or geographical space, virtual space is a range of computer-generated environments that could not exist without computers. These environments, in turn, include virtual communities as well as virtual reality (VR) games and applications.

Although we now have a working definition of a virtual space or a virtual environment, we have yet to define "virtual." This term can be used in three senses. Sometimes it is contrasted with "real," as in distinguishing virtual objects from real ones. At other times the term is contrasted with "actual," as when a person says that she has "virtually finished" her project (i.e., she has not actually, or literally, finished it, but she believes that for practical purposes, she has finished it). The term "virtual" can also express feeling "as if" physically present in a situation, as when you are conversing with a friend in an electronic chat room or on a telephone; even though you could be literally thousands of miles away from each other, the sense that you are interacting in "real time" makes you feel "as if" you are both in the same room. Contrast this experience with radio communications, where messages can only be transmitted in one direction at a time. We should keep these three different senses of "virtual" in mind as we examine ethical aspects of virtual environments, including VR technologies.

11.3.1   Defining Virtual Reality and VR Technologies

Philip Brey (1999) defines virtual reality, or VR, as "a three-dimensional interactive computer-generated environment that incorporates a first-person perspective." Notice three important features in Brey's definition of VR:

- interactivity,
- a three-dimensional environment,
- a first-person perspective.

How does this distinguish VR from other computer-mediated environments? First, *interactivity* requires that users navigate and manipulate the represented environment. Because a *three-dimensional environment* is required in VR, neither text-based computer-generated environments nor two-dimensional graphic environments will qualify. As Brey points out, a *first-person perspective* requires a single locus from which the environment is perceived and interacted with; the first-person perspective also requires an "immersion in" the virtual world rather than simply an "experience of" that world as an "object that can be (partially) controlled by the outside."

We can distinguish between Brey's notion of VR technologies and applications in the strict sense of VR, and a more broadly defined notion of "virtual environment." Recall our discussion of on-line communities, and note that these can be two-dimensional or three-dimensional environments. For example, LambdaMOO would be considered a two-dimensional environment in that it was a text-based forum. So LambdaMOO would not qualify as a VR environment as Brey defines it. As an on-line community, however, it is a type of virtual environment. We use this broader sense of virtual environment in our analysis of ethical aspects of virtual behavior.

Figure 11-1 illustrates some manifestations of virtual environments.

In Section 11.1.3 we noted that many actions that are considered morally objectionable in the physical world can be performed easily in VR environments, including on-line communities. For example, some VR games enable users to engage in morally objectionable acts, including murder, mutilation, and torture, in virtual space. We next consider some ethical implications of this kind of virtual behavior.

11.3.2 Ethical Aspects of Virtual Reality Technologies and Virtual Environments

Are ethical issues involving virtual behavior different from those associated with morally controversial acts displayed on television or played out in board games? Consider that television programs sometimes display violent acts and some board games allow participants to act out morally controversial roles—how are VR applications different? Brey points out that in VR applications, users are actively engaged, while television viewers are passive. VR users are not spectators; rather, they are more like actors, as are board game players, who

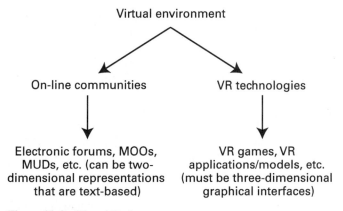

Figure 11-1   Virtual Environments

also act out roles in certain board games. This common feature suggests that there might not be much difference between the two kinds of games; however, Brey notes that VR applications, unlike board games, simulate the world in a way that gives it a much greater appearance of reality. And in VR, the player has a first-person perspective of what it is like to perform certain acts and roles, including some that are criminal or immoral, or both.

Is it wrong to perform acts in VR environments that would be considered immoral in real life? On the one hand, we can argue that no one can be physically harmed in a virtual world; therefore, any harm caused in the virtual realm is not "real harm" but only *virtual harm*. In our discussion of logical fallacies in Chapter 3, we saw that this reasoning commits the *virtuality fallacy*. Earlier in this chapter, we saw that "virtual" is ambiguous in at least three ways. We noted that sometimes "virtual" is contrasted with "real" in a way that might suggest that a "virtual harm" is equivalent to an "unreal harm." Because a harm caused in a virtual environment might not result in physical harm to a "flesh-and-blood" person, however, it doesn't follow that the harm caused is not real. Consider that an insulting e-mail message you receive consists of electronic bits that may ultimately reside in virtual space, yet the harm you suffer by that message is no less real than the harm you suffer by the same message written on paper in a letter received via the physical mail (postal) system. The LambdaMOO incident, described earlier, can help us see why harm caused in virtual space is not itself limited to virtual characters in a virtual environment.

11.3.3   Two Arguments for Evaluating Virtual Harm

Recall the case illustration we presented in Section 11.1.3 involving a rape in cyberspace. That incident, involving LambdaMOO, occurred in a forum that is not a three-dimensional VR application. However, we noted that the ethical aspects of behavior in virtual environments apply to (two-dimensional) on-line communities as well.

Why is Bungle's behavior in LambdaMOO morally objectionable? After all, it was not a "real" rape, and it did not result in physical harm to any "flesh-and-blood" individuals. Brey (1999) believes that we can use two arguments to show why it is wrong to engage in immoral acts in VR environments: One is the "argument from moral development," and the other is the "argument from psychological harm."

To illustrate the argument from moral development, Brey suggests that we can extend an argument advanced by Immanuel Kant for the treatment of animals to the treatment of virtual characters. Kant argued that even if we have no direct moral obligation to treat animals kindly, we should, because our treating animals kindly can influence our development of moral attitudes and behaviors for treating human beings. Similarly, then, the way we treat virtual characters may ultimately affect the way we treat real-life characters—raping virtual characters in virtual space, or even viewing such a rape, could desensitize us to the act of rape itself as it affects flesh-and-blood individuals in physical space.

The argument from psychological harm suggests that the way we refer to characters who represent a particular group can cause harm to actual members of the group. Consider a cartoon depicting a woman being raped: Actual (flesh-and-blood) women may suffer psychological harm from seeing, or possibly even knowing about this cartoon image, even though none of them, as flesh-and-blood individuals, is being raped, either physically or as represented by the cartoon. Extending this analogy to virtual space, it would follow that the "rape" of a virtual woman in a virtual environment such as a MOO or aVR game can also cause psychological harm to flesh-and-blood women.

11.3.4 Misrepresentation and Bias in Virtual Environments

Brey argues that we can analyze two aspects of VR environments from an ethical perspective. We have already examined some problems (such as the LambdaMOO incident) involving what Brey calls the *behavioral*, or interactive, aspect of VR. The other ethical aspect of VR involves the ways that virtual characters and objects are *represented* in virtual environments.

Problems can result from both *misrepresentation* and *bias* in virtual environments. Brey believes that misrepresentation ranges from cases in which there is no correspondence between the virtual entity and its corresponding physical (or nonvirtual) entity to cases in which the correspondence is almost, but not fully, accurate. When a VR application does not accurately portray all of the characteristics or features of the physical (or nonvirtual) entities represented—whether by intention or as a result of an oversight—the application *mis*represents reality.

Misrepresenting entities with respect to descriptive features, however, can be distinguished from (otherwise accurate) representations that favor certain values or interests over others. Brey calls the latter "biased" representation; it can result from the choice of model. For example, *softbots* (or "bots") and *avatars* can display human qualities. Paul Ford (2001) defines bots as "virtual reality robots" and avatars as "graphical forms that act as on-line embodiments." Bots and avatars appearing in a VR application could represent a member of a racial or minority group; even though the representation may be structurally accurate, if the bot is used in a way that suggests a racial stereotype, it can fail to accurately portray a member of the racial group. Ford considers a bot that represents an African-American "shoe shine boy." Note here that the bot does not misrepresent any physical characteristics of the particular African-American represented, yet the depiction is also a biased caricature of African-Americans.

Brey argues that VR model builders are morally obligated to avoid both misrepresentation and biased representation in designing VR applications. Extending an analytical scheme developed by Richard Mason (1994), Brey suggests that developers of VR systems need to both recognize who the stakeholders are in those systems and take into account their values and interests as they develop VR models. Mason's scheme works well for understanding and analyzing moral responsibility issues involved in developing VR systems that misrepresent or bias stakeholders; however, Brey notes that the locus of moral responsibility for the unethical behavior of individuals in virtual environments (such as in LambdaMOO) is more difficult to pinpoint. Perhaps the responsibility for behavior-related moral issues spans both (a) users who abuse and misuse VR environments by engaging in morally objectionable acts and (b) developers of VR systems who design applications that facilitate morally questionable forms of virtual conduct.

Figure 11-2 summarizes Brey's scheme.

We have examined positive and negative features of virtual environments, including both VR games and virtual, or on-line, communities. We have also seen that while virtual communities empower individuals by giving them choices regarding which communities they can decide to join, these communities can also have a darker side (illustrated in the

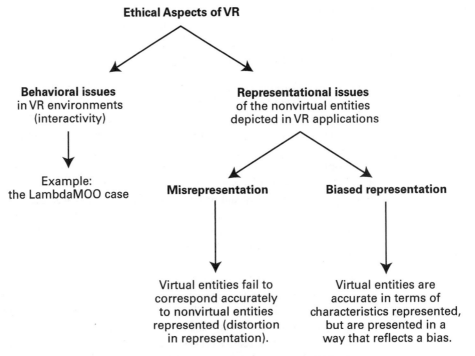

Figure 11-2 Brey's Scheme for Analyzing Ethical Issues in Virtual Environments

incident involving LambdaMOO). Thus far, we have considered the social impact of virtual environments. It is also worth examining the implications of cybertechnology for personal identity as well as community.

▶ 11.4 PERSONAL IDENTITY AND CYBERTECHNOLOGY

Some social scientists have analyzed the effect that computers and cybertechnology have had on personal identity. One of the earliest cases involved a male psychologist in an online forum; his alter ego (or "cyberego") was a woman who had become crippled as a result of an automobile accident. Under this alias "she" joined an on-line forum for disabled persons and quickly struck up romantic exchanges with a few of the forum's members. When participants eventually learned "her" true identity, they were outraged. Some felt manipulated by the psychologist's use of a fraudulent identity, and others complained that they were victims of "gender fraud" and "mind rape." Lindsy Van Gelder (1991) describes this incident as "the strange case of the electronic lover."

In one sense, the "electronic lover" case could be examined under the category of online communities (discussed in Section 11.1) because of the impact of the psychologist's behavior on the electronic forum and its members. Yet we can also reflect on the implications this case has for personal identity; for example, was the male psychologist simply acting out his "would-be personality" in cyberspace instead of in physical space, as some might suggest? Or does cyberspace make a difference for understanding the identities that can emerge in different on-line forums?

11.4.1   The Computer as a Medium of Self-expression and Self-discovery

Shery Turkle (1984) suggests that a computer can be a model for analyzing and constructing one's identity. She also suggests that the computer has become a medium through which people can discover their personal identity. Turkle believes that computers provide a context in which individuals can try out different cognitive styles and different methods of problem solving to ultimately discover which style or method they prefer. Turkle argues that as people develop their own unique style of computing, the computational environment becomes an extension of themselves, in much the same way that their manner of dress is an extension of their personality. In this sense, she believes, the computer is a medium of self-expression as well as self-discovery.

Turkle's early studies focused mainly on the role that stand-alone, or non-networked, computers played in the relationship between personal identity and computers. Noting that computers have evolved from "calculators to simulators," or from calculating machines to a networked communications medium, Turkle's more recent research focuses on interactions involving networked computers; in particular, her studies examine how behavior in networked environments significantly impacts our relationships with our "selves" as we conceive them. To illustrate several of her key points, she uses examples involving MUDs (Multiuser Dimensions).

What are MUDs? MUDs are similar to MOOs (defined in Section 11.1.3) in that they are simulated or virtual environments in which members participate. Both forums enable users to construct "rooms" in cyberspace and to converse and interact with others in those rooms. In our LambdaMOO case we saw how objectionable behavior in MOO environments can raise ethical concerns; similar issues arise in MUDs as well. In our discussion of LambdaMOO, we saw the virtual characters assumed cyberidentities such as "Bungle," "Legba," and "Starsinger"; characters that participate in MUDs also assume virtual (or MUD) identities.

11.4.2   "MUD Selves" and Distributed Personal Identities

In MUDs and MOOs, participants can construct new identities and selves. Turkle (1995) maintains that as people participate, or "play characters," in MUDs, they "construct new selves" through social interaction. As Turkle notes, however, "Mud selves" are constituted by and dependent upon interaction with machines; if the machine is taken away, the "Mud self" ceases to exist.

Users participate in MUDs anonymously; they are known only by the names of their MUD character or characters. In MUDs, users can *be* (i.e., represent themselves textually or graphically as) characters as different from their "actual selves" as they like; the obese can be slender, and the old can be young. Turkle points out that MUD users can also express multiple and often unexplored aspects of the self, and they can "play with their identity by trying out new roles." In different MUDs the same physical person can represent himself as a seductive woman, a macho man, or even a creature of unspecified gender; so one's identity on the computer can be, Turkle suggests, the "sum of one's distributed presence."

Individuals assuming different identities or different gender roles is hardly unique to computers and the world of MUDs; transvestites in physical space can selectively represent themselves as member of the opposite sex in contexts of their choosing. Perhaps you are familiar with the movie and, later, Broadway musical *Victor, Victoria* in which a woman pretends to be a man playing the part of a woman. But gender-role reversals in the physical world do not seem to have the same significant social impact as they do in cyberspace. Turkle notes that since traditional theater and role-playing games take place in physical space, thy enable one to "step in and out of character." MUDs, on the other hand, offer parallel identities and parallel lives, and this parallelism encourages treating off-screen and on-screen lives as equally real.

Turkle notes that some of her research subjects experience their world through interactions in "multiple windows"; real life (or RL) is considered by some MUDders as simply "one window." One of Turkle's research subjects, whom she refers to as Doug, remarked: "RL isn't usually my best window." Turkle points out that in computer screens we can project ourselves into dramas in which we are at once producer, director, and star; computer screens have become the "new location for acting out our fantasies." So we can ask, as Turkle does, "Are we living life *on* the screen or *in* the screen?"

▶ 11.5 OUR SENSE OF SELF IN THE CYBERERA

We have considered arguments that behavior in computer-mediated environments has affected, and possibly even altered, the personal identity of some individuals. In this section, we focus on the question as to the more general impact of cybertechnology on our *sense of self*, especially in our relation to nature and the universe. Social scientists often describe three major epochs in human civilization: the agricultural age, the industrial age, and the information age. Each has been characterized by revolutionary technological breakthroughs in gaining control over nature.

At the dawn of the agricultural age, people who had previously led nomadic lives developed technology that enabled them to control the production of crops by controlling elements of nature rather than conforming to nature's seasonal rotations, which often required migrating to different locations. In the industrial age, humans harnessed steam power. With steam power people were no longer compelled to set up communities close to large bodies of water that provided the much of their energy. We have now entered the information age, the third great epoch. Citing Alvin Toffler (1980), some also refer to this period as the "third wave." In this section, we consider the impact that our shift to this third major wave of technological development has for the way we conceive of ourselves as human beings.

Scientific discoveries resulting from technological innovations have deeply affected our sense of self in relation to nature and the universe. The invention of the telescope made possible discoveries by Copernicus, Galileo, and other Renaissance scientists that shifted our view of the universe from geocentric (or earth-centered) to heliocentric (or sun-centered). This dramatic shift in worldview compelled humans to come to terms with the fact that they inhabit a proportionately small and relatively insignificant planet, which is not even at the center of our own solar system. Mary Williams (1997) considers three discoveries that have had a significant impact on our sense of self in relation to the universe:

> The first such milestone, a great (and greatly humbling) challenge to our sense of human beings as uniquely important, came when the Copernican revolution established that Earth, the human home, was not at the center of the universe. The second milestone was Charles Darwin's conclusion that emergence of Homo sapiens was . . . the result of evolution from lower species by the process of natural selection. The third milestone resulted from the work of Karl Marx and Sigmund Freud, which showed intellectual, social, and individual creativity to be the result

of nonrational (unconscious) libidinal or economic forces—not, as has been believed, the products of the almost god-like powers of the human mind.

As a result of these three milestones, Williams concludes, we have a much humbler view of our place in the universe than our ancestors did. The interesting question for us, of course, is whether computerization and cybertechnology might join the other milestone events in deeply changing the way we see ourselves.

11.5.1 Cybertechnology as a Defining Technology

Although cybertechnology may be the latest in a series of technologies to have a significant influence on the way human beings have come to see themselves, it is not, as we have noted, the first technology to do so. J. David Bolter (1984) claims that many people in Western cultures have come to see themselves in terms of what he calls a *defining technology*, which "develops links, metaphorical or otherwise, with a culture's science, philosophy, or literature." As such, defining technologies have been used by philosophers and humanists to "define" both human beings and their universe in a given age or time period. Bolter describes three ages in Western culture when humans have used a defining technology: the ancient Greek world, the Renaissance, and the contemporary computer age.

Bolter notes that in the classical Greek world, philosophers described nature as an organic, rotating system. Rotating technologies, such as the drop spindle or the potter's wheel, were used to describe the universe, even though technologies such as masonry and woodworking were more important to daily life during that period. For example, Plato compared the created universe to a spindle. Bolter refers to anyone who endorses this view of nature and humanity as "Plato's man."

In the early seventeenth century, many humanists constructed metaphors comparing various important concepts (such as the workings of the natural world, or the relationship between humanity and the universe) with the weight-driven clock. Again, there were more important technologies at that time for day-to-day living, such as the moldboard plow and crop rotation. The clock and its intricate mechanisms of gears and levers, however, captivated humanists and scientists such as philosopher Renè Descartes (1596–1650), who employed a clock metaphor in his notion of a mechanistic universe that obeyed the laws of mathematics. Bolter refers to anyone who subscribes to this worldview as "Descartes's man" or "Cartesian man."

In the twentieth century we became fascinated with computer technology. Again, other technologies such as electricity, indoor plumbing, automobiles, etc., have arguably been more important for day-to-day living than computers, but philosophers and scientists tend to use computer and computing metaphors to describe humans and their relationship to the universe. Twentieth-century computer science pioneer Alan Turing was one of the first to articulate interesting connections between the computer and the human mind as a manipulator of logical symbols. Acknowledging Turing's insight, Bolter uses the phrase "Turing's man" to depict those who subscribe to the computer as the defining metaphor of our age. Turing's man sees nature as *information* and humans (or human brains) as *information-processing engines*. We examine Turing's contribution to the field of artificial intelligence in Section 11.5.2.

To support Bolter's thesis that we see ourselves more and more in terms of the computer, we have only to reflect on the language we use to describe ourselves. When, for example, psychologists speak of input and output states of the brain, or of the brain's hardware and software, they exemplify Turing's men. When cognitive psychologists study the mind's algorithm for searching long-term memory, or when linguists treat human language as if it were a programming code, they too are Turing's men. Consider too that psychologists and cognitive scientists who suggest that the human mind is like a computer in that it encodes, stores, retrieves, and processes information are also Turing's men (Bolter 1984).

Not only do we think of ourselves in computer terms, but we also now describe many objects and events in our environment in the language of computer technology. Consider the economist who draws up "input-output diagrams" of the nation's business; the person who describes her automobile, which cannot be used because it is in the repair shop, as "down"; the manager running a business meeting who requests that a certain discussion should be taken "off-line"; the psychiatrist who reports that a patient referred to his spouse as a "peripheral"; and a cartoon portraying an expectant mother impatiently complaining that she has to wait nine months to "download her baby." These uses of computer language confirm Bolter's point that we increasingly see ourselves in terms of a computer metaphor.

11.5.2   Recent Developments in Artificial Intelligence

The view that only humans have intelligence and are rational can be challenged on two fronts. First, research in animal intelligence suggests that many primates, dolphins, and whales demonstrate skills we typically count as rational while many humans cannot demonstrate these same skills. Second, work in artificial intelligence (AI) and cognitive science shows that computers can exhibit certain forms of rational activity. In fact, questions that have surfaced in AI research cause some philosophers and scientists to reconsider our definitions of rationality, intelligence, knowledge, and learning.

Research and development in AI also question the nature of consciousness; for example, cognitive scientists now ask whether consciousness is a uniquely human attribute or whether it might be an *emergent property*—that is, capable of "emerging" in "highly intelligent" AI systems. Stanley Kubrick's classic 1967 film *2001: A Space Odyssey* portrays a computer named HAL with higher-order thinking functions resembling human consciousness. In addition to performing ordinary computational tasks, HAL engages in sophisticated conversations with members of the space ship's crew, plays chess, and criticizes art. To take control of the space ship from HAL, the sole surviving member of the crew removes the logic components of HAL's higher-order ("mental") functions: HAL is forced to undergo a sort of "lobotomy." Of course, HAL is merely science fiction, but then AI has progressed considerably since HAL's film debut in 1967.

Today, cognitive scientists and AI researchers working with *neural network (computer) systems* are on the verge of modeling higher-order thinking in these systems. Suppose that we reach general agreement that human consciousness can be understood as an "emergent property" and that conscious activity—similar to that of humans—emerges whenever a sufficient number of neurons (or "connection strengths" in neural network computer systems) are present. If this were to happen, consider the implications for our sense of self.

Are computers indeed capable of exhibiting human-like intelligence? In 1950, computer science pioneer Alan Turing confidently predicted that by the year 2000 computers would be able to pass a test, which has come to be called the *Turing Test*, demonstrating their intelligence. Turing envisioned a person engaged in a conversation with a computer (located in a room not visible to the human), unable to tell whether he or she was conversing with another human or with a machine. And while most AI experts would concede that Turing's prophecy has not yet been fully realized, few working in AI doubt that computers can now exhibit some form of intelligence and in some cases, emulate aspects of human rationality. In 1997 an IBM computer program called *Deep Blue* defeated Gary Kasparov, then reigning champion, in the competition for the world chess title.

Unfortunately, an in-depth discussion of the current debate in AI regarding the question of machine intelligence is beyond the scope of this chapter; however, let us assume that computers possess some intelligence. Because historically many people have believed that intelligence is a distinguishing characteristic for humans, we can see how developments in AI raise profound questions for our notions of self and what it means to be human.

Before concluding this section, we consider implications of softbot, or "bot," technology. Bots in the form of avatars (defined in Section 11.3.4) and personal digital assistants have already begun to appear on computer screens and are designed to assist users in organizing their work schedules, reminding them of important scheduled meetings, arranging travel, and so forth. Even though they are virtual entities, some bots exhibit human-like features when they appear on computer screens and can easily be confused with representations of actual flesh-and-blood characters that can also appear on computer screens. Can we tell the difference between them? Consider that some bots exhibit characteristics and stereotypic traits associated with certain professions. For example, a bot designed to interact with other bots, as well as with humans as a "negotiation agent," may have the persona of a broker, and after interacting with your personal bot (or human-like, digital agent) over a period of time, you may sense that you are dealing with an actual person.

At present, we can only speculate about the implications that AI bots, as well as other "intelligent entities" of the future, will have for our sense of what it means to be a human being. Should we proceed with developments in AI, realizing that we may create intelligences vastly superior to our own? Perhaps John Weckert (2002) articulates this concern best when he asks:

> Can we, or do we want to, live with artificial *intelligences*? We can happily live with fish that swim better than we do, with dogs that hear better, hawks that see and fly better, and so on, but things that can reason better seem to be in a different and altogether more worrying category . . . What would such [developments mean for] our view of what it is to be human?

11.5.3 Will We Need to Expand Our Sphere of Moral Consideration?

We have examined AI in respect to its impact on our sense of self and on what it means to be human. AI research and development raises two questions about moral responsibility: (a) Should we develop intelligent agents and entities? and (b) If we do, what are our moral responsibilities to them? We examine question (a) in Section 11.6.3, where we discuss future directions in computing and the corresponding impact for computer professionals. Here we focus on question (b).

Will we expand our current domain of moral consideration to include artificial creatures and artificial objects? To understand this question, we first consider (i) which things deserve moral consideration, and (ii) why they warrant it. Prior to the twentieth century, ethicists and lay persons in the Western world generally assumed that only human beings deserved ethical consideration; all other entities—animals, trees, natural objects, etc.—were merely resources for humans to use (and abuse) as they saw fit. In other words, humans viewed these resources simply as something to be used and disposed of as they saw fit, because they believed they had no moral obligations toward these "resources."

By the mid-twentieth century, however, the assumption that moral consideration should be granted only to humans had been challenged on two separate fronts. One challenge comes from animal-rights groups, who argue that animals, like humans, are sentient creatures and thus capable of feeling pleasure and pain. Some activists have further argued that we should also grant ethical consideration to animals. In this sense, it would be morally wrong for humans to abuse animals or to treat them simply as resources. On a second front, some environmentalists made an even bolder claim, arguing that we should extend ethical consideration to include "objects," or entities such as trees and plants as well as the entire ecosystem itself. Philosopher Hans Jonas (1984) argued that because modern technologies involving atomic and nuclear power had presented us with tools of destruction that could devastate our planet on a scale never before imaginable, we have to expand our sphere of moral obligation to include "new objects of moral consideration" such as the environment and even abstract objects such as "future generations of humans" who will inherit the planet.

In the past fifty years our thinking about who and what should be included in the sphere of moral obligation has evolved significantly. We have moved from a morality that grants consideration only to human beings to one that at least debates whether animals, land, and yet-to-be-born future generations of humans are granted consideration as well. The question before us is whether there is now or soon will be compelling reasons to once again expand our sphere of moral consideration to include "artificial objects."

Luciano Floridi and J. W. Sanders (2001) have suggested that we need to take seriously whether or not to grant moral consideration to at least certain kinds of "information entities" such as "artificial autonomous agents." Initially, one might find this assertion strange, perhaps even preposterous, but we have already noted that sophisticated electronic agents exhibit a rationality that parallels, and in some cases exceeds, that of humans. If we base the essential criterion for granting moral consideration to humans on the premise that humans are rational entities, and if certain artificial electronics agents and bots are also "rational agents," then we can make a compelling case for granting moral consideration to those artificial agents.

Robots of the future will most likely exhibit sentient, as well as rational characteristics; that is, robots, like humans and animals, will be capable of experiencing sensation and feeling. Perhaps, then, we will need to take criteria in addition to rationality itself into consideration in determining whether to grant at least some degree of moral status to robots of the future.

▶ **SCENARIO:** Artificial Children

The movie *AI* is a story of an artificial boy who is physically indistinguishable from human boys and who is capable of experiencing human-like emotion as well as displaying human-like intelligence. This "boy" needs the love of human parents and displays that need in a way that seems genuine and convincing. He is adopted by human parents, who later abandon him. Does this "boy" deserve any moral consideration? Do the parents who adopted "him" have any clear moral obligations to their "child?"? For example, do they have the right to discard "him" at their convenience? Should such a creature have been developed in the first place?

In one sense, these questions merge with questions about artificial life and so might seem beyond the scope of cyberethics; however, they are relevant because they arise from certain uses of cybertechnology. So ethical questions traditionally associated with distinct categories of applied ethics, such as computer ethics and bioethics, are beginning to blur, and this blurring will likely increase with the convergence of research and development in biotechnology and cybertechnology.

▶ 11.6 FUTURE DIRECTIONS AND ETHICAL CHALLENGES

We have seen that current developments and future directions in AI raise serious questions about human nature and what it means to be a human being, as well as questions about moral responsibility and whether the spheres of moral consideration should be extended to include at least some forms of artificial entities. They also raise questions about the moral obligations of those who manufacture, research, and develop such entities. We now examine ethical challenges likely to arise with developments in nanotechnology and nanocomputers from the perspective of computer professionals engaged in research and development.

11.6.1 What Is Nanotechnology and Why Is It Significant?

Nanotechnology was coined by K. Eric Drexler in the 1980s; it refers to a branch of engineering dedicated to the development of extremely small electronic circuits and mechanical devices, built at the molecular level of matter. Current microelectricomechanical systems (or MEMS), tiny devices such as sensors embedded in conductor chips used in airbag systems to detect collisions, are one step away from the molecular machines envisioned by nanotechnology. Andrew Chen (2002) notes that a primary goal of this technology is to provide us with tools, analogous to what we have at the macroscale, for work at the molecular and atomic levels. Drexler (1991) believes that developments in this field will result in nanoscale computers—no bigger in size than bacteria—called *nanocomputers*.

Nanocomputers can be designed using various architectures; for example, an electronic nanocomputer would operate similarly to present-day computers but differ in size and scale. A *quantum nanocomputer*, on the other hand, would store data in the form of atomic quantum states or spin. John Weckert (2002) points out that quantum computers would be much more powerful than any computing systems available today; he notes that according to one estimate, a quantum computer could be more powerful than all existing computers networked together to perform a single task.

To appreciate the scale of future nanocomputers, imagine a mechanical or electronic device whose dimensions are measured in nanometers (billionths of a meter, or units of 10^{-9} meter). Ralph Merkle (1997) envisions nanocomputers having "mass storage devices that can store more than 100 billion bytes in a volume the size of a sugar cube." He also predicts that these nanoscale computers will be able to "deliver a billion billion instructions per second—a billion times faster than today's desktop computers." Although they are still in an early stage of research and development, some primitive nanodevices have already been tested. In 1989, physicists at the IBM Almaden Laboratory demonstrated the feasibility of development in nanotechnology by manipulating atoms to produce the IBM logo.

Those who advocate continued research in nanoscience and nanotechnology are quick to point out its advantages for both the medical field and the environment. For example, nanoparticles inserted into bodies could diagnose diseases and directly treat diseased cells. Doctors could use nanomachines (or *nanites*) to make microscopic repairs on areas of the body that are difficult to operate on with conventional surgical tools. And nanotechnology tools could better monitor patients' life signs. With respect to the environment, nanites could clean up toxic spills as well as eliminate other environmental hazards. They could also dismantle, or "disassemble," garbage at the molecular level and recycle it again at the molecular level via "nanite assemblers."

Those who worry about future developments in nanotechnology and quantum computing see things quite differently. Since nanite assemblers and disassemblers could theoretically disassemble and reassemble all matter (objects and organisms), some worry about what would happen if strict "limiting mechanisms" were not built into those nanites: if nanomachines were created to be self-replicating and there was a problem with their limiting mechanisms, they could multiply endlessly like viruses. Another concern is that nanite assemblers and disassemblers could be used to create weapons or that nanites themselves could be used as weapons. As Chen (2002) points out, guns, explosives, and electronic components of weapons could all be miniaturized. A third concern is the likelihood that privacy and freedom would be eroded if governments, businesses, and ordinary citizens could use molecular-sized microphones, cameras, and homing beacons to track and monitor people. Weckert (2002) notes that people with microscopic implants could be tracked using Global Positioning Systems (GPS), just as cars can. On the one hand, children would never get lost; on the other hand, we would have very little privacy since we could so easily be tracked.

11.6.2   Ethical Aspects of Nanotechnology and Nanocomputers

Are claims about the future of nanotechnology plausible? If so, what kinds of ethical issues do they raise? And finally, do the potential dangers outweigh the benefits likely from future developments in nanotechnology and nanocomputing? We consider each question.

First, many claims and predictions regarding nanotechnology are plausible. Whether quantum computers will be able to compute at the speeds predicted by some of nanotechnology's proponents is currently being debated. But reputable scientists and researchers tend to agree with the projection that nanocomputers of some sort will be available around the middle of the twenty-first century. Weckert (2002) suggests that because the evidence is so credible, it would be prudent for us to look at the ethical implications now while there is still time to anticipate them. He believes that while some traditional computer-ethics problems will be exacerbated by nanotechnology, new problems will also arise; for example, issues associated with privacy and data mining will likely be exacerbated while issues pertaining to bionic chip implants will likely arise.

Weckert points out that conventional implants in the form of devices designed to correct deficiencies have been used for some time to assist patients to achieve normal vision, hearing, heartbeat, etc; they are "therapeutic implants." Future chip plants in the form of "enhancement implants" could make a normal person superhuman, raising an "enhancement vs. therapy" debate. James Moor (2004) points out that this distinction might suggest policy that would limit unnecessary implants. He also notes that because the human body has "natural functions," some will argue that implanting chips in a body is acceptable as long as these implants "maintain and restore the body's natural functions." Although Moor does not argue for a policy along the lines of a therapeutic-enhancement distinction, he believes that such a policy would appeal to many because in this scheme

> pacemakers, defibulators, and bionic eyes that maintain and restore natural bodily functions are acceptable. But giving patients added arms or infrared vision would be prohibited. It would endorse the use of a chip that reduced dyslexia but would forbid the implanting of a Deep Blue chip for superior chess play. It would permit a chip implant to assist memory of Alzheimer patients but would not license implanting of a miniature digital camera that would record and playback what a person had just seen.

We will have to frame clear policies and laws as more and more bionic parts become available. Some worry that with bionic parts, humans and machines could merge into cyborgs. Ray Kurzweill (1999) has suggested that in the near future the distinction between machines and humans may no longer be useful. And Moor (2004) believes we must continually re-evaluate "not whether we should become cyborgs, but rather what sort of cyborgs should we become." Describing advantages and disadvantages of bionic implants of the future, Weckert (2002) invites us to consider the question: "Do we want to be 'superhuman' relative to our current abilities with implants that enhance our senses, our memories, and our reasoning ability? What would such implants do to our view of what it is to be human?"

It is difficult to determine at this point whether the potential advantages of developments in nanotechnology and nanocomputers will outweigh the dangers. We might be tempted to argue that because this technology could be abused, and could be used in warfare, it should not be developed. We would be guilty of committing a logical fallacy (see the slippery slope fallacy in Chapter 3), however, if we reasoned that merely because something could be abused or could result in unintended tragedies, it should not be allowed. For example, automobiles and medical drugs can both be abused, resulting in unintended deaths. In the United States there are more than 40,000 deaths each year from automobile accidents. And some individuals abuse medical drugs that save lives; this abuse results in many deaths each year. Should we ban the development of automobiles? Should we stop research on medical drugs? You can no doubt see the fallacy in such reasoning. The question before us here is whether we should continue research in nanotechnology and nanocomputing, and an important corollary question is whether continued development in nanocomputing presents a moral dilemma for computer professionals engaged in that research.

11.6.3 Nanocomputing and the Challenge for Computer Professionals

We need to address whether computer professionals should participate in research projects involving nanotechnology, given the ethical implications for its future development. As might be expected, opinions differ. On one side, Joseph Weizenbaum (1984) argues certain kinds of computer science research should not be undertaken—specifically, research that can easily be seen to have "irreversible and not entirely unforeseeable side effects." And Bill Joy (2000) suggests that because developments in nanotechnology threaten to make us an "endangered species," the only realistic alternative is to limit its development. Ralph Merkle (2001), however, disagrees with Joy, arguing that if research in nanotechnology is prohibited, or even restricted, it will be done underground and therefore would not be regulated by governments and social policies.

Weckert (2001) believes that if Joy is correct about the dangers of nanotechnology, then we must seriously consider whether computer scientists should engage in nano-technology research. Furthermore, if computer scientists elect to carry out such research and development, Weckert believes that we must determine whether they should be held morally responsible for its outcomes. So should computer professionals currently working on projects related to nanocomputers and quantum computers discontinue their work? And should aspiring computer scientists who plan to enter the field be discouraged, or perhaps prevented, from doing so? Weckert (2001) argues that all things being equal, poten-tial disadvantages from research in a particular field are not in themselves sufficient grounds for halting research altogether. Rather he suggests that there should be a presump-tion in favor of freedom in research; however, he also argues that we should be allowed to restrict or even forbid research where it can be clearly shown that harm is more likely than not to result. Weckert offers us the following strategy: "If a prima facie case can be made that some research will likely cause harm, . . . then the burden of proof should be on those who want the research carried out to show that it is safe." He goes on to say, however, that there should be

> a presumption in favour of freedom until such time a prima facie case is made that the research is dangerous. The burden of proof then shifts from those opposing the research to those supporting it. At that stage the research should not begin or be continued until a good case can be made that it is safe.

So if Weckert is correct, until a prima facie, or self evident, case can be made to show that nanotechnology poses a dangerous threat, there are no compelling grounds for halting nanocomputing research. Of course, if future evidence were to suggests otherwise, we would need to reassess that position.

As we go forward with research in nanocomputing, it would be prudent to establish strict ethical guidelines. But who should formulate them? "Molecular Nanotechnology Guidelines" have been suggested by the Foresight Institute, a nonprofit educational organ-ization. The United States government has created the National Nanotechnology Initiative (NNI) to monitor and guide research, but some fear NNI monitoring might not be objective because government agencies, such as the National Science Foundation (NSF) and the Defense Advanced Research Projects Agency (DARPA), fund much of the nanotechnology research. Others worry that government-formulated guidelines would not represent all of the stakeholders. Andrew Chen (2002) believes that in addition to NSF and DARPA, other stakeholders include both independent and privately funded researchers, as well as users of nanotechnology; and, insofar as we all may eventually be affected by nanotechnology, everyone is ultimately a stakeholder. Chen proposes forming a nongovernment advisory council to monitor research and help formulate ethical guidelines and policies

Before work was able to proceed on the Human Genome Project in the late 1980s, eth-ical, legal, and social implications (ELSI) had to be addressed and formal ELSI guidelines established; genomic research was able to continue only after the ELSI requirements were in place. Similar ethical guidelines could help direct researchers and computer professionals in nanocomputing. And clear guidelines that address the future development of nanocomput-ing—beyond the specific concerns of researchers and computer professionals—would benefit every member of the human race.

▶ 11.7 CHAPTER SUMMARY

In this chapter we have examined social issues that relate to community and identity in cyberspace. In particular, we have seen how cybertechnology has affected our traditional notions of community and democracy as well as our concept of personal identity and our sense of self. We have also examined ethical and social issues that arise from the development and use of AI and VR technologies. Finally, we speculated about the future direction of cybertechnology, especially nanotechnology and nanocomputing, and the ethical issues that may arise with the development of those fields.

▶ REVIEW QUESTIONS

1. What are on-line communities?
2. How do they differ from traditional communities?
3. What does Gordon Graham mean when he says that on-line communities increase social fragmentation?
4. Does the Internet facilitate democracy?
5. Should the Internet be used to promote democracy? Explain.
6. What are some differences between direct and indirect democracies?
7. What does Graham mean when he says that the Internet may promote the "worst aspects" of direct and representative democracies?
8. Describe some of the implications that computers and cybertechnology have for our sense of personal identity.
9. What does Sherry Turkle mean when she says that the computer is a medium for self-discovery and self-expression?
10. What are MUDs, and what are their implications for our sense of personal identity in the age of the Internet?
11. What is virtual reality (VR)?
12. Describe three senses in which "virtual" is often used ambiguously.
13. What ethical challenges do VR environments pose?
14. What does Philip Brey mean when he suggests that ethical aspects of VR involve two distinct categories: (virtual) interaction and behavior, and misrepresentation and bias?
15. How does Brey propose that the philosophical argument found in Kant involving the treatment of animals and the argument involving psychological harm be applied to ethical issues involving VR environments?
16. What does Bolter mean by a defining technology and by the expression "Turing's man"?
17. Describe some implications of recent developments in the field of artificial intelligence (AI) for our sense of self.
18. What ethical issues do softbots raise? Do we have any moral obligations to artificial entities, especially those who behave as "autonomous agents," who make decisions on our behalf?
19. What is nanotechnology, and what moral issues do research and development in nanocomputing raise?
20. How can a model of ethical guidelines similar to the ones established for the Human Genome Project inform policies for nanocomputing and guide researchers in this field?

▶ DISCUSSION QUESTIONS

1. Assess the arguments advanced by Gordon Graham, Cass Sunstein, and Richard Sclove (in Section 11.2.1) as to whether Internet technology should be used to promote and spread democracy and democratic ideals. Whose argument do you find most convincing? Should the Internet be used to enhance democracy? Defend your answer.

2. Compare Philip Brey's arguments in Section 11.3.4 regarding misrepresentation and bias in virtual environments, especially in virtual reality (VR) applications, to Elizabeth's Buchanan's argument in Chapter 10 (Section 10.4.2) concerning gender bias in the representation (or lack of it) in video games. How are their arguments similar? How are they different?

3. Howard Rheingold (1991), who speculates about what VR may mean for the future of social relationships, raises an interesting questions involving *teledildonics* (or simulated sex at a distance). Though not yet a marketable technology, current work in *interactive tactile presence* (or touch feedback) will, Rheingold believes, make it possible for computer users to have sex at a distance. Inviting us to imagine this not-too-distant phenomenon, Rheingold asks us to picture ourselves "dressing for a hot night in the virtual village," where people wear a "cybersuit" made of "smart skin." Whether Rheingold's account turns out to be cyberfiction or whether it turns out to be factual, it is difficult to avoid considering the implications that teledildonics-related technology could have for future social relationships. Apply Philip Brey's model for analyzing ethical issues in virtual environments, described in Section 11.3.3, to Rheingold's scenario.

4. In addition to his critiques of on-line communities and on-line democracy that we examined in this chapter, Gordon Graham (1999) argues that experiences in VR will never have the same character as everyday experiences. He believes that one disadvantage of VR is that we will miss the joys of comparable "real" experiences, such as falling in love; he concludes that VR is an "impoverished reality" relative to life in the real world. Douglas Birsch (2002) critiques Graham's views and suggests that he seriously shortchanges VR. Birsch acknowledges that VR experience may be inferior to the "real life" one, but he points out that a VR experience is far superior to not having the experience at all. Birsch claims that he would rather ski the Alps in Switzerland than ski in a VR application, but he would rather have the virtual experience than none at all. He also points out that the virtual experience may be the only one available to physically challenged people. If Birsch is correct, then VR may not be as impoverished a form of reality as Graham suggests. Do you agree with Birsch or with Graham? Explain.

5. Evaluate the arguments that we examined for and against future research in nanotechnology. Given the potential advantages and disadvantages of future development in this area, which side's arguments do you find more convincing? Do the criteria provided by John Weckert for when research in a particular area should and should not be allowed offer us any guidelines for research in nanotechnology? Which kinds of ethical guidelines need to be built into research and development in this field?

▶ REFERENCES

Birsch, Douglas (2002). "Gordon Graham's *The Internet: A Philosophical Inquiry*: Review Article," *Ethics and Information Technology*, Vol. 4, No. 4, pp. 325–328.

Bolter, J. David (1984). *Turing's Man: Western Culture in the Computer Age*, Chapel Hill, NC: University of North Carolina Press.

Brey, Philip (1999). "The Ethics of Representation and Action in Virtual Reality," *Ethics and Information Technology*, Vol. 1, No. 1, pp. 5–14.

Chen, Andrew (2002). "The Ethics of Nanotechnology." Available at http://www.actionbioscience.org/newfrontiers/chen.html.

Dibbell, Julian (1993). "A Rape in Cyberspace," *Village Voice*, December 21, pp. 36–42.

Drexler, K. Eric (1991). *Unbounding the Future*. New York: Quill.

Epstein, Richard G. (2000). "The Fragmented Public Square," *Computers and Society*. Available at: http://www.cs.wcupa.edu/~epstein.fragmented.htm.

Floridi, Luciano, and J. W. Sanders (2001). "On the Mortality of Artificial Agents." In R. Chadwick, L. Introna, and A. Marturano, eds. *Proceedings of the Fourth International Conference on Computer Ethics: Philosophical Enquiry (CEPE 2001)*. Lancaster University, UK, pp. 84–107.

Ford, Paul J. (2001). "A Further Analysis of the Ethics of Representation in Virtual Reality–Multi-User Environments," *Ethics and Information Technology*, Vol. 3, No. 2, pp. 113–121.

Graham, Gordon (1999). *The Internet: A Philosophical Inquiry*. New York: Routledge.

Johnson, Deborah G. (2000). "Democratic Values and the Internet." In D. Langford, ed. *Internet Ethics*. New York: St. Martin's Press, pp. 180–199.

Jonas, Hans (1984). *The Imperative of Responsibility: In Search of an Ethics for the Technological Age*. Chicago: University of Chicago Press.

Joy, Bill (2000). "Why the Future Doesn't Need Us," *Wired*, Vol. 8, No. 4.

Kurzweill, Ray (1999). *The Age of Spiritual Machines: When Computers Exceed Human Intelligence*. New York: Penguin.

Mason, Richard O. (1994). "Morality and Models." In W. Wallace, ed. *Ethics in Modeling*. Oxford: Elsevier Science.

Merkle, Ralph (1997). "It's a Small, Small, Small World," *Technology Review*, Vol. 25, February/March.

Merkle, Ralph (2001). "Nanotechnology: What Will it Mean?" *IEEE Spectrum*, January.

Mill, John Stuart (1861). *Considerations on Representative Government*. London.

Moor, James H. (2004). "Should We Become Cyborgs?" In R. Cavalier, ed. *The Impact of the Internet on Our Moral Lives*. Albany, NY: State University of New York Press.

Negroponte, Nicholas (1995). *Being Digital*. New York: Alfred A. Knopf.

Plato's Republic (1980). Trans. by G. M. A. Grube. New York: Hackett.

Rheingold, Harold (1991). *Virtual Reality*, New York: Touchstone Books.

Rheingold, Harold (2001). *The Virtual Community: Homesteading on the Electronic Frontier*, revised ed. Cambridge, MA: MIT Press.

Sclove, Richard E. (1995). *Democracy and Technology*. New York: Guilford Press.

Sunstein, Cass R. (2002). *Republic.com*. Princeton, NJ: Princeton University Press.

Toffler, Alvin (1980). *The Third Wave*. New York: William Morrow.

Turkle, Shery (1984). *The Second Self: Computers and the Human Spirit*. New York: Simon and Schuster.

Turkle, Shery (1995). *Life on the Screen: Identity in the Age of the Internet*. New York: Simon and Schuster.

Ulen, Thomas S. (2001). "Democracy on the Line: A Review of *Republic.com* by Cass Sunstein," *Journal of Law Technology and Policy*, Vol. 2001, No. 2, pp. 317–346.

Van Gelder, Lindsy (1991). "The Strange Case of the Electronic Lover." In C. Dunlop and R. Kling, eds. *Computerization and Controversy: Value Conflicts and Social Choices*. San Diego, CA, pp. 364–375.

Weckert, John (2001). The Control of Scientific Research: The Case of Nanotechnology," *Australian Journal of Professional and Applied Ethics*, Vol. 3, No. 2, pp. 29–44.

Weckert, John (2002). "Lilliputian Computer Ethics," *Metaphilosophy*, Vol. 33, No. 3, pp. 366–375.

Weizenbaum, Joseph (1984). *Computer Power and Human Reason: From Judgment to Calculation*. New York: Penguin Books.

White, Michelle (2002). "Regulating Research: The Problem of Theorizing Research in LambdaMOO," *Ethics and Information Technology*, Vol. 4, No. 1, pp. 55–70.

Williams, Mary B. (1997). "Ethical Issues in Computing: Work, Privacy, and Justice." In M. D. Ermann, M. B. Williams, and M. S. Shauf, eds. *Computers, Ethics, and Society*. 2nd ed. New York: Oxford University Press, pp. 3–19.

▶ FURTHER READINGS

Adam, Alison (1998). *Artificial Knowing: Gender and the Thinking Machine*. New York: Routledge.

Bakardjeiva, Maria, and Andrew Feenberg (2000). "Involving the Virtual Subject," *Ethics and Information Technology*, Vol. 2, No. 4, pp. 233–240.

Brothers, Robyn (1998). "'Deindividuation' and the Ethical Imperative: Rethinking Selfhood in the Information Age." In M. J. van den Hoven, ed. *Proceedings of the Conference on Computer Ethics:Philosophical Enquiry (CEPE 97)*. Rotterdam, The Netherlands: Erasmus University Press, pp. 76–84.

Cerqui, Daniela (2002). "The Future of Human Kind in the Era of Human and Computer Hybridization: An Anthropological Analysis," *Ethics and Information Technology*, Vol. 4, No. 2, pp. 101–108.

Cocking, Dean, and Steve Matthews (2000). "Unreal Friends," *Ethics and Information Technology*, Vol. 2, No. 4. pp. 223–231.

Edgar, Stacey L. (2003). "The Artificial Intelligensia and Virtual Worlds." Chap. 12 in *Morality and Machines: Perspectives on Computer Ethics*. 2d ed. Sudbury, MA: Jones and Bartlett.

Epstein, Richard G. (1999). "Now Hiring: Dogs and Humans Need Not Apply," *Ethics and Information Technology*, Vol. 1, No. 3, pp. 227–236.

Ess, Charles (2002). "Computer-mediated Colonization, the Renaissance, and Educational Imperatives for an Intercultural Global Village," *Ethics and Information Technology*, Vol. 4, No. 1, pp. 11–22.

Green, Eileen, and Alison Adam, eds. (2002). *Virtual Gender: Technology, Consumption, and Identity*. New York: Routledge.

Heim, Michael (1998). *Virtual Realism*. New York: Oxford University Press.

Johnson, Deborah G. (1997). "Is the Global Information Infrastructure a Democratic Technology?" *Computers and Society*, Vol. 27, No. 3, pp. 20–26.

Kapor, Mitch (1996). "Where is the Digital Highway Really Heading? The Case for a Jeffersonian Information Policy," *Wired*, Vol. 3, No. 1.

Moor, James H. (2001). "The Future of Computer Ethics: You Ain't Seen Nothin' Yet!" *Ethics and Information Technology*, Vol. 3, No. 2, pp. 89-91.

Moravec, Hans (1999). *Robot: Mere Machine to Transcendent Mind*. New York: Oxford University Press.

Paglia, Camille (1998). "The Internet and Sexual Personae." In K. Schellenberg, ed. *Computers in Society*. 7th ed. New York: Dushkin/McGraw Hill, pp.13–15.

Tavani, Herman T. (2004). "The Impact of the Internet on Our Moral Condition: Do We Need a New Ethical Framework for the Internet Age?" In R. Cavalier, ed. *The Impact of the Internet on Our Moral Lives*. Albany, NY: State University of New York Press.

Weckert, John (2001). "Computer Ethics: Future Directions," *Ethics and Information Technology*, Vol. 3, No. 2, pp. 93–96.

Winner, Langdon (1997). "Cyberlibertarian Myths and the Prospects for Community," *Computers and Society*, Vol. 27, No. 3, pp. 14–19.

APPENDIX

A

IEEE CODE OF ETHICS

We, the members of the IEEE, in recognition of the importance of our technologies in affecting the quality of life throughout the world, and in accepting a personal obligation to our profession, its members, and the communities we serve, do hereby commit ourselves to the highest ethical and professional conduct and agree

1. to accept responsibility in making engineering decisions consistent with the safety, health, and welfare of the public, and to disclose promptly factors that might endanger the public or the environment;

2. to avoid real or perceived conflicts of interest whenever possible, and to disclose them to affected parties when they do exist;

3. to be honest and realistic in stating claims or estimates based on available data;

4. to reject bribery in all its forms;

5. to improve the understanding of technology, its appropriate application, and potential consequences;

6. to maintain and improve our technical competence and to undertake technological tasks for others only if qualified by training or experience, or after full disclosure of pertinent limitations;

7. to seek, accept, and offer honest criticism of technical work, to acknowledge and correct errors, and to credit properly the contributions of others;

8. to treat fairly all persons regardless of such factors as race, religion, gender, disability, age, or national origin;

9. to avoid injuring others, their property, reputation, or employment by false or malicious action;

10. to assist colleagues and coworkers in their professional development and to support them in following this code of ethics.

Approved by the IEEE Board of Directors, August 1990.

B

ACM CODE OF ETHICS AND PROFESSIONAL CONDUCT

Adopted by ACM Council on October 16, 1992.

▶ PREAMBLE

Commitment to ethical professional conduct is expected of every member (voting members, associate members, and student members) of the Association for Computing Machinery (ACM).

This Code, consisting of 24 imperatives formulated as statements of personal responsibility, identifies the elements of such a commitment. It contains many, but not all, issues professionals are likely to face. Section 1 outlines fundamental ethical considerations, while Section 2 addresses additional, more specific considerations of personal conduct. Statements in Section 3 pertain more specifically to individuals who have a leadership role, whether in the workplace or in a volunteer capacity such as with organizations like ACM. Principles involving compliance with this code are given in Section 4.

The Code shall be supplemented by a set of Guidelines, which provide explanation to assist members in dealing with the various issues contained in the Code. It is expected that the Guidelines will be changed more frequently than the Code.

The Code and its supplemented Guidelines are intended to serve as a basis for ethical decision making in the conduct of professional work. Secondarily, they may serve as a basis for judging the merit of a formal complaint pertaining to violation of professional ethical standards.

It should be noted that although computing is not mentioned in the imperatives of Section 1, the Code is concerned with how these fundamental imperatives apply to one's conduct as a computing professional. These imperatives are expressed in a general form to emphasize that ethical principles which apply to computer ethics are derived from more general ethical principles.

It is understood that some words and phrases in a code of ethics are subject to varying interpretations, and that any ethical principle may conflict with other ethical principles in specific situations. Questions related to ethical conflicts can best be answered by thoughtful considerations of fundamental principles, rather than reliance on detailed regulations.

▶ CONTENTS AND GUIDELINES

1. General Moral Imperatives.
2. More Specific Professional Responsibilities.
3. Organizational Leadership Imperatives.
4. Compliance with the Code.

▶ 1. GENERAL MORAL IMPERATIVES

As an ACM member I will . . .

1.1 Contribute to society and human well-being

This principle concerning the quality of life of all people affirms an obligation to protect fundamental human rights and to respect the diversity of all cultures. An essential aim of computing professionals is to minimize negative consequences of computing systems, including threats to health and safety. When designing or implementing systems, computing professionals must attempt to ensure that the products of their efforts will be used in socially responsible ways, will meet social needs, and will avoid harmful effects to health and welfare.

In addition to a safe social environment, human well-being includes a safe natural environment. Therefore, computing professionals who design and develop systems must be alert to, and make others aware of, any potential damage to the local or global environment.

1.2 Avoid harm to others

"Harm" means injury or negative consequences, such as undesirable loss of information, loss of property, property damage, or unwanted environmental impacts. This principle prohibits use of computing technology in ways that result in harm to any of the following: users, the general public, employees, employers. Harmful actions include intentional destruction or modification of files and programs leading to serious loss of resources or unnecessary expenditure of human resources such as the time and effort required to purge systems of computer viruses.

Well-intended actions, including those that accomplish assigned duties, may lead to harm unexpectedly. In such an event the responsible person or persons are obligated to undo or mitigate the negative consequences as much as possible. One way to avoid unintentional harm is to carefully consider potential impacts on all those affected by decisions made during design and implementation.

To minimize the possibility of indirectly harming others, computing professionals must minimize malfunctions by following generally accepted standards for system design and testing. Furthermore, it is often necessary to assess the social consequences of systems to project the likelihood of any serious harm to others. If system features are misrepresented to users, coworkers, or supervisors, the individual computing professional is responsible for any resulting injury.

In the work environment the computing professional has the additional obligation to report any signs of system dangers that might result in serious personal or social damage. If one's superiors do not act to curtail or mitigate such dangers, it may be necessary to "blow the whistle" to help correct the problem or reduce the risk. However, capricious or misguided reporting of violations can, itself, be harmful. Before reporting violations, all relevant aspects of the incident must be thoroughly assessed. In particular, the assessment of risk and responsibility must be credible. It is suggested that advice be sought from other computing professionals. (See imperative 2.5 regarding thorough evaluations.)

1.3   Be honest and trustworthy

Honesty is an essential component of trust. Without trust an organization cannot function effectively. The honest computing professional will not make deliberately false or deceptive claims about a system or system design, but will instead provide full disclosure of all pertinent system limitations and problems.

A computer professional has a duty to be honest about his or her own qualifications, and about any circumstances and might lead to conflicts of interest.

Membership in volunteer organizations such as ACM may at times place individuals in situations where their statements or actions could be interpreted as carrying the "weight" of a larger group of professionals. An ACM member will exercise care to not misrepresent ACM or positions and policies of ACM or any ACM units.

1.4   Be fair, and take action not to discriminate

The values of equality, tolerance, and respect for others and the principles of equal justice govern this imperative. Discrimination on the basis of race, sex, religion, age, disability, national origin, or other such factors is an explicit violation of ACM policy and will not be tolerated.

Inequities between different groups of people may result from the use or misuse of information and technology. in a fair society all individuals would have equal opportunity to participate in, or benefit from, the use of computer resources regardless of race, sex, religion, age, disability, national origin, or other such similar factors. However, these ideals do not justify unauthorized use of computer resources nor do they provide an adequate basis for violation of any other ethical imperatives of this Code.

1.5   Honor property rights including copyrights and patents

Violation of copyrights, patents, trade secrets, and the terms of license agreements is prohibited by law in most circumstances. Even when software is not so protected, such violations are contrary to professional behavior. Copies of software should be made only with proper authorization. Unauthorized duplication of materials must not be condoned.

1.6 Give proper credit for intellectual property

Computing professionals are obligated to protect the integrity of intellectual property. Specifically, one must not take credit for other's ideas or work, even in cases where the work has not been explicitly protected, for example, by copyright, patent, etc.

1.7 Respect the privacy of others

Computing and communication technology enables the collection and exchange of personal information on a scale unprecedented in the history of civilization. Thus there is increased potential for violating the privacy of individuals and groups. It is the responsibility of professionals to maintain the privacy and integrity of data describing individuals. This includes taking precautions to ensure the accuracy of data as well as protecting it from unauthorized access or accidental disclosure to inappropriate individuals. Furthermore, procedures must be established to allow individuals to review their records and correct inaccuracies.

This imperative implies that only the necessary amount of personal information be collected in a system, that retention and disposal periods for that information be clearly defined and enforced, and that personal information gathered for a specific purpose not be used for other purposes without consent of the individual(s). These principles apply to electronic communications, including electronic mail, and prohibit procedures that capture or monitor electronic user data, including messages, without the permission of users or bona fide authorization related to system operation and maintenance. User data observed during the normal duties of system operation and maintenance must be treated with strictest confidentiality except in cases where it is evidence for the violation of law, organizational regulations, or this Code. In these cases, the nature or contents of that information must be disclosed only to proper authorities.

1.8 Honor confidentiality

The principle of honesty extends to issues of confidentiality of information whenever one has made an explicit promise to honor confidentiality or, implicitly, when private information not directly related to the performance of one's duties becomes available. The ethical concern is to respect all obligations of confidentiality to employers, clients, and users unless discharged from such obligations by requirements of the law or other principles of this Code.

► 2. MORE SPECIFIC PROFESSIONAL RESPONSIBILITIES

As an ACM computing professional I will . . .

2.1 Strive to achieve the highest quality, effectiveness, and dignity in both the process and products of professional work

Excellence is perhaps the most important obligation of a professional. The computing professional must strive to achieve quality and to be cognizant of the serious negative consequences that may result from poor quality in a system.

2.2 Acquire and maintain professional competence

Excellence depends on individuals who take responsibility for acquiring and maintaining professional competence. A professional must participate in setting standards for appropriate levels of competence, and strive to achieve those standards. Upgrading technical knowledge and competence can be achieved in several ways: doing independent study; attending seminars, conferences, or courses; and being involved in professional organizations.

2.3 Know and respect existing laws pertaining to professional work

ACM members must obey existing local, state, province, national, and international laws unless there is a compelling ethical basis not to do so. Policies and procedures of the organization in which one participates must also be obeyed. But compliance must be balanced with the recognition that sometimes existing laws and rules may be immoral or inappropriate and therefore must be challenged.

Violation of a law or regulation may be ethical when that law or rule has inadequate moral basis or when it conflicts with another law judged to be more important. If one decides to violate law or rule because it is viewed as unethical, or for any other reason, one must fully accept responsibility for one's actions and for the consequences.

2.4 Accept and provide appropriate professional review

Quality professional work, especially in the computing profession, depends on professional reviewing and critiquing. Whenever appropriate, individual members should seek and utilize peer review as well as provide critical review of the work of others.

2.5 Give comprehensive and thorough evaluations of computer systems and their impacts, including analysis of possible risks

Computer professionals must strive to be perceptive, thorough, and objective when evaluating, recommending, and presenting system descriptions and alternatives. Computer professionals are in a position of special trust and therefore have a special responsibility to provide objective, credible evaluations to employers, clients, users, and the public. When providing evaluations the professional must also identify any relevant conflicts of interest, as stated in imperative 1.3.

As noted in the discussion of imperative 1.2 on avoiding harm, any signs of danger from systems must be reported to those who have opportunity and/or responsibility to resolve them. (See the guidelines for imperative 1.2 for more details concerning harm, including the reporting of professional violations.)

2.6 Honor contracts, agreements, and assigned responsibilities

Honoring one's commitments is a matter of integrity and honesty. For the computer professional this includes ensuring that system elements perform as intended. Also, when one contracts for work with another party, one has an obligation to keep that party properly informed about progress toward completing that work.

A computing professional has a responsibility to request a change in any assignment that he or she feels cannot be completed as defined. Only after serious consideration and with full disclosure of risks and concerns to the employer or client, should one accept the assignment. The major underlying principle here is the obligation to accept personal accountability for professional work. On some occasions other ethical principles may take the greater priority.

A judgment that a specific assignment should not be performed may not be accepted. Having clearly identified one's concerns and reasons for that judgment, but failing to procure a change in that assignment, one may yet be obligated, by contract or by law, to proceed as directed. The computing professional's ethical judgment should be the final guide in deciding whether or not to proceed. Regardless of the decision, one must accept the responsibility for the consequences.

However, performing assignments "against one's own judgment" does not relieve the professional of responsibility for any negative consequences.

2.7   Improve public understanding of computing and its consequences

Computing professionals have a responsibility to share technical knowledge with the public by encouraging understanding of computing, including the impacts of computer systems and their limitations. This imperative implies an obligation to counter any false views related to computing.

2.8   Access computing and communication resources only when authorized to do so

Theft or destruction of tangible and electronic property is prohibited by imperative 1.2: "Avoid harm to others." Trespassing and unauthorized use of a computer or communication system is addressed by this imperative. Trespassing includes accessing communication networks and computer systems, or accounts and/or files associated with those systems without explicit authorization to do so. Individuals and organizations have the right to restrict access to their systems so long as they do not violate the discrimination imperative (see 1.4). No one should enter or use another's computing system, software, or data files without permission. One must always have appropriate approval before using system resources, including communication ports, file space, other system peripherals, and computer time.

▶ 3. ORGANIZATIONAL LEADERSHIP IMPERATIVES

Background Note: This section draws extensively from the Draft IFIP Code of Ethics, especially its sections on organizational ethics and international concerns. The ethical obligations of organizations tend to be neglected in most codes of professional conduct, perhaps because these codes are written from the perspective of the individual member. This dilemma is addressed by stating these imperatives from the perspective of the organizational leader. In this context "leader" is viewed as any organizational member who has leadership or educational responsibilities. These imperatives generally may apply to organizations as well as their leaders. In this context "organizations" are corporations, government agencies, and other "employers," as well as volunteer professional organizations.

As an ACM member and an organizational leader, I will . . .

3.1 Articulate social responsibilities of members of an organizational unit and encourage full acceptance of those responsibilities

Because organizations of all kinds have impacts on the public, they must accept responsibilities to society. Organizational procedures and attitudes oriented toward quality and the welfare of society will reduce harm to members of the public, thereby serving public interest and fulfilling social responsibility. Therefore, organizational leaders must encourage full participation in meeting social responsibilities as well as quality performance.

3.2 Manage personnel and resources to design and build information systems that enhance the quality of working life

Organizational leaders are responsible for ensuring that computer systems enhance, not degrade, the quality of working life. When implementing a computer system, organizations must consider the personal and professional development, physical safety, and human dignity of all workers. Appropriate human-computer ergonomic standards should be considered in system design and in the workplace.

3.3 Acknowledge and support proper and authorized uses of an organization's computing and communications resources

Because computer systems can become tools to harm as well to benefit an organization, the leadership has the responsibility to clearly define appropriate and inappropriate uses of organizational computing resources. While the number and scope of such rules should be minimal, they should be fully enforced when established.

3.4 Ensure that users and those who will be affected by a system have their needs clearly articulated during the assessment and design of requirements; later the system must be validated to meet requirements

Current system users, potential users, and other persons whose lives may be affected by a system must have their needs assessed and incorporated in the statement of requirements. System validation should ensure compliance with those requirements.

3.5 Articulate and support policies that protect the dignity of users and others affected by a computing system

Designing or implementing systems that deliberately or inadvertently demean individuals or groups is ethically unacceptable. Computer professionals who are in decision-making positions should verify that systems are designed and implemented to protect personal privacy and enhance personal dignity.

3.6 Create opportunities for members of the organization to learn the principles and limitations of computer systems

This complements the imperative on public understanding (2.7). Educational opportunities are essential to facilitate optimal participation of all organizational members. Opportunities must be available to all members to help them improve their knowledge and skills in computing, including courses that familiarize them with the consequences and limitations of particular types of systems. In particular, professionals must be made aware of the dangers of building systems around oversimplified models, the improbability of anticipating and designing for every possible operating condition, and other issues related to the complexity of this profession.

▶ 4. COMPLIANCE WITH THE CODE

As an ACM member I will . . .

4.1 Uphold and promote the principles of this Code

The future of the computing profession depends on both technical and ethical excellence. Not only is it important for ACM computing professionals to adhere to the principles expressed in this Code, each member should encourage and support adherence by other members.

4.2 Treat violations of this code as inconsistent with membership in the ACM

Adherence of professionals to a code of ethics is largely a voluntary matter. However, if a member does not follow this code by engaging in gross misconduct, membership in ACM may be terminated.

This Code and the supplemental Guidelines were developed by the Task Force for the Revision of the ACM Code of Ethics and Professional Conduct: Ronald E. Anderson, Chair, Gerald Engel, Donald Gotterbarn, Grace C. Hertlein, Alex Hoffman, Bruce Jawer, Deborah G. Johnson, Doris K. Lidtke, Joyce Currie Little, Dianne Martin, Donn B. Parker, Judith A. Perrolle, and Richard S. Rosenberg. The Task Force was organized by ACM/SIGCAS and funding was provided by the ACM SIG Discretionary Fund. This Code and the supplemental Guidelines were adopted by the ACM Council on October 16, 1992.

IEEE-CS/ACM SOFTWARE ENGINEERING CODE OF ETHICS AND PROFESSIONAL PRACTICE

(Version 5.2) as recommended by the IEEE-CS/ACM Joint Task Force on Software Engineering Ethics and Professional Practices.

► SHORT VERSION

Preamble

The short version of the Code summarizes aspirations at a high level of abstraction. The clauses that are included in the full version give examples and details of how these aspirations change the way we act as software engineering professionals. Without the aspirations, the details can become legalistic and tedious; without the details, the aspirations can become high sounding but empty; together, the aspirations and the details form a cohesive code.

Software engineers shall commit themselves to making the analysis, specification, design, development, testing, and maintenance of software a beneficial and respected profession. In accordance with their commitment to the health, safety, and welfare of the public, software engineers shall adhere to the following eight Principles:

1. PUBLIC—Software engineers shall act consistently with the public interest.

2. CLIENT AND EMPLOYER—Software engineers shall act in a manner that is in the best interests of their client and employer, consistent with the public interest.

3. PRODUCT—Software engineers shall ensure that their products and related modifications meet the highest professional standards possible.

4. JUDGMENT—Software engineers shall maintain integrity and independence in their professional judgment.

5. MANAGEMENT—Software engineering managers and leaders shall subscribe to and promote an ethical approach to the management of software development and maintenance.

6. PROFESSION—Software engineers shall advance the integrity and reputation of the profession consistent with the public interest.

7. COLLEAGUES—Software engineers shall be fair to and supportive of their colleagues.

8. SELF—Software engineers shall participate in lifelong learning regarding the practice of their profession and shall promote an ethical approach to the practice of the profession.

▶ FULL VERSION

Preamble

Computers have a central and growing role in commerce, industry, government, medicine, education, entertainment, and society at large. Software engineers are those who contribute by direct participation or by teaching, to the analysis, specification, design, development, certification, maintenance, and testing of software systems. Because of their roles in developing software systems, software engineers have significant opportunities to do good or cause harm, to enable others to do good or cause harm, or to influence others to do good or cause harm. To ensure, as much as possible, that their efforts will be used for good, software engineers must commit themselves to making software engineering a beneficial and respected profession. In accordance with that commitment, software engineers shall adhere to the following Code of Ethics and Professional Practice.

The Code contains eight Principles related to the behavior of and decisions made by professional software engineers, including practitioners, educators, managers, supervisors, and policy makers, as well as trainees and students of the profession. The Principles identify the ethically responsible relationships in which individuals, groups, and organizations participate and the primary obligations within these relationships. The Clauses of each Principle are illustrations of some of the obligations included in these relationships. These obligations are founded in the software engineer's humanity, in special care owed to people affected by the work of software engineers, and in the unique elements of the practice of software engineering. The Code prescribes these as obligations of anyone claiming to be or aspiring to be a software engineer.

It is not intended that the individual parts of the Code be used in isolation to justify errors of omission or commission. The list of Principles and Clauses is not exhaustive. The Clauses should not be read as separating the acceptable from the unacceptable in professional conduct in all practical situations. The Code is not a simple ethical algorithm that generates ethical decisions. In some situations, standards may be in tension with each other or with standards from other sources. These situations require the software engineer to use ethical judgment to act in a manner that is most consistent with the spirit of the Code of Ethics and Professional Practice, given the circumstances.

Ethical tensions can best be addressed by thoughtful consideration of fundamental principles, rather than blind reliance on detailed regulations. These Principles should influence software engineers to consider broadly who is affected by their work; to examine if they and their colleagues are treating other human beings with due respect; to consider how the public, if reasonably well informed, would view their decisions; to analyze how the least empowered will be affected by their decisions; and to consider whether their acts would be judged worthy of the ideal professional working as a software engineer. In all these judgments concern for the health, safety, and welfare of the public is primary; that is, the "Public Interest" is central to this Code.

The dynamic and demanding context of software engineering requires a code that is adaptable and relevant to new situations as they occur. However, even in this generality, the Code provides support for software engineers and managers of software engineers who need to take positive action in a specific case by documenting the ethical stance of the profession. The Code provides an ethical foundation to which individuals within teams and the team as a whole can appeal. The Code helps to define those actions that are ethically improper to request of a software engineer or teams of software engineers.

The Code is not simply for adjudicating the nature of questionable acts; it also has an important educational function. As this Code expresses the consensus of the profession on ethical issues, it is a means to educate both the public and aspiring professionals about the ethical obligations of all software engineers.

Principles

Principle 1. PUBLIC—Software engineers shall act consistently with the public interest. In particular, software engineers shall, as appropriate:

1.01. Accept full responsibility for their own work.

1.02. Moderate the interests of the software engineer, the employer, the client, and the users with the public good.

1.03. Approve software only if they have a well-founded belief that it is safe, meets specifications, passes appropriate tests, and does not diminish quality of life, diminish privacy or harm the environment. The ultimate effect of the work should be to the public good.

1.04. Disclose to appropriate persons or authorities any actual or potential danger to the user, the public, or the environment, that they reasonably believe to be associated with software or related documents.

1.05. Cooperate in efforts to address matters of grave public concern caused by software, its installation, maintenance, support, or documentation.

1.06. Be fair and avoid deception in all statements, particularly public ones, concerning software or related documents, methods, and tools.

1.07. Consider issues of physical disabilities, allocation of resources, economic disadvantage, and other factors that can diminish access to the benefits of software.

1.08. Be encouraged to volunteer professional skills to good causes and to contribute to public education concerning the discipline.

Principle 2. CLIENT AND EMPLOYER—Software engineers shall act in a manner that is in the best interests of their client and employer, consistent with the public interest. In particular, software engineers shall, as appropriate:

2.01. Provide service in their areas of competence, being honest and forthright about any limitations of their experience and education.

2.02. Not knowingly use software that is obtained or retained either illegally or unethically.

2.03. Use the property of a client or employer only in ways properly authorized, and with the client's or employer's knowledge and consent.

2.04. Ensure that any document upon which they rely has been approved, when required, by someone authorized to approve it.

2.05. Keep private any confidential information gained in their professional work, where such confidentiality is consistent with the public interest and consistent with the law.

2.06. Identify, document, and collect evidence and report to the client or the employer promptly if, in their opinion, a project is likely to fail, to prove too expensive, to violate intellectual property law, or otherwise to be problematic.

2.07. Identify, document, and report significant issues of social concern, of which they are aware, in software or related documents, to the employer or the client.

2.08. Accept no outside work detrimental to the work they perform for their primary employer.

2.09. Promote no interest adverse to their employer or client, unless a higher ethical concern is being compromised; in that case, inform the employer or another appropriate authority of the ethical concern.

Principle 3. PRODUCT—Software engineers shall ensure that their products and related modifications meet the highest professional standards possible. In particular, software engineers shall, as appropriate:

3.01. Strive for high quality, acceptable cost, and a reasonable schedule, ensuring significant tradeoffs are clear to and accepted by the employer and the client, and are available for consideration by the user and the public.

3.02. Ensure proper and achievable goals and objectives for any project on which they work or propose.

3.03. Identify, define, and address ethical, economic, cultural, legal, and environmental issues related to work projects.

3.04. Ensure that they are qualified for any project on which they work or propose to work, by an appropriate combination of education, training, and experience.

3.05. Ensure that an appropriate method is used for any project on which they work or propose to work.

3.06. Work to follow professional standards, when available, that are most appropriate for the task at hand, departing from these only when ethically or technically justified.

3.07. Strive to fully understand the specifications for software on which they work.

3.08. Ensure that specifications for software on which they work have been well documented, satisfy the users' requirements and have the appropriate approvals.

3.09. Ensure realistic quantitative estimates of cost, scheduling, personnel, quality, and outcomes on any project on which they work or propose to work and provide an uncertainty assessment of these estimates.

3.10. Ensure adequate testing, debugging, and review of software and related documents on which they work.

3.11. Ensure adequate documentation, including significant problems discovered and solutions adopted, for any project on which they work.

3.12. Work to develop software and related documents that respect the privacy of those who will be affected by that software.

3.13. Be careful to use only accurate data derived by ethical and lawful means, and use it only in ways properly authorized.

3.14. Maintain the integrity of data, being sensitive to outdated or flawed occurrences.

3.15. Treat all forms of software maintenance with the same professionalism as new development.

Principle 4. JUDGMENT—Software engineers shall maintain integrity and independence in their professional judgment. In particular, software engineers shall, as appropriate:

4.01. Temper all technical judgments by the need to support and maintain human values.

4.02. Only endorse documents either prepared under their supervision or within their areas of competence and with which they are in agreement.

4.03. Maintain professional objectivity with respect to any software or related documents they are asked to evaluate.

4.04. Not engage in deceptive financial practices such as bribery, double billing, or other improper financial practices.

4.05. Disclose to all concerned parties those conflicts of interest that cannot reasonably be avoided or escaped.

4.06. Refuse to participate, as members or advisors, in a private, governmental, or professional body concerned with software related issues, in which they, their employers, or their clients have undisclosed potential conflicts of interest.

Principle 5. MANAGEMENT—Software engineering managers and leaders shall subscribe to and promote an ethical approach to the management of software development and maintenance. In particular, those managing or leading software engineers shall, as appropriate:

5.01. Ensure good management for any project on which they work, including effective procedures for promotion of quality and reduction of risk.

5.02. Ensure that software engineers are informed of standards before being held to them.

5.03. Ensure that software engineers know the employer's policies and procedures for protecting passwords, files, and information that is confidential to the employer or confidential to others.

5.04. Assign work only after taking into account appropriate contributions of education and experience tempered with a desire to further that education and experience.

5.05. Ensure realistic quantitative estimates of cost, scheduling, personnel, quality, and outcomes on any project on which they work or propose to work and provide an uncertainty assessment of these estimates.

5.06. Attract potential software engineers only by full and accurate description of the conditions of employment.

5.07. Offer fair and just remuneration.

5.08. Not unjustly prevent someone from taking a position for which that person is suitably qualified.

5.09. Ensure that there is a fair agreement concerning ownership of any software, processes, research, writing, or other intellectual property to which a software engineer has contributed.

5.10. Provide for due process in hearing charges of violation of an employer's policy or of this Code.

5.11. Not ask a software engineer to do anything inconsistent with this Code.

5.12. Not punish anyone for expressing ethical concerns about a project.

Principle 6. PROFESSION—Software engineers shall advance the integrity and reputation of the profession consistent with the public interest. In particular, software engineers shall, as appropriate:

6.01. Help develop an organizational environment favorable to acting ethically.

6.02. Promote public knowledge of software engineering.

6.03. Extend software engineering knowledge by appropriate participation in professional organizations, meetings, and publications.

6.04. Support, as members of a profession, other software engineers striving to follow this Code.

6.05. Not promote their own interest at the expense of the profession, client, or employer.

6.06. Obey all laws governing their work, unless, in exceptional circumstances, such compliance is inconsistent with the public interest.

6.07. Be accurate in stating the characteristics of software on which they work, avoiding not only false claims but also claims that might reasonably be supposed to be speculative, vacuous, deceptive, misleading, or doubtful.

6.08. Take responsibility for detecting, correcting, and reporting errors in software and associated documents on which they work.

6.09. Ensure that clients, employers, and supervisors know of the software engineer's commitment to this Code of Ethics, and the subsequent ramifications of such commitment.

6.10. Avoid associations with businesses and organizations that are in conflict with this Code.

6.11. Recognize that violations of this Code are inconsistent with being a professional software engineer.

6.12. Express concerns to the people involved when significant violations of this Code are detected unless this is impossible, counterproductive, or dangerous.

6.13. Report significant violations of this Code to appropriate authorities when it is clear that consultation with people involved in these significant violations is impossible, counterproductive, or dangerous.

Principle 7. COLLEAGUES—*Software engineers shall be fair to and supportive of their colleagues. In particular, software engineers shall, as appropriate:*

7.01. Encourage colleagues to adhere to this Code.

7.02. Assist colleagues in professional development.

7.03. Credit fully the work of others and refrain from taking undue credit.

7.04. Review the work of others in an objective, candid, and properly documented way.

7.05. Give a fair hearing to the opinions, concerns, or complaints of a colleague.

7.06. Assist colleagues in being fully aware of current standard work practices including policies and procedures for protecting passwords, files, and other confidential information, and security measures in general.

7.07. Not unfairly intervene in the career of any colleague; however, concern for the employer, the client, or public interest may compel software engineers, in good faith, to question the competence of a colleague.

7.08. In situations outside of their own areas of competence, call upon the opinions of other professionals who have competence in that area.

Principle 8. SELF—Software engineers shall participate in lifelong learning regarding the practice of their profession and shall promote an ethical approach to the practice of the profession. In particular, software engineers shall continually endeavor to:

8.01. Further their knowledge of developments in the analysis, specification, design, development, maintenance, and testing of software and related documents together with the management of the development process.

8.02. Improve their ability to create safe, reliable, and useful quality software at reasonable cost and within a reasonable time.

8.03. Improve their ability to produce accurate, informative, and well-written documentation.

8.04. Improve their understanding of the software and related documents on which they work and of the environment in which they will be used.

8.05. Improve their knowledge of relevant standards and the law governing the software and related documents on which they work.

8.06. Improve their knowledge of this Code, its interpretation, and its application to their work.

8.07. Not give unfair treatment to anyone because of any irrelevant prejudices.

8.08. Not influence others to undertake any action that involves a breach of this Code.

8.09. Recognize that personal violations of this Code are inconsistent with being a professional software engineer.

This Code was developed by the IEEE-CS/ACM joint task force on Software Engineering Ethics and Professional Practices (SEEPP):

Executive Committee: Donald Gotterbarn (Chair), Keith Miller, and Simon Rogerson; Members: Steve Barber, Peter Barnes, Ilene Burnstein, Michael Davis, Amr El-Kadi, N. Ben Fairweather, Milton Fulghum, N. Jayaram, Tom Jewett, Mark Kanko, Ernie Kallman, Duncan Langford, Joyce Currie Little, Ed Mechler, Manuel J. Norman, Douglas Phillips, Peter Ron Prinzivalli, Patrick Sullivan, John Weckert, Vivian Weil, S. Weisband, and Laurie Honour Werth.

GLOSSARY

ACM Code of Ethics and Professional Conduct: A code of ethics endorsed by the Association for Computing Machinery.

anonymity: In the context of cybertechnology, the ability to navigate the Internet and participate in on-line forums without having to reveal one's true identity.

Anti-Cybersquatting Act: The Anti-Cybersquatting Act, passed in 1999, is intended to protect the interests of those who hold trademarks in physical space as well as the interests of celebrities from having their names registered as Internet domain names by others. See also *cybersquatting*.

antivirus software: A security countermeasure designed to "inoculate" computer systems against viruses, worms, and other forms of malicious or rogue computer programs.

applied ethics: A branch of ethical inquiry that examines practical (as opposed to theoretical) moral issues and problems from the vantage point of ethical theory. See also *ethical theory*.

artificial intelligence (AI): The field of study that examines relationships between "machine intelligence" and human intelligence. One branch of AI attempts to shed light on human intelligence by using cybertechnology to simulate it; another branch is concerned with constructing "intelligent tools" to assist humans in complex tasks. See also *expert system*.

back door: A hole in a security system deliberately left in place by designers and maintainers. See also *trap door*.

biometrics: The biological identification of a person, which includes eyes, voice, hand prints, finger prints, retina patterns, and handwritten signatures.

Carnivore: A "packet sniffing" computer program used by the United States government to monitor data communicated between networked computers. See also *packet sniffing program*.

computer security: A branch of computer science concerned with both safeguarding computer systems (hardware and software resources) from attacks by malicious programs, such as viruses and worms, and protecting the integrity of the data resident in and transmitted between those systems from unauthorized access.

consequentialism: An ethical theory that appeals to consequences, outcomes, or ends as the essential criterion, or standard, used to justify particular actions and policies in a moral system. See also *utilitarianism*.

contract theory of ethics: A theory that ties a moral obligation to assist others to an express contract to do so. Contract theory is sometimes viewed as a minimalist theory of morality, because without an explicit contract, one would simply be required to "do no harm" to others; there is no obligation to actively assist others.

cookies: Text files that Web sites send to and retrieve from a Web visitor's computer system. Cookies technology enables Web site owners to collect information about a visitor's preferences while the visitor interacts with their Web sites.

cryptography: The technique of converting the information in a message composed in ordinary text (plain text) into "ciphertext" and then back into plain text. In cybertechnology, a data-encryption technique involving a system of "keys" (private and public) is used to encode and decode the data. See also *data encryption*.

cybercrime: Criminal activity that is either made possible or significantly exacerbated by the use of computers and cybertechnology.

cyberethics: The field of study that examines moral, legal, and social issues involving cybertechnology.

cybersquatting: The act of registering Internet domain names that are either identical to or closely resemble the names of celebrities or the names of trademarks previously registered in physical space. See also *Anti-Cybersquatting Act*.

cyberstalking: The use of cybertechnology to clandestinely track the movement and whereabouts of one or more individuals.

cybertechnology: A range of computing and information/communication technologies, from stand-alone computer systems to privately owned computer networks to the Internet.

cyberterrorism: The convergence of cyberspace and terrorism, covering a range of politically motivated hacking operations that can result in loss of life, severe economic loss, or both.

data encryption: A security countermeasure designed to ensure the confidentiality and integrity of information transmitted on the Internet, especially in e-mail applications, using a system of cryptography. See also *cryptography*.

data mining: A computerized technique for unearthing implicit patterns in large databases to reveal statistical data and corresponding associations that can be used to construct consumer profiles.

dataveillance: A term coined by Roger Clarke to describe the combination of data-monitoring (surveillance) techniques with data-recording techniques made possible by computer technology.

deductive argument: An argument form in which the premises, if assumed true, are sufficient to guarantee the truth of the conclusion.

denial-of-service attacks: Repeated spurious requests to a Web site that are intended to disrupt services at that site. Denial-of-service attacks can be sent via third-party sites, from computer systems located in universities and organizations, to confuse the targeted sites about the source of the attacks.

deontological ethics: A theory of ethics that bases its moral system in duty or obligation rather than in consequences and outcomes that result from actions. Deontological ethical theories can be contrasted with consequentialist theories. See also *consequentialism.*

descriptive ethics: A branch of ethical inquiry that reports or describes the ethical principles and values held by various groups and individuals. Descriptive ethics is usually contrasted with normative ethics. See also *normative ethics.*

digital divide: The disparity between those who have (information "haves") and those who do not have (information "have-nots") computers and access to the Internet.

Digital Millennium Copyright Act (DMCA):   Public Law 304, 1998, which contains a clause that forbids the development of any software or hardware technology that circumvents copyrighted digital media.

domain name: A convention for naming Web sites that allows each site to have a unique identification. The domain name is included as part of an Internet URL. See also *URL.*

Echelon: A once-secret system that monitors voice and data communication worldwide; it has been used by the United States government to track the movements of professional criminals in on-line activities. See also *carnivore.*

e-commerce: Electronic commerce, usually conducted on Web sites.

ethical theory: A branch of ethical inquiry dedicated to the study of philosophical frameworks for determining when actions and policies are morally right or morally wrong. Ethical theory, or theoretical ethics, is often contrasted with applied ethics. See also *applied ethics.*

ethics: The study of morality or a moral system. Normative ethics approaches the study of a moral system, from the perspective of philosophy, religion, or law, while descriptive ethics typically examines morality from the perspective of social science. See also *morality*, *descriptive ethics,* and *normative ethics.*

expert system (ES):   A computer program or a computer system that is "expert" at performing one particular task traditionally performed by humans; developed from research in Artificial Intelligence. Because it is a computer program, an ES is different than a robot, which is a physical or mechanical system. See also *artificial intelligence* and *robotics.*

firewall: A system or combination of systems that enforces a boundary between two or more networks and is designed to secure systems from unauthorized external access. Firewalls do not necessarily ensure against unauthorized access by those inside the protected network.

hacktivism: The convergence of political activism and computer hacking by which activists use computer and Internet technology to disrupt the operations of organizations.

IEEE Code of Ethics: An ethical code sanctioned by the Institute of Electrical and Electronics Engineering.

inductive argument: An argument form in which the premises, when assumed true, are strong enough to suggest the likelihood of the argument's conclusion, but unlike deductive, or valid, arguments, the premises of an inductive argument cannot guarantee the conclusion.

informal logical fallacies: Fallacious arguments that commonly occur in everyday discourse. Because these fallacies are so common, they have familiar names such as *ad hominem*, *ad populum*, *begging the question*, and *slippery slope*.

information warfare (IW):   Operations that target or exploit information media in order to win some objective over an adversary. IW, unlike conventional warfare, can be more disruptive than destructive; it can also use false information to deceive the enemy.

intellectual property: An intangible form of property that is protected by a system of laws such as patents, copyrights, trademarks, and trade secrets, through which authors and inventors are given ownership rights over their creative works (e.g., books, poems, songs) and inventions.

keystroke-monitoring software: A specialized form of audit-trail software that records every keystroke entered by a user and every character of the response that the system returns to the user.

legal liability: Required by law that the party found liable compensate for costs and injuries involved, but unlike moral responsibility, liability does not necessarily attribute blame to that party.

logical argument: A form or structure of reasoning in which one or more statements (called premises) are used as evidence to support another statement, the conclusion.

macroethics: Concerned with the analysis of moral rules and policies at the societal level, as opposed to the level of individuals. See also *microethics*.

microethics: Concerned with the analysis of moral rules and directives at the level of individuals, as opposed to the societal level. See also *macroethics*.

moral relativism: The view that there are no universal moral norms and standards and that only the members of a particular group or culture are capable of evaluating the moral principles used within that group; sometimes contrasted with cultural relativism, a descriptive thesis that different groups, in fact, have different views about what is morally right or wrong. Many philosophers have argued that even if cultural relativism is true, it does not logically imply moral relativism, which is a normative position.

morality: A system that comprises rules, principles, and values; at its core are rules of conduct for guiding action, and principles of evaluation for justifying those rules.

MOO/MUD: Multi-user Object Oriented environment/Multi-User Dimension. MOOs and MUDs are simulated or virtual environments in which members assume characters and identities other than their own. One of the best known examples of this is LambdaMOO.

MP3:   A standard file digital format developed in 1987 by the **M**oving **P**icture **E**xports **Group** and used for the compression of music so that it can be stored in a computer hard drive.

nanotechnology: A branch of engineering dedicated to the development of extremely small electronic circuits and mechanical devices built at the molecular level of matter.

normative ethics: A branch of ethical inquiry that is concerned with evaluating moral rules and principles by asking what *ought to be* the case, as opposed to descriptive ethics which simply reports what *is* the case (i.e., what individuals and cultures happen to believe) with respect to morally right and wrong behavior. See also *descriptive ethics*.

on-line communities: Computer-mediated social groups that interact in virtual space, as contrasted with traditional communities in which interaction occurs in physical space.

open source software: Software for operating systems and applications in which the source code is made freely available to use, modify, improve, and redistribute. Open source software, such as the Linux operating system, is contrasted with proprietary operating system software such as MS Windows.

packet-sniffing program: A program used to capture data (packets) across a computer network. Packet sniffers (sometimes referred to as "sniffers") have been used to capture user IDs and passwords. See also *Carnivore*.

PETs (Privacy-Enhancing Technologies):   Tools that *both* protect a user's personal identity while the user interacts with the Web and protect the privacy of communications (such as e-mail) sent over the Internet.

PICS (Platform for Internet Content Selection):   A labeling scheme for Internet users who wish to self-rate (or, depending on one's point of view, self-censor) Web sites.

P2P technology: Peer-to-peer technology, which enables two or more computers to share files through either a centralized directory such as Napster, or through a decentralized system such as Morpheus, KaZaA, and Gneutella.

remote work: A generic term that refers both to telework (organizational work performed outside the organizational confines), and telecommuting (the use of computer and communications technologies to transport work to the worker as a substitute for physical transportation of the worker to the workplace).

risk analysis: A methodology used to make an informed decision about a product based on considerations such as cost. A costs-benefits model of risk assessment for software can include safety, reliability, schedule, budget, consumer demand, and so forth.

robotics: The field of research and development in robots and robotic parts/limbs. A robot is essentially the integration of computer and electromechanical parts; it can be just a mobile robotic limb or arm or it can be as a full-fledged robotic system. See also *expert system*.

softbots: Software robots and artificial agents (sometimes called "bots") that perform highly specialized tasks on the Web. Meta-search engines (Web crawlers) and "negotiation agents" are examples of softbots.

Sonny Bono Copyright Term Extension Act (SBCTEA):   Legislation that extends the protection granted in the 1976 Copyright Act from the life of the author plus fifty years to the life of the author plus seventy years and also extends the protection of "works of hire" produced before 1978 from seventy-five years to ninety-five years. A "work of hire" can be a literary or artistic work in which the work's creator(s) receives payment from a corporation or organization that commissioned the work.

spam: E-mail that is unsolicited, promotional, and sent in bulk to multiple users.

trap door: A hidden software or hardware mechanism used to circumvent security. See *back door.*

Uniform Computer and Information Transactions Act (UCITA):   A law enacted at the state level (in Virginia and Maryland) designed to govern all contracts for the development, sale, licensing, maintenance, and support of computer software. UCITA's critics argue that it grants too much control to software vendors.

URL (Universal Resource Locator):   A string of alpha-numeric characters that points to a unique location on the Internet. For commercial Web applications, a URL usually has the form http://www.domainname.com. See also *domain name.*

utilitarianism: A consequentialist ethical theory based on the principle that an act or policy is morally permissible if it produces the greatest good (usually measured in terms of happiness) for the greatest number of people affected by it. See also *consequentialism.*

virtual environment: An on-line environment, such as an Internet chatroom, which is contrasted with an environment in physical space. Virtual environments, as opposed to "virtual-reality" environments and applications, can be either two-dimensional (e.g., text-only) or three-dimensional. See also virtual reality.

virtue ethics: A theory that stresses character development and the acquisition of moral habits as opposed to duty-based (deontological) and consequence-based (utilitarian) ethical theories, which stress obligation or duty and conformance with certain rules of action.

virtual reality: A three-dimensional, interactive computer-generated environment, as contrasted with physical reality. See also *virtual environment.*

virus: A program that can insert executable copies of itself into other programs; also generically referred to as a "malicious program" or a "rogue computer program." See also *worm.*

worm: A program or program segment that searches computer systems for idle resources and then disables them by erasing various locations in memory; also generically referred to as a "malicious program" or a "rogue computer program." See also *virus.*

INDEX